# 1,000,000 Books
are available to read at

# Forgotten Books

## www.ForgottenBooks.com

Read online
Download PDF
Purchase in print

ISBN 978-1-330-01555-1
PIBN 10004497

This book is a reproduction of an important historical work. Forgotten Books uses state-of-the-art technology to digitally reconstruct the work, preserving the original format whilst repairing imperfections present in the aged copy. In rare cases, an imperfection in the original, such as a blemish or missing page, may be replicated in our edition. We do, however, repair the vast majority of imperfections successfully; any imperfections that remain are intentionally left to preserve the state of such historical works.

Forgotten Books is a registered trademark of FB &c Ltd.
Copyright © 2018 FB &c Ltd.
FB &c Ltd, Dalton House, 60 Windsor Avenue, London, SW19 2RR.
Company number 08720141. Registered in England and Wales.

For support please visit www.forgottenbooks.com

# 1 MONTH OF FREE READING

## at

## www.ForgottenBooks.com

By purchasing this book you are eligible for one month membership to ForgottenBooks.com, giving you unlimited access to our entire collection of over 1,000,000 titles via our web site and mobile apps.

To claim your free month visit: www.forgottenbooks.com/free4497

\* Offer is valid for 45 days from date of purchase. Terms and conditions apply.

English
Français
Deutsche
Italiano
Español
Português

# www.forgottenbooks.com

**Mythology** Photography **Fiction** Fishing Christianity **Art** Cooking Essays Buddhism Freemasonry Medicine **Biology** Music **Ancient Egypt** Evolution Carpentry Physics Dance Geology **Mathematics** Fitness Shakespeare **Folklore** Yoga Marketing **Confidence** Immortality Biographies Poetry **Psychology** Witchcraft Electronics Chemistry History **Law** Accounting **Philosophy** Anthropology Alchemy Drama Quantum Mechanics Atheism Sexual Health **Ancient History** **Entrepreneurship** Languages Sport Paleontology Needlework Islam **Metaphysics** Investment Archaeology Parenting Statistics Criminology **Motivational**

# THE
# MAGICIAN'S OWN BOOK,

OR THE

# WHOLE ART OF CONJURING.

BEING A

COMPLETE HAND-BOOK OF PARLOR MAGIC,

AND CONTAINING

## OVER ONE THOUSAND

OPTICAL, CHEMICAL, MECHANICAL, MAGNETICAL, AND MAGICAL EXPERIMENTS, AMUSING TRANSMUTATIONS, ASTONISHING SLEIGHTS AND SUBTLETIES, CELEBRATED CARD DECEPTIONS, INGENIOUS TRICKS WITH NUMBERS, CURIOUS AND ENTERTAINING PUZZLES, TOGETHER WITH ALL THE MOST NOTED TRICKS OF MODERN PERFORMERS.
THE WHOLE

**ILLUSTRATED WITH OVER 500 WOOD CUTS,**

AND INTENDED AS A SOURCE OF AMUSEMENT FOR

## ONE THOUSAND AND ONE EVENINGS.

NEW YORK:
DICK & FITZGERALD, 18 ANN STREET.
1862.

Entered according to Act of Congress, in the year 1857, by
DICK & FITZGERALD,
In the Clerk's Office of the District Court for the Southern District of New York.

# PREFACE.

The publishers of this interesting volume do not conceive that it requires an elaborate introduction to the reading public. Some brief remarks, however, may not be inappropriate as a preface to THE MAGICIAN'S OWN BOOK, since the "black art," as in lessen lightened ages the practice of all these innocent and interesting feats was termed, is not yet as popularly understood in this country as it is abroad. There is a charm in legerdemain, or sleight of hand, that all, whether young or old, can readily appreciate. There is a mystery in it that piques the understanding as well as provokes the curiosity of the spectator. If the trick be executed with address, it excites our admiration; and the simpler it appears, the more it engages our fancy and fascinates our attention. And it is not only when we are mystified in public, cajoled in great saloons, and in the presence of crowds, that these effects are developed. They are called forth by the performances even of some humble artist in the family circle, whose ingenuity of mind has enabled him to gather up the more available of these practical puzzles. It would seem, therefore, a useful thing to place this source of harmless amusement within the reach of all who can relish its eccentricities, and instead of leaving it in the hands of "professors," as a pecuniary speculation, to enable the domestic group to master and enjoy it in all its ever-varying phases of novelty and gratification. To do this is what the publishers propose in the issue of this volume; and they flatter themselves, that if carefully studied, it will prepare the Young Conjuror to convert the parlor, at any desirable moment, into a place of genuine entertainment for himself and his companions, and ample repay him for the little time and thought he may devote to the acquisition of the necessary skill and dexterity.

Sleight of hand, magic, necromancy, &c., are all terms of art applicable to the same series of performances. The parlor student, therefore, once familiar with the general principles upon which these "experiments" are effected, will find little difficulty in comprehending at a glance, notwithstanding all the show of gorgeous paraphernalia and auxiliary machinery employed, the *modus operandi* of every one of them he may witness in public. This will be a new source of pleasure to him, independent of his ability to turn "Conjuror" on his own account at home. Nor can we well conceive of any rational objection likely to be urged against a kind of knowledge, so unimpeachable in its nature, and so mirth provoking in its results. Acting Charades are common, even among the most fastidious families. Enigmas and puzzles, in pantomime and speech, afford innoxious amusement to thousands. The publishers only consider THE MAGICIAN'S OWN BOOK a new addition to the current list of entertainments of that character; for what is a sleight of hand feat but an enigma placed before the spectator for solution? What is a trick in "natural magic" but a puzzle repeated to those who behold it, each one of whom is tacitly expected to guess how it is accomplished, while the little practitioner only holds the key to the mystery? In truth, the parlor needs some increase in its means of social amusement. The number it embraces is extremely limited. They soon weary. This weariness creates an appetite for outside attractions, not always wholesome, and too often insidiously pernicious. THE MAGICIAN'S OWN BOOK nicely fills up, therefore, the void in the category of parlor recreations. It may be made to present an ever-changing, always tempting, stay-at-home inducement, and in this shape becomes a moral assistant of no unimportant description, as well as the piquant source of good humored bamboozlement.

In conclusion we would say, that the MAGICIAN'S OWN BOOK contains a great variety of curious tricks and deceptions, many of which have never before appeared in print, and for many of which the publishers beg to acknowledge their indebtedness to Mr. John Wyman, Junior, the celebrated magician, that gentleman having kindly furnished clear and simple explanations to many of his most surprising parlor feats and fancies.

# INDEX.

### Sleight of Hand Tricks.

| | PAGE |
|---|---|
| The Flying Dime, | |
| The Flying Dime, (another method,) | |
| The Beads and Strings, | |
| To get a Ring out of a Handkerchief, | 5 |
| To tie a Knot in a Handkerchief which Cannot be drawn Tight, | 6 |
| The Three Cups, | 7 |
| To tie a Handkerchief round your Leg, and get it off Without Untying the Knot, | 8 |
| The Magic Bond, | 8 |
| The Old Man and his Chair, | 8 |
| To tie a Knot on the Left Wrist, without letting the right hand approach it, | 10 |
| The Magic Handcuffs, | 11 |
| To pull a String through your Buttonhole, | 11 |
| The Cut String Restored, | 12 |
| The Gordian Knot, | 12 |
| The Knot Loosened, | 13 |
| To Conjure Nuts in your Ear, | 13 |
| To Crack Walnuts in your Elbow, | 14 |
| To Take Feathers out of an Empty Handkerchief, | 14 |
| The Knotted Handkerchief, | 14 |
| Houdin's Nut Trick, | 16 |
| Conjuring a Ring, | 17 |
| The Erratic Egg, | 18 |
| The Obedient Dime, | 19 |
| The Prisoner Released, | 19 |
| Advantageous Wager | 19 |
| The Double Meaning, | 20 |
| The Three Spoons, | 20 |
| The Juggler's Joke, | 20 |
| To Cause Water and Wine to Change Places, | 21 |
| The Wizard's Wit, or Is it Possible, | 21 |
| The Toper's Stratagem, | 21 |
| The Impossible Omelet, | 21 |
| New Perpetual Rotary Motion, | 22 |
| The Miraculous Apple, | 22 |
| An Omelet Cooked in a Hat, | 23 |
| The Infallible Prophet, | 23 |
| Philosophy Cheated, | 24 |
| The Disappearing Dime, | 26 |
| The Hat and Die Trick, | 27 |
| The Penetrative Cents, | 27 |
| The Doll Trick, | 29 |
| The Flying Coins, | 30 |
| The Vanished Half Dime, | 30 |
| The Restored Document, | 30 |
| The Magic Rings, | 31 |
| The Fish and Ink Trick, | 32 |
| The Hat and Cannon Ball Trick, | 32 |
| The Dime in the Ball of Cotton, | 33 |
| The Egg and Bag Trick, | 33 |
| The Dancing Egg, | 34 |
| The Bell and Shot Trick. | 34 |

| | PAGE |
|---|---|
| The Burned Handkerchief Restored, | 35 |
| The Fire Eater, | 35 |
| The Egg Box Trick, | 36 |
| The Globe Box Trick, | 36 |
| The Coffee Trick, | 37 |
| The Handkerchief Trick, | 38 |
| The Magic Funnel, | 41 |
| The Magic Bottle, | 41 |
| The Bottle Trick, | 42 |
| The Magic Quarter, | 44 |
| To change a Dime to a Quarter, | 44 |
| Wyman's Gun Trick, | 46 |
| The Hatched Bird, | 46 |
| The Apple and Orange Trick, | 47 |
| A Magician's Box Explained, | 47 |
| The Enchanted Coin, | 48 |
| The Mysterious Coin, or How to Make Dollars pass through a Wine Glass, a China Plate, a Table, and fall into the Hand, | 49 |
| The Egyptian Fluids, or Impossibilities Accomplished, | 50 |
| The Magician's Snow Ball, | 51 |
| The Magnetized Cane, | 52 |
| Wyman's Mode of performing the Egg Bag Trick. | 52 |
| The Dancing Automaton, | 354 |
| The Invisible Springs, | 355 |
| The Flight of the Ring, | 356 |
| The Magic Book, | 360 |
| The Tape Trick, | 360 |
| The Knotted Thread, | 361 |
| The Transposable Pieces, | 362 |

### Tricks and Deceptions with Cards.

| | PAGE |
|---|---|
| To Make the Pass, | 55 |
| To Tell a Card by its Back, | 55 |
| The Card named without being seen, | 56 |
| The Card told by an Opera Glass, | 56 |
| The Four Kings, | 58 |
| The Four Accomplices, | 58 |
| To Tell the Card thought of, in a Circle of Ten, | 59 |
| To guess the Card thought of, | 59 |
| To tell the number of Cards by Weight, | 60 |
| Audacity, | 61 |
| The Card found at the second guess | 61 |
| The Card found under the Hat, | 61 |
| To call the Cards out of the Pack, | 61 |
| Heads and Tails, | 62 |
| The Surprise, | 62 |
| The Revolution, | 63 |
| The Slipped Card, | 63 |
| The Nailed Card, | 63 |
| To ascertain the number of Points on three unseen Cards, | 64 |
| To tell the numbers on two unseen Cards, | 64 |
| The Knaves and the Constable, | 64 |

(v)

# INDEX.

| | PAGE |
|---|---|
| The Pairs Re-paired, | 65 |
| The Queens Digging for Diamonds, | 66 |
| The Triple Deal, | 67 |
| The Quadruple Deal, | 67 |
| The Card Discovered by the Touch or Smell, | 67 |
| The Ingenious Confederacy, | 67 |
| Hold it Fast, | 69 |
| The Charmed Twelve, | 69 |
| The Trick of "Thirty-one," | 70 |
| To tell the Names of the Cards by their Weight, | 71 |
| The Cards in the Vase, | 73 |
| The Metamorphosis, | 74 |
| To hold Four Kings, or Four Knaves in your Hand, and to Change them suddenly into Blank Cards, and then to Four Aces, | 76 |
| To Change a Card in a Person's Hand, | 76 |
| The Card in the Egg, | 77 |
| The Fifteen Thousand Livres, | 78 |
| Hints to Amateurs, | 79 |
| Cure for Troublesome Spectators | 80 |
| To make a Card jump out of the Pack, | 357 |
| The Tell-Tale Cards, | 357 |
| The Double Dozen, | 358 |
| The Housebreakers, | 359 |

### The Magic of Chemistry.

| | |
|---|---|
| Sympathetic or Invisible Inks, | 84 |
| The Silver Tree, | 85 |
| Cleopatra's Pearls, | 86 |
| Wonderful Experiments in Combustion, | 86 |
| Mimic Rain, | 86 |
| Marine Illumination, | 87 |
| The Mimic Explosion, | 88 |
| The Shower of Fire, | 88 |
| The Magical Heat, | 88 |
| The Magic Lamp, | 89 |
| Surprising Experiments with Potassium, | 89 |
| The Water Demon, | 89 |
| A Flame produced with Ice, | 89 |
| The Chemical Chimney Sweep, | 90 |
| The Magical Illumination, | 90 |
| The Chemical Chameleon, | 91 |
| Crystallizations of Metals, | 92 |
| Beauties of Crystallization, | 93 |
| To Crystallize Camphor, | 93 |
| To do. Tin, | 94 |
| Crystals in Hard Water, | 94 |
| Varieties of Crystals, | 94 |
| A Liquid Changed to a Solid, and Heat from Crystallization, | 94 |
| Beautiful Experiment, | 95 |
| A Solid Changed to a Liquid, and intense Cold from the Liquefaction, | 95 |
| Magic of Heat, | 95 |
| Sublimation by Heat, | 96 |
| Heat Passing through Glass, | 96 |
| Metals unequally Influenced by Heat, | 97 |
| Spontaneous Combustion, | 97 |
| Inequality of Heat in Fire Irons, | 97 |
| Expansion of Metal by Heat, | 97 |
| Evaporation of a Metal, | 98 |
| A Floating Metal on Fire, | 98 |
| Ice Melted by Air. | 98 |
| Splendid Sublimation, | 98 |

| | PAGE |
|---|---|
| Magic Inks, | 98 |
| Chameleon Liquids, | 99 |
| The Magic Dyes, | 99 |
| Wine Changed into Water, | 99 |
| Two colorless Transparent Liquids become Black and Opaque, | 100 |
| Two colorless Fluids, Make a colored one, | 100 |
| Change of Color, by colorless Fluids, | 100 |
| To Change Blue Liquid to White, | 100 |
| Veritable "Black" Tea, | 100 |
| Restoration of Color by Water, | 101 |
| Two Liquids Make a Solid, | 101 |
| Two Solids Make a Liquid, | 101 |
| A Solid, Opaque Mass, Makes a Transparent Liquid, | 101 |
| Two cold Liquids Make a Hot one, | 101 |
| Quintuple Transmutation, | 102 |
| The Same Agent may Produce and Destroy Color, | 102 |
| Union of two Metals without Heat, | 102 |
| Magic Breath, | 102 |
| Two Bitters Make a Sweet, | 103 |
| Visible and Invisible, | 103 |
| To Form a Liquid of two Solids, | 103 |
| The Spectral Lamp, | 104 |
| Curious Change of Colors, | 105 |
| The Protean Light, | 105 |
| The Chameleon Flowers, | 105 |
| To Change the Colors of Flowers, | 105 |
| Changes of the Poppy, | 106 |
| Changes of the Rose, | 106 |
| Light changing White into Black, | 106 |
| The Visibly Growing Acorn, | 106 |
| Colored Flames, | 107 |
| Orange colored Flame, | 107 |
| Emerald Green Flame, | 107 |
| Instantaneous Flame, | 107 |
| To Cool Flame by Metal, | 108 |
| Proof that Flame is Hollow, | 108 |
| To Hold a Hot Tea Kettle on the Hand, | 108 |
| Incombustible Linen, | 108 |
| The Burning Circle, | 108 |
| Water of different Temperatures in the same Vessel, | 109 |
| Warmth of Different Colors, | 109 |
| Substitute for Fire, | 109 |
| Laughing Gas, | 109 |
| Flame from Cold Metals, | 110 |
| Phosphorus in Chlorine, | 110 |
| Magic Vapor, | 111 |
| Gas from the Union of Metals, | 111 |
| Camphor Sublimated by Flame, | 111 |
| Green Fire, | 111 |
| Brilliant Red Fire, | 112 |
| Purple Fire, | 112 |
| Silver Fire, | 112 |
| Fiery Fountain, | 112 |
| Combustion without Flame, | 112 |
| Combustion of Three Metals, | 113 |
| To Make Paper Apparently Incombustible, | 113 |
| Heat not to be estimated by Touch, | 113 |
| Flame upon Water, | 113 |
| Rose Colored Flame upon Water, | 113 |
| To Set a Mixture on Fire by Water, | 114 |
| Waves of Fire on Water, | 114 |
| Water from the Flame of a Candle, | 114 |

# INDEX.

| | PAGE |
|---|---|
| Formation of Water by Fire, | 114 |
| Boiling upon Cold Water, | 114 |
| Currents in Boiling Water, | 114 |
| Hot Water Lighter than Cold, | 115 |
| Expansion of Water by Cold, | 115 |
| The Cup of Tantalus, | 115 |
| The Magic Whirlpool, | 116 |
| Artificial Fire Balls, | 117 |
| To Melt Steel as Easily as Lead, | 118 |
| To Tell a Lady if She is in Love, | 118 |
| To put an Egg in a Phial, | 118 |
| To Astonish a Large Party, | 118 |
| Magical Test Papers, | 119 |
| Infinite Divisibility, | 119 |
| Chemistry an Agent in Secret Writing, | 327 |
| To Melt a Piece of Money in a Walnut Shell, without Injuring the Shell, | 355 |
| The Pyramid of Alum, | 354 |

## Experiments in Electricity.

| | |
|---|---|
| The Rotary Tobacco Pipe, | 123 |
| The Erratic Feather, | 123 |
| The Attractive Sealing Wax, | 124 |
| The Unneighborly Balls, | 124 |
| The Electrified Paper, | 124 |
| The Sociable Feather, | 124 |
| The Eccentric Feather, | 124 |
| The Discontented Pith Ball, | 124 |
| The Dancing Bran, | 124 |
| The Electrical Cat, | 124 |
| Electrical Shock from a Sheet of Paper, | 125 |
| Light under Water, | 126 |
| Simple means of Producing Electricity, | 126 |
| Attraction and Repulsion Exhibited, | 127 |
| How to Make an Electrical Machine, | 127 |
| Conductor, | 128 |
| The Plate Electrical Machine, | 129 |
| How to Draw Sparks from the Tip of the Nose, | 129 |
| How to Get a Jar full of Electricity, | 129 |
| The Electrical Battery, | 130 |
| Dancing Balls and Dolls, | 131 |
| The Electrical Kiss, | 131 |
| Ringing Bells, | 131 |
| Working Power of Electricity, | 132 |
| The Electrified Wig, | 132 |
| Imitation Thunder Clouds, | 133 |
| The Lightning Stroke Imitated, | 133 |
| The Sportsman, | 134 |

## Experiments in Galvanism.

| | |
|---|---|
| Singular Galvanic Shock, | 135 |
| The Flash of Light, | 135 |
| The Magical Cup, | 135 |
| The Prisoner Leech, | 136 |
| The Metamorphosed Knife, | 136 |
| With Plates in Water, | 136 |
| To Make a Magnet by Galvanism, | 137 |
| Effects of Galvanism on a Magnet, | 137 |
| Change of Color by Galvanism, | 137 |
| The Galvanic Shock, | 138 |
| A Galvanic Tongue, | 138 |
| Influence of Galvanism on Porter and Ale, | 188 |
| The Galvanized Flounder, | 188 |

## Experiments in Magnetism.

| | PAGE |
|---|---|
| The Impromptu Magnet, | 139 |
| The Merry Iron Filings, | 140 |
| Test of Magnetic Power, | 140 |
| To Make Artificial Magnets, | 140 |
| How to Magnetize a Poker, | 140 |
| To Show Magnetic Attraction and Repulsion, | 141 |
| Variation of the Needle, | 141 |
| Dip of the Needle, | 141 |
| To Suspend a Needle in the Air, by Magnetism, | 141 |
| Magnetism by Hammering, | 142 |
| Power of the Electro-Magnet, | 142 |
| The Mariner's Compass, | 142 |
| To Make Artificial Magnets without the Aid of either Natural Loadstone, or Artificial Magnets, | 143 |
| The Watch Magnetized, | 144 |
| North and South Poles of the Magnet, | 144 |
| Polarity of the Magnet, | 144 |
| Magnetic Action and Reaction, | 145 |
| To Pass Magnetism through a Table, | 145 |
| The Magnetic Table, | 145 |
| Interesting Particulars Concerning the Magnet, | 145 |
| Exaggerated Magnetism, | 146 |

## The Magic of Pneumatics and Aerostatics.

| | |
|---|---|
| Weight of the Air Proved by a Pair of Bellows, | 148 |
| The Pressure of Air Shown by a Wine Glass, | 148 |
| The Pressure of Air Shown by a Glass Jar, | 148 |
| Elasticity of the Air, | 149 |
| The Air Pump, | 149 |
| To Prove that Air has Weight, | 150 |
| To Prove Air Elastic, | 150 |
| Air in the Egg, | 150 |
| The Descending Smoke, | 151 |
| Half Eagle and Feather, | 151 |
| The Soundless Bell, | 152 |
| The Floating Fish, | 152 |
| The Mysterious Circles, | 152 |
| The Diving Bell, | 154 |
| The Air Balloon, | 154 |
| How to Make an Air Balloon, | 155 |
| How to Fill a Balloon, | 156 |
| To Make Fire Balloons, | 156 |
| The Mysterious Bottle, | 157 |
| How to Make a Parachute, | 157 |
| Caoutchouc Balloons, | 157 |
| The Bacchus Experiment, | 362 |

## The Magic of Optics.

| | |
|---|---|
| Light as an Effect, | 159 |
| Refraction, | 159 |
| The Invisible Coin Made Visible, | 159 |
| The Multiplying Glass, | 160 |
| Transparent Bodies, | 160 |
| The Prism, | 160 |
| To Make a Prism, | 161 |
| Composition of Light, | 161 |

# INDEX.

| | PAGE |
|---|---|
| A Natural Camera Obscura, | 162 |
| Bullock's Eyes Experiment, | 162 |
| The Camera Obscura, | 162 |
| The Magic Lantern, | 163 |
| The Camera Lucida, | 164 |
| Painting the Slides, | 164 |
| To Exhibit the Magic Lantern, | 165 |
| Effects of the Magic Lantern, | 165 |
| Tempest at Sea, | 165 |
| The Phantasmagoria, | 166 |
| Dissolving Views, | 167 |
| How to Raise a Ghost, | 167 |
| The Thaumatrope, | 168 |
| The Bird in the Cage, | 168 |
| Construction of the Phantasmascope, | 168 |
| Curious Optical Illusion, | 169 |
| Another, | 170 |
| Another, | 170 |
| The Picture in the Air, | 171 |
| Breathing Light and Darkness, | 171 |
| To Show what Rays of Light do not Obstruct each other, | 172 |
| To See through a Philadelphia Brick, | 172 |
| The Stereoscope, | 173 |
| Ocular Spectra, | 175 |
| Brilliant Water Mirror, | 175 |
| Optics of a Soap Bubble, | 176 |
| The Kaleidoscope, | 176 |
| Simple Solar Microscope, | 177 |
| Anamorphoses, | 178 |
| The Cosmorama, | 180 |
| Distorted Landscapes, | 180 |
| The Magic Coin, | 181 |
| The Magician's Mirror, | 344 |
| The Perspective Mirror, | 345 |
| The Artificial Landscape, | 348 |
| The Boundless Prospect, | 350 |
| The Enchanted Palace, | 352 |

## Tricks in Mechanics.

| | |
|---|---|
| Importance of Mechanics, | 182 |
| The Laws of Motion, | 182 |
| Experiment of the Law of Motion, | 182 |
| Balancing, | 183 |
| The Prancing Horse, | 183 |
| To Construct a Figure, which, being Placed on a Curved Surface, and Inclined in any Position, shall, when left to itself, Return to its Former Position, | 183 |
| To Make a Carriage Run in an Inverted Position, without Falling, | 183 |
| To Cause a Cylinder to Roll of its own Weight, up Hill, | 184 |
| The Balanced Stick, | 184 |
| The Chinese Mandarin, | 184 |
| To Make a Quarter Dollar Turn on its Edge on the Point of a Needle, | 184 |
| The Self-Balanced Pail, | 185 |
| To Lift a Bottle with a Straw, | 185 |
| The Dancing Pea, | 186 |
| The Toper's Tripod, | 186 |
| The Magical Snake, or the Obliquity of Motion, | 187 |
| The Bridge of Knives, | 187 |
| Sand in the Hour Glass, | 188 |

| | PAGE |
|---|---|
| Resistance of Sand, | 188 |
| The Magical Gyroscope, | 846 |

## Tricks in Hydraulics and Hydrostatics.

| | |
|---|---|
| The Science of Hydraulics, | 189 |
| The Fountain and Pump, | 189 |
| The Hydraulic Dancer, | 190 |
| The Syphon, | 191 |
| The Water Snail, or Archimedean Screw, | 191 |
| The Bottle Ejectment, | 192 |
| The Magic of Hydrostatics with the Ancients, | 192 |
| To Empty a Glass under Water, | 192 |
| The Mysterious Bottle, | 157 |
| Boiling upon Cold Water, | 114 |
| Currents in Boiling Water, | 114 |
| Hot Water Lighter than Cold, | 115 |
| Expansion of Water by Cold, | 115 |
| The Magic Whirlpool, | 116 |
| The Cup of Tantalus, | 116 |
| To Weigh Water without Scales, | 852 |
| More than Full, | 861 |

## Tricks in Acoustics.

| | |
|---|---|
| The Science of Acoustics, | 193 |
| Difference between Sound and Noise, | 193 |
| Visible Vibration, | 193 |
| Transmitted Vibration, | 194 |
| Double Vibration, | 194 |
| Champagne and Sound, | 194 |
| Music of the Snail, | 195 |
| The Tuning Fork a Flute Player, | 195 |
| Musical Bottles, | 195 |
| Theory of Whispering, | 195 |
| Theory of the Voice, | 196 |
| To Tune a Guitar without the Assistance of the Ear, | 196 |
| Progress of Sound, | 196 |
| To Make an Æolian Harp, | 196 |
| The Invisible Girl, | 197 |
| Magic of Acoustics with the Ancients, | 198 |
| The Secret of Ventriloquism, | 81 |
| To Show how Sound Travels through a Solid, | 198 |
| To Show that Sound depends upon Vibration, | 198 |
| Musical Figures Resulting from Sound, | 857 |

## The Magic of Numbers, or Curious Tricks in Arithmetic.

| | |
|---|---|
| Aphorisms of Number, | 199 |
| Palpable Arithmetic, | 200 |
| The Abacus, | 201 |
| Napier's Rods, | 202 |
| The Arithmetical Boomerang, | 203 |
| To Find a Number Thought of, | 203 |
| Second Method, | 204 |
| Third Method, | 205 |
| Fourth do., | 205 |
| Fifth do., | 206 |
| Sixth do., | 206 |
| To Discover two or more Numbers that a Person has Thought of, | 206 |

# INDEX.

| | PAGE |
|---|---|
| How many Counters have I in my Hands? | 207 |
| The Mysterious Halvings, to tell a Number a Person has Thought of, | 208 |
| Second Method, | 209 |
| Who Wears the Ring? | 211 |
| What is Probable? | 212 |
| Variations, | 213 |
| Amusing Combinations, | 214 |
| The Visitors to the Crystal Palace, | 217 |
| How many Changes can be Given to Seven Notes of a Piano? | 217 |
| The Arithmetical Triangle, | 217 |
| How many Different Deals can be made with Thirteen Cards out of Fifty-two, | 218 |
| The Three Graces, | 218 |
| Second Method, | 219 |
| Third Method, | 220 |
| The Fortunate Ninth, | 221 |
| The Ten Ten's, | 222 |
| Dividing the Beer, | 223 |
| The Difficult Case of Wine, | 224 |
| Decimation of Fruit, | 224 |
| The Wine and the Tables, | 225 |
| The Three Travelers, | 225 |
| What Counter has been Thought of out of Sixteen, | 226 |
| Magic Squares | 227 |
| Odd Magic Squares, | 227 |
| The Square of Gotham, | 229 |
| The Mathematical Blacksmith, | 230 |
| Curious Properties of some Figures, | 230 |
| The Industrious Frog, | 234 |
| The Council of Ten, | 235 |
| The Two Travelers, | 235 |
| Arithmetical Trick, | 237 |
| The Money Trick, | 237 |
| The Philosopher's Pupils, | 237 |
| To Discover a Square Number, | 238 |
| The Sheep, and the Sheep Fold, | 238 |
| The Countrywoman and the Eggs, | 238 |
| To Rub out Twenty Chalks at Five Times, Rubbing out every Time an Odd one, | 239 |
| The Impossible Triangle, | 239 |
| Odd or Even, | 239 |
| The Figures, up to 100, arranged as to make 505 in each Column, when Counted in Ten Columns Perpendicularly, and the Same when Counted in Ten Files Horizontally, | 240 |
| The Old Woman and Her Eggs, | 240 |
| The Mathematical Fortune Teller | 241 |
| The Dice Guessed Unseen, | 242 |
| The Sovereign and the Sage, | 242 |
| The Knowing Shepherd, | 243 |
| The Certain Game, | 243 |
| The Astonished Farmer, | 244 |
| The Magical Century, | 244 |
| The Hatter Cheated, | 245 |
| The Basket of Nuts, | 245 |
| The United igits, | 246 |
| December and May, | 246 |
| The Two Drovers, | 246 |
| The Basket and Stones, | 246 |
| The Famous Forty-Five, | 247 |
| Trick in Subtraction, | 247 |

| | PAGE |
|---|---|
| The Expunged Figure, | 247 |
| The Mysterious Addition, | 248 |
| To tell at what Hour a Person Intends to rise, | 249 |
| To find the Difference between Two Numbers, the Greater of which is Unknown, | 249 |
| The Magic Remainder, | 250 |
| A Person having an equal Number of Counters, or Pieces of Money, in each Hand, to find how many he has altogether, | 250 |
| The Three Jealous Husbands, | 251 |
| The False Scales, | 251 |
| The Apple Woman, | 252 |
| The Graces and Muses, | 252 |
| The Jesuitical Teacher, | 252 |
| Nine Quaint Questions, | 253 |
| The Fox, Goose and Corn, | 253 |
| Multiplying Money by Money, | 253 |
| The Unfair Division, | 255 |
| A Popular Fallacy, | 255 |

## Curious Tricks in Geometry.

| | |
|---|---|
| The Inventor of Geometry, | 256 |
| Geometrical Definitions, | 256 |
| The Five Geometrical Solids, | 257 |
| How to Make Five Squares into a large one without any Waste of Stuff, | 258 |
| Deceptive Vision, | 258 |
| The Carpenter Puzzled, | 259 |
| The Bricklayer Puzzled, | 260 |
| Triangular Problem, | 260 |
| To Form a Square, | 261 |
| Squaring the Circle, | 262 |
| The Perplexed Cabinet Maker, | 277 |

## Curious and Amusing Puzzles.

| | |
|---|---|
| Alexander the Great's Puzzle, | 266 |
| The Chinese Cross, | 266 |
| The Parallelogram, | 267 |
| The Divided Garden, | 267 |
| The Endless String, | 267 |
| Chinese Maze, the Willow Pattern Plate, | 268 |
| The Vertical Line Puzzle, | 268 |
| The Three Rabbits, | 269 |
| The Accommodating Square, | 269 |
| The Circle Puzzle, | 269 |
| The Cardboard Puzzle, | 269 |
| The Button Puzzle, | 269 |
| The Quarto Puzzle, | 269 |
| The Puzzle of Fourteen, | 270 |
| The Square and Circle Puzzle, | 270 |
| The Scale and Ring Puzzle, | 270 |
| The Heart Puzzle, | 271 |
| The Cross Puzzle, | 272 |
| The Yankee Square, | 272 |
| The Card Puzzle, | 272 |
| The Three Square Puzzle, | 273 |
| The Cylinder Puzzle, | 273 |
| The Four Tenants, | 273 |
| The Puzzle Wall, | 274 |
| The Twenty-Four Nuns, | 274 |
| The Horse Shoe Puzzle, | 274 |
| The Card Square, | 275 |

# INDEX.

| | PAGE |
|---|---|
| The Dog Puzzle, | 275 |
| Puzzle of the Two Fathers, | 275 |
| The Triangular Puzzle, | 276 |
| Cutting out a Cross, | 276 |
| Another Cross Puzzle, | 276 |
| The Fountain Puzzle, | 276 |
| The Puzzle of the Stars, | 277 |
| The Counter Puzzle, | 277 |
| Japan Square Puzzle, | 277 |
| The Cabinet Maker's Puzzle, | 277 |
| String and Balls Puzzle, | 277 |
| Double Headed Puzzle, | 278 |
| Arithmetical Puzzle, | 278 |
| Grammatical Puzzle, | 278 |
| The Tree Puzzle, | 279 |
| Puzzling Epitaph, | 279 |
| Curious Letter, | 279 |
| A Puzzling Inscription, | 279 |
| Puzzling Rings, | 279 |
| The Knight's Puzzle, | 283 |
| Another Method, | 284 |
| Another Method, | 287 |
| Rosamond's Bower, | 287 |
| The Labyrinth, | 288 |
| The Chinese Puzzle, | 289 |
| Trouble-Wit, | 290 |

### Answers to Puzzles.

| | |
|---|---|
| The Chinese Cross, | 291 |
| The Parallelogram. | 291 |
| The Divided Garden, | 292 |
| The Endless String, | 292 |
| Chinese Maze, | 292 |
| The Vertical Line Puzzle, | 293 |
| The Three Rabbits | 293 |
| The Accommodating Square, | 293 |
| The Circle Puzzle, | 293 |
| The Cut Card Puzzle, | 294 |
| The Button Puzzle, | 294 |
| The Quarto Puzzle, | 294 |
| The Puzzle of Fourteen, | 294 |
| The Square and Circle Puzzle, | 295 |
| The Scale and Ring Puzzle, | 295 |
| The Heart Puzzle, | 295 |
| The Cross Puzzle, | 295 |
| The Yankee Square, | 295 |
| The Card Puzzle, | 296 |
| The Three Square Puzzle, | 296 |
| The Cylinder Puzzle, | 296 |
| The Four Tenants, | 296 |
| The Puzzle Wall, | 297 |
| The Twenty-Four Nuns, | 297 |
| The Horse Shoe Puzzle, | 297 |
| The Card Square, | 297 |
| The Dog Puzzle, | 298 |
| The Two Fathers, | 298 |
| The Triangular Puzzle, | 298 |
| Cutting out a Cross, | 299 |
| Another Cross Puzzle, | 299 |
| The Fountain Puzzle, | 299 |
| The Star Puzzle, | 300 |
| The Counter Puzzle, | 300 |
| Japan Square Puzzle, | 300 |
| Cabinet Maker's Puzzle, | 300 |
| String and Balls Puzzle, | 301 |
| Double Headed Puzzle, | 301 |
| Arithmetical Puzzle, | 301 |

| | PAGE |
|---|---|
| Grammatical Puzzle, | 301 |
| The Tree Puzzle, | 301 |
| Puzzling Epitaph, | 302 |
| A Curious Letter, | 302 |
| A Puzzling Inscription, | 302 |

### The Magic of Art.

| | |
|---|---|
| To Trace an Oval, | 303 |
| An Endless Source of Amusement, | 303 |
| The Magic of the Oval, | 303 |
| Variations of the Oval, | 304 |
| What may be done with a Square, | 305 |
| How to make a Circle, | 306 |
| Importance of the Circle in Drawing, | 307 |
| Variation of the Square and Circle, | 307 |
| Importance of the Triangle, | 308 |
| How to Construct a Triangle, | 309 |
| The Triangle Works Wonders in Perspective, | 810 |
| Exaggerated Drawing, | 311 |
| The Parallelogram and Triangle in Combination, | 312 |
| Two Parallelograms in Combination, | 312 |
| Magic of the Parallelogram, | 313 |
| The Secret of Comic Drawing, | 313 |
| Caricature Sketching, | 314 |
| Simple Elements of the Profile, | 315 |
| Comic Profiles, | 316 |
| "Punch," and "Mother Hubbard," | 316 |
| Comical Beards, | 316 |
| The Human Figure, | 317 |
| Proportions of the Human Figure, | 318 |
| Standard Height of the Body, | 318 |
| Comical Drawing of the Human Figure, | 319 |
| The Centre of Gravity, | 320 |
| A Central Line through Everything, | 320 |
| The Curved Line Pervades all Nature, | 821 |
| The Droll Landscape, | 823 |
| Attitude Formed upon the Curved Line, | 824 |
| How to Draw upon Glass, for Magic Lantern Slides, | 825 |

### The Magic of Secret Writing.

| | |
|---|---|
| The Art of Secret Writing very Ancient, | 326 |
| Various Modes of Communicating Secret Intelligence, | 327 |
| Chemistry an Agent in Secret Writing, | 327 |
| Ingenious Mode of Secret Writing, | 328 |
| The Chiffre Indéchiffrable, | 328 |
| A Lock for Mr. Hobbs to Pick, | 330 |
| The Circular Cypher, | 831 |
| Another Method, | 832 |
| The Musical Cypher, | 833 |

### The Magic of Strength.

| | |
|---|---|
| Mechanical Inventions of the Ancients few in Number, | 334 |
| Ancient and Modern Feats of Strength, | 334 |
| Feats of Eckeberg particularly described, | 335 |
| One Man Drawing against Two Horses, | 335 |
| Breaking the Rope, | 336 |

# INDEX.

| | PAGE |
|---|---|
| The Anvil Feat, | 336 |
| Breaking Stones, | 337 |
| The Chair Feat, | 337 |
| The Knee Feat, | 338 |
| The Cannon Feat, | 338 |
| Twisting Iron Bars, | 339 |
| General Explanation on all the Above Feats, | 339 |
| Real Feats of Strength Performed by Thomas Topham, | 340 |
| Remarkable Power of Lifting Heavy Persons when the Lungs are Inflated, | 341 |
| Pyramids of Men, | 342 |

## Miscellaneous Curious Tricks and Fancies.

| | |
|---|---|
| An Artificial Memory, | 343 |
| The Magician's Mirror, | 344 |
| The Perspective Mirror, | 345 |
| The Magical Gyroscope, | 346 |
| Artificial Landscape, | 348 |
| Easy and Curious Method of Foretelling Rainy or Fine Weather, | 349 |
| The Magical Measure, | 350 |
| The Boundless Prospect, | 350 |
| The Magical Watch Lamp, | 352 |

| | PAGE |
|---|---|
| The Hour of the Day or Night told by a Suspended Shilling, | 351 |
| The Enchanted Palace, | 352 |
| To Know which of Two Different Waters is the Lightest, without any Scales, | 353 |
| To Know if a Suspicious Piece of Money is Good or Bad, | 353 |
| The Pyramid of Alum, | 354 |
| The Dancing Automaton, | 354 |
| To Melt a Piece of Money in a Walnut Shell without Injuring the Shell, | 355 |
| The Invisible Springs, | 355 |
| The Flight of the Ring, | 356 |
| Musical Figures resulting from Sound, | 357 |
| To Make a Card Jump out of the Pack, | 357 |
| The Tell-Tale Cards, | 357 |
| The Double Dozen, | 358 |
| The Housebreakers, | 359 |
| The Magic Book, | 360 |
| The Tape Trick, | 360 |
| More than Full, | 361 |
| Floating Needles, | 361 |
| The Knotted Thread, | 361 |
| The Bacchus Experiment, | 362 |
| Curious Method of Measuring the Height of a Tree, | 362 |
| The Transposable Pieces, | 363 |

# THE YOUNG CONJUROR.

**INCLUDING SLEIGHT OF HAND, WITH OBJECTS OR CARDS, WITH AND WITHOUT APPARATUS.**

That there has been "Jugglery" in all ages of the world, the pages of history abundantly prove. The ancient religions of the heathen were mixed up with an extensive system of legerdemain, and were, more or less, tissues of trickery. Sleight of hand, tricks of the tongue by which the word was kept to the ear, but broken to the hope, and various miraculous deceptions, were the means by which the priests of Egypt, Greece, and Rome used to subjugate mankind. Happy ought we to be, in living in an age when humbug of every kind is sure to meet exposure by the daylight beams of truth.

The Eastern nations, from the earliest times, possessed,

besides these religious jugglers, others who made a livelihood by going from place to place, and performing various tricks and feats by which the judgement was bewildered and the reason bamboozled; and even now the performers of the East infinitely exceed those of the West. In the Norman times the juggler was termed jongleur, or joculator, and united in one the minstrel, astrologer, and merry-andrew. In the fourteenth century, he seems to have become more entirely a performer of tricks and feats, and bore the name of Tregetour. The tregetours were adepts at every kind of sleight of hand, and by the assistance of machinery of various kinds, deceived the eyes of the spectators, and produced such illusions as were usually supposed to be the effect of enchantment, for which reason they were frequently ranked with sorcerers, magicians, and witches. Chaucer, who no doubt had frequently an opportunity of seeing the tricks exhibited by the tregetours of his time, says, "There I sawe playenge jogelours, magyciens, trageteours, phetonysses, charmeresses, old witches, and sorceresses;" and the old poet goes on to say to them, "Sometimes they will bring on the similitude of a grim lion, or make flowers spring up as in a meadow; sometimes they cause a vine to flourish, bearing white and red grapes, or show a castle built with stone, and when they please, they cause the whole to disappear:" and in another part of his work, he says:

> "There saw I Coll Tregetour,
> Upon a table of sycamour,
> Play an uncouthe thynge to tell;
> I sawe hym cary a wyndemell,
> Under a walnot shale."—*House of Fame*, book iii.

The learned monarch, James I, was perfectly convinced that these and other inferior feats exhibited by the tregetours of his day, could only be performed by the agency of the "old gentleman," whom it is not polite to name. The profession had already fallen very low, and at the close of the reign of Queen Elizabeth, the performers were ranked by the moral writers of that time, not only with ruffians, blasphemers, thieves, and vagabonds, but also with Jews, Turks, heretics, pagans, and sorcerers; and in more modern times, by way of derision, the juggler was called a mocus-pocus, or hocus-pocus, a term applicable to a pick-pocket, or a common cheat.

The following pages are not intended to make the young reader either a cheat or a trickster; there is nothing, per haps, so utterly contemptible in every-day life, as trickery and deception, and we would caution our young master not to obtain by these amusements a love of deception, which is only allowable in such feats of amusement, and which is in no way culpable, when every one knows he is deceived. But we would advise him strongly to cultivate in his own mind the virtues of sincerity, straightforwardness, candor, openness, and truth; to shun subterfuge and deception as he would a venomous reptile; and to hate a lie as he would hate that same old gentleman whom we were too polite to name, and who is the father of it.

With this sage advice, we shall present a collection of amusing conjuring tricks.

## SLEIGHT OF HAND.

It is my intention, in the following pages, to lay more stress upon those tricks which require no apparatus, than upon those for which special apparatus, or the assistance of a confederate, is required. No one is nearly so well pleased by a trick whose essence evidently lies in the machinery, while every one feels pleasure at seeing a sleight of hand trick neatly executed. For my own part, I despise all the numerous boxes, bottles, variegated covers, and other gimcracks which are generally seen on a conjuror's table; and I have never been so pleased with any performer as with one who did not even require a table, but pressed into his service articles borrowed from his audience, as he stood before them, or walked among them. The spectators should never be able to say, "Ah! the trick lies in the box; he dares not show it to us!"

The following tricks have almost all been successfully performed by myself, and have caused me some reputation in the magic art. Some are my own invention:

### 1. THE FLYING DIME.

This trick must be frequently practiced before it is produced in public.

Borrow two colored silk handkerchiefs from the company, and have *three* dimes in your hand, but only show *two*, keeping the other one firmly fixed against the first joint of the second and third fingers. You must also have a fine needle and thread stuck inside the cuff of your coat. Then take one of the handkerchiefs, and put in *both* dimes, but pretend that only *one* is in the handkerchief; then put the handkerchief into a hat, leaving one corner hanging out. Now hold up the *third* dime (which the spectators imagine is the *second*), and ask one of the company to lay the second handkerchief over it. You then ask him to hold the dime tight between his finger and thumb, while you twist up the handkerchief. While doing so, with both hands concealed under the handkerchief, you pass a few stitches under the dime, and replace the needle. This being done, spread one corner of the handkerchief over the hand of the person who is still holding the dime, and, taking hold of another corner, tell him to drop the dime when you have counted three. At the word "three," he lets go the dime, and you whisk the handkerchief into the air, when the dime appears to have vanished, but is really held in the handkerchief. You then tell the astonished individual to draw the other handkerchief out of the hat by the corner that is hanging out. The two dimes are heard to fall into the hat, and every one is persuaded that you have conjured one of the dimes out of a person's hand, and sent it into the hat.

## 2. ANOTHER METHOD.

Perhaps the spectators may ask to see it again, or demand to mark the dime. In this case, vary it as follows. Ask some one (always choose the most incredulous of the party) to mark a dime of his own, and give it you. Take the same handkerchief, and give him the dime to hold that is already enclosed in it, as in the last trick, dropping the marked dime into the palm of your hand. Twist it up as before, and then leave it entirely in his hands. Direct him to place it on a table, and cover it with a basin or saucer. Ask him to give you a cup or tumbler, and hold it under the table, beneath the place where the saucer is. Then tell him to knock three times on the saucer, and at the third knock let the marked dime fall into the tumbler. Hand him the tumbler, and while he is examining the dime to see if it is the same one that he marked, take up the saucer, and shake out the handkerchief that is lying under it, as in the last trick. You must then return the handkerchief, and while you pretend to be searching for the marks, draw out the thread that held the dime, and drop the coin into the palm of your hand, taking care to rub between your finger and thumb the spot where the threads had been, in order to eradicate the marks. This variation seldom fails to confuse the company.

You must remember to keep talking the whole time, and always try to make a joke, or otherwise to distract the attention of the audience, while you are executing the necessary changes.

### 3. THE BEADS AND STRINGS.

Ask some lady to lend you the beads off her bracelet, or have by you five or six beads, which you may hand round for examination. Then get some one to cut two pieces of thin string of equal length, and twist them about your fingers, appearing to lay them side by side, but in reality placing 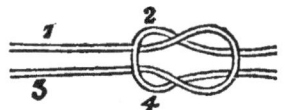 them as in the figure, and then, by twisting them together with apparent carelessness, the manner in which they are arranged will not be seen, particularly if you keep the point of junction hidden either by a finger, or by throwing the shade of your hand upon it.

When the beads are returned, thread them all, taking care to pass the center bead over the point of juncture. You then bring the ends of the string 1 and 2 together, and tie them so, doing the same with 3 and 4. Now give the tied ends to two persons, directing them to hold them tight. You need not fear that the beads will come off, even if they pull hard. Then grasp the beads with both hands, directing the holders to slacken the strings. You then, under cover of the left hand, which is placed above the beads, slip the center bead to one side, and draw out the two loops which have been hidden in it. The beads will then easily come off into your right hand. Tell the holders to pull hard, which they will do, and the same moment remove your hands, showing the empty strings, and all the beads in your right hand. Then hand round the beads and strings as before. Remember to rub out the marks in the strings caused by the loops, before you remove your hands.

### 4. TO GET A RING OUT OF A HANDKERCHIEF.

Bend a piece of gold wire into the form of a ring, having previously sharpened both ends. You have a real ring made of the same piece of wire, and concealing the false ring in the palm of your hand, offer the real one to be inspected. When it is returned, borrow a handkerchief, and while taking it from the lender, slip the real ring into your left hand, and take the false one at its point of junction. Throw the handkerchief over the ring, and give it to some one to hold between his finger and thumb. Let the handkerchief fall over it, and give a piece of string to a second spectator, directing him to tie it round the handkerchief, about two inches below the ring, so as to enclose it in a bag, and tell him to do so as tightly as he can. While he is doing this, take up your conjuring wand, a rod of some hard wood, about eighteen inches long, and when the knot is tied, step forward, passing the rod into your left hand, taking care to slip over it the real ring, which has lain concealed there. Slip your left hand to the center of the rod, and direct each of the two persons to hold one end of it in his right hand. Then tell the one who has the ring and handkerchief, to lay them on your left hand, which you immediately cover with your right. Then tell them to spread another handkerchief over your hands, and to say after you any nonsense that you like to invent.

While they are so doing, unbend the false ring, and draw it through the handkerchiefs by one of its points, carefully rubbing between the thumb and finger the place where it came through. Hang the empty handkerchief over the ring which is on the rod, and take away your hands, which you exhibit empty, as you have stuck the false ring inside your cuff. Take away the upper handkerchief, and let a third person come to examine, when he will find the ring gone out of the handkerchief, and hung upon the rod.

### 5. TO TIE A KNOT IN A HANDKERCHIEF WHICH CANNOT BE DRAWN TIGHT.

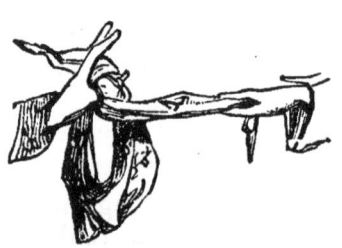

Cast an ordinary knot on a handkerchief, and give the end out of your right hand to some spectator, and tell him to pull hard and sharp when you count three. Just as he pulls, slip your left thumb under the handkerchief, as drawn in the cut, and it will be pulled out quite straight, without any knot at all. You must let go the end that hangs over the left hand, and grasp the handkerchief between the thumb and fore finger.

### 6. THE THREE CUPS.

This is an admirable delusion, but requires very careful management, and should be practiced repeatedly before it is exhibited publicly. You get three tin cups, of the shape shown in the cut. They should have two or three ridges running round them at the mouth, in order to give a better hold. Four balls should now be made of cork, and carefully blackened. One of the balls is held concealed between the roots of the third and fourth fingers, while the other three are handed round for examination, together with the cups. 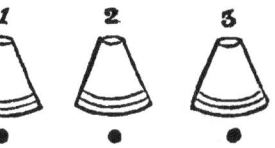 When they are returned, the young conjuror begins by placing each ball under a cup, or, if he chooses, asking one of the spectators to do so for him. While this is being done, he slips the fourth ball to the tips of the second and third fingers. He then lifts up cup No. 1, replaces it on the table a few inches from its first position, and at the same time slips the fourth ball under it. He takes up ball No. 1, and pretends to throw it away, but in reality he slips it into the place which the fourth ball had occupied. He does the same with the three cups, and then commences a sham search after the lost ball, in which he accidentally (!) knocks over one of the cups, and, to his pretended astonishment, finds a ball under it. He then knocks over both the other cups, and finds in them the two missing balls.

He again places the balls under the cups, taking care to slip the fourth ball under cup No. 3. He then takes up cup No. 1, and pretends to throw the ball into No. 3, but hides it as before. As there are already two balls in No. 3, the spectators imagine that he really has thrown the ball into it. He replaces cup No. 3 over both balls, and slips among them ball No. 1. He then takes up cup No. 2, and goes through the same process, and on knocking over cup No. 3, all three balls are found together under it, and while the spectators are being astonished, ball No 2 can be quickly got rid of.

A rather startling termination to this trick can be managed by taking up one of the cups, with its mouth upwards.

holding the finger and thumb close to its mouth. Then by throwing another cup into it, letting go the first and catching the second, you appear to have thrown the second cup through the first.

### 7. TO TIE A HANDKERCHIEF ROUND YOUR LEG, AND GET IT OFF WITHOUT UNTYING THE KNOT.

Hold the handkerchief by both ends, lay the center of the handkerchief on your knee, and pass the two ends below, appearing to cross them, but in reality hitching them within  each other, as represented in the engraving, which shows the manner in which this is managed. Draw this loop tight, and bring back the ends to the same side on which they were originally, and tie them above. If the loop is properly made, it will stand a good pull. Then, after showing the spectators how firmly it is tied, put your hand under the knot, and by giving it a sharp pull, it will come off.

The engraving represents the manner in which the loop is made, but it must be made considerably smaller than it is shown, or it will be seen. In fact, it ought not to be a loop at all, as it should be almost concealed under the fold of the handkerchief. Do not show this in public until you can tie it with rapidity and precision.

### 8. THE MAGIC BOND.

 Take a piece of string, and tie the two ends together with a weaver's knot, as that holds the best, and arrange it over the fingers, as represented in the engraving. Having done so, let the long loop hang loose, lift both loops off the thumb, draw them forward until the string is quite tight, and then put them behind the hand, by passing them between the second and third fingers. Then pull the part of the string that lies across the roots of the fingers, and the whole affair will come off.

### 9. THE OLD MAN AND HIS CHAIR.

Take the same piece of string as in the last trick, hold your left hand with the palm uppermost, and hang the string over the palm. Spread all the fingers, and with the right hand bring forward the loops that hang behind, by passing it over the second and third fingers. Loose the loop, take hold of the part of the string that crosses the hand, and pull it forwards. When tight, pass it to the back of the hand, the reversal of the movement that brought it forwards. Loose the loop, insert the fore-finger and little finger of the right hand under the string that encircles the left fore-finger and little finger, and pass the two loops to the back of the hand, as shown in the cut, Fig. 1. Tuck both loops under the cross-strings at the back, and your preliminaries are completed. Then begin your story: "There was once upon a time, an old man, who stole a pound of candles. Here they are." You then hold your left hand as at the commencement, hook the right fore-finger under the cross-piece at the back, and draw it downward until it is long enough to be passed over the second and third fingers to the front. Pass it over, and draw it slowly upwards, when the similitude of a pound of candles hanging by their strings will be seen. (See Fig. 2.) "The old man being tired hung up his candles," you then hang the long loop over your thumb, " and sat down in his high-backed chair, which you see here." You then hitch the right fore finger and middle finger under the two loops that will be found hanging behind the left hand, bring them to the front, raise them perpendicularly, and the chair will be seen as in Fig. 3. The thumb must be raised perpendicularly, and brought as much as possible into the center of the hand, or the chair will be all aside.

"When the old man was rested, it began to become dark, and he took a pair of scissors to cut down a candle for himself. Here are the scissors." While you are saying this, you slip the loop off the thumb, and you get Fig. 4. Move the blades and handles of the scissors, as if cutting something with them. "Just as

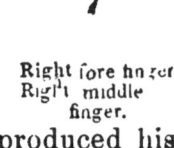
1. Right fore finger.
2. Right middle finger.

he had lighted it, in came a policeman, and produced his

1*

staff, with the Queen's crown at the top." Now let go the
little finger of the left hand and the loop will run up the

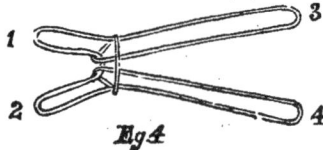

1. Fore finger of left hand.
2. Little finger of left hand.
3. Fore finger of right hand.
4. Middle finger of right hand.

Fig 4

string towards the right hand, producing Fig. 5. "The old
man in vain tried to resist, for the policeman called a com-
rade to his assistance, and they tied a cord round the old

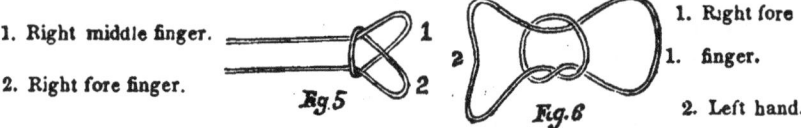

1. Right middle finger.
2. Right fore finger.

Fig. 5

1. Right fore finger.
2. Left hand.

Fig. 6

man's arms in a tight knot, like this"—slip the right middle
finger out of its loop, and you will obtain Fig. 6—"and
carried him off to prison."

10. TO TIE A KNOT ON THE LEFT WRIST, WITHOUT LETTING THE RIGHT HAND APPROACH IT.

Take a piece of thick pliant string by each end, and with
a quick jerk of the right hand cast a loop on it as in Fig. 1.
The jerk must be given upwards and towards the left hand,

Fig. 1

and its impetus will cause the loop to run up the string
until it falls over the left wrist, as in Fig. 2. The moment
that the forward jerk is given the right hand should be

Fig. 2

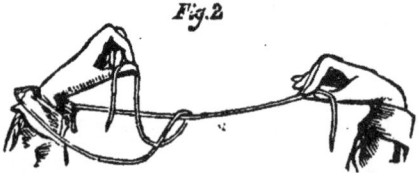

drawn back, so that the loop is drawn tight directly it has

settled on the wrist. Both ends should be let fall when the knot is firm. This is a very nice little sleight of hand trick to practice in the intervals between more showy ones, and, although rather difficult to learn, is soon acquired.

### 11. THE HANDCUFFS.

Let two persons, A and B, have their hands tied together with string, so that the strings cross, as represented in the engraving  The object is, to free themselves from each

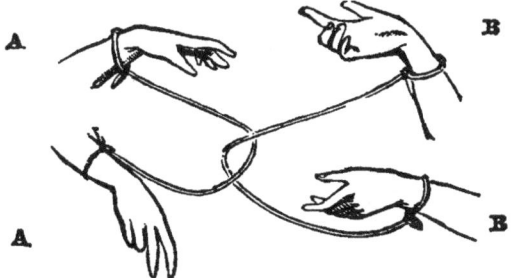

other without untying the knot. It is executed in the following manner :

Let B gather up the string that joins his hands, pass the loop under the string that binds either of A's wrists, slip it over A's hand, and both will be free. By a reversal of the same process, the string may be replaced.

### 12. TO PULL A STRING THROUGH YOUR BUTTON-HOLE.

Take a piece of string about two feet in length, and tie the ends together. Pass it through a button-hole of your coat; hitch one thumb at each end, hook the little fingers into the upper strings of the opposite hand. Then draw the hands well outward, and the string will look very complicated, as in the engraving.

To get out the string, loose the hold of the right thumb and left little finger, and separate the hands smartly, when the string will appear to have been pulled out *through* the substance of your coat.

It is an improvement of the trick, if, immediately on loosing the hold of the right thumb, you change the string from the right little finger on to the thumb.

### 13. THE CUT STRING RESTORED.

Tie together the ends of a piece of string, pass one hand through each end, twist it once round, and put both ends into the left hand. Draw the right hand rapidly along the double strings until you come to the place where the strings have crossed each other, as seen in the engraving. Conceal the junction with the thumb and finger of the right hand; hold the strings in a similar manner with the left hand, and tell some one to cut the string between them. You show that the string has been divided into two pieces, and say that you will join them with your teeth. Put all four ends into

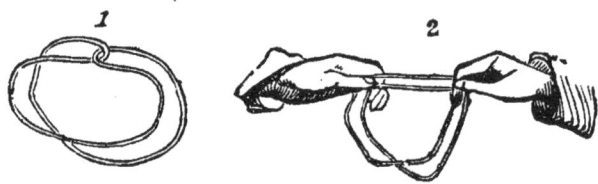

1. The twisted string.    2. The manner of holding it.

your mouth, and remove with your tongue the little loop that has been cut off. When you take the string out of your mouth, the spectators will not notice the absence of so small a portion of its length, and will fancy that you really have joined them.

### 14. THE GORDIAN KNOT.

Take a silk handkerchief, and lay it on a table. Take each of the corners, and lay them across each other in the mid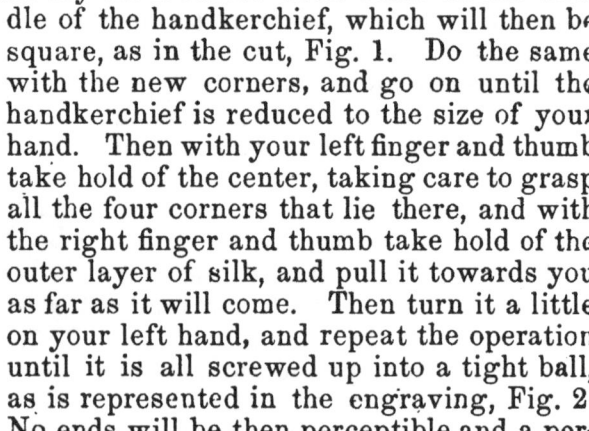dle of the handkerchief, which will then be square, as in the cut, Fig. 1. Do the same with the new corners, and go on until the handkerchief is reduced to the size of your hand. Then with your left finger and thumb take hold of the center, taking care to grasp all the four corners that lie there, and with the right finger and thumb take hold of the outer layer of silk, and pull it towards you as far as it will come. Then turn it a little on your left hand, and repeat the operation until it is all screwed up into a tight ball, as is represented in the engraving, Fig. 2 No ends will be then perceptible, and a person who is unacquainted with the mode will never be able to untie it. Of course you must prepare it previously. When the person to whom you give it has failed to untie it, you take the ball in your hand, and holding it behind your back, you reverse the method by which it was tied, and when it is loose a good shake will release it.

### 15. THE KNOT LOOSENED.

This is a very amusing deception. You ask any one for a handkerchief, and tie the ends firmly together in a double knot, allowing him to feel it, or pull the ends as tight as he pleases. You then throw the center of the handkerchief over the knot, ask the person to hold it tight between his finger and thumb. You ask him if the knot is still there, to 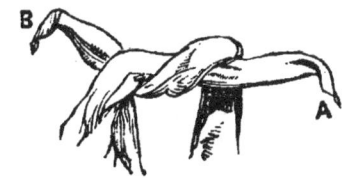 which he will answer in the affirmative. You then take hold of any part of the handkerchief, and direct the holder to drop the handkerchief at the word "three." You count, "one, two, three," at which word he looses his hold of the handkerchief, and there is no vestige left of the knot.

The method of managing this trick is as follows: Take the handkerchief and tie the ends in a simple knot, keeping *one end tight*, and the other end loose. We will call the tight end A, and the loose one B. Keep A *always* in the right hand, and on the stretch horizontally, and the handkerchief will look as in the cut. Do this when you tie it the second time, and draw B tight, which will then form a double tie round A, but will not hold it firm. When you throw the handkerchief over the knot, you draw out A with the finger and thumb of the left hand, and the knot will apparently remain firm, although in reality it is nothing but a double twist of silk, which of course falls loose when the handkerchief is dropped.

### 16. TO PUT NUTS INTO YOUR EAR.

Take three nuts in the left hand, show them, and take out one of them between your right finger and thumb, and another between the first and third finger. This latter is not seen by the company. You then put one of them in your mouth and retain it there, unknown to the spectators, while you exhibit the second as the one that you put into your mouth. This second one you carry to your ear, as if you meant to insert it there, and on replacing it in your left hand, only two nuts will be left instead of three, the third of which appears to have gone into your ear.

### 17. TO CRACK WALNUTS IN YOUR ELBOW.

Conceal a very strong walnut in your right hand, and take two other walnuts out of the dish. Place one of them on the joint of your arm, and say that you are going to break it by the power of your muscles. You will now have one walnut in your arm and two in your right hand. Close your left arm, and strike it an apparently violent blow with the right hand, at the same time clenching the right hand violently, which will smash the second walnut in it, and the spectators hearing the crash will be sure to fancy that it is caused by the demolition of the walnut in your arm. Then open your arm very gently (for fear of dropping any of the fragments, you must say), and, when pretending to take out the walnut which you had placed there, you substitute for it the broken one from your right hand.

### 18. TO TAKE FEATHERS OUT OF AN EMPTY HANDKERCHIEF.

Procure at the military clothier's four or five large plumes, such as are worn by officers. Take off your coat, and lay the plumes along your arms, the stem being toward your hand Now put on your coat again, and the feathers will lie quite smoothly and unsuspected. Borrow a handkerchief from one of the spectators, and wave it about to show that it is empty. Throw it over your left hand, and with the right draw out one of the plumes from up the coat-sleeve, at the same time giving it a flourish in the air, which will loosen all the fibers of the feather, and make it appear much too large to have been concealed about the person. Wave the handkerchief again, and repeat the operation until all the plumes are gone. You can carry enough plumes under the sleeve to cover a table with, and if you prepare a board or an ornamental vase full of holes, you can place the plumes upright as you take them out.

### 19. THE KNOTTED HANDKERCHIEF.

This feat consists in tying a number of hard knots in a pocket-handkerchief borrowed from one of the company, then letting any person hold the knots, and by the operator merely shaking the handkerchief, all the knots become unloosened, and the handkerchief is restored to its original state.

To perform this excellent trick, get as soft a handkerchief as possible, and taking the opposite ends, one in each hand, throw the right hand over the left, and draw it through, as if you were going to tie a knot in the usual way. Again throw the right-hand end over the left, and give the left-hand end to some person to pull, you at the same time pulling the right-hand end with your right hand, while your left hand holds the handkerchief just behind the knot. Press the thumb of your left hand against the knot to prevent its slipping, always taking care to let the person to whom you gave one end pull first: so that, in fact, he is only pulling against your *left hand*.

You now tie another knot exactly in the same way as the first, taking care always to throw the right-hand end over the left. As you go on tying the knots, you will find the right-hand end of the handkerchief decreasing considerably in length, while the left-hand one remains nearly as long as at first; because, in fact, you are merely tying the right-hand end *round the left*. To prevent this from being noticed, you should stoop down a little after each knot, and pretend to pull the knots tighter; while, at the same time, you press the thumb of the right hand against the knot, and with the fingers and palm of the same hand, draw the handkerchief, so as to make the left-hand end shorter, keeping it at each knot as nearly the length of the right-hand end as possible.

When you have tied as many knots as the handkerchief will admit of, hand them round for the company to feel that they are firm knots; then hold the handkerchief in your right hand, just below the knots, and with the left hand turn the loose part of the center of the handkerchief over them, desiring some person to hold them. Before they take the handkerchief in hand, you draw out the right-hand end of the handkerchief, which you have in the right hand, and which you may easily do, and the knots being still held together by the loose part of the handkerchief, the person who holds the handkerchief will declare he feels them: you then take hold of one of the ends of the handkerchief which hangs down, and desire him to repeat after you, one, two, three; then tell him to let go, when, by giving the handkerchief a smart shake, the whole of the knots will become unloosed.

Should you, by accident, whilst tying the knots, give the wrong end to be pulled, a hard knot will be the consequence, and you will know when this has happened the instant you try to draw the left-hand end of the handkerchief shorter. You must, therefore, turn this mistake to the best advantage, by asking any one of the company to see how long it will take him to untie one knot, you counting the seconds. When he has untied the knot, your other knots will remain right as they were before. Having finished tying the knots, let the same person hold them, and tell him that, as he took two minutes to untie one knot, he ought to allow you fourteen minutes to untie the seven; but as you do not wish to take any advantage, you will be satisfied with fourteen seconds.

You may excite some laughter during the performance of this trick, by desiring those who pull the knots along with you, to pull as hard as they please, and not to be afraid, as the handkerchief is not yours; you may likewise go to the owner of the handkerchief, and desire him to assist you in pulling a knot, saying, that if the handkerchief is to be torn, it is only right that he should have a share of it; you may likewise say that he does not pull very hard, which will cause a laugh against him.

### 20. HOUDIN'S NUT TRICK.

To perform a clever trick with dexterity before a "small party" is at once to become the hero of the evening. If you cannot sing, you must solve conundrums, or dance a hornpipe; if neither of these be "your forte," a good trick or two will give equal pleasure to the "bright blue eyes" peering at you. The nut trick is exhibited thus: The professor hands the audience a dessert plate and a cambric handkerchief for examination; these being returned, he places the plate upon a table near to him; the handkerchief is then spread out quite flat over the plate. At command, sugared almonds, nuts, and comfits pour into the dessert plate the instant the kerchief is lifted up, producing an effect that would have astonished the magi of old. The way in which it is done is this: Make a calico bag large enough to hold the nuts and sweetmeats you intend to distribute, exactly to the pattern of a nightcap, or the letter A: a small selvage is turned up at the bottom of the bag; procure two pieces of watch spring, and bend them quite flat, each spring to be exactly half the diameter of the bag. These are put into the selvage, and sewn up firm. When the bag is opened, it will close itself in consequence of the springs. A long pin is passed through the top of the bag and bent round hook-shape. If the bag be now filled with nuts, &c., it may be suspended by the hook, without any danger of the nuts or anything else falling out; because, although the mouth of the bag is downwards, the springs keep it shut. When this trick is to be shown, the prepared bag is hung on the side of the table that is away from the audience. The plate is also placed on that side; and when the handkerchief is laid over the plate a portion is left to fall over the side of the table. Now the kerchief is picked up with the *right* hand in the center (just as a lady does when she wishes to exhibit the lace edge), and with it the bag of nuts; the folds of the cambric hide the bag. The left hand is now used to draw over the handkerchief and to press the bag; this causes the springs to open, and out fall the " good things" upon the plate. This causes sufficient diversion for the merest tyro of a conjuror to drop the bag behind the table unseen, while he advances to the audience, politely inquiring, "Will you take a few nuts or sweetmeats?"

### 21. CONJURING A RING.

Several very marvelous tricks can be shown with an ordinary finger ring, such as passing it through the table, through a basin, an ale-glass or a plate, then into a box or nest of boxes, and other feats of legerdemain of a similar kind. These tricks are so good that they are always shown by the professors of magic at evening parties, but are never explained; however, we will attempt it. Procure a soft clean silk handkerchief and a sham gold ring; now a needleful of black silk, double; sew the silk to the middle of the handkerchief, and let the ring hang from it, suspended by the end of the silk, say at about three or four inches from the kerchief. When the handkerchief is held up by two corners, the suspended ring must always hang on the side facing the magician; the handkerchief can then be shaken, folded, and crumpled up in the hands, so as to make it appear "all fair." Now, to pass a ring through a drinking-glass and plate, and through the table on which it is placed. "If any lady or gentleman will kindly lend me a ring, I shall be happy to exhibit the electric and magnetic action of metallic substances on diaphonous bodies and ceramic manufactures, by showing their imperviousness, and the porosity of ligneous products of the Honduras." "Hem!" says Aunt Caroline, "what an extraordinary youth!" Do not, however, allow yourself to be carried away by any flattery of this kind, but determine to do the trick well, and *deserve* praise. Take the borrowed ring in the LEFT hand, and keep it there; pretend to pass it to the right hand, and say, "I will place it in the handkerchief. Who will kindly hold it for me while I put the glass on the plate in the center of the table?" While you thus freely ask who will hold the kerchief, you will secure the most bashful lady or gentleman in the company to hold the (your) ring in the handkerchief. "You will perceive, ladies and gentlemen, that the glass and the plate are now quite empty. I shall now place the glass in the plate on to the center of the table, and request the lady (or gent) to place the ring and the handkerchief over the glass. I particularly draw your attention to the fact that you will *hear* the ring fall into the glass when I request it to be released. You will then be certain that it is in the glass; but at my command it shall pass into this box (show the box round), which I shall place under the table. Now, miss (or sir) be good enough to let the ring fall into the glass. Silence! Ting! You heard it fall?" "Yes," all must reply, except the deaf Presto! It is now in the box. You lift the handkerchief, smooth down your brow with it, and put it into your pocket. The audience are now left to themselves. They rush to the plate and glass, it is not there; now the box, behold! it is as sound as ever: how it got there Aunt Carry could never tell, but you could, for you put it there out of your left hand when you placed the box under the table.

#### 22. THE ERRATIC EGG.

Transfer the egg from one wine-glass to the other, and back again to its original position, without touching the egg or glasses, or allowing any person or any thing to touch them. To perform this trick, all that you have to do, is to blow smartly on one side of the egg, and it will hop into the next glass; repeat this and it will hop back again.

## 23. THE OBEDIENT DIME.

### A CAPITAL TRICK AT THE DINNER TABLE.

Lay a dime between two half-dollars, and place upon the larger coins a glass, as in the diagram. Remove the dime without displacing either of the half-dollars or the glass. After having placed the glass and coins as indicated, simply scratch the tablecloth with the nail of the fore finger in the direction you would have the dime to move, and it will answer immediately. The table cloth is necessary; for this reason the trick is best suited to the breakfast or dinner table. The amusement will be heightened by reciting the following words prior to moving the finger:

" Little dime, do not stay
In a place so out-of-the-way;
But when my finger moved shall be,
Like a good fellow come to me."

## 24. THE PRISONER RELEASED.

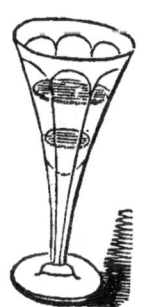

Place a dime in the bottom of a glass, and over the latter put a quarter, as in the diagram. The puzzle is to remove the small coin from beneath the larger one, without touching either of the coins, or touching or upsetting the glass. To do this capital trick you must blow with considerable force down one side of the glass upon the edge of the quarter. The dime will be expelled by the force of the air, and will fall either upon the upper surface of the quarter or upon the table. A little practice will render the performance of this feat very easy.

## 25. ADVANTAGEOUS WAGER.

Request a lady to lend you a watch. Examine it, and give a guess as to its value; then offer to lay the owner a wager, considerably below the real value of the watch, that she will not answer to three questions which you will put to her consecutively, "My watch." Show her the watch, and say, "What is this which I hold in my hand?" she, of course, will not fail to reply, "My watch." Next present to her notice some other object, repeating the same question. If she name the object you present, she loses the wager; but if she be on her guard, and remembering her stake, she says, "My watch," she must, of course, win; and you, therefore, to divert her attention, should observe to her, "You are certain to win the stake, but supposing I lose, what will you give me?" and if, confident of success, she replies for the third time, "My watch," then take it and leave her the wager agreed on.

### 26. THE DOUBLE MEANING.

Place a glass of any liquor upon the table, put a hat over it, and say, "I will engage to drink the liquor under that hat, and yet I'll not touch the hat." You then get under the table, and after giving three knocks, you make a noise with your mouth as if you were swallowing the liquor. Then getting from under the table, you say, "Now, gentlemen, be pleased to look." Some one, eager to see if you drank the liquor, will raise up the hat, when you instantly take the glass, and drink the contents, saying, "Gentlemen, I have fulfilled my promise. You are all witnesses that *I* did not touch the hat."

### 27. THE THREE SPOONS.

This is a most capital trick, but it requires a confederate's aid. Place three silver spoons crosswise on a table, request any person to touch one, and assure him you will find out the one he touches by a single inspection; although you will leave the room while he does so, and even if he touches it so gently as not to disarrange the order in which they are once put in the slightest degree. You retire; and when he gives you notice to enter, walk up to the table and inspect the spoons, as if trying to ascertain whether there are any finger-marks upon them, and then decide. Your confederate, of course, makes some sign, previously agreed upon, to give you notice which is the identical spoon; the actions may be, touching a button of his jacket for the top spoon, touching his chin for the second, and putting his finger to his lips may signify the lowest; but the precise actions are immaterial, so that the spoon they indicate be understood.

### 28. THE JUGGLER'S JOKE.

Take a little ball in each hand, and stretch your hands as

far apart as you possibly can, one from the other; then tell the company that you will make both the balls come into whichever hand they please, without bringing the hands into contact with each other. If any of the lookers-on challenge your ability of achieving this feat, all you have to do is to lay one of the balls down upon a table, turn yourself round, and take it up with your other hand. Both the balls will thus be in one of your hands, without the latter approaching the other, agreeably to your promise.

### 29. TO CAUSE WINE AND WATER TO CHANGE PLACES.

Fill a small narrow-necked bulb with port wine, or with water and colored spirit of wine, and put the bulb into a tall, narrow glass jar, which is then to be filled up with cold water: immediately, the colored fluid will issue from the bulb, and accumulate on the surface of the water in the jar, while colorless water will be seen accumulating at the bottom of the bulb. By close inspection, the descending current of the water may also be observed, and the colored and the colorless liquids be seen to pass each other in the narrow neck of the bulb without mixing. The whole of the colored fluid will shortly have ascended, and the bulb will be entirely filled with clear water.

### 30. IS IT POSSIBLE?

Side by side place three pieces of anything, (money is most convenient,) then take away the middle piece without touching it.

By removing the right hand piece to the side of the left, you thus take away the center without touching it.

### 31. THE TOPER'S STRATAGEM.

Get a bottle full of water, with the cork driven tightly in, and the top of it level with the neck of the bottle. You must remove the cork from the bottle without touching the cork with anything, and without injuring the bottle.

Wrap a towel round the bottom of the bottle, and strike it evenly and repeatedly, but not too hard, against a wall, post, or tree, and after some time the cork will be driven out of the bottle.

### 32. THE IMPOSSIBLE OMELET.

Produce some butter, eggs, and other ingredients for making an omelet, together with a frying-pan, in a room where there is a fire, and offer to bet a wager, that the cleverest cook will not be able to make an omelet with them. The wager is won by having previously caused the eggs to be boiled very hard.

### 33. NEW PERPETUAL ROTARY MOTION.

By an accidental occurrence, it has recently been discovered that a piece of rock-crystal, or quartz, cut in a peculiar form, produces, upon an inclined plane, and without any apparent impetus, an extraordinary rotary motion, which may be kept up for an indefinite period of time. The curiosity of this philosophical toy having excited general interest in the scientific world, Professor Leslie, in his lecture, thus explains the phenomenon:

"The crystal has six sides, and being cut accurately from the faces to a perfect convex surface, if placed upon a wetted smooth surface, and held parallel, no motion will take place, because the center of gravity of each face is balanced and supported in this position of the plane surface; but if a slight inclination is given to the plane, a rotary motion commences, in consequence of the support being removed from the center of gravity. The impetus once given, the centrifugal force increases the rotary motion to such a degree, as for an observer to be unable to distinguish the form of the crystal.

"*To produce the effect.*—Place the crystal on a piece of plate or common window glass, a china or glazed plate, or any smooth surface, perfectly clean, as grease or a particle of dust would impede its motion. Wet the surface, and give the plane a slight inclination, when, if properly managed, a rotatory motion will commence, which may be kept up for any length of time by giving alternate inclinations to the plane surface, according to the movements of the crystal; to heighten the pleasing effect of which, a variety of paper figures, harlequins, waltzers, &c., may be attached. The first trial of the experiment had better be made by giving a slight rotatory motion to the crystal."

### 34. THE MIRACULOUS APPLE.

To divide an apple into several parts, without breaking the rind. Pass a needle and thread under the rind of the apple, which is easily done by putting the needle in again at the same hole it came out of; and so passing on till you have gone round the apple. Then take both ends of the thread in your hands and draw it out, by which means the apple will be divided into two parts. In the same manner, you may divide it into as many parts as you please, and yet the rind will remain entire. Present the apple to any one to peel, and it will immediately fall to pieces.

#### 35. AN OMELET COOKED IN A HAT, OVER THE FLAME OF A CANDLE

State that you are about to cook an omelet; then you break four eggs in a hat, place the hat for a short time over the flame of a candle, and shortly after produce an omelet, completely cooked, and quite hot.

Some persons will be credulous enough to believe that by the help of certain ingredients you have been enabled to cook the omelet without fire; but the secret of the trick is, that the omelet had been previously cooked and placed in the hat, but could not be seen, because the operator, when breaking the eggs, placed it too high for the spectators to observe the contents. The eggs were empty ones, the contents having been previously extracted, by being sucked through a small aperture; but to prevent the company from suspecting this, the operator should, as if by accident, let a full egg fall on the table, which breaking, induces a belief that the others are also full.

#### 36. THE INFALLIBLE PROPHET.

In this trick one of three articles being taken by each of three persons, you propose to tell the article each person has taken. We will suppose the articles to be a ring, dime or shilling, and a key. The performer must in his own mind, term the ring *a*, the shilling or dime *e*, and key *i*: (this being the alphabetical order of the vowels, can be easily recollected) and he must also mentally distinguish the persons as first, second and third. Then taking twenty-four counters or cards, he gives one to the first person, two to the second and three to the third; and placing the remainder of the counters on the table, he turns his back or leaves the room, telling the persons each to take an article, and that whoever takes the ring is to take also as many counters as he already has; he who takes the shilling, twice as many; and he who takes the key, four times as many. This being done, the performer advances, and reckons the remaining counters, and according to their number and the underneath line, which he must have previously acquired, he tells who has taken each of the different articles.

| 1. | 2. | 3. | 5. | 6. | 7. |
|---|---|---|---|---|---|
| Salve | certa | animæ | semita | vita | quies. |

Thus, if there had been a remainder of six counters, the position of the vowels in the corresponding word *vita*, shows that the first person took *i*, the key; and the second person took *a*, the ring; and, consequently, the third person must have taken the shilling. It must be observed, that in no instance can there be a remainder of four counters; and that the first syllable of each word represents the first person, and the second syllable the second person. This ingenious feat is founded on the permutation of the three articles, or their representative vowels, which can only be placed in six different positions, and the corresponding numerical arrangement of the counters, thus:

1. *a e i*  salve.
2. *e a i*  certa.
3. *a i e*  animæ.
5. *e i a*  semita.
6. *i a e*  vita.
7. *i e a*  quies.

The three vowels, in their different positions, are made easy of recollection, by being united with consonants and formed in their regular succession into the above Latin line, or into this similarly constructed French one:

| 1. | 2. | 3. | 5. | 6. | 7. |
|---|---|---|---|---|---|
| Par fer | Cesar | jadis | devint | si grand | prince. |

### 37. PHILOSOPHY CHEATED.

This feat is really an excellent one, and has astonished crowds of spectators in different parts of the United States. It was one of the favorites of a late professor, by whom it was promulgated. Before you perform it in public, you must practice it until you are quite perfect, in private, for it would be a pity to spoil its effect by making a blunder in it. Begin by stating that you are about performing what you have no doubt will be regarded as a very extraordinary maneuver, and you will leave the company to decide upon what principle of natural philosophy it is accomplished. The mode of performance is as follows: Lay the piece of wood across the palm of your left hand, which keep wide open, with the thumb and all the fingers far apart, lest you be suspected of supporting the wood with them. Next, 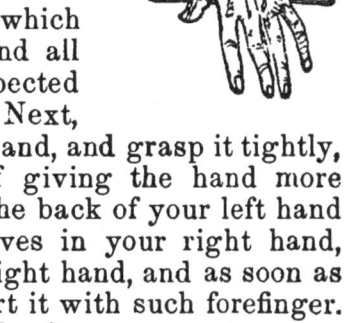 take your left wrist in your right hand, and grasp it tightly, for the purpose, as you state, of giving the hand more steadiness. Now, suddenly turn the back of your left hand uppermost, and as your wrist moves in your right hand, stretch out the forefinger of your right hand, and as soon as the wood comes undermost, support it with such forefinger. You may now shake the hand, and, after a moment or two, suffer the wood to drop. It is two to one but the spectators will suppose it to be produced by the action of the air, and try to do it themselves; but, of course, they must, unless you have performed the feat so awkwardly as to be discovered, fail in its performance. If you have no objection to reveal the secret, you can do it again, and while they are gravely philosophizing upon it, suddenly lift up your hand (*vide* Cut), and expose the trick. This will, doubtless, create much amusement. Observe that, in doing this feat, you must keep your fingers so low that no one can see the palm of your left hand; and move your finger so carefully, that its action may not be detected; 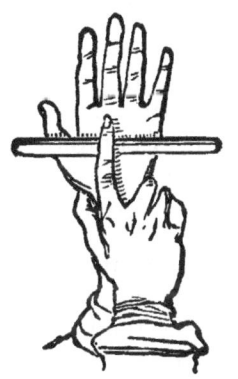 and if it be not, you may rest satisfied that its absence from round the wrist of the left hand will not be discovered, some of the fingers being naturally supposed to be under the coat; so that, if the spectators only see two or even one, they will imagine the others are beneath the cuff. When you have turned your hand over, do not keep the stick too long upheld, lest the spectators should take hold of your hands, and discover the trick; before their surprise is over, remove your forefinger, and suffer the stick to fall.

### 38. THE DISAPPEARING DIME.

Provide yourself with a piece of India rubber cord about twelve inches long, and a dime with a hole on the edge; attach the dime to the cord with a piece of white sewing silk, and after having done this, sew the cord to your coat sleeve lining, but be very careful and ascertain that the end upon which the dime is attached does not extend lower than within two inches of the extreme end of the sleeve when the coat is on. It is better to have the dime in the left arm sleeve. Having done this, bring down the dime with the right hand, and place it between the thumb and index finger of the left hand, and, showing it to the company, tell them that you will give the coin to any one present who will not let it slip away. You must then select one of the audience to whom you proffer the dime, and just as he is about to receive it you must let it slip from between your fingers, and the contraction of the elastic cord will make the coin disappear up your sleeve, much to the astonishment of the person who thinks he is about to receive it. This feat can be varied by pretending to wrap the coin in a piece of paper, or a handkerchief. Great care should be taken not to let any part of the cord be seen, as this would, of course, discover the trick. This is one of the most surprising feats of legerdemain, and its chief beauty consists in its extreme simplicity. The writer has frequently astonished a whole room full of company by the performance of this trick.

## TRICKS REQUIRING SPECIAL APPARATUS.

I admit no tricks that are wholly managed by the apparatus, as I think they are unworthy of notice. Therefore, every trick mentioned in the following pages must be carefully practiced in private before it is produced in public. The apparatus, of course, cannot be inspected by the audience, and for that reason it is better to mix them with those tricks that have been already mentioned, in order that suspicious persons may be quieted by an occasional permission to inspect the objects used in the performances.

The young conjuror should always vary the mode of performance in the non-essentials, and should study combinations of one trick with another, by which means he will produce more astonishing results than if he restricted himself to the methods mentioned in this work. He should also invariably make a little speech, acknowledging that he is only deceiving the eye and not the mind, and should therefore request the company not to ask any questions, or to demand inspection of any of his apparatus.

### 39. THE DIE TRICK.

Get a wooden die about two inches and a half square (1), and a hollow tin die exactly the size of the wooden one, but without one of the sides (2). Then paint them both exactly alike, as in the engraving. It will be better to let an *accidental* flaw appear on the same side of each. Then get a tin cover (4) that exactly fits the dice. Now for the trick itself.

Borrow two hats, and while you turn your back upon the audience as you go to your table, slip into one of them the false die. Place both hats on the table, and send round the real die and cover for inspection. When they are returned, say, "Now, ladies and gentlemen, it is my intention to place these hats one above another, thus." You then place the two hats as in No. 3, the hollow die being in the bottom hat. "I shall then cover the die thus," which you do, "and after I have knocked on the cover, I shall take it off, and you will find that the die is not under the cover, as it is now," taking it off, "but inside the hat, like this." You then put the real die into the hat. "You do not believe me, ladies and gentlemen, but I will soon convince you." You then take out the false die, and replacing the upper hat, put the die on the upper hat (of course, with the open side downward,) and place the cover over it. Pick up your conjuring wand, give it a few flourishes, and bring it down on the cover. Grasp the cover tightly near the bottom, when both cover and false die will come up together; put the end of your wand into them, and give them a good rattle. Then knock off the upper hat with a blow of the wand, and push the lower one off the table, so that the die tumbles out of it. Always use plenty of gesture about your tricks.

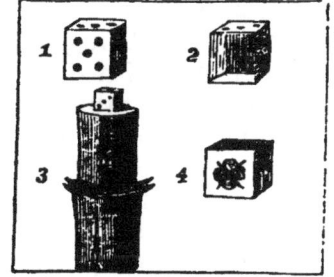

### 40. THE PENETRATIVE CENTS.

Get a brazier to cut out all the interior of five cents, only leaving the rims. He must then bore out nearly all the interior of a sixth cent, merely leaving a shell of copper at the top. A long rivet must then be let into the rim, as shown in Fig. 1, No. 2, and a hole must be drilled in each of the five rings, as in No. 3. The rivet is to be passed through the holes in the rings, and fastened below, so that all the rings can play easily upon it. Fig. 1, No. 1, is a section of the entire apparatus, the dotted lines representing the rivet. They can then be placed as shown in Fig. 2, No. 1, and no one will imagine that they are only shams, as you can rattle them or move them about upon each other. A leathern cover, Fig. 2, No. 2, is then made, which passes easily over the heap of cents, but being pliable, is capable of picking up the hollow cents with it, when it is held firmly. To the under surface of the table you fasten a little shelf, Fig. 2, No. 3, which moves on a hinge, and is let fall by placing the foot on the pedal, Fig. 2, No. 4, which draws the catch.

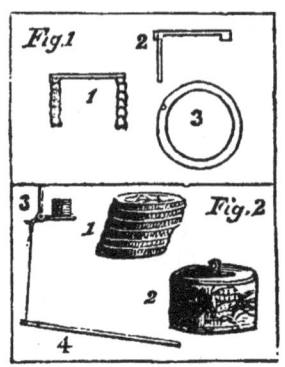

To perform the trick, place six real cents on the little shelf, and have the sham cents on the table. Take them up and rattle them, and put them down as in Fig. 2, No. 1. Keep a sixpence in the palm of your hand, pick up the sham cents, and as you put them down, slip the sixpence under them, as you do the ball in trick 6. Take the cover, and put it over the sham cents, make a short speech, and knock the cover with your wand, at the same time pressing the pedal with your foot, which will cause all the six real cents to tumble down with a great crash. Take up the cover and false cents together, put the end of your wand into them and hold them up triumphantly, showing the spectators that the six cents have been replaced by a silver sixpence. While you are picking up the cents, slip the sham ones out of the cover into your left hand, and take some opportunity of letting the empty cover roll towards the audience, one of whom you ask to pick it up and bring it to you. This maneuver generally disarms all suspicion, for the picker-up is sure to examine it very closely.

I have only given mere outlines of this really excellent trick, which may be varied in a hundred ways, and is capable of combination with other tricks to a large extent. For the pedal may be substituted a lever running immediately under the surface of the table, if the performer prefers to have a short cloth on it. There should be always two cloths on the table; the lower one thick and soft, to prevent jingling of objects, and the upper one white, as it displays everything better than a colored one. The ingenuity of the young conjuror will easily find methods of varying this trick. *See Trick* 67, *page* 48.

### 41. THE DOLL TRICK.

Get a comical looking doll, and cut off his head diagonally, taking care to do it very neatly. Drive a peg into the neck, and bore a hole in the body, into which the peg fits, as in the cut. Paint his body and head carefully, and if you put a gold chain or two round his neck, it will conceal the line of junction. Make also a coat of silk, and sew a pocket inside the edge of the skirt.

Take up the doll, and say, "Now, ladies and gentlemen, here is a very learned man. Observe the development of his forehead, the sagacity of his nose, the eloquence of his lips, the dignity of his spectacles, and the philosophy of his pigtail. He is professor of astronomy at Timbuctoo, and here is his gown of office. See how handsome he looks in it. He is going to Amsterdam to see the eclipse of the last new comet. He has the honor to wish you all farewell before starting on his journey. Now, professor, we are waiting to see you go. Oh! you want funds, do you? I beg your pardon; here it a quarter for you." So saying, you take your right hand from under the gown, taking with it the body, and put the body into your pocket, while you jingle some silver. The head is now supported by your left hand. Pretend to give him some money, and then say, "What! you won't go unless you have more! Get along!" Hit the head a hard rap with your right hand, which drives it into the pocket, which you hold open for it with your left thumb and little finger. "O dear! the doctor is dead, and cannot be found." Saying this, you grasp the gown by the place where the head is, and shake it about to show that it is empty. If you like.

you can make another oration and hold a dialogue, making the doctor resuscitate himself, which is of course done by taking the head out of the pocket with the left hand, and working it about by the peg.

### 42. THE FLYING COINS.

Take two eagles, or rather brass imitations, and grind them down until they are reduced to half their thickness. Do the same with two quarter dollars, and fasten them accurately together, so that you will have two coins, each having one silver face, and one brass face. Take one of them in each hand, showing the silver side of one and the brass side of another, and offer to change them without moving your arms. Shut your hands and the coins will turn over. Then, on opening them again, they will appear to have changed from one hand into the other.

### 43. THE VANISHED HALF-DIME.

Put a little wax on the nail of the middle finger of the right hand, and take a half-dime into the palm of the same hand. Close the hand, pressing the wax on the coin. Then rapidly open it, and the silver piece will adhere to the wax, and be quite concealed behind the finger when you hold your hand up.

### 44. THE RESTORED DOCUMENT.

Make a memorandum book, and line the cover with paper which has been previously rubbed with a mixture of lamp-black and oil. The paper must be loosely affixed, so that it can be raised up, and a leaf from the memorandum book placed under it. You must also make a flat box, having a double opening.

You now take a leaf out of the memorandum book, and ask some one to write a sentence, at the same time offering him the book to write upon. The pencil with which you furnish him is very hard, and he is forced to press upon the paper in order to mark. In so doing, the black is transferred by the pressure of the pencil from the blackened paper to the white leaf that has been placed under it, and of course makes an exact copy of the writing. You then give the man his document, put the memorandum book in your pocket, and go out of the room to fetch your box, which you have *forgotten*. While you are out of the room, you take out the leaf from under the black paper, and put it into one side of the flat box, and shut down the cover that hides it. You bring in the box, apologising for your absence, and give the box, open at the *other* side, into the writer's hands. Tell him to burn his writing in a candle, and to place the ashes in the box. He does so, and closing the box, returns it to you. You then flourish about a little with the box, wave it in the air, bring it down with a bang on the table, strike it with your wand, and then, opening it as at first, you produce the duplicate leaf, which the writer acknowledges to be in his own hand-writing. If the lamp-black should have come off and smeared the paper, you can account for it by observing that it is very difficult to get rid of all traces of the burning.

### 45. THE MAGIC RINGS.

Get a blacksmith to make a number of rings, about six or seven inches in diameter, as in the cut. A is made with a spring opening on one side, B is a set of two rings forged permanently within each other, C is a set of three rings formed in the same manner, and D D are two simple rings. The rings should be about the thickness of a rather large black-lead pencil.

Lay the rings on one another, and they will all appear to be separate and distinct : D D should be the uppermost rings, then B, then A, and then C. Hand round D for inspection, and if any more are desired, hand round the other D. When returned, hang them over your left arm, or grasp them in your hand, and tell the company that you are going to weave all the rings together. You clash them together, and after going through some complicated movements, bring out B, which the spectators will think you have just fastened together. Hand them round. When they are returned 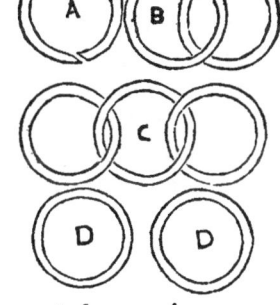 mix them all up, and bring out C. Then take A in your hand, and passing one of the outer rings of C through the opening, you have four rings together. Then add D and you have five. Take off D and substitute B which will give you six. So you go on weaving them into all kinds of fantastic shapes. You must always conceal the joint in A with your thumb, and contrive as often as you can to have one at least of the rings D at liberty

This is a capital trick, and may be diversified to any extent, especially if the number of rings is increased.

### 46. THE FISH AND INK TRICK.

This is really a first-rate delusion. You bring before the spectators a glass vase, full of ink. You dip a ladle into it, and pour out some of the ink upon a plate, in order to convince the audience that the substance in the vase is really ink. You then throw a handkerchief over the vase and instantly withdraw it, when the vase is found to be filled with pure water, in which a couple of gold fish are swimming.

This apparent impossibility is performed as follows. To the interior of the vessel is fitted a black silk lining, which adheres closely to the sides when pressed by the water, and which is withdrawn inside the handkerchief during the performance of the trick. The ladle has a hollow handle with an opening into the bowl. In the handle is a spoonful or so of ink, which runs into the bowl when it is held downward, during the act of dipping it into the vase.

### 47. THE CANNON BALLS.

The performer of this trick borrows a number of hats, and places them on the table. He then returns each person his hat, and on turning it over, a thirty-two pounder cannon ball rolls out.

The method of performing this delusion is as follows. Get a turner to make a number of wooden balls, each the size of a thirty-two pounder cannon ball, and let a hole be bored in each which will admit the middle finger. The balls are arranged hole upwards on a shelf on your table on the side opposite to your audience, so that the balls are nearly level with the top of the table. When you take a hat off the table, you slip your fore or middle finger into the ball just as you would into a thimble, and by bending the finger, bring the ball into the hat.

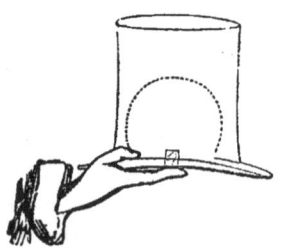

Any object may be brought into a hat in this manner, a great cabbage, for instance, having a hole cut in the stall

### 48. THE DIME IN THE BALL OF COTTON.

Get a tinman to make a flat tin tube, which will just allow a dime to pass through it. Wind a quantity of worsted round it, so as to make it into a ball.

These preliminaries having been accomplished, perform any trick that will get a dime out of sight, such as number 1 or 2. Then tell the spectators that you will bring the marked dime into the middle of a ball of worsted. Take down the ball from the place where it is lying, drop the dime into the tube, and withdraw the tube, leaving the dime in the ball. A good squeeze or two will hold it tight, and obliterate every mark of the tube. Place the ball in a tumbler, take the end of the worsted, and give it to some one to unwind. This being done, the dime will be found in the very center of the ball, with the end of the worsted wrapped tightly round it.

### 49. THE EGG AND BAG TRICK.

Get a chintz or cloth bag made double,*and between the two bags make six or seven pockets, each of which will hold an egg, and have an opening into the bag. Fill the pockets with eggs, and you are ready for the performance.

Hold the bag by the place where the eggs are, shake it, turn it inside out, and show that there is nothing in it. Then tell the spectators, that you are sure there is a hen in the bag. Put your head near the mouth of the bag, and make a clucking like a hen. You then say "I knew I was right, and she has laid an egg." So saying, you put your hand into the bag and take out one of the eggs, taking care to pretend to grope in one of the corners for it.

This is repeated until all the eggs but one are gone. You then, after taking out the last egg, say that some people think the eggs are not real, but you will convince them by ocular inspection. Saying this, you break the egg in a saucer with your right hand, and while the people are occupied with it, you drop the bag behind your table, or hang it on a hook out of sight, and take up another exactly like it, into which you have put a hen. "These are real eggs," you then say, "and if any one doubts their reality, they cannot doubt that this is a real hen." You then turn the bag upside down, and shake out the hen. If any one wishes to inspect that bag, he can do so without being much wiser for it.

* That is, make two bags and sew the edges together, so that actually there will be a third bag between the two.

## 50. THE DANCING EGG.

Send for some eggs, and take care to place among them one which has been emptied of its contents, and to which is fastened a long hair, at the other end of which is tied a crooked pin. Borrow a small stick from one of the spectators, and as you go behind your table contrive to hook the bent pin into your coat, passing it over the stick. Then place the egg on an inverted hat, and ask for some music, and directly it begins to sound, a slight and imperceptible depression or elevation of the stick will cause the egg to twist and roll about upon it as if it had life. You must be careful to turn gently round now and then, so as apparently to vary the distance of the egg from the body.

## 51. BELL AND SHOT.

Get a wooden bell made, so thick that there is a considerable space between the outer and inner surfaces, especially on the upper part of the bell. A hollow must be cut in this, and the handle so made, that when it is at rest, it is forced upwards by a spring, and draws up the round piece of wood to which the clapper chain is attached, and closes the aperture, as shown in the engraving.

You have a cardboard measure, which is of precisely the same capacity as the cavity in the bell, and just wide enough to hold a cent. Into this you privately put a cent, and then fill up the measure with shot, heaping it a little, to compensate for the cent. You make up a tale about a man going out shooting, and ringing the bell of the gunmaker's shop. (You then ring your wooden bell.) How the man bought a measure full of shot for a cent, (you pour the shot into the bell and back again two or three times,) but was so long haggling over three shots, that the gunmaker took away the shot, (here you again pour the shot into the bell, and by pressing on the handle, allow them all to run into the hollow,) and kept the cent for his trouble. The man went out of the shop, but soon came in again, and rang furiously. (Here you again ring the bell which is now apparently empty, and invert the measure on the table. The cent not being held by the finger and thumb, will now fall on the tablecloth.) Then finish the story with an account of the manner in which the man got back his cent. When you have finished, invert the bell over the empty measure, and on pressing the handle, the shots will refill it. Do not touch it until you have done another trick or two, and then, when you put the bell aside, ring it again, and remark that the purchaser was a silly fellow ofter all, for here are his shots in his measure.

### 52. THE BURNED HANDKERCHIEF RESTORED.

Get a tinman to make a double canister, such as is shown in the cut, with an opening at each end. This must so slide within a tin tube, that either end can be concealed within it alternately, as seen in the engraving, where the end A is shown, and B is concealed. In this position it looks like an ordinary canister. The interior is divided into two parts. Into B put a piece of cambric made to look like a handkerchief.

Borrow a cambric handkerchief, and say, "Now ladies and gentlemen, I shall burn this handkerchief to ashes, place them in this canister," (so saying you put it into A,) "and when I have uttered a spell, it will be restored perfectly whole. Will the owner say what mark it has?" While the audience are looking towards the owner, you turn the canister over, and push up the canister until the shoulder of B is on a level with the top of the tube. When the mark has been declared, you open B, take out the cambric, and pretend to verify the mark. You then put it into a candle flame, and when it has burned entirely to ashes, put the ashes into B, shut it up, and rapidly reverse it as you turn round to your audience, so that A is uppermost again. Then utter any nonsense you like, open A, and take out the handkerchief uninjured. It rather adds to the trick if you drop a little eau de cologne into A before commencing.

### 53. THE FIRE EATER.

If the young conjuror is desirous of appearing in the character of a fire-eater, it is very easily managed. He must prepare a piece of thick string, by soaking it in a solution of niter, and then drying it. He cuts off a piece about an inch in length, lights one end, and wraps it up in a piece of tow which he holds in his left hand. The trifling smoke will be concealed by a huge bundle of loose tow also carried in the left hand.

He takes a handful of tow in his right hand, puts it into his mouth, chews it up, and appears to swallow it. He then takes another handful, and with it the piece in which is the string. As he puts this into his mouth, he takes out the piece which he has already chewed. By taking breath through the nostrils, and breathing it out through the mouth, smoke begins to issue forth, and the whole interior of the mouth is soon lighted up with a glow. When the mouth is shut, and the tow pressed together, the fire goes out, except the piece of prepared string. More tow is then taken into the mouth, and treated in the same manner.

### 54. THE EGG-BOX.

A, the egg-box ; B, the upper shell ; C, the inner shell, covered over with the shell of an egg ; D, the lower part of the box. To do the trick, call for an egg, then bid all the 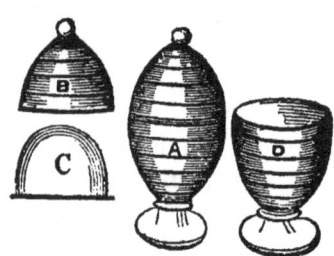 by-standers look at it, and see that it is a real egg, set the box on the table, take off the upper part, with your fore finger and thumb, then placing the egg in the box, say, "You see it fairly in," and uncovering it again, likewise say, "You shall see me take it out, and put it in my pocket in your sight ;" open your box again and say, "There is nothing," close your hand about the middle of your box, and taking B by the bottom, say, "There is the egg again," which it appears to the spectators to be, so clapping that in again, and taking the lid of C in your finger and thumb, say, "There it is gone again."

### 55. THE GLOBE-BOX.

This trick is not inferior to the best that is shown with boxes. It is done with a box made of four pieces, and a ball as big as may be conveniently contained therein ; the ball serves as the egg does in the egg-box, to deceive the nand and eyes of spectators. This ball, made of wood or ivory, is thrown out of the box upon the table, for every one to see that it is substantial; then put the ball into the box, which close up with all the pieces one within another; remove the upper shell with your fore finger and thumb, and there will appear another of a different color, red, blue, yellow, or any other color you may fancy; this will seem

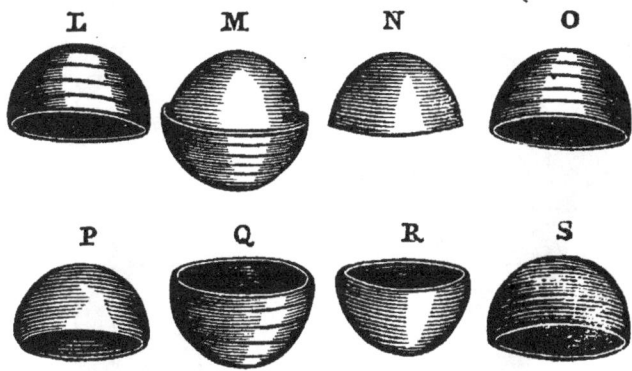

to be another ball, though, in fact, it is no more than a shell of wood, ingeniously turned and fitted to the box, as you may perceive by the cuts. L is the outer shell of the globe, taken off the figure M, the top of which represents the ball; N is an inner shell; O, the cover of the same; P, another inner shell; Q, the cover of the same; R, a third shell; S, that which covers it. These globes may be made with more or less varieties, according to the desire of the practitioner.

### 56. THE COFFEE AND HANDKERCHIEF TRICKS.

One of the greatest means of wonder-working is that of *ingenious contrivance*. We will illustrate this by two popular feats. A number of handkerchiefs taken from the audience by more than one popular performer, were placed in a small washing tub, into which water was poured, and they were washed for a few minutes. They were then placed in a vessel like the figure (\*) on the next page, and immediately afterwards the performer said to the persons in front: "I will give you these;" and taking off the top, when he was expected to throw out the wet handkerchiefs, all that fell was a number of flowers. He now brought out a box, which he opened, and shoved it to be empty; then shutting it, and uttering a few cabalistic words, he opened it again.

and there were the handkerchiefs, all dry, folded, and scented, which he distributed to their respective claimants.

Another experiment of a popular performer was called "coffee for the million." Producing a vessel like the diagram A, the performed filled it with unground coffee, and

placing it under a cover B, he said, "There, when you have done that, let it simmer for three quarters of an hour; but, perhaps, you will not like to wait so long; here then it is;" and on removing the cover, the vessel appeared full of hot liquid coffee. In another vessel of the same kind he obtained lump-sugar from rape-seed; and in a third, warm milk from horse-beans; and pouring out the coffee into cups, sent them round to regale his auditory, amidst their loud and approving shouts at so great a transformation.

These feats are the result of considerable ingenuity. It is probable that the devices employed would not readily occur to spectators in general, while they would utterly escape those whose object is merely amusement, and who, if they thought at all, would be likely to describe the result as supernatural. We proceed, then, to the unraveling of the mystery. Let it be observed, in reference to the first experiment, that a number of handkerchiefs are collected in the early part of the evening for various illusions, and that many of them appear for a time on the performer's table. Provided with a collection of these articles, from the handsome silk handkerchief to one trimmed with lace, used by a fashionable lady, he could easily substitute his own of the same kind for those of his auditory, as the curtain falls, according to the arrangements of the evening, between the collection of the handkerchiefs and the subsequent processes. His own handkerchiefs, therefore, are washed and placed in the vase already described; and the so-called change into flowers is nothing more than the retention of the handkerchiefs in the lower part of the apparatus, which the figure illustrates, while the upper part holds the flowers till they are scattered among the spectators. Meanwhile, all that is required is done to their handkerchiefs. It is not absolutely necessary that they should be washed; for folding, pressing, and a little eau-de-Cologne, would complete the preparation; but granting that they are washed, there is still no difficulty, though this mystifies the spectators, who have the idea that drying is a long affair; for it may be effected in a minute or two by a machine that is readily obtained. The box brought out has them deposited in it, but as it is double, one interior is first shown, which, of course, contains nothing, for the inner drawer holding the handkerchiefs remains in the case; but when a few sounds are uttered, and the professor touches a secret spring behind, which disengages the inner box, he draws it out with the outer one, and presents the handkerchiefs to the audience. In the diagram A, the box is shown as empty. At B, we have a representation of the box containing the handkerchiefs. It is only necessary to add that the box is very nicely made; the part within the other drawn out to the end, defies detection. *See Trick No.* 65.

The preparation of coffee, milk, and sugar, may be easily explained; for if the vessels containing respectively the unground coffee, the rape-seed, and the horse-beans, always placed under a cover, be put on a part of the table having

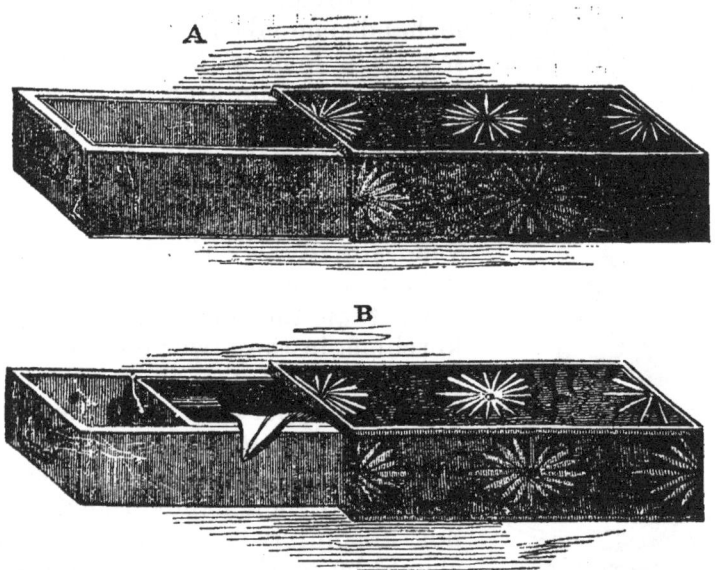

a circular trap-door—and for this there is full provision in the cover of the table extending to the floor—a confederate may readily substitute one for the other.

## 57. THE MAGIC FUNNEL.

This favorite and simple trick is carried out by the assistance of a double funnel, that is to say, one funnel soldered into the other so as to leave a space between them for water, and communicating with the hollow of the funnel by a hole in the tube. Our drawing will assist the explanation.

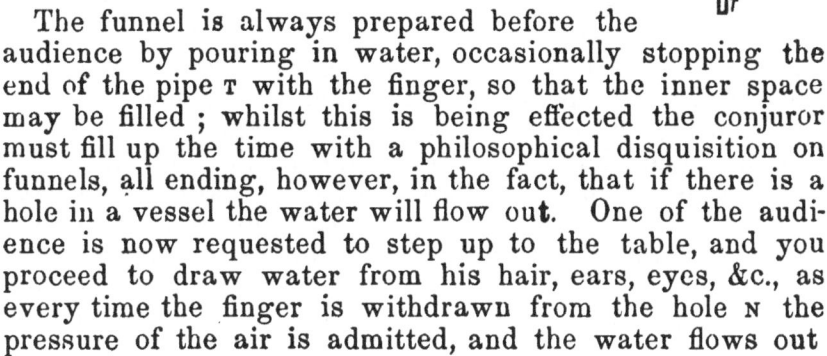

s s, space for water between the funnels, which is filled by stopping end of tube T with the finger: the water flows in and out at K.

N, a pin-hole at the top, which is covered with the finger. When the funnel is prepared for use, every time the finger is withdrawn water flows out from tube T.

The funnel is always prepared before the audience by pouring in water, occasionally stopping the end of the pipe T with the finger, so that the inner space may be filled; whilst this is being effected the conjuror must fill up the time with a philosophical disquisition on funnels, all ending, however, in the fact, that if there is a hole in a vessel the water will flow out. One of the audience is now requested to step up to the table, and you proceed to draw water from his hair, ears, eyes, &c., as every time the finger is withdrawn from the hole N the pressure of the air is admitted, and the water flows out

## 58. THE MAGIC BOTTLE.

This trick, if well managed, is one of the most wonderful that can be performed in a drawing-room without apparatus; but it requires dexterity at the conclusion.

The person performing the trick offers to pour from a common wine bottle, port wine, sherry, milk, and champagne in succession, and in any order.

To accomplish the trick, you must make solutions of the following chemicals, and label the bottles with numbers, thus:

1 A saturated solution of the sulphocyanate of potash.

2 A diluted solution of the above—one part of the solution to four of water.

3. A saturated solution of nitrate of lead.

4. A saturated solution of perchloride of iron.

5. A saturated solution of bicarbonate of potash.

6 Sulphuric acid.

7 A clear solution of gum-arabic.

Procure a champagne bottle, and wash it out well, then pour three teaspoonfuls of No. 4 into it. As the quantity is very small, it will not be observed, especially if you are quick in your movements. Pour some distilled or rain water into a common water-bottle or jug, and add a tablespoonful of No. 7 to it; then set it aside ready for use.

Provide some wine glasses of four different patterns, and into one pattern pour the solution marked No. 1, into another that marked No. 2, and so on for Nos. 3 and 5. Return the solutions to their respective bottles, and arrange the glasses on a small tray, remembering the solutions that were poured into each pattern.

Everything being ready, take the champagne bottle that you have prepared, from two or three others, and holding it up to show the company that it is clear and empty, you must desire some person to hand you the water bottle or jug, and then fill up the bottle with the water.

Pour some of the contents of the bottle into an unprepared glass, in order to show that it is water; then say, "change to champagne," and pour the liquid from the bottle into one of the glasses rinsed with No. 5; then pour into a glass rinsed with No. 1, and it will change to port wine; but if poured into No. 3, it will change to milk, and if into No. 2, it will produce sherry. Be careful in pouring the fluid from the bottle, not to hold it high above the glasses, but to keep the mouth of it close to the edges of the glasses, otherwise persons will observe that it undergoes change of color after it is poured into the wine glasses, and on this account the glasses should be held rather high.

*\** As the solutions used in the above trick are deleterious, they must not be left about in the way of children, and of course the fluid in the wine glasses must not even be tasted; but if any of the company wish to drink the wines you have made, then the tray must be adroitly exchanged for another with the proper wines placed on it.

This is an excellent parlor trick if well managed, and is not difficult to comprehend.

### 59. THE BOTTLE TRICK.

The chemical method of performing this delusion has been already explained, the mechanical one will be easily understood from the "Magic Funnel Trick." It is usually carried out with a bottle, the body of which is constructed of tin, the neck of glass ; the body is divided into sundry compartments, three of which are sufficient, with a center one, for ordinary use : by cutting the bottle in two, the arrangement will be understood as shown beneath.

o, center of bottle, from which milk may be poured.  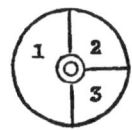  1, 2, 3, compartments holding port, sherry, and alcohol.

It must be understood that little tubes from each compartment terminate in the neck, and they are filled with their respective liquids by the pear-shaped vessel already explained. Each compartment is perforated with a little hole at the top, so that when the fingers are placed over them (as on the holes of a flute) the liquid cannot run out on inverting the bottle.

On showing the trick, the performer alludes to his wonderful bottle full of the milk of human kindness, which he pours out carefully from the center compartment, keeping the three holes tight with his fingers, the center being filled and emptied in the ordinary manner ; after pouring out and handing round a few glasses of milk, he may pour the rest into a jug, in the bottom of which some milk has been already placed, so that the company may believe the bottle was originally filled with it; he may now wash out the bottle (that is to say, the center compartment), still keeping his fingers over the holes, and for the sake of a little mystification put the bottle upright under a hat, commanding the bottle to change its temperance habits. He may now ask the company to call for port, sherry, gin, brandy, noyeau, &c.

The sherry and port are poured from their compartments, the spirit supplies the others, as a number of wine-glasses can be prepared with drops of burnt sugar for brandy, syrup and juniper for gin. A small drop of oil of almonds or other flavoring materials may be used for the different liquors. A thick wine-glass must be employed, holding a very small quantity of fluid.

A magic coffee-pot may be arranged in a similar manner, with three compartments to hold hot tea, coffee, and punch ; the middle compartment may hold the tea and coffee berries, into which the assistant may pour by mistake the contents of the bottle labeled "*Ink*." The performer, after scratching his head, as if in deep thought, will take a lump of whiting and powder up, placing it in the center compartment, which can be fastened up with a cork or proper lid. Then, if the holes from the compartments terminate in the handle and the pipes in the spout, when the fingers are removed the three liquids pour out separately, as in the Bottle Trick. This mode of showing the trick is good, because, however large your audience, you can provide everybody with something to drink, and it is displayed with great effect by Signor Blitz, and Wyman.

### 60. THE MAGIC QUARTER.

Procure a small round box, about one inch deep, to which fit accurately a quarter or cent: line the box with any dark paper (crimson, for instance), and paste some of it on one side of the coin, so that when it lies in the lower part of the box it shall appear like the real box. This quarter or cent is concealed in the hand, and before performing the trick, it will heighten the effect if a number of single quarters or cents are hidden about the room, in places known to yourself. Having borrowed a coin, you dexterously place this on one side, and substitute the prepared one; and putting it gravely into the box, ask all to be sure they have seen it enter: when the lid is on, shake up and down—the noise betrays the metal; now command it to disappear, and shake laterally from side to side; as the quarter is made to fit accurately, no noise is apparent—the coin seems to be gone; in proof of which you open the box, and display the interior; the paper on the coin conceals it, whilst you direct the audience to look into a book, or a pair of slippers, for the missing quarter; the prepared coin can be slipped out, and the box handed round for examination, in which, of course, nothing will be found. This trick may be repeated two or three times with the greatest success, and is so simple that nobody guesses the manner of performance.

### 61 TO CHANGE A DIME TO A QUARTER.

This is quite a simple parlor trick, but when performed with dexterity is calculated to produce much astonishment at an evening party. In fact, it surprises on account of its very simplicity. Procure two pieces of marbled paper about seven inches square, and having put the marble backs of the paper together, cut them the shape of diagram

Fig. 1. Be very careful to have them exactly the same size, as the success of the trick depends in a great measure upon the regularity of the paper. After cutting the paper in the manner described, place a dime in the center of one of the pieces at the place marked A, then fold it carefully over at the crease on the side marked B, and also again at the side marked C. When you have done this turn down the end marked D upon the center A, and again fold over on E. When this is accomplished, you will discover that you have formed a small parcel the same shape as Fig. 2, with a dime in the center. You must then place a quarter of a dollar

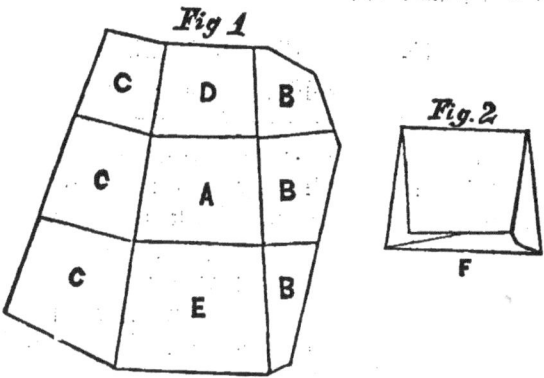

in the center of the other piece of paper, and fold it up exactly the same size and shape as the first piece. When you have done this, gum the two parcels together at the back of the ends marked F, in Fig. 2, and the sides will be so even that both parcels will appear as one. You can then open the side of the paper containing the dime and show it to your audience, at the same time informing them that you are going to open a mint on a small plan, and coin a quarter from a dime. Having done this, mutter some cabalistic words and dexterously turn over the side containing the quarter, and upon opening the paper, to the astonishment of the company, instead of a dime they will behold a genuine quarter. I have seen much merriment created by this excellent feat.

## 62. DESCRIPTION OF THE MAGICIAN'S TABLE.

When a secret confederate is required, have a table four and a half feet long, two feet eight inches high, two feet nine inches wide, with a curtain round it, twenty-two inches deep. In the top of this table are several secret square holes, of different sizes, from three to five inches across; these having covers which exactly fit, and hung upon concealed hinges, so that they may be let down; but when lying flat, the top of the table appears to present a perfect surface. Under this surface are buttons, which prevent those lids from falling down when not made use of. Under the top of the table is fastened a box, or drawer, open at the top, and at the side which is farthest from the spectators. This box is about twenty inches deep, and concealed by the curtain; and in this box is placed the secret agent who assists the performer

### 63. WYMAN'S GUN TRICK.

Having provided yourself with a fowling-piece, permit any person to load it, retaining for yourself the privilege of putting in the ball, to the evident satisfaction of the company, but instead of which you must provide yourself with an artificial one made of black lead, which may be easily concealed between your fingers, and retain the real ball in your possession, producing it after the gun has been discharged; and a mark having been previously put upon it, it will instantly be acknowledged. This trick is quite simple, as the artificial ball is easily reduced to a powder on the application of the ramrod; besides the smallness of the balls preclude all discovery of the deception.

### 64. THE HATCHED BIRD.

Separate an egg in the middle as nearly as possible, empty it, and then, with a fine piece of paper and a little glue, join the two halves together, having first put a live canary bird inside it, which will continue unhurt in it for some time, provided you make a small pinhole in the shell to supply the bird with air; have, also, a whole egg in readiness. Present the two eggs for one to be chosen; put the egg, which contains the bird, next to the person who is to choose, and for this purpose be sure to select a lady; she naturally chooses the nearest to her, because, having no idea of the trick to be performed, there is no apparent reason to take the further one; at any rate, if the wrong one be taken, you do not fail in the trick, for you break the egg, and say, "You see that this egg is fair and fresh madam;

so you would have found the other, if you had chosen it. Now, do you choose to find in it a mouse, or a canary bird?" She naturally declares for the bird; nevertheless, if she ask for the mouse, there are means to escape; you ask the same question of several ladies, and gather the majority of votes, which, in all probability, will be in favour of the bird which you then produce.

### 65. THE APPLE AND ORANGE TRICK.

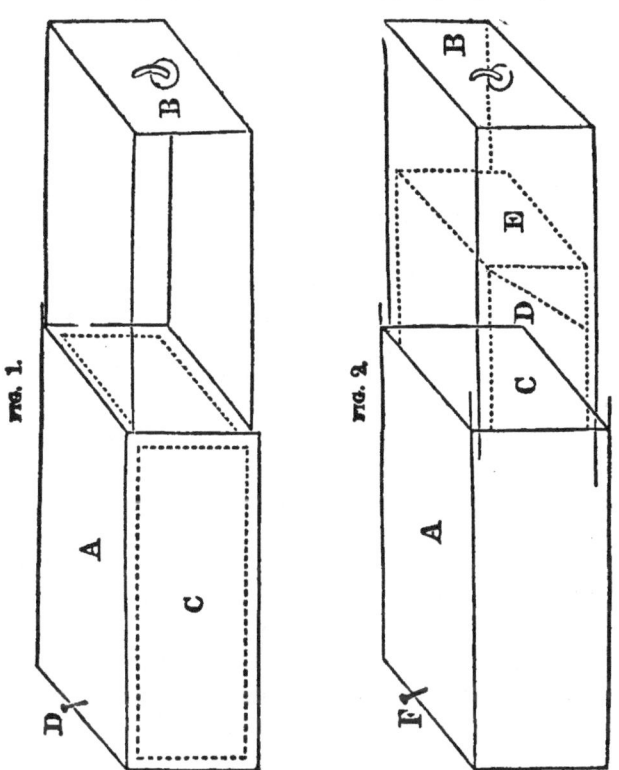

Have a box made with a drawer fitted to it as in the figure No. 2, marked A. The back part of the drawer B, which slides into the box A, has no end piece; then have another drawer made, marked C, open at the top, that will fit the drawer B rather easy, when put into it the sides and ends of the drawer C, made of rather thin wood, with their end and sides sloping towards the sides of the drawer B, so that when it is in the drawer B, it cannot be discovered without minute examination; then push them both into the box A, and have a small hole bored through the top of the box A, in which you put a small pin with a flat top, as marked D in the plate ; this pin is so long that it will just catch drawer C, inside of the box A, to prevent it from coming out with the drawer B, when not necessary to be exposed. It is now ready to perform experiments with. You are aware, as has already been described, that the drawer B is open at the inner end, consequently, when that with the loose drawer C is pushed into the box A, and you put the pin D in its place, the drawer B may be pulled out, or pushed back, without interruption ; but if you remove the pin out of the box, C will come out inside of the drawer B without the trick being discovered ; it being understood that the false drawer C is invariably concealed from the spectator. When the drawer C is in the box A, and the drawer B has been drawn out, the end of the drawer C will then appear as if it was the end of the drawer B as represented in the plate. You can then show it to the company, and you may also measure the inside of the drawer B, and the outside of the box A, and convince them that, apparently, nothing is concealed. Care must be taken in pulling the drawer C out alone, that the drawer C will not slip from the bottom of the drawer B, which otherwise would prevent it from being pushed back. A little catch may be affixed in the bottom of the drawer C, so as to prevent the same from slipping out of its place.

*To Perform the Experiment.*—Fill, privately, the drawer C with fruit, close the drawer B, and exhibit it ; then pull the drawer B out, alone, as represented in the plate, figure 2, which will convince the spectators that it is empty. When you have satisfied them on that point, slide back the drawer B, then place the left hand on the secret pin D, and take it out ; then with the right hand pull out the drawer B, with the secret drawer C, which is full of fruit, to the great astonishment of the company ; take the fruit out and present it to the spectators. This concludes the performance.

### 66. ENCHANTED COIN, AS PERFORMED BY PROFESSOR WYMAN.

Put fifteen pieces of money into a hat, take out five and mysteriously pass them back into the hat and it covered. To do this trick you must have in your left hand a plate, and under the plate and in your left hand have previously placed five pieces of coin such as you will have placed in the hat; after you have counted the fifteen pieces into the hat, you then ask the person whom you have selected from the audience to assist you in performing the tricks, to count the money out of the hat into the plate, to see that there is no mistake, after which you turn the money out of the plate into the hat, and at the same time let fall the five pieces you have secreted in your hand under the plate; you then ask him to draw out five pieces, which will still leave fifteen, you take the five that is drawn out and place them in a drawer (see the orange and apple trick), then you go through the magic words, *Presto, Pacillo, Pass,* you then open the drawer, (after placing your finger on the spring to hold the inside drawer in which the five pieces were placed,) and show the audience that the five pieces are gone, you then tell him to get the hat and see how many pieces are in it; he gets the hat, and to the surprise of all, he counts the original number, fifteen.

**67. MYSTERIOUS COIN, OR HOW TO MAKE DOLLARS PASS THROUGH A WINE GLASS, A CHINA PLATE, A TABLE, AND FALL INTO THE HAND.**

After performing trick 40, (p. 27,) you may address the company again, and say: "I will show you the nature of this trick, if you will only look sharp enough to see how it is done. Therefore, watch closely, and if you have *very* penetrating eyes, you may see the money go through this glass and fall upon the plate, and from that through the table into my hand. I will do it deliberately, so that you may have every opportunity of detecting the deception, which will make you as wise as myself."

Now you take a plate and place it on the table, place upon that a wine glass upside down, and take the empty leathern case and hold it before the audience, to convince them that nothing is inside. Place it, in a careless manner, over the riveted money, which you had before put a little aside from the view of the spectators. Place a small ball on the bottom of the glass, then take the case with the concealed coins therein, and place them over the ball, which will be secreted therein. Now tell the company to keep a sharp look out, and they may discover the whole process. Take the loose coins and throw them on the table; bring them again under the table, and exchange them for a ball previously deposited on the shelf, and lay the same upon the table. Remove the case alone, which, of course, will leave the money exposed on the top of the glass. "Now," says the performer, "I presume that you have discovered the whole mystery; but if not, I will give you another opportunity, and will return the money whence it came." Cover the money with the case, and bring the ball which you previously exposed to the spectator under the table, and exchange it for the money on the shelf, which you again toss upon the table. Remove the case with the coins concealed therein, and the ball will appear on the top of the glass, as at first. Our performer makes the following concluding speech: "Now, as you have, I suppose, discovered the whole mystery, I hope, ladies, that *you* will not set up an opposition line against me; since, if you do, you will very seriously injure my pockets, and, of course, *attract* all the company, and leave me in an empty house with empty pockets."

#### 68. PROFESSOR WYMAN'S GREAT TRICK OF THE EGYPTIAN FLUIDS, OR IMPOSSIBILITIES ACCOMPLISHED

Mix wine and water together, then separate them by means of a red and white tape. To perform this trick you must have three covers (tin) made, of an obeliatic form, terminating at about one inch and a half on top, upon the top of two of these covers is soldered a piece of thick brass, copper, or lead, say about a quarter of an inch in thickness, in the center make a hole about the same in diameter, about two inches from the top, and on the inside will be a partition or floor, through the center of which make a small a hole, (this partition must be water tight.) Previous to performing the trick fill the two covers (the tops of them) one with water, the other with wine, then cork them well which excludes the air, consequently keeps the liquid from coming out at the small hole made in the center of the partition, then take two sound tumblers and put about as much water in one as there is water in one of the covers, place the cover over that, the tumbler that has the water, then put about the same quantity of wine in the other tumbler, as there is in the other cover, and place that cover over it; now have a tumbler with a hole through the center of the bottom (made with a drill), have this hole closed with a long peg from the under side, then through your trick table have a small auger hole made to admit the peg, this tumbler must also be covered with a similar cover in external appearance ; you then take the covers off the tumblers containing water and wine, and in presence of the audience mix the two liquids, then pour both into the tumbler that has the hole through the bottom, place the tumblers back and cover them over, now lift the tumbler up containing the mixture that the audience may see it, (keeping your hand in front of the peg,) place it back with peg through the hole, cover it over, then take a red and white tape string that has previously been fastened to a small stick, and place it in the top of the cover that is over the false tumbler, then take the end of the red tape, which has a small wire to it, and after removing the cork from the cover over the wine, drop the end of the wire into the whole ; the air is then let into the wine, which lets it run down into the tumblers underneath, do likewise with the white tape, then reach your hand under the table and draw the peg out of the tumbler and let the mixture run down into a tumbler or cup secreted there for that purpose ; now remove the covers and show the audience that the tumbler you poured the mixture into is empty, and the one you poured it out of contains it again, which will greatly astonish them. That accomplished magician, Professor Wyman, has astonished applauding and delighted thousands in every city in the United States and Canada, by the performance of this wonderful experiment.

**69. THE MAGICIAN'S SNOW BALL. ONE OF THE FAKER OF AVA'S FEATS.**

Take a cup and fill it with rice, then change it into a handkerchief. To do this trick you have two cups (tin) made to fit one within the other, but let the outside cup be about two inches deeper than the inside one, let the rims be turned square down all round, but let that of the inside cup be a trifle larger than the outside one, so that when the tin cover (which you must also have) is put over them it will fit sufficiently tight to lift out the inside cup when it is taken off. Previous to performing this trick you must place in the bottom of the deep cup a white pocket handkerchief, then place the other cup in it, after which bring it out in presence of the audience, then fill the inside cup (which to the audience appears to be the only cup) with rice, place the cover over it, after which repeat the mystic words *Presto, Pacillo, Pass*, then remove the cover and the inside cup will have stuck to it and be concealed from view, now take out the handkerchief, and it will greatly astonish those who see it.

### 70. THE MAGNETIZED CANE.

Is a very surprising little fancy, and is calculated to create much astonishment in the parlor or drawing room. To perform this trick, take a piece of black silk thread or horse hair, about two feet long, and fasten to each end of the same bent hooks of a similar color. When unobserved, fasten the hooks in the back part of your pantaloon-legs, about two inches below the bend of the knees. Then place the cane (it should be a dark one and not too heavy), within the inner part of the thread, as represented in the engraving, and by a simple movement of the legs, you can make the cane dance about, and perform a great variety of fantastic movements. At night your audience cannot perceive the thread, and apparently the cane will have no support whatever. The performer should inform the company before commencing this trick, that he intends to magnetize the cane, and by moving his hands as professors of magnetism do, the motion of the legs will not be noticed.

### 71. PROFESSOR WYMAN'S MODE OF PERFORMING THE EGG BAG TRICK.

Take a bag and exhibit it to the audience, turn the bag inside out, then back again, after which take several eggs out of it. To perform this trick, have you a bag about a half yard wide, and about five eighths deep, made of black cambric, then take strips of the same cloth about three inches wide and sew them on each side of the strip lengthwise of the bag, these are called cells, it is in these that the eggs are placed; let the end of the cells be closed at the mouth of the large bag, so that the mouth of the cells will be the reverse of that of the large bag, these are filled with eggs made of wood, with the exception of one or two natural eggs, which you take out first, and break, to convince the audience that they are genuine. When you turn the bag you keep these cells next to you, and as the large bag is turned upside down, the eggs are in the bottom of the cells at the mouth of the large bag. The performer will then catch the bag just above the eggs, and give it a few wraps across the other hand, to convince the audience that there is nothing in it, after which he turns the bag again and takes out several eggs, which to the audience is a great mystery.

In this account of conjuring, I have purposely avoided such tricks as require expensive apparatus. Such apparatus is either entirely beyond a boy's reach, or at all events he ought not to be encouraged in the notion of spending much money on objects of no real use. A boy of any ingenuity will make the greater part of the apparatus himself, or at least he can do the painting and polishing of his machinery. I have mentioned no machinery that need cost more than a dollar at the outside, and not that, if a boy is acquainted with the use of tools. It has also been my especial care to introduce only such experiments as are adapted for performance at the parlor or drawing-room table or fireside, and by imparting interesting facts, to stimulate the young experimentalist to inquire into the laws that regulate them ; by aiding him to acquire dexterity of practice, to smoothe the road to the development of principles ; and, above all, to enable him to escape an imputation which every boy of spirit would consider the depth of disgrace— that of being

## "No Conjuror!"

# TRICKS WITH CARDS.

ALTHOUGH proficiency in games with cards, is, in our opinion, a most pernicious accomplishment for youth, and one which cannot be too severely reprobated, we do not consider SLEIGHT-OF-HAND TRICKS with a pack of cards, at all objectionable, but rather a source of much harmless amusement ; and, under this impression, we do not hesitate to insert the following series of excellent deceptions and sleight-of-hand tricks.

Playing cards are believed to have been invented in Spain as early as the fourteenth century ; for, in 1378, John the First, king of Castile, forbade card-playing in his dominions, in an edict which is anterior to any similar legislative measure in other parts of Europe. The figures upon the cards themselves, add to the strength of the supposition; for the suits answering to those of spades and clubs have not the same inverted heart and trefoil shape which ours of the present day display, but *espadas*, or swords, and *bastos*, or cudgels, or clubs; so that in fact we retain their names, though we have altered the figures. At the present time, too, cards are a favorite diversion of the Spaniards, and the monopoly of selling them is vested in the hands of the sovereign.

In the reign of Henry the Seventh, card-playing was a very fashionable court amusement in England. The cards then used, differed materially in their figures from those now in vogue, as instead of clubs, spades, diamonds, and hearts, they had rabbits, pinks, roses, and the flowers called columbines, upon them ; as also bells, hearts, leaves, acorns, deer, &c. Let us now turn to the tricks that can be played with cards.

In accordance with my rule, I shall lay the principal stress on card tricks that require no apparatus, and may be performed with ordinary cards.

TRICKS WITH CARDS. 55

### 1. TO MAKE THE PASS.

This is a necessary beginning for card tricks. "Making the pass," is the technical term for shifting either the top or the bottom card to any place in the pack that you like. It is almost impossible to describe it, and I can only say that it will be learned better in five minutes from a friend, than in as many hours from a book. As, however, a friend is not always to be found who can perform the pass, I will endeavor to describe it.

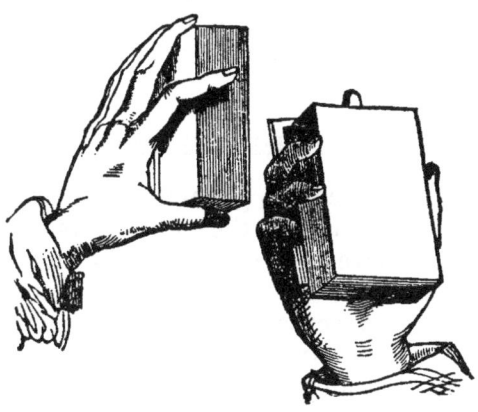

The cards are held in both hands, right hand underneath and left above, as in the engraving, where, as the *bottom* card is to be raised to the top, the little finger is seen between that card and those above it. By a quick movement of the right hand, the bottom card is slipped away towards the left, and is placed upon the top card, under shadow of the left hand, which is raised for the moment to allow of its passage.

This movement must be assiduously practiced before it is exhibited in public, as nothing looks more awkward than to see it clumsily performed, in which case two or three cards generally tumble on the floor.

### 2. TO TELL A CARD BY ITS BACK.

While shuffling the pack, cast a glance at the bottom card, make the pass, and bring it to the top. Continue to shuffle, and lay upon it by degrees as many cards as you like, say six. Then lay the pack on the table, face downwards, and divide it into seven heaps, beginning at the bottom, and leave the seventh heap larger than any of the others.

When you have done this, take one card from the top of the seventh heap, appear to calculate, and lay it, face upwards, on one of the other heaps. Do so with five more cards, thus leaving your slipped card at the top of the seventh heap. You then announce that by the aid of the six cards you will name the seventh. You name it accordingly, after carefully studying the other cards, and on asking a spectator to take it up, it will be seen that you are right.

If you place five cards above the slipped card, you will lay out six heaps, and if eight cards, there will of course be nine heaps.

### 3. THE CARD NAMED WITHOUT BEING SEEN.

As in the last trick, cast a glance at the bottom card, say the ace of spades. Lay out the pack in as many heaps as you like, noting where that one is laid which contains that bottom card. Ask any one to take up the top card of any heap, look at it, and replace it. You then gather up the heaps apparently by chance, but you take care to put the heap containing the bottom card upon the card which has been chosen. You then give any one the cards to cut, and on counting them over, the card that immediately follows the ace of spades is the card chosen.

If by any accident the two cards should be separated when cut, the upper card of the pack is the chosen one, and can be picked out with seeming care.

### 4. THE CARD TOLD BY THE OPERA GLASS.

Make out a table, such as is given in Fig. 1, and place it in an opera-glass, so that the figures will be visible when you look through it. For convenience, I have made mine as seen in Fig. 2, the numbers 1, 2, 3 in each series being understood. The best plan is to write the numbers, or cut them out of a book, and paste them on a circular piece of cardboard, which must then be soaked in oil, so as to make it semi-transparent. The light will then easily pierce through it, and the figures will be better visible than if it were opaque.

It will be seen that Fig. 2 contains as much matter as Fig 1, and that two thirds of the figures are saved by it.

TRICKS WITH CARDS. 57

These preliminaries being arranged, tell any one to take any twenty-seven cards out of a pack, and to think of any one of them. Deal them into three heaps, and ask him in which heap it is, and what number from the top he would

| 1. 131 | 10. 132 | 19. 133 |
| 2. 231 | 11. 232 | 20. 233 |
| 3. 331 | 12. 332 | 21. 333 |
| 4. 121 | 13. 122 | 22. 123 |
| 5. 221 | 14. 222 | 23. 223 |
| 6. 321 | 15. 322 | 24. 323 |
| 7. 111 | 16. 112 | 25. 113 |
| 8. 211 | 17. 212 | 26. 213 |
| 9. 311 | 18. 312 | 27. 313 |

Fig. 1.

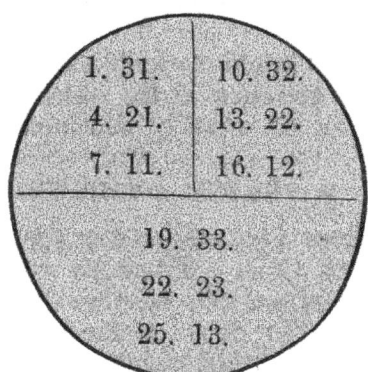

Fig. 2.

like it to come after the third deal. Suppose he chooses it to be the twenty-sixth card, you take up your opera-glass and look for the number 26. This you will find last but one, arranged thus—26 213 The meaning is, that if the chosen

3*

card is to be the twenty-sixth, the heap in which it was found must be for the first time placed second, the second time first, and the last time third. So you pick up the cards, taking care to keep that heap number two. You again deal them in three heaps, and this time you place the heap in which is the chosen card at the top, being number one. Deal them a third time, and on gathering up the heaps, place it at the bottom.

Then, on counting from the top, the chosen card will be found to be the twenty-sixth.

### 5. THE FOUR KINGS.

Take the four kings out of a pack of cards, and also two other court cards, which are not to be shown. Spread out the kings before the spectators, but conceal the two court cards between the third and fourth kings. Lay the cards face downwards on the table. Take off the bottom card, which is, of course one of the kings; show it as if by accident, and place it on the top. Take the next card, (which is one of the court cards.) and place that in the middle of the pack. Take the third card, (i. e., the second court card,) and place that also near the middle of the pack. There will then be one king at the top and three at the bottom. Ask any one to cut the cards, and to examine them, when he will find all four kings together in the middle of the pack.

It is better to use court cards to place between the third and fourth kings, because if the cards should slip aside, they would not be so readily distinguished as common cards.

### 6. THE FOUR ACCOMPLICES.

Let a person draw four cards from the pack, and tell him to think of one of them. When he returns you the four cards, dexterously place two of them under the pack, and two on the top. Under those at the bottom you place four cards of any sort, and then, taking eight or ten from the bottom cards, you spread them on the table, and ask the person if the card he fixed on be among them. If he say no, you are sure it is one of the two cards on the top. You then pass two cards to the bottom, and drawing off the lowest of them, you ask if that be not his card. If he again say no, you take that card up, and bid him draw his card from the bottom of the pack. If the person say his card is among those you first drew from the bottom, you must dexterously take up the four cards that you put under them, and placing those on the top, let the other two be the bottom cards of the pack, which draw in the manner before described.

### 7. TO TELL THE CARD THOUGHT OF IN A CIRCLE OF TEN.

Place the first ten cards of any suit in a circular form, as in the annexed figure; the ace being counted as one. Request a person to think of a number or card, and to touch also any other number or card; desire him to add to the number of the card he touched the number of the cards laid out, that is, ten; then bid him count that sum backward, beginning at the card he touched, and reckoning that card at the number he thought of; when he will thus end it at the card or number he first thought of, and thereby enable you to ascertain what that was. For example, suppose he thought of the number three, and touched the sixth card, if ten be added to six, it will of course make sixteen; and if he count that number from the sixth card, the one touched, in a retrograde order, reckoning three on the sixth, four on the fifth, five on the fourth, six on the third cards, and so on; it will be found to terminate on the third card, which will therefore show you the number the person thought of. When the person is counting the numbers, he should not, of course, call them out aloud.

### 8. TO GUESS THE CARD THOUGHT OF.

To perform this trick, the number of cards must be divisible by 3, and it is more convenient that the number should be odd. Desire a person to think of a card; place the cards on the table with their faces downward, and, taking them up in order, arrange them in three heaps, with their faces upward, and in such a manner that the first card of the pack shall be first in the first heap, the second the first in the second heap, and the third the first of the third; the fourth the second of the first, and so on. When the heaps are completed, ask the person in which heap the card he thought of is, and when he tells you, place that heap in the middle ; then turning up the packet, form three heaps, as before, and again inquire in which heap the card thought of is ; form the three heaps afresh, place the heap containing the card thought of again in the center, and ask which of them contains the card. When this is known, place it as before, between the other two, and again form three heaps, asking the same question. Then take up the heaps for the last time, put that containing the card thought of in the middle, and place the packet on the table with the faces downward, turn up the cards till you count half the number of those contained in the packet ; twelve, for example, if there be twenty-four, in which case the twelfth card will be the one the person thought of. If the number of the cards be at the same time odd, and divisible by three, such as fifteen, twenty-one, twenty-seven, &c., the trick will be much easier, for the card thought of will always be that in the middle of the heap in which it is found the third time, so that it may be easily distinguished without counting the cards ; in reality, nothing is necessary but to remember, while you are arranging the heap for the third time, the card which is the middle one of each. Suppose, for example, that the middle card of the first heap be the ace of spades ; that the second be the king of hearts ; and that the third be the knave of hearts : if you are told that the heap containing the required card is the third, that card must be the knave of hearts. You may therefore have the cards shuffled, without troubling them any more ; and then, looking them over for form's sake, may name the knave of hearts when it occurs.

### 9. TO TELL THE NUMBER OF CARDS BY THE WEIGHT.

Take a pack of cards, say forty, and privately insert among them two cards rather larger than the others; let the first be the fifteenth, and the other the twenty-sixth, from the top. Seem to shuffle the cards, and cut them at the first long card ; poise those you have taken off in your hand, and say, "There must be fifteen cards here ;" then cut them at the second long card, and say, "There are but eleven here ;" and poising the remainder, exclaim, "And here are fourteen cards." On counting them, the spectators will find your calculations correct

## AUDACITY.

Several tricks may be successfully played by sheer audacity. I once astonished a whole party by holding a pack of cards over my head, and naming each. The fact was, that I was standing exactly opposite a large mirror, in which the cards were reflected, while the spectators, having their backs to the mirror, suspected nothing.

I will give one or two tricks that depend on audacity for success.

### 10. THE CARD FOUND AT THE SECOND GUESS.

Offer the cards to any one, and let him draw one. You then hold the cards behind your back, and tell him to place his card on the top. Pretend to make a great shuffling, but only turn that card with its back to the others, still keeping it at the top. Then hold up the cards with their faces towards the spectator, and ask him if the bottom card is his. While doing so, you inspect his card at your leisure. He of course denies it, and you begin shuffling again furiously. "Let me do that," he will probably say; so, as you are perfectly acquainted with his card, you let him shuffle as much as he likes, and then, when you get the cards back again, shuffle until his card is at the bottom. Then pass them behind your back, make a ruffling noise with them, and show him his own card at the bottom.

### 11. THE CARD FOUND UNDER THE HAT.

Have a needle stuck just inside your sleeve. Hand the cards, &c., just as in the preceding trick, and tell the taker to put the card on the top. Take out the needle, and prick a hole nearly through the top *left*-hand corner. Replace the needle, shuffle the cards, or let any one shuffle them. Place the pack on the table, cover them with a hat, and the marked card will be known by a little raised knob on the *right*-hand top corner. Draw out card by card, saying whether it is that card or not, until you come to the marked one, which you throw on the table carelessly, and when you are about taking out another card, stop suddenly, and pretend to find, by some magic process, that it is the chosen card.

### 12. TO CALL THE CARDS OUT OF THE PACK.

Tell the spectators that you will call six cards out of the

pack. Secure a card, say the ace of spades, in the palm of your hand. Throw the pack on the table, face downwards, spread out the cards, give one of the spectators your conjuring wand, and tell him, when you name a card to touch one, which you will take up.

First name the ace of spades. He touches a card, which you take up without showing the face of it. This card may be, say the eight of diamonds. Put it into your left hand, and place it upon the ace of spades, which is already there, so that the two look like one card. Then call for the eight of diamonds. Another card is touched, say the queen of clubs. This you put with the others, and, after pretending to calculate, call for the queen of clubs.

Proceed in this manner until six cards have been drawn. Then substitute the last card drawn (which is of course a wrong one) for the ace of spades, and conceal it in the palm of your hand. Then strew the others on the table, and while the eyes of the spectators are fixed upon them, get rid of the card in your left hand.

It is a good plan to ask some one to write down the names of the cards as they are called, and then to have the list called over, in order that every one may see that there has been no mistake.

### 13. HEADS AND TAILS.

While you are shuffling the cards, contrive to arrange quietly all their heads one way, or as many as possible, rejecting all the diamonds except the king, queen, knave, and seven, and passing them to the bottom. Put the pack upon the table, take off a number of the upper cards, and offer them for some one to choose a card from. While he is looking at it, turn the cards round, and offer them to him, in order that he may replace it. Shuffle the cards, and on looking them over, the chosen card will be standing with its head one way, while the others are reversed.

### 14. THE SURPRISE.

When you have discovered a card, the following plan will make a *striking* termination to the trick. Get the card to the bottom of the pack, and tell one of the spectators to hold the cards by one corner as tightly as he can. Give them a sharp rap with your finger, not with your hand, and all the cards will be struck out of his hold, and fall on the floor, except the bottom card, which will remain between his finger and thumb. It has a rather more dashing effect, if you put the chosen card at the top, and strike them upwards, when the whole pack will fly about the room, like a flock of butterflies, only leaving the top card in the person's grasp.

### 15. THE REVOLUTION.

Another neat way of finishing a trick is as follows. Get the card to the top of the pack ; and taking care that all the cards are even, drop the pack on the floor, taking care just as you let go, to slip the top card a little off the rest of the pack. In falling, the resistance of the air will turn the card over, and it will rest with its face upwards on the top of the pack.

### 16. THE SLIPPED CARD.

Ascertain the bottom card of the pack ; hold the cards in your left hand, with their faces downwards. Place your right hand upon them, and with your right fore finger slide them slowly over each other, asking some one to stop any card he chooses, by putting his finger upon it. When he has done so, open the pack at that card, but while opening it, make the pass, and bring the bottom card under the one touched. Hold up the cards, and ask the chooser to be sure of his card ; hand all the cards to him, and let him shuffle as much as he chooses. Afterwards discover the card in any manner that you prefer. The following is a good plan.

### 17. THE NAILED CARD.

Take a flat-headed nail, and file it down until its point is as sharp as a needle, and the head quite flat. The nail should be about half an inch long, or even shorter if anything. Pass the nail through the center of any card, say the ace of spades, and conceal it in your left hand.

Take another pack of cards, get the ace of spades to the bottom, and perform the preceding trick. When the cards are returned, shuffle them about, and exchange the pierced card for the other. Put the pierced card at the bottom of the pack, and throw the cards violently against a door, when the nail will be driven in by the pressure of the other cards against its head, and the chosen card will be seen nailed to the door The nail should be put through the face of the card, so that when the others fall on the floor, it remains facing the spectators.

### 18. TO ASCERTAIN THE NUMBER OF POINTS ON THREE UNSEEN CARDS.

In this amusement the ace counts eleven, the court cards ten each, and the others according to the number of their spots.

Ask any one to choose any three cards, and lay them on the table, with their faces downwards. On each of these he must place as many as with the number of the card will make fifteen. He gives you the remaining cards, and when you have them in your hand, you count them over on the pretence of shuffling them, and by deducting four, you will have the number of points on the three cards.

For example, the spectator chooses a four, an eight, and a king. On the four he places eleven cards, on the eight seven, and on the king five. There will then be twenty-six cards left. Deduct from this twenty-six four, and the result will be twenty-two, which is the number of points on the three cards, the king counting ten, added to the eight and the four.

### 19. TO TELL THE NUMBERS ON TWO UNSEEN CARDS.

As in the preceding trick, the ace counts eleven, and the court cards ten each. Let the person who chooses the two cards lay them on the table with their faces downward, and place on each as many as will make their number twenty-five.

Take the remaining cards and count them, when they will be found to be just as many as the points in the two cards. For example, take an ace and a queen, *i. e.* eleven and ten, and lay them on the table. On the ace you must put fourteen cards, and on the queen fifteen. There will be then fifteen cards in one heap, and sixteen in the other: these added together make thirty-one cards: these subtracted from the number of cards in the pack, *i. e.* fifty-two, leave twenty-one, the joint number of the ace and queen.

### 20. THE KNAVES AND THE CONSTABLE.

Select the four knaves from a pack of cards, and one of the kings to perform the office of constable. Secretly place one of the knaves at the bottom of the pack, and lay the other three, with the constable, down upon the table. Proceed with a tale to the effect that three knaves once were to rob a house; one got in at the parlor window (putting a knave at the bottom of the pack, taking care not to lift the pack so high that the one already at the bottom can be seen); one effected his entrance at the first floor window (putting another knave in the middle of the pack); and the other, by getting on the parapet from a neighboring house, contrived to scramble in at the garret window (placing the third knave at the top of the pack); the constable vowed he would capture them, and closely followed the last knave (putting the king likewise upon the top of the pack). Then request as many of the company to cut the cards as please; and tell them that you have no doubt the constable has succeeded in his object, which will be quite evident, when you spread out the pack in your hands; as the king and three knaves will, if the trick is neatly performed, be found together. A very little practice only is required to enable you to convey a knave or any other card secretly to the bottom of the pack.

### 21. THE PAIRS RE-PAIRED.

Tell out twenty cards in pairs, and ask ten people to take a pair each, and remember them. Take up the pairs in their order, and lay them on the table in order, according to the accompanying table, which forms a memoria technica, and may be construed, "Mutus gave a name to the Coci," (a people who have yet to be discovered.)

| M | U | T | U | S* |
|---|---|---|---|---|
| 1 | 2 | 3 | 2 | 4 |
| D | E | D | I | T |
| 5 | 6 | 5 | 7 | 3 |
| N | O | M | E | N |
| 8 | 9 | 1 | 6 | 8 |
| C | O | C | I | S |
| 10 | 9 | 10 | 7 | 4 |

Arranging these words in your mind on the table, take the first card of the first pair, lay it on M in Mutus, and the second on the M in Nomen. The next pair goes entirely in Mutus, being two U's. The first card of the second pair

* The figures represent the pairs, *i.e.*, the 1 under M signifies that M belongs to the *first* pair.

goes on T in Mutus, and the second on T in Dedit; and so on until all the cards are laid in their places.

Ask each person in succession in which rows his cards are, and you can immediately point them out. For example, if he says the second and third row, you point out the second and fourth cards in those rows, because they both represent the letter E. If another says the first and last rows, you point out the last cards in each, because the cards represent s in Mutus and s in Cocis. It will be seen that the whole table consists of ten letters, each repeated, which will always point out the positions of the pairs if they are put in the places of those letters. Any number of bystanders may choose pairs, and to make the trick more mysterious, the pairs may be placed on the table back upwards.

### 23. THE QUEENS DIGGING FOR DIAMONDS.

Select from a pack the aces, kings, queens, and knaves, together with four common cards of each suit. Lay down the four queens in a row, and say, "Here are four queens going to dig for diamonds. *(Lay a common diamond over each queen.)* They each took a spade with them *(place a common spade on each diamond)* and dug until they were nearly tired. Their four kings, thinking that they might be attacked by robbers, sent four soldiers to keep guard. *(Lay an ace on each spade.)* Evening came, and the queens had not returned, so the kings, fearing that they might have come to harm, became uneasy and set off themselves. *(Place a king on each ace.)* They were only just in time, for as they came along, they met their queens being carried off by four villains *(lay a knave on each king)*, who, although only armed with clubs *(place a common club on each knave)*, had overpowered the guards and driven them off. But the four kings, being possessed of bold hearts *(lay a common heart over each king)*, soon vanquished the villains, and bound them." Gather up the cards, place the heaps upon each other and direct some one to cut them. Have them cut four or five times, and continue to do so until a common heart appears at the bottom. Then continue the tale, and say, "The party then returned home in the following order. First the queen, *(lay down the top card)* with the diamonds which she had found *(lay down the second card, which will be a diamond)* in one hand, and her spade *(the third card will be a spade)* in the other, &c

&c." You continue dealing out the cards in that manner, and it will be found that they will be in precisely the same order as when they were taken up.

### 24. THE TRIPLE DEAL.

Take any twenty-one cards, and ask some person to choose one from them. Lay them out in three heaps, and ask the person who took the card in which heap it is. You may turn your back while he searches. Gather them up and put that heap between the other two. Do this twice more, and the chosen card will always be the eleventh from the top.

### 25. THE QUADRUPLE DEAL.

This is a variation of the preceding. Take twenty-four cards, and lay them in four heaps. Act as in No. 24, putting the heap in which is the chosen card second. The tenth card will be the one thought of.

### 26. THE CARD DISCOVERED BY THE TOUCH OR SMELL.

Offer the long card, or any other that you thoroughly well know; and, as the person who has drawn it holds it in his hand, pretend to feel the pips or figures on the under side with your fore finger, or smell it, and then sagaciously declare what card it is.

If it be the long card, you may give the pack to the person who drew it, and allow him either to replace it or not. Then take the pack, and feel whether it be there or not; shuffle the cards in a careless manner, and without looking at it, decide accordingly.

### 27. THE INGENIOUS CONFEDERACY.

Lay sixteen cards on the table, in four divisions, four cards in each, with their faces upwards. You then state that you will leave the room, and, on your return, will name any one card which may have been touched in your absence, on one of the company (your confederate) pointing out a passage from any author to be read to you, on your return, by any person present. To perform this trick, the cards should be placed in the order in which they appear in the cut inserted on the next page, you previously making your confederate acquainted with your mode of proceeding, which is thus: The cards are supposed to be divided into four classes, as A, B, C, D; you likewise agree to class every-

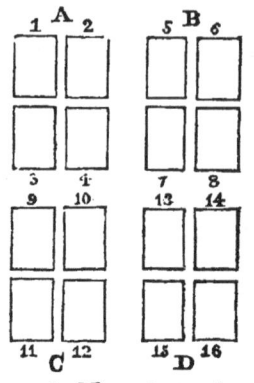

thing in the world under the four denominations of biped, quadruped, vegetable, and mineral: class A stands for bipeds, B for quadrupeds, C for vegetables, and D for minerals. Each class must now be subdivided in the same manner: in class A, No. 1 is the biped, 2 the quadruped, 3 the vegetable, and 4 the mineral; and so with the other classes. When performing the trick, your confederate must take care to select an appropriate passage. For example, we will suppose the card No. 4 to have been touched, and that a volume of Moore having been presented to your confederate to select from, he gives the following lines to be read:

> "Breathes there the *slave* so lowly,
> Condemned to *chains* unholy,
> Who, could he burst his bonds at first,
> Would pine beneath them slowly?" &c.

The first word which can be classed as above is *slave*, you may thus be certain that the card touched is in class A, a slave being a biped. The next word you can fix upon is *chains*, which being commonly made of some metal, you rank in the mineral class, and know that card No. 4 was the one touched, it being the mineral of the biped class.

Supposing the trick to be repeated, as is very likely, and that a volume of Byron is given to your confederate, who selects the passage commencing—

> "Know ye the land, where the cypress and myrtle
> Are emblems of deeds that are done in their clime?" &c.

you know, "cypress" being the first word that can be classed, the card touched must be in class C (vegetable), and the next word "myrtle" being also a vegetable, the card touched must have been No. 11, which is the vegetable of the vegetable class. Many appropriate passages may be easily selected, and your confederate should select a long passage to be read, as it gives greater scope, and helps to mislead the rest of the company; for should they imagine that the card is discovered by the number of lines read, and they touch the same card again, he can select another passage, desiring them to read only as many lines as they choose.

## 29. "HOLD IT FAST."

You commence by asking the most athletic person in company whether he is nervous ; he will most probably answer in the negative ; you then ask whether he thinks he can hold a card tightly. If he answers, No, ask the question of some one else, till you obtain an answer in the affirmative. You then desire the party to stand in the middle of the room, and holding up the pack of cards, you show him the bottom card, and request him to proclaim what card it is ; he will say it is the knave of hearts ; you then tell him to hold the card tightly at the bottom, and look to the ceiling. While he is looking up, you ask him if he recollects his card ; if he says, Yes, desire him to draw it away, and ask him what it is ; he will, of course, answer, the knave of hearts ; tell him he has made a mistake, for if he look at his card, he will find it to be the knave of spades, which will be the case. You then give him the remainder of the pack, telling him that if he looks over it, he will find the knave of hearts in quite a different situation.

This feat, though it excites much admiration, is very simple. You procure an extra knave of hearts, and cut it in half, keeping the upper part, and throwing away the lower When commencing your feat, get the knave of spades to the bottom of the pack, and lay over the upper part of it, unperceived, your half knave of hearts ; and, under pretence of holding the pack very tight, throw your thumb across the middle of the knave, so that the joining may not be perceived, for the legs of those two knaves are so much alike that there is no danger of detection. You, of course, give him the legs of the knave of spades to hold, and when he has drawn the card away, hold your hand so that the faces of the cards will be turned towards the floor, and take an opportunity of removing the half-knave : you may vary the feat by having a half-knave of spades.

## 30. THE CHARMED TWELVE.

Let any one take a pack of cards, shuffle, take off the upper card, and, having noticed it, lay it on the table, with its face downward. and put so many cards upon it as will make up twelve with the number of spots on the noted card. For instance : if the card which the person drew was king, queen knave, or ten, bid him lay that card, with its face downward, calling it ten ; upon that card let him lay another, calling it eleven, and upon that card, another, calling it twelve; then bid him take off the next uppermost card : suppose it to be nine, let him lay it down on another part of the table, calling it nine, upon it let him lay another, calling it ten, upon the latter another, calling it eleven, and upon that another, calling it twelve; then let him go to the next uppermost card, and so proceed to lay out in heaps, as before, until he has gone through with the whole pack.

If there be any cards at the last, that is, if there be not enough to make up the last noted card, the number twelve, bid him give them to you; then, in order to tell all the number of spots contained in all the bottom cards of the heaps, do thus : from the number of heaps subtract four, multiply the remainder by thirteen, and, to the product, add the number of remaining cards, which he gave you; but if there were but four heaps, then those remaining cards alone will show the number of spots on the four bottom cards. You need not see the cards laid out, nor know the number of cards in each heap, it being sufficient to know the number of heaps, and the number of remaining cards, if there be any, and therefore you may perform this feat as well standing in another room, as if you were present.

### 31. THE TRICK OF THIRTY-ONE.

A trick often introduced by "*sporting men*," for the purpose of deceiving and making money by it. It is called "thirty-one." I caution all not to play or bet with a man who introduces it : for, most probably, if he does not propose betting on it at first, he will after he gets you interested, and pretend to teach you all the secrets of it, so that you can play it with him; and perhaps he will let you beat him if you should play in fun; but if you bet, he will surely beat you. It is played with the first six of each suit—the *aces* in one row, the *deuces* in another, the *threes* in another; then the *fours*, *fives* and *sixes*—all laid in rows. The object now will be to turn down cards alternately, and endeavor to make thirty-one points by so turning, or as near to it as possible, without overrunning it; and the man who turns down a card, the spots of which make him thirty-one, or so near it that the other cannot turn down one without overrunning it, wins. This trick is very deceiving, as all other tricks are, and requires much practice to be well understood.

The persons using it I have known to attach great importance to it, and say that Mr. Fox, of England, was the first to introduce it; and that it was a favorite amusement of his. The chief point of this celebrated trick is to count so as to end with the following numbers, viz., 3, 10, 17 or 24. For example, we will suppose it your privilege to commence the count: you would commence with 3, and your adversary would add 6, which would make 9; it would then be your policy to add 1, and make 10; then, no matter what number he adds, he cannot prevent you counting 17, which number gives you the command of the trick. We will suppose he add 6, and make 16; then, you add 1, and make 17, then he to add 6, and make 23, you add 1, and make 24, then he cannot possibly add any number to count 31; as the highest number he can add is 6, which would only count 30, so that you can easily add the remaining 1, or ace, and make 31. There are, however, many variations to the trick.

### 32. TO TELL THE NAMES OF THE CARD BY THE WEIGHT.

You desire any person to cut a pack of cards as often as he pleases, and undertake, by weighing each card for a moment on your finger, not only to tell the color, but the suit and number of spots, and, if a court-card, whether it be king, queen, or knave.

You must have two packs of cards exactly alike: one pack to be constantly in use during the evening in performing your other tricks; the second, or prepared pack, in your pocket, which take an opportunity of exchanging, so that it may be believed that the pack of cards of which you tell the names is the same as that you have been using with your other tricks, and which they must know have been well shuffled.

The manner of preparing your pack (which must be done previously) is by the following line, which you commit to memory, the words in italics forming the key:

Eight Kings threa-tened to save nine fair Ladies for one sick Knave.
*Eight King three ten two seven nine five Queen four ace six Knave,*

You will perceive that this is a kind of artificial memory, formed by the circumstances of the initial letter of the words in the line and the names of the cards being identical, as well as the near resemblance of some of the words. The word "threatened" is divided into two words, in order that it may answer for the three and ten; you should pay attention to this, or you will be very likely to forget the ten altogether, which would set you entirely wrong; you should likewise commit to memory the order in which the suits come. viz.: *hearts—spades—diamonds—clubs.*

You should now separate the different suits, and lay them on the table, face upwards, placing heart first, spades next, diamonds next, and clubs last. Having done so, begin to sort (to yourself), according to your key: take up the eight of hearts, placing it in the left hand with its back to the palm; then the king of spades, which you lay over it, next the three of diamonds, next the ten of clubs, then the two of hearts, and so on, until you finish your line, which will terminate with the knave of hearts. You then take up the eight of spades, and go on in the same way till you come to the knave of spades, when you begin again with the eight of diamonds, and go on until you come to the knave of diamonds, and beginning again with the eight of clubs, you go on until you come to the knave of clubs, which finishes the pack, and which is now ready for use; when you have made your exchange, and brought forward your prepared pack, hand it round to be cut.

You now want to know the first card, as a clue to the rest; and therefore take off the top card, and holding it up between you and the light, you see what the card is, saying at the same time, that the old way of performing the trick was by doing so, but that this was very easily detected.

Having thus obtained a knowledge of the first card, which we will suppose to be the ten of diamonds, you then take the next card on your finger, and while pretending to weigh it, you have time to recollect what is the next word in your key, to *ten'd*, which is *to*—you consequently know that this card is a *two;* you must then recollect what suit comes after diamonds, which is *clubs;* you, therefore, declare the card you are now weighing on your finger to be the *two of clubs*; the next will of course be the seven of hearts, the next to that the nine of spades, and so on as long as you please.

## TRICKS WITH CARDS, THAT REQUIRE APPARATUS

I shall only give one or two of these tricks, because, in general, the apparatus required for cards is exceedingly expensive. Those that I shall give require but little apparatus, and any boy with the use of his hands can make it.

### 33. THE CARDS IN THE VASE.

Make a vase with five divisions, two of which hold an entire pack of cards, and the remaining three are only large enough just to admit one card each, as in the figure. A strong silk thread is fastened at A, passes over the three little compartments, through the bottom of the vase, and running over two pulleys, terminates in the weight at B.

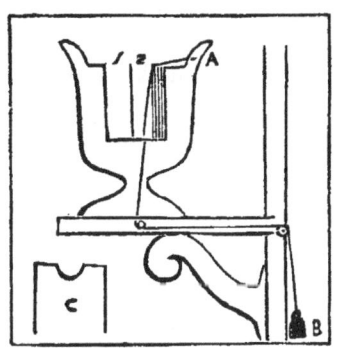

Take three cards, say the ace of spades, the ten of diamonds, and the king of hearts, out of a pack of cards, and put one into each of the little divisions pressing the thread down into the bottom of each division. If the cards are left, the weight will descend, and the string being tightened, will push the cards upwards. So a kind of trigger shelf is made, on which the weight rests. The remainder of the pack you put into division 2.

When you show the trick, you take another pack of cards exactly like that which is already in the vase, and handing it to three persons successively, compel them to choose the ace of spades, the ten of diamonds, and the king of hearts.* Let some one shuffle the cards, and when this is done, put the pack into division 1  Tell the spectators that when you

* This may be done by making the pass.

have struck three times on the table, the cards will come **out** of the vase. At the third stroke, loosen the catch on which the weight stands, by means of the string that communicates with your table, and the three cards will rise slowly up. In order to show that the cards have really vanished from the pack, take the pack out of division 2 and let any one examine it.

If you prefer, you can draw the thread yourself, by having a kind of a pedal under your table, to which the other end of the string is attached, instead of being fastened to the weight B. If you prefer the weight, you must have a small shelf for the weight to rest upon, when it has descended sufficiently low, or the cards will be forced entirely out by the thread. c is a representation of one of the divisions, showing the semi-circular cut that is made in them for the convinience of taking out the cards.

### 34. THE METAMORPHOSIS.

In this most excellent trick you choose from the pack the four eights and the two of diamonds; you put the four eights in your left hand and the two on the table; you take in the two, placing an eight on the table, and they are all twos. You exchange the two for the eight, and they all become black cards; you again exchange the eight for the two, and they all turn red; and after again exchanging, you have, as before, the four eights and the two of diamonds.

The method of accomplishing this trick is as follows: Get three plain white cards, exactly like playing cards, and paint them as in the engraving. Mix them with an ordinary

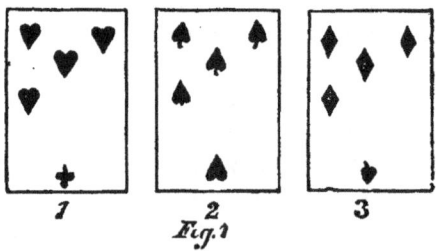

*Fig. 1*

dinary pack, and when you are searching for the four eights, with which you say you are going to perform a trick, take them from the pack, and with them an ordinary eight of clubs and a two of diamonds.

## TRICKS WITH CARDS.

Show the cards as in fig. 2, making the spectators observe that there are the four eights. Put the two of diamonds behind the eight of clubs, and lay the eight on the table. The two must be inserted before the eight is removed, or the mystery of the marking will be apparent Close the cards, turn them over, and spread them out, when they will appear as in Fig. 3. Take in the eight and lay the two on the table; close the cards, and while shuffling them, turn card No. 2 the other way upwards. The cards will

then all appear black, as in Fig. 4. Take in the two and remove the eight, turn them over, and spread them out, when they will appear all red, as in Fig. 5. Finally, take the

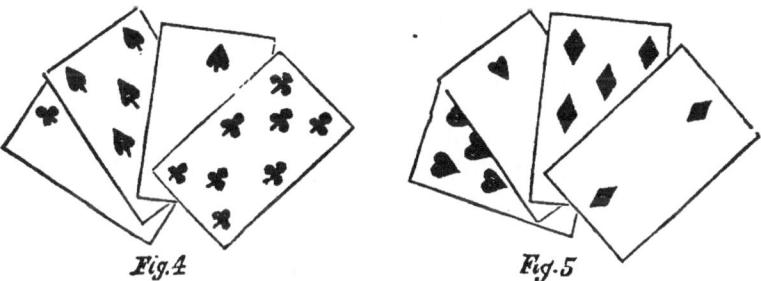

eight, replacing the two on the table, reverse No. 2, and you will have the four eights and the two of diamonds, just as they were at first. You must invent plenty of talk during your changes. If the spectators say that the cards are double, spread them out, and hold them up to the light, (for the light cannot penetrate through the places where the cards are placed over each other,) and if they are still skeptical, hand them the two of diamonds to look at, and in a moment or two hand them the eight of clubs, asking them whether they would like to examine a black card also. This will effectually disarm supicion.

### 35. TO HOLD FOUR KINGS OR FOUR KNAVES IN YOUR HAND, AND TO CHANGE THEM SUDDENLY INTO BLANK CARDS, AND THEN TO FOUR ACES.

It is necessary to have cards made on purpose for this trick; half cards, as they may be properly termed, that is, one half kings or knaves, and the other half aces. When you lay the aces one over the other, of course nothing but the kings or knaves can be seen; and on turning the kings or knaves downward, the four aces will make their appearance. You must have two perfect cards, one a king or knave, to put over one of the aces, else it will be seen; and the other an ace, to lay over the kings or knaves. When you wish to make them all appear blank, lay the cards a little lower, and by hiding the aces, they will appear white on both sides; you may then ask which they wish to have, and may show kings, aces, or knaves, as they are called for.

### 36. TO CHANGE A CARD IN A PERSON'S HAND.

Cut very neatly the spots from a three of spades. Lay the pierced card on an ace of diamonds, and rub pomatum on the ace of diamonds through the places which the spades occupied. Remove the pierced card, and sprinkle the ace of diamonds with jet powder, which adhering to the pomatum, will transform the card into a three of spades.

Place the transformed card at the bottom of the pack, and show a person what card it is. Make him declare it that every one may hear, then place it on the table, face downwards, and push it over the cloth to the spectator, which action will rub off all the jet powder. Tell him to place his hand on the card. Let a three of spades be at the top of the pack, and an ace of diamonds the second from the bottom. Show another person the ace of diamonds, and ask him to tell the name of the card openly. Put the pack down, face downwards, and in so doing make the pass, and bring the three of spades to the bottom.

Tap the hand of the person who is guarding the card, and then tell him to take up the card and show it to the spectators, when it will be seen to be the ace of diamonds. Simultaneously, you take up the pack, and show the three of spades at the bottom.

### 37. THE CARD IN THE EGG.

To perform this feat, provide a round hollow stick, about ten inches long and three quarters of an inch in diameter, the hollow being three eighths of an inch in diameter. Also, have another round stick to fit this hollow, and slide in it easily, with a knob to prevent its coming through. Our young readers will clearly understand our meaning, when we say, that in all respects it must resemble a pop-gun, with the single exception that the stick which fits the tube, must be of the full length of the tube exclusively of the knob

Next steep a card in water for a quarter of an hour, peel off the face of it, and double it twice across, till it becomes one fourth of the length of a card, then roll it up tightly, and thrust it up the tube till it becomes even with the bottom. You then thrust in the stick at the other end of the tube till it just touches the card.

Having thus provided your magic wand, let it lie on the table until you have occasion to make use of it, but be careful not to allow any person handle it.

Now take a pack of cards, and let any person draw one; but be sure to let it be a similar card to the one which you have in the hollow stick. This must be done by forcing. The person who has chosen it will put it into the pack again, and, while you are shuffling, you let it fall into your lap. Then, calling for some eggs, desire the person who drew the card, or any other person in the company, to choose any one of the eggs. When he has done so, ask if there be anything in it? He will answer there is not. Place the egg in a saucer; break it with the wand, and pressing the knob with the palm of your right hand, the card will be driven into the egg. Then show it to the spectators.

A great improvement may be made in this feat, by presenting the person who draws the card with a saucer and a pair of forceps, and instead of his returning the card to the pack, desire him to take it by the corner with the forceps and burn it, but to take care and preserve the ashes; for this purpose you present him with a piece of paper (prepared as hereafter described), which he lights at the candle; but a few seconds after, and before he can set the card on fire, it will suddenly divide in the middle and spring back, burning his fingers if he do not drop it quickly. Have another paper ready and desire him to try that ; when he will most likely beg to be excused, and will prefer lighting it with the candle.

When the card is consumed, say that you do not wish to fix upon any particular person in company to choose an egg, lest it might be suspected he was a confederate ; therefore, request any two ladies in company to choose each an egg, and having done so, to decide between themselves which shall contain the card ; when this is done, take a second saucer, and in it receive the rejected egg, break it with your wand, and show the egg round to the company ; at the same time drawing their attention to the fact of those two eggs having been chosen from among a number of others, and of its not being possible for you to have told which of them would be the chosen one.

You now receive the chosen egg in the saucer containing the ashes, and having rolled it about until you have blacked it a little, blow the ashes from around it into the grate ; you then break the egg with the same wand, when, on touching the spring, the card will be found in the egg.

The method of preparing the paper mentioned in the above feat is as follows : Take a piece of letter paper, about six inches in length and three quarters of an inch in breadth, fold it longitudinally, and with a knife cut it in the crease about five inches down ; then take one of the sides which are still connected at the bottom, and with the back of the knife under it, and the thumb of the right hand over it, curl it outwards as a boy would the tassels of his kite ; repeat the same process with the other side, and lay them by for use. When about using them, (but not till then, as the papers will soon lose their curl if stretched,) draw them up so as to make them their original length, and turn the ends over a little, in order that they may remain so ; when set on fire, they will burn for a minute or two, until the turn-over is burnt out, when the lighted ends will turn over quickly, burning the fingers of the holder : this part of the trick never fails to excite the greatest merriment.

### 38. THE FIFTEEN THOUSAND LIVRES.

For this trick, prepare two cards like the accompanying engraving ; and have a common ace and five of diamonds. Hold down the five of diamonds and the two prepared cards,

as shown in the next engraving; and say, "A certain Frenchman left fifteen thousand livres, which are represented by these three cards, to his three sons; the two youngest agreed to leave their five thousand, each of them, in the hands of the elder, that he might improve it." While you are telling this story lay the five on the table, and put the ace in its place; at the same time artfully change the position of the other two cards, so that the three cards appear as in this engraving. Then, resuming the tale, relate that "The eldest brother, instead of improving the money, lost it all by gaming, except three thousand livres, as you here see (laying the ace on the table, and taking up the five). Sorry for having lost the money, he went to the East Indies with these three thousand, and brought back fifteen thousand." Then show the cards in the same position as at first. To render this deception agreeable, it must be performed with dexterity, and should not be repeated, but the cards immediately put in the packet; and you should have five common cards ready to show, if any one desire to see them.

## HINTS TO AMATEURS.

THE following hints are of considerable importance to the amateur exhibitor.

1. Never acquaint the company beforehand with the particulars of the feat you are about to perform, as it will give them time to discover your mode of operation.

2. Endeavor, as much as possible, to acquire various methods of performing the same feat, in order that if you should be likely to fail in one, or have reason to believe that your operations are suspected, you may be prepared with another.

3. Never yield to the request of any one to repeat the same feat, as you thereby hazard the detection of your mode of operation; but do not absolutely refuse, as that would appear ungracious. Promise to perform it in a different

way, and then exhibit another which somewhat resembles it. This maneuver seldom fails to answer the purpose.

4. Never venture on a feat requiring manual dexterity, till you have previously practiced it so often, as to acquire the necessary expertness.

5. As diverting the attention of the company from too closely inspecting your maneuvers is a most important object, you should manage to talk to them during the whole course of your proceedings. It is the plan of vulgar operators to gabble unintelligible jargon, and attribute their feats to some extraordinary and mysterious influence. There are few persons at the present day credulous enough to believe such trash, even among the rustic and most ignorant ; but, as the youth of maturer years might inadvertently be tempted to pursue this method, while exhibiting his skill before his younger companions, it may not be deemed superfluous to caution him against such a procedure. He may state, and truly, that everything he exhibits can be accounted for on rational principles, and is only in obedience to the unerring laws of Nature ; and although we have just cautioned him against enabling the company themselves to detect his operations, there can be no objection (particularly when the party comprises many younger than himself) to occasionally show by what simple means the most apparently marvelous feats are accomplished.

### CURE FOR TROUBLESOME SPECTATORS.

It will sometimes happen at an early stage of the performance, that the ultimate success of the whole is likely to be endangered by a troublesome person, (generally a naughty boy,) who will persist in crying out, " I know how it is done !"—at the same time continually advancing to the table, from which it is, of course, the business of the conjurer to keep his youthful admirers. Should this be the case, the magic whistles may be produced, and the remark made, that now the troublesome boy shall show the company a trick. Having taken up one of the whistles, which has previously been filled with flour or magnesia, dust or soot, proceed to give a few directions, particularly impressing on him the necessity of blowing hard, because the whistle you place in his hand is perforated with a number of holes. The would-be magician is, therefore, excessively mortified, on applying his mouth and blowing hard, to receive the powder in his face. Any turner will make such a whistle, it being nothing more than the usual shaped toy perforated at the top with a number of holes.

## THE SECRET OF VENTRILOQUISM.

The main secret of this surprising art simply consists in first making a strong, deep inspiration, by which a considerable quantity of air is introduced into the lungs, to be afterwards acted upon by the flexible powers of the larynx, or cavity situated behind the tongue, and the trachea, or windpipe ; thus prepared, the expiration should be slow and gradual. Any person, by practice, can, therefore, obtain more or less expertness in this exercise ; in which, though not apparently, the voice is still modified by the mouth and tongue ; and it is in the concealment of this aid, that much of the perfection of ventriloquism lies.

But the distinctive character of ventriloquism consists in its imitations being performed by the voice *seeming* to come from the stomach : hence its name, from *venter*, the stomach, and *loquor*, to speak. Although the voice does not actually come from that region, in order to enable the ventriloquist to utter sounds from the larynx without moving the muscles of his face, he strengthens them by a powerful action of the abdominal muscles. Hence, he speaks by means of his stomach ; although the throat is the real source from whence the sound proceeds. It should, however, be added, that this speaking distinctly, without any movement of the lips at all, is the highest perfection of ventriloquism, and has but rarely been obtained. Thus, MM. St. Gille and Louis Brabant, two celebrated French ventriloquists, appeared to be absolutely mute while exercising their art, and no change in their countenances could be discovered.

It has lately been shown, that some ventriloquists have acquired by practice the power of exercising the veil of the palate in such a manner, that, by raising or depressing it, they dilate or contract the inner nostrils. If they are closely contracted, the sound produced is weak, dull, and seems to be more or less distant; if, on the contrary, these cavities are widely dilated, the sound will be strengthened, the voice become loud, and apparently close to us.

Another of the secrets of ventriloquism, is the uncertainty with respect to the direction of sounds. Thus, if we place a man and a child in the same angle of uncertainty, and the man speaks with the accent of a child, without any corresponding motion in his mouth or face, we shall necessarily believe that the voice comes from the child. In this case, the belief is strengthened by the imagination; for if we were directed to a statue, as the source from which we were to expect sounds to issue, we should still be deceived, and refer the sounds to the lifeless stone or marble. This illusion will be greatly assisted by the voice being totally different in tone and character from that of the man from whom it really comes. Thus, we see how easy is the deception when the sounds are required to proceed from any given objects, and are such as they actually yield.

The ventriloquists of our time have carried their art still further. They have not only spoken by the muscles of the throat and the abdomen, without moving those of the face, but have so far overcome the uncertainty of sound, as to become acquainted with modifications of distance, obstruction, and other causes, so as to imitate them with the greatest accuracy. Thus, each of these artists has succeeded in carrying on a dialogue; and each, in his own single person and with his own single voice, has represented a scene apparently with several actors. These ventriloquists have likewise possessed such power over their faces and figures that, aided by rapid changes of dress, their personal identity has scarcely been recognized among the range of personations.

Vocal imitations are much less striking and ingenious than the feats of ventriloquism. Extraordinary varieties of voice may be produced, by speaking with a more acute or grave pitch than usual, and by different contractions of the mouth. Thus may be imitated the grinding of cutlery on a wheel, the sawing of wood, the frying of a pancake, the uncorking of a bottle, and the gurgling noise in emptying its contents.

# THE MAGIC OF CHEMISTRY.

CHEMISTRY is one of the most attractive sciences. From the beginning to the end, the student is surprised and delighted with the developments of the exact discrimination, as well as the power and capacity, which are displayed in various forms of chemical action. Dissolve two substances in the same fluid, and then by evaporation, or otherwise, cause them to reassume a solid form, and each particle will unite with its own kind, to the entire exclusion of all others. Thus, if sulphate of copper and carbonate of soda are dissolved in boiling water, and then the water is evaporated, each salt will be re-formed as before. This phenomenon is the result of one of the first principles of the science, and as such is passed over without thought; but it is a wonderful phenomenon, and made of no account only by the fact that it is so common and so familiar.

It is by the action of this same principle, "chemical affinity," that we produce the curious experiments with

SYMPATHETIC INKS. By means of these, we may carry on a correspondence which is beyond the discovery of all not in the secret. With one class of these inks, the writing becomes visible only when moistened with a particular solution. Thus, if we write to you with a solution of sulphate of iron, the letters are invisible. On the receipt of our letter, you rub over the sheet a feather or sponge, wet with a solution of nut-galls, and the letters burst forth into sensible being at once, and are permanent.

2. If we write with a solution of sugar of lead, and you moisten with a sponge or pencil dipped in water impregnated with sulphuretted hydrogen, the letters will appear with metallic brilliancy.

3. If we write with a weak solution of sulphate of copper, and you apply ammonia, the letters assume a beautiful blue. When the ammonia evaporates, as it does on exposure to the sun or fire, the writing disappears, but may be revived again as before.

4. If you write with oil of vitriol very much diluted, so as to prevent its destroying the paper, the manuscript will be invisible except when held to the fire, when the letters will appear black.

5. Write with cobalt dissolved in diluted muriatic acid; the letters will be invisible when cold, but when warmed they will appear a bluish green.

We are almost sure that our secrets thus written will not be brought to the knowledge of a stranger, because he does not know the solution which was used in writing, and therefore knows not what to apply to bring out the letters.

Other forms of elective affinity produce equally novel results. Thus, two invisible gases, when combined, form sometimes a *visible solid*. Muriatic acid and ammonia are examples, also ammonia and carbonic acid.

On the other hand, if a solution of sulphate of soda be mixed with a solution of muriate of lime, the whole becomes solid.

Some gases when united form liquids, as oxygen and hydrogen, which unite and form water. Some solids, when combined, form liquids.

Chemical affinity is sometimes called *elective*, or the effect of *choice*, as if one substance exerted a kind of *preference* for another, and chose to be united to it rather than to that with which it was previously combined; thus, if you pour some vinegar, which is a weak acetic acid, upon some pearlash, (a combination of potassa and carbonic acid,) or some carbonate of soda, (a combination of the same acid with soda,) a violent effervescence will take place, occasioned by the escape of the carbonic acid, displaced in consequence of the potash or soda preferring the acetic acid, and forming a compound called an acetate. Then, if some sulphuric acid be poured on this new compound, the acetic acid will in its turn be displaced by the greater attachment of either of the bases, as they are termed, for the sulphuric acid. Again, if into a solution of blue vitriol, (a combination of sulphuric acid with oxide of copper,) the bright blade of a knife be introduced, the knife will speedily be covered with a coat of copper, deposited in consequence of the acid *preferring* the iron of which the knife is made, a quantity of it being dissolved in exact proportion to the quantity of copper deposited.

It is on the same principle that a very beautiful preparation, called a silver-tree, or a lead-tree, may be formed, thus: Fill a wide bottle, capable of holding from half a pint to a pint, with a tolerably strong solution of nitrate of silver, (lunar caustic,) or acetate of lead, in pure distilled water; then attach a small piece of zinc by a string to the cork or stopper of the bottle, so that the zinc shall hang about the middle of the bottle, and set it by where it may be quite undisturbed; in a short time, brilliant plates of

silver or lead, as the case may be, will be seen to collect around the piece of zinc, assuming more or less of the crystalline form. This is a case of elective affinity; the acid with which the silver or lead was united *prefers* the zinc to either of those metals, and in consequence discards them in order to attach the zinc to itself; and this process will continue until the whole of the zinc is taken up, or the whole of the silver or lead deposited.

Again, many animal and vegetable substances consist for the most part of carbon or charcoal, united with oxygen and hydrogen in the proportion which forms water. Now oil of vitriol (strong sulphuric acid) has so powerful an affinity, or so great a *thirst* for water, that it will abstract it from almost any body in which it exists; if you then pour some of this acid on a lump of sugar, or place a chip of wood in it, the sugar or wood will speedily become quite black, or be *charred*, as it is called, in consequence of the oxygen and hydrogen being removed by the sulphuric acid, and only the carbon, or charcoal, left.

When Cleopatra dissolved pearls of wondrous value in vinegar, she was exhibiting unwittingly an instance of chemical elective affinity; the pearl being simply carbonate of lime, which was decomposed by the greater affinity or fondness of lime for its new acquaintance, (the acetic acid of the vinegar,) than for the carbonic acid, with which it had been united all its life; an example of inconstancy in strong contrast with the conduct of its owner, who chose death rather than become the mistress of her lover's conqueror.

### EXPERIMENTS ON COMBUSTION.

Into an ordinary wine bottle put some pieces of granulated zinc, and pour on them a mixture of sulphuric acid and water, in the proportion of about one part of acid to fou· of water, then close the bottle with a cork having a hole bored through the middle, in which a piece of glass tube is inserted; wait some minutes that the atmospheric air in the bottle may be expelled by the hydrogen gas set free by the decomposition of the water, then apply a lighted taper to the end of the tube, when the gas will inflame, giving out so little light as to be barely visible by daylight, but producing so intense a heat that a piece of platinum wire instantly becomes white hot when held in the flame. If you hold a glass tumbler inverted over the flame, it becomes covered with minute drops of water, the result of the union of the hydrogen with the oxygen of the air, and in this case water is the only product.

If a piece of charcoal, which is pure carbon or nearly so, be ignited, and introduced into a jar, containing oxygen or common atmospheric air, the product will be carbonic acid gas only. As most combustible bodies contain both carbon and hydrogen, the result of their combination is carbonic acid and water. This is the case with the gas used for illumination; and in order to prevent the water so produced from spoiling goods in shops, various plans have been devised for carrying off the water when in the state of steam. This is generally accomplished by suspending over the burners glass bells, communicating with tubes opening into the chimney, or passing outside the house.

To show that oxygen, or some equivalent, is necessary for the support of combustion, fix two or three pieces of wax taper on flat pieces of cork, and set them floating on water in a soup-plate, light them, and invert over them a glass jar ; as they burn, the heat produced may perhaps at first expand the air so as to force a small quantity out of the jar, but the water will soon rise in the jar, and continue to do so until the tapers expire, when you will find that a considerable portion of the air has disappeared, and what remains will no longer support flame ; that is, the oxygen has been converted partly into water, and partly into carbonic acid gas, by uniting with the carbon and hydrogen of which the taper consists, and the remaining air is principally nitrogen, with some carbonic acid : the presence of the latter may be proved by decanting some of the remaining air into a bottle, and then shaking some lime-water with it, which will absorb the carbonic acid and form chalk.

Into an ale-glass, two thirds full of water at about 140°, drop one or two pieces of phosphorus about the size of peas, and they will remain unaltered. Then take a bladder containing oxygen gas, to which is attached a stop-cock and a long fine tube ; pass the end of the tube to the bottom of the water, turn the stop-cock, and press the bladder gently ; as the gas reaches the phosphorus it will take fire, and burn under the water with a brilliant flame, filling the glass with brilliant flashes of light dashing through the water.

Into another glass put some cold water ; introduce carefully some of the salt called chlorate of potassa, upon that drop a piece of phosphorus ; then let some strong sulphuric acid (oil of vitriol) trickle slowly down the side of the glass, or introduce it by means of a dropping bottle. As soon as it touches the salt it decomposes it, and liberates a gas which ignites the phosphorus, producing much the same appearance as in the last experiment.

Into the half of a broken phial put some chlorate of potassa, and pour in some oil of vitriol. The phial will soon be filled with a heavy gas of a deep yellow color. Tie a small test tube at right angles to the end of a stick not less than a yard long, put a little ether into the tube, and pour it gently into the phial of gas, when an instantaneous explosion will take place, and the ether will be set on fire. This experiment should be performed in a place where there are no articles of furniture to be damaged, as the ingredients are often scattered by the explosion, and the oil of vitriol destroys all animal and vegetable substances.

Into a jar containing oxygen gas, introduce a coil of soft iron wire, suspended to a cork that fits the neck of the jar, and having attached a small piece of charcoal to the lower part of the wire, ignite the charcoal. The iron will take fire and burn with a brilliant light, throwing out bright scintillations, which are oxide of iron, formed by the union of the gas with the iron; and they are so intensely hot, that some of them will probably *melt* their way into the sides of the jar, if not through them.

But by far the most intense heat, and most brilliant light, may be produced by introducing a piece of phosphorus into a jar of oxygen. The phosphorus may be placed in a small

copper cup, with a long handle of thick wire passing through a hole in a cork that fits the jar. The phosphorus must first be ignited; and as soon as it is introduced into the oxygen, it gives out a light so brilliant that no eye can bear it, and the whole jar appears filled with an intensely luminous atmosphere. It is well to dilute the oxygen with about one fourth part of common air, to moderate the intense heat, which is nearly certain to break the jar, if pure oxygen is used.

The following experiment shows the production of heat by chemical action alone. Bruise some fresh prepared crystals of nitrate of copper, spread them over a piece of tin foil, sprinkle them with a little water; then fold up the foil tightly, as rapidly as possible, and in a minute or two it will become red hot, the tin apparently burning away This heat is produced by the energetic action of the tin on the nitrate of copper, taking away its oxygen in order to unite with the nitric acid, for which, as well as for the oxygen, the tin has a much greater affinity than the copper has.

Combustion without flame may be shown in a very elegant and agreeable manner, by making a coil of platinum wire by twisting it round the stem of a tobacco pipe, or any cylindrical body, for a dozen times or so, leaving about an inch straight, which should be inserted into the wick of a spirit lamp; light the lamp, and after it has burned for a minute or two, extinguish the flame quickly; the wire will soon become red hot, and, if kept from draughts of air, will  continue to burn until all the spirit is consumed. Spongy platinum, as it is called, answers rather better than wire, and has been employed in the formation of fumigators for the drawing-room, in which, instead of pure spirit, some perfume, such as lavender water, is used; by its combustion an agreeable odor is diffused through the apartment. These little lamps were much in vogue a few years ago, but are now nearly out of fashion.

Experiments on combustion might be multiplied, almost to any amount, but the above will be sufficient for our purpose.

### POTASSIUM.

Potassium was discovered by Sir H. Davy, in the beginning of the present century, while acting upon potash with the enormous galvanic battery of the Royal Institution, consisting of two thousand pairs of four inch plates. It is a brilliant white metal, so soft as to be easily cut with a penknife, and so light as to swim upon water, on which it acts with great energy, uniting with the oxygen, and liberating the hydrogen, which takes fire as it escapes.

#### EXPERIMENT.

Trace some continuous lines on paper with a camel's-hair brush, dipped in water, and place a piece of potassium about the size of a pea, on one of the lines, and it will follow the course of the pencil, taking fire as it runs, and burning with a purplish light. The paper will be found covered with a solution of ordinary potash. If turmeric paper be used, the course of the potassium will be marked with a deep brown color. Corollary: hence, if you touch potassium with *wet* fingers, you will burn them!

If a small piece of the metal be placed on a piece of ice, it will instantly take fire, and form a deep hole, which will be found to contain a solution of potash.

In consequence of its great affinity for oxygen, potassium must be kept in some fluid destitute of it, such as naphtha.

Saltpeter, or niter, is a compound of this metal (or rather its oxide) with nitric acid. It is one of the ingredients of gunpowder, and has the property of quickening the combustion of all combustible bodies.

#### EXPERIMENT.

Rub together in a *warm* mortar, three parts of powdered niter, two of dry carbonate of potash, and one of flour of brimstone ; place a small quantity of the mixture in an iron ladle, and heat it over the fire, when it will speedily melt, and then explode with a very loud noise ; and if held under a foul chimney, will save the expense of a chimney sweep : but avoid cooking time.

Another salt of potash remarkable for the same property, in even a greater degree, is the *chlorate* of potash.

#### EXPERIMENTS.

1. Triturate together in a *dry* mortar a few grains of flowers of sulphur, with a small quantity of the chlorate of potash, and a succession of sharp explosions, like the crack of a whip, will be produced.

2. Substitute half a grain of phosphorus for the sulphur, and the action will be much more violent. The hand should be defended by a thick glove, and the eyes carefully guarded, in making this experiment.

3. Mix very carefully a little of this salt, reduced to powder, with a little lump sugar, also powdered, and drop on the mixture a little strong sulphuric acid, and it will instantly burst into a flame. This experiment also requires caution.

Want of space precludes us from considering the individual metals and their compounds in detail ; it must suffice to describe some experiments, showing some of their properties.

The different affinities of the metals for oxygen, may be exhibited in various ways. The silver or zinc tree has already been described.

#### EXPERIMENTS.

1. Into a solution of nitrate of silver, in distilled water, immerse a clean plate or slip of copper. The solution, which was colorless, will soon begin to assume a greenish tint, and the piece of copper will be covered with a coating of a light gray color, which is the silver formerly united to the nitric

acid, which has been displaced by the greater affinity or *liking* of the oxygen and acid for the copper.

2. When the copper is no longer coated, but remains clean and bright when immersed in the fluid, all the silver has been deposited, and the glass now contains a solution of *copper.*

Place a piece of clean iron in the solution, and it will almost instantly be coated with a film of *copper*, and this will continue until the whole of that metal is removed, and its place filled by an equivalent quantity of *iron*, so that nitrate of *iron* is found in the liquid. The oxygen and nitric acid remain unaltered in quantity or quality during these changes, being merely transferred from one metal to another.

A piece of zinc will displace the iron in like manner, leaving a solution of nitrate of zinc.

Nearly all the colors used in the arts, are produced by metals and their combinations; indeed, one is named *chromium,* from a Greek word signifying color, on account of the beautiful tints obtained from its various combinations with oxygen and the other metals. All the various tints of green, orange, yellow, and red, are obtained from this metal.

Solutions of most of the metallic salts give precipitates with solutions of alkalies and their salts, as well as with many other substances, such as what are usually called prussiate of potash, hydro-sulphuret of ammonia, &c.; and the colors differ according to the metal employed; and so small a quantity is required to produce the color, that the solutions before mixing may be nearly colorless.

### EXPERIMENTS.

1. To a solution of sulphate of iron, add a drop or two of a solution of prussiate of potash, and a blue color will be produced.

2. Substitute sulphate of copper for iron, and the color will be a rich brown.

3. Another blue, of quite a different tint, may be produced by letting a few drops of a solution of ammonia fall into one of sulphate of copper, when a precipitate of a light blue falls down, which is dissolved by an additional quantity of the ammonia, and forms a transparent solution of the most splendid rich blue color.

4. Into a solution of sulphate of iron, drop a few drops of a strong infusion of galls, and the color will become a bluish-

black—in fact, *ink*. A little *tea* will answer as well as the infusion of galls. This is the reason why certain stuffs formerly in general use for dressing gowns for gentlemen were so objectionable ; for as they were indebted to a salt of iron for their color, buff, as it was called, a drop of tea accidentally spilled, produced all the effect of a drop of ink.

5. Put into a largish test tube, two or three small pieces of granulated zinc, fill it about one third full of water, put in a few grains of iodine, and boil the water, which will at first acquire a dark purple color, gradually fading as the iodine combines with the zinc. Add a little more iodine from time to time, until the zinc is nearly all dissolved. If a few drops of this solution be added to an equally colorless solution of corrosive sublimate (a salt of mercury), a precipitate will take place of a splendid scarlet color, brighter, if possible, than vermilion, which is also a preparation of mercury.

### CRYSTALLIZATION OF METALS.

Some of the metals assume certain definite forms in return from the fluid to the solid state. Bismuth shows this property more readily than most others.

#### EXPERIMENT.

Melt a pound or two of bismuth in an iron ladle over the fire ; remove it as soon as the whole is fluid ; and when the surface has become solid break a hole in it, and pour out the still fluid metal from the interior ; what remains will exhibit beautifully-formed crystals of a cubic shape.

Sulphur may be crystallized in the same manner, but its fumes, when heated, are so very unpleasant, that few would wish to encounter them.

One of the most remarkable facts in chemistry—a science abounding in wonders—is the circumstance that the mere contact of hydrogen, the *lightest* body known, with the metal platinum, the heaviest, when in a state of minute division, called spongy platinum, produces an intense heat, sufficient to inflame the hydrogen : of course this experiment must be made in the presence of atmospheric air or oxygen. If a small piece of the metal in the state above named be introduced into a mixture of oxygen and hydrogen, it will cause them to explode. A very small quantity of gas should be employed, and placed in a jar lightly covered with a card, or the explosion would be dangerous.

## BEAUTIES OF CRYSTALLIZATION.

Dissolve alum in hot water until no more can be dissolved in it; place in it a smooth glass rod and a stick of the same size; next day, the stick will be found covered with crystals, but the glass rod will be free from them: in this case, the crystals cling to the rough surface of the stick, but have no hold upon the smooth surface of the glass rod. But if the rod be roughened with a file at certain intervals, and then placed in the alum and water, the crystals will adhere to the rough surfaces, and leave the smooth bright and clear.

Tie some threads of lamp-cotton irregularly around a copper wire or glass rod; place it in a hot solution of blue vitriol, strong as above, and the threads will be covered with beautiful blue crystals, while the glass rod will be bare.

Bore a hole through a piece of coke, and suspend it by a string from a stick, placed across a hot solution of alum; it will float; but, as it becomes loaded with crystals, it will sink in the solution according to the length of the string. Gas-coke has mostly a smooth, shining, and almost metallic surface, which the crystals will avoid, while they will cling only to the most irregular and porous parts.

If powdered turmeric be added to the hot solution of alum, the crystals will be of a bright yellow; litmus will cause them to be of a bright red; logwood will yield purple; and common writing ink, black; and the more muddy the solution, the finer will be the crystals.

To keep colored alum crystals from breaking or losing their color, place them under a glass shade with a saucer of water; this will preserve the atmosphere moist, and prevent the crystals getting too dry.

If crystals be formed on wire, they will be liable to break off, from the expansion and contraction of the wire by changes of temperature.

## TO CRYSTALLIZE CAMPHOR.

Dissolve camphor in spirit of wine, moderately heated, until the spirit will not dissolve any more; pour some of the solution into a cold glass, and the camphor will instantly crystallize in beautiful tree-like forms, such as we see in the show-glasses of camphor in druggists' windows.

## CRYSTALLIZED TIN.

Mix half an ounce of nitric acid, six drams of muriatic acid, and two ounces of water; pour the mixture upon a piece of tin plate previously made hot, and after washing it in the mixture it will bear a beautiful crystalline surface, in feathery forms. This is the celebrated *moirée métallique*, and, when varnished, is made into ornamental boxes, &c. The figures will vary according to the degree of heat previously given to the metal.

## CRYSTALS IN HARD WATER.

Hold in a wine-glass of hard water a crystal of oxalic acid, and white threads, *i. e.* oxalate of lime, will instantly descend through the liquid suspended from the crystal.

## VARIETIES OF CRYSTALS.

Make distinct solutions of common salt, niter, and alum; set them in three saucers in any warm place, and let part of the water dry away or evaporate; then remove them to a warm room. The particles of the salts in each sacer will begin to attract each other, and form crystals, but not all of the same figure: the common salt will yield crystals with six square and equal faces, or sides; the niter six-sided crystals; and the alum, eight-sided crystals; and if these crystals be dissolved over and over again, they will always appear in the same forms.

## A LIQUID CHANGED TO A SOLID, AND HEAT FROM CRYSTALLIZATION.

A strong saline solution excluded from the *air* will frequently crystallize the instant that air is admitted. For this purpose make a solution of Glauber's salt (sulphate of soda) in boiling water (3 lbs. of the salt to 2 lbs. of water); bottle and cork quickly; also tie over the neck a piece of wet bladder. When perfectly cold, or even a few days afterwards, remove the cork, and the salt will immediately crystallize, shooting out the most beautiful crystals, at last becoming nearly solid: at the same time the whole becomes warm, in consequence of the latent heat generated by the change of the liquid to the solid state. If the liquid will not crystallize quickly on removing the cork, tie a crystal of Glauber's salt to a bit of wire, touch the surface of the liquid, and the crystallization will then generally occur

### ANOTHER EXPERIMENT.

Heat some blue vitriol (sulphate of copper) in an iron ladle till all the water contained in the crystals is driven off, and the color changes to a gray. Take the lumps out without breaking them, and lay the dried blue vitriol on a plate; if this be moistened with water, steam is produced; and if a slice of phosphorus is then laid on the sulphate of copper, it ignites, demonstrating again that the condensation of a liquid produces heat. The addition of the water restores the blue color, thus proving that water was necessary to the composition of blue vitriol.

### A SOLID CHANGED TO A LIQUID, AND INTENSE COLD FROM THE LIQUEFACTION.

Mix five parts by weight of powdered muriate of ammonia, commonly termed sal ammoniac, five parts of niter in powder, and sixteen parts of water. A temperature of twenty-two degrees below the freezing point of water is produced; and if a phial of water, or any convenient metallic cylinder containing water, be surrounded with a sufficient quantity of the freezing mixture, ice is obtained. The ice clings to the interior of the tube, but may easily be removed by dipping it in tepid water.

This experiment is the reverse of the last, and proves that a sudden reduction of a solid to the liquid condition always affords cold.

An amusing combination of two experiments may be made by putting some fresh-burned lime into one tea-pot and this freezing mixture into another. When water is poured on the one containing lime, it gives out steam from the spout; while the addition of water to the other produces so much cold, that it can hardly be kept in the hand. Thus heat and cold are afforded by the same medium, water.

### MAGIC OF HEAT.

Melt a small quantity of the sulphate of potassa and copper in a spoon over a spirit lamp; it will be fused at a heat just below redness, and produce a liquid of a dark green color. Remove the spoon from the flame, when the liquid will become a solid of a brilliant emerald green color, and so remain till its heat sinks nearly to that of boiling water; when suddenly a commotion will take place throughout the mass, beginning from the surface, and each atom, as if animated, will start up and separate itself from the rest, till, in a few moments, the whole will become a heap of powder.

### SUBLIMATION BY HEAT.

Provide two small pieces of glass; sprinkle a minute portion of sulphur upon one piece, lay thin slips of wood around it, and place upon it the other piece of glass. Move them slowly over the flame of a lamp or candle, and the sulphur will become sublimed, and form gray nebulous patches, which are very curious microscopic objects. Each cluster consists of thousands of transparent globules, imitating in miniature the nebulæ which we see figured in treatises on astronomy. By observing the largest particles, we shall find them to be flattened on one side. Being very transparent, each of them acts the part of a little lens, and forms in its focus the image of a distant light, which can be perceived even in the smaller globules, until it vanishes from minuteness. If they are examined again after a certain number of hours, the smaller globules will generally be found to have retained their transparency, while the larger ones will have become opaque, in consequence of the sulphur having undergone some internal spontaneous change. But the most remarkable circumstance attending this experiment is, that the globules are found adhering to the upper glass only; the reason of which is, that the upper glass is somewhat cooler than the lower one: by which means we see that the vapor of sulphur is very powerfully repelled by heated glass. The flattened form of the particles is owing to the force with which they endeavor to recede from the lower glass, and their consequent pressure against the surface of the upper one. This experiment is considered by its originator, Mr. H. F. Talbot, F.R.S., England, to be a satisfactory argument in favor of the repulsive power of heat.

### HEAT PASSING THROUGH GLASS.

The following experiment is also by Mr. Talbot: Heat a poker bright red hot, and having opened a window, apply the poker quickly very near to the outside of a pane, and the hand to the inside ; a strong heat will be felt at the instant, which will cease as soon as the poker is withdrawn, and may be again renewed, and made to cease as quickly as before. Now, it is well known that if a piece of glass be so much warmed as to convey the impression of heat to the hand, it will retain some part of that heat for a minute or more ; but in this experiment the heat will vanish in a moment. It will not, therefore, be the heated pane of glass that we shall feel, but heat which has come through the glass, in a free or radiant state.

### METALS UNEQUALLY INFLUENCED BY HEAT.

All metals do not conduct heat at the same rate, as may be proved by holding in the flame of a candle at the same time, a piece of silver wire and a piece of platina wire, when the silver wire will become too hot to hold, much sooner than the platina. Or, cut a cone of each wire, tip it with wax, and place it upon a heated plate, (as a fire-shovel,) when the wax will melt at different periods.

### SPONTANEOUS COMBUSTION.

Mix a small quantity of chlorate of potassa with spirit of wine in a strong saucer ; add a little sulphuric acid, and an orange vapor will arise and burst into flame with a loud crackling sound.

### INEQUALITY OF HEAT IN FIRE-IRONS.

Place before a brisk fire a set of polished fire-irons, and beside them a rough unpolished poker, such as is used in a kitchen, instead of a bright poker. The polished irons will remain for a long time without becoming warmer than the temperature of the room, because the heat radiated from the fire is all reflected, or thrown off, by the polished surface of the irons, and none of it is absorbed. The rough poker will, however, become speedily hot, so as not to be used without inconvenience. Hence, the polish of fire-irons is not merely ornamental, but useful.

### EXPANSION OF METAL BY HEAT

Provide an iron rod, and fit it exactly into a metal ring : heat the rod red hot, and it will no longer enter the ring.

Observe an iron gate on a warm day, when it will shut with difficulty ; whereas it will shut loosely and easily on a cold day.

### EVAPORATION OF A METAL.

Rub a globule of mercury upon a silver spoon, and the two metals will combine with a white appearance; heat the spoon carefully in the flame of a spirit lamp, when the mercury will volatilize and disappear, and the spoon may then be polished until it recovers its usual luster: if, however, the mercury be left for some time on the spoon, the solid texture of the silver will be destroyed throughout, and then the silver can only be recovered by heating it in a ladle. Care must be taken to avoid the fumes of mercury, which are very poisonous.

### A FLOATING METAL ON FIRE.

Throw a small piece of that marvelous substance, potassium, into a basin of water, and it will swim upon the surface and burn with a beautiful light, of a red color mixed with violet. When moderately heated in the air, potassium takes fire, and burns with a red light.

### ICE MELTED BY AIR.

If two pieces of ice be placed in a warm room, one of them may be made to melt much sooner than the other, by blowing on it with a pair of bellows.

### SPLENDID SUBLIMATION.

Put into a flask a small portion of iodine; hold the flask over the flame of a spirit-lamp, and from the state of bluish-black crystals, the iodine, on being heated, will become a violet-colored transparent gas; but, in cooling, will resume its crystalline form.

### MAGIC INKS.

Dissolve oxide of cobalt in acetic acid, to which add a little niter: write with this solution; hold the writing to the fire, and it will be of pale rose color, which will disappear on cooling.

Dissolve equal parts of sulphate of copper and muriate of ammonia in water; write with the solution, and it will give a yellow color when heated, which will disappear when cold.

Dissolve nitrate of bismuth in water; write with the solution, and the characters will be invisible when dry, but will become legible on immersion in water.

Dissolve, in water, muriate of cobalt, which is of a

bluish-green colour, and the solution will be pink ; write with it, and the characters will be scarcely visible : but, if gently heated, they will appear in brilliant green, which will disappear as the paper cools.

Dissolve in water a few grains of prussiate of potash ; write with this liquid, which is invisible when dry ; wash over with a dilute solution of iron, made by dissolving a nail in a little aqua fortis ; a blue and legible writing is immediately apparent.*

### CHAMELEON LIQUIDS.

Put a small portion of the compound called mineral chameleon into several glasses, pour upon each water at different temperatures, and the contents of each glass will exhibit a different shade of color. A very hot solution will be of a beautiful green color ; a cold one, a deep purple.

Make a colorless solution of sulphate of copper ; add to it a little ammonia, equally colorless, and the mixture will be of an intense blue color ; add to it a little sulphuric acid, and the blue color will disappear ; pour in a little solution of caustic ammonia, and the blue color will be restored. Thus may the liquor be changed at pleasure.

### THE MAGIC DYES.

Dissolve indigo in diluted sulphuric acid, and add to it an equal quantity of solution of carbonate of potassa. If a piece of white cloth be dipped in the mixture, it will be changed to blue ; yellow cloth, in the same mixture, may be changed to green ; red to purple ; and blue litmus paper to red.

Nearly fill a wine-glass with the juice of beet-root, which is of a deep red color ; add a little lime-water, and the mixture will be colorless ; dip into it a piece of white cloth, dry it rapidly, and in a few hours the cloth will become red.

### WINE CHANGED INTO WATER.

Mix a little solution of subacetate of lead with port wine ; filter the mixture through blotting-paper, and a colorless liquid will pass through ; to this add a small quantity of dry salt of tartar ; distil in a retort, when a spirit will arise, which may be inflamed.

* See also page 84.

### TWO COLORLESS TRANSPARENT LIQUIDS BECOME BLACK AND OPAQUE.

Have in one vessel some dilute hydrosulphate of ammonia, and in another a solution of acetate of lead; they are both colorless and transparent; mix them, and they will become black and opaque.

### TWO COLORLESS FLUIDS MAKE A COLORED ONE.

Put into a wine-glass of water a few drops of prussiate of potash, and into a second glass of water a little weak solution of sulphate of iron in water; pour the colorless mixtures together into a tumbler, and they will be immediately changed to a bright deep blue.

Or, mix the solution of prussiate of potash with that of nitrate of bismuth, and a yellow will be the product.

Or, mix the solution of prussiate of potash with that of sulphate of copper, and the mixture will be of a reddish-brown color.

### CHANGE OF COLOR BY COLORLESS FLUIDS.

Three different colors may be produced from the same infusion, merely by the addition of three colorless fluids. Slice a little red cabbage, pour boiling water upon it, and when cold decant the clear infusion, which divide into three wine-glasses: to one, add a small quantity of solution of alum in water; to the second, a little solution of potash in water; and to the third, a few drops of muriatic acid. The liquor in the first glass will assume a purple color, the second a bright green, and the third a rich crimson.

### TO CHANGE A BLUE LIQUID TO WHITE.

Dissolve a small lump of indigo in sulphuric acid by the aid of moderate heat, and you will obtain an intense blue color; add a drop of this to half a pint of water, so as to dilute the blue; then pour some of it into strong chloride of lime, and the blue will be bleached with almost magical velocity.

### VERITABLE "BLACK" TEA.

Make a cup of strong green tea; dissolve a little green copperas in water, which add to the tea, and its color will be black.

### RESTORATION OF COLOR BY WATER.

Water being a colorless fluid, ought, one would imagine, when mixed with other substances of no decided color, to produce a colorless compound. Nevertheless, it is to water only that blue vitriol, or sulphate of copper, owes its vivid blueness, as will be plainly evinced by the following simple experiment. Heat a few crystals of the vitriol in a fire-shovel, pulverize them, and the powder will be of a dull and dirty white appearance. Pour a little water upon this, when a slight hissing noise will be heard, and at the same moment the blue color will instantly reappear.

Under the microscope the beauty of this experiment will be increased, for the instant that a drop of water is placed in contact with the vitriol, the powder may be seen to shoot into blue prisms. If a crystal of prussiate of potash be similarly heated, its yellow color will vanish, but reappear on being dropped into water.

### * TWO LIQUIDS MAKE A SOLID.

Dissolve muriate of lime in water until it will dissolve no more; measure out an equal quantity of oil of vitriol; both will be transparent fluids; but if equal quantities of each be slowly mixed and stirred together, they will become a solid mass, with the evolution of smoke or fumes of muriatic acid.

### TWO SOLIDS MAKE A LIQUID.

Rub together in a mortar, equal quantities of the crystals of Glauber salts and nitrate of ammonia, and the two salts will slowly become a liquid.

### A SOLID OPAQUE MASS MAKES A TRANSPARENT LIQUID.

Take the solid mixture of the solutions of muriate of lime and carbonate of potash, pour upon it a very little nitric acid, and the solid opaque mass will be changed to a transparent liquid.

### TWO COLD LIQUIDS MAKE A HOT ONE.

Mix four drams of sulphuric acid (oil of vitriol) with one dram of cold water, suddenly, in a cup, and the mixture will be nearly half as hot again as boiling water.

* All experiments marked thus, *, should be performed on the hob of the grate, to permit the fumes to escape up the chimney.

## QUINTUPLE TRANSMUTATION.

Take five ale-glasses: place into the first a solution of iodide of potassium; into the second, a solution of corrosive sublimate, sufficiently strong to yield a scarlet precipitate with the iodide in the first glass, without redissolving, as the effect of the experiment depends on the adjustment of this beforehand; into the third, a strong solution of iodide of potassium with some oxalate of ammonia; into the fourth, a solution of muriate of lime; into the fifth, a solution of hydrosulphate of ammonia. The following changes occur.

No. 1 added to No. 2 produces a yellow, quickly changing to a scarlet; No. 2, poured into No. 3, becomes clear and transparent again; No. 3, into No. 4, changes a milky white; No. 4, poured into No. 5, produces a black precipitate.

Thus, a clear and colorless liquid is changed to scarlet; the scarlet again becomes colorless; the colorless liquid, milky white; and the white, black.

## THE SAME AGENT MAY PRODUCE AND DESTROY COLOR.

Procure a bottle of chlorine, and arrange two tall cylindrical glasses: fill one half full with a dilute solution of iodide of potassium and starch, and the other with a very dilute solution of sulphate of indigo; provide each vessel with a plate glass or cardboard valve, laid on the top; carefully open the bottle of chlorine, invert it slowly over one cylindrical vessel, so as to pour out half the gas, which is very heavy; add the remainder to the other, and shake up both vessels. The chlorine will bleach the indigo, and afford a magnificent purple in the iodide of potassium and starch, because it sets free iodine, which combines with the starch, producing a purple compound.

## UNION OF TWO METALS WITHOUT HEAT.

Cut a circular piece of gold leaf, called "dentists' gold," about half an inch in diameter; drop upon it a globule of mercury, about the size of a small pea, and if they be left for a short time, the gold will lose its solidity and yellow color, and the mercury its liquid form, making a soft mass of the color of mercury.

## MAGIC BREATH.

Half fill a glass tumbler with lime-water; breathe into it frequently, at the same time stirring it with a piece of glass. The fluid, which before was perfectly transparent, will presently become quite white, and if allowed to remain at rest, real chalk will be deposited.

### TWO BITTERS MAKE A SWEET.

It has been discovered, that a mixture of nitrate of silver with hyposulphate of soda, both of which are remarkably bitter, will produce the sweetest known substance.

### VISIBLE AND INVISIBLE.

Write with French chalk on a looking-glass; wipe it with a handkerchief, and the lines will will disappear; breathe on it, and they will reappear. This alternation will take place for a great number of times, and after the lapse of a considerable period.

### TO FORM A LIQUID FROM TWO SOLIDS.

Rub together in a Wedgewood mortar a small quantity of sulphate of soda and acetate of lead, and as they mix they will become liquid.

Carbonate of ammonia and sulphate of copper, previously reduced to powder separately, will also, when mixed, become liquid, and acquire a most splendid blue color.

The greater number of salts have a tendency to assume regular forms, or become *crystallized*, when passing from the fluid to the solid state; and the size and regularity of the crystals depends in a great measure on the slow or rapid escape of the fluid in which they were dissolved. Sugar is a capital example of this property; the ordinary loaf-sugar being rapidly boiled down, as it is called: while to make rock-candy, which is nothing but sugar in a crystallized form, the solution is allowed to evaporate slowly, and as it cools it forms into those beautiful crystals termed rock-candy. The threads found in the center of some of the crystals are merely placed for the purpose of hastening the formation of the crystals.

EXPERIMENT No. 1.—Make a strong solution of alum, or of sulphate of copper, or blue vitriol, and place in them rough and irregular pieces of clinker from stoves, or wire baskets, and set them by in a cool place, where they will be free from dust, and in a few days crystals of the several salts will deposit themselves on the baskets, &c. They should then be taken out of the solutions, and dried in an oven not too hot. when they form very pretty ornaments for a room.

Experiment No. 2.—Fill a Florence flask up to the neck with a strong solution of sulphate of soda, or Glauber salt, boil it, and tie the mouth over with a piece of moistened bladder while boiling, and set it by in a place where it cannot be disturbed. After twenty-four hours it will probably still remain fluid. Pierce the bladder covering with a penknife, and the percussion of the air will cause the whole mass instantly to crystallize, and the flask will become quite warm from the latent caloric, of which we have spoken before, given out by the salt in passing from the fluid to the solid state. It is better to prepare two or three flasks at the same time, to provide against accidents, for the least shake will often cause the crystallization to take place before the proper time.

### THE SPECTRAL LAMP.

Mix some common salt with spirit of wine in a platinum or metallic cup; set the cup upon a wire frame over a spirit-lamp, which should be inclosed on each side, or in a dark-lantern: when the cup becomes heated, and the spirit ignited, it will burn with a strong yellow flame: if, however, it should not be perfectly yellow, throw more salt into the cup. The lamp being thus prepared, all other lights should be extinguished, and the yellow lamp introduced, when an appalling change will be exhibited; all the objects in the room but of one color, and the complexions of the several persons, whether old or young, fair or brunette, will be metamorphosed to a ghastly, death-like yellow; whilst the gayest dresses, as the brightest crimson, the choicest lilac, the most vivid blue or green—all will be changed into one monotonous yellow: each person will be inclined to laugh at his neighbor, himself insensible of being one of the spectral company.

Their astonishment may be heightened by removing the yellow light to one end of the room, and restoring the usual or white light at the other; when one side of each person's dress will resume its original color, while the other will remain yellow; one cheek may bear the bloom of health, and the other, the yellow of jaundice. Or if, when the yellow light only is burning, the white light be introduced within a wire sieve, the company and the objects in the apartment will appear yellow, mottled with white.

Red light may be produced by mixing with the spirit in

the cup over the lamp, salt of strontian instead of common salt; and the effect of the white or yellow lights, if introduced through a sieve upon the red light, will be even more striking than the white upon the yellow light.

### CURIOUS CHANGE OF COLORS.

Let there be no other light than a taper in the room; then put on a pair of dark green spectacles, and having closed one eye, view the taper with the other. Suddenly remove the spectacles, and the taper will assume a bright red appearance; but if the spectacles be instantly replaced, the eye will be unable to distinguish anything for a second or two. The order of colors will, therefore, be as follows. green, red, green, black.

### THE PROTEAN LIGHT.

Soak a cotton wick in a strong solution of salt and water, dry it, place it in a spirit lamp, and when lit it will give a bright yellow light for a long time. If you look through a piece of blue glass at the flame, it will loose all its yellow light, and you will only perceive feeble violet rays. If, before the blue glass, you place a pale yellow glass, the lamp will be absolutely invisible, though a candle may be distinctly seen through the same glasses.

### THE CHAMELEON FLOWERS.

Trim a spirit lamp, add a little salt to the wick, and light it. Set near it a scarlet geranium, and the flower will appear yellow. Purple colors, in the same light, appear blue.

### TO CHANGE THE COLORS OF FLOWERS.

Hold over a lighted match a purple columbine, or a blue larkspur, and it will change first to pink, and then to black. The yellow of other flowers, held as above, will continue unchanged. Thus, the purple tint will instantly disappear from a heart's-ease, but the yellow will remain; and the yellow of a wall-flower will continue the same, though the brown streak will be discharged. If a scarlet, crimson, or maroon dahlia be tried, the color will change to yellow; a fact known to gardeners, who by this mode variegate their growing dahlias.

### CHANGES OF THE POPPY.

Some flowers, which are red, become blue by merely bruising them. Thus, if the petals of the common corn-poppy be rubbed upon white paper, they will stain it purple, which may be made green by washing it over with a strong solution of potash in water. Put poppy petals into very dilute muriatic acid, and the infusion will be of a florid red color ; by adding a little chalk, it will become of the color of port wine ; and this tint, by the addition of potash, may be changed to green or yellow.

### TO CHANGE THE COLOR OF A ROSE.

Hold a red rose over the blue flame of a common match, and the color will be discharged wherever the fume touches the leaves of the flower, so as to render it beautifully variegated, or entirely white. If it be then dipped into water, the redness, after a time, will be restored.

### LIGHT CHANGING WHITE INTO BLACK.

Write upon linen with permanent ink (which is a strong solution of nitrate of silver), and the characters will be scarcely visible ; remove the linen into a dark room, and they will not change ; but expose them to a strong light. and they will be of an indelible black.

### THE VISIBLY GROWING ACORN.

Cut a circular piece of card to fit the top of a hyacinth-glass, so as to rest upon the ledge, and exclude the air. Pierce a hole through the center of the card, and pass through it a strong thread, having a small piece of wood tied to one end, which, resting transversely on the card, prevents its being drawn through. To the other end of the thread attach an acorn ; and having half filled the glass with water, suspend the acorn at a short distance from the surface.

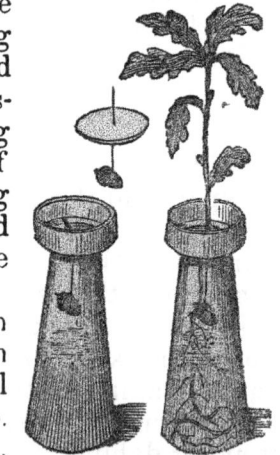

The glass must be kept in a warm room ; and, in a few days, the steam which has generated in the glass will hang from the acorn in a large drop. Shortly afterwards the acorn will burst, the root will protrude and thrust itself into the water; and in a few days more a stem will shoot out at the other end, and rising upwards, will press against the card, in which an orifice must be made to allow it to pass through. From this stem, small leaves will soon be observed to sprout; and in the course of a few weeks you will have a handsome oak plant, several inches in height.

### COLORED FLAMES.

A variety of rays of light are exhibited by colored flames, which are not to be seen in white light. Thus, pure hydrogen gas will burn with a blue flame, in which many of the rays of light are wanting. The flame of an oil lamp contains most of the rays which are wanting in the sunlight. Alcohol, mixed with water, when heated or burned, affords a flame with no other rays but yellow. The following salts, if finely powdered, and introduced into the exterior flame of a candle, or into the wick of a spirit lamp, will communicate to the flame their peculiar colors:

| | |
|---|---|
| Muriate of Soda (common salt) | Yellow. |
| Muriate of Potash | Pale violet. |
| Muriate of Lime | Brick red, |
| Muriate of Strontia | Bright crimson. |
| Muriate of Lithia | Red. |
| Muriate of Baryta | Pale apple-green. |
| Muriate of Copper | Bluish green. |
| Borax | Green. |

Or, either of the above salts may be mixed with spirit of wine, as directed for Red Fire.

### ORANGE COLORED FLAME.

Burn spirit of wine on chloride of calcium, a substance obtained by evaporating muriate of lime to dryness.

### EMERALD GREEN FLAME.

Burn spirit of wine on a little powdered nitrate of copper

### INSTANTANEOUS FLAME.

Heat together potassium and sulphur, and they will instantly burn very vividly.

Heat a little niter on a fire-shovel, sprinkle on it flour of sulphur, and it will instantly burn. If iron filings be thrown upon red-hot niter, they will detonate and burn.

Pound, separately, equal parts of chlorate of potash and lump sugar; mix them, and put upon a plate a small quantity; dip a glass rod into sulphuric acid, touch the powder with it, and it will burst into a brilliant flame.

Or, put a few grains of chlorate of potash into a tablespoonful of spirit of wine; add one or two drops of sulphuric acid, and the whole will burst into a beautiful flame.

### TO COOL FLAME BY METAL.

Encircle the very small flame of a floating night light, with a cold iron wire, which will instantly cause its extinction.

### PROOF THAT FLAME IS HOLLOW.

Pour some spirit of wine into a watch-glass, and inflame it; place a straw across this flame, and it will only be ignited and charred at the outer edge; the middle of the straw will be uninjured, for there is no ignited matter in the center of the flame.

### TO HOLD A HOT TEA KETTLE ON THE HAND.

Be sure that the bottom of the kettle is well covered with soot; when the water in it boils, remove it from the fire, and place it upon the palm of the hand; no inconvenience will be felt, as the soot will prevent the heat being transmitted from the water within and the heated metal, to the hand.

### INCOMBUSTIBLE LINEN.

Make a strong solution of borax in water, and steep in it linen, muslin, or any article of clothing; when dry, they cannot easily be inflamed. A solution of phosphate of ammonia with sal ammoniac answers much better.

### THE BURNING CIRCLE.

Light a stick, and whirl it round with a rapid motion, when its burning end will produce a complete circle of light, although that end can only be in one part of the circle at the same instant. This is caused by the duration of the impression of light upon the retina. Another example is, that during the winking of the eye we never lose sight of the object we are viewing.

## WATER OF DIFFERENT TEMPERATURES IN THE SAME VESSEL.

Of heat and cold, as of wit and madness, it may be said that "thin partitions do their bounds divide." Thus, paint one half of the surface of a tin pot with a mixture of lamp black and size, and leave the other half, or side, bright; fill the vessel with boiling water, and by dipping a thermometer, or even the finger, into it shortly after, it will be found to cool much more rapidly upon the blackened than upon the bright side of the pot.

## WARMTH OF DIFFERENT COLORS.

Place upon the surface of snow, as upon the window sill, in bright daylight or sunshine, pieces of cloth of the same size and quality, but of different colors, black, blue, green, yellow, and white: the black cloth will soon melt the snow beneath it, and sink downwards; next the blue, and then the green; the yellow but slightly; but the snow beneath the white cloth will be as firm as at first.

## SUBSTITUTE FOR FIRE.

Put into a cup a lump of quicklime, fresh from the kiln, pour water upon it, and the heat will be very great. A pailful of quicklime, if dipped in water, and shut closely into a box constructed for the purpose, will give out sufficient heat to warm a room, even in very cold weather. This is the source of steam vapor in theatrical representations.

## LAUGHING GAS.

The above fanciful appellation has been given to nitrous oxide, from the very agreeable sensations excited by inhaling it. In its pure state it destroys animal life, but loses this noxious quality when inhaled, because it becomes blended with the atmospheric air which it meets in the lungs. This gas is made by putting three or four drams of nitrate of ammonia, in crystals, into a small glass retort, which being held over a spirit lamp, the crystals will melt, and the gas be evolved.

Having thus produced the gas, it is to be passed into a large bladder, having a stop-cock; and when you are desirous of exhibiting its effects, you cause the person who wishes to experience them, to first exhale the atmospheric air from the lungs, and then quickly placing the cock in his mouth, you turn it, and bid him inhale the gas. Immedi ately, a sense of extraordinary cheerfulness, fanciful flights of imagination, an uncontrollable propensity to laughter, and a consciousness of being capable of great muscular exertion, supervene. It does not operate in exactly the same manner on all persons; but in most cases the sensations are agreeable, and have this important difference from those produced by wine or spirituous liquors, that they are not succeeded by any depression of mind.

### FLAME FROM COLD METALS.

Provide a bottle of the gas chlorine, which may be purchased of any operative chemist, and with it you may exhibit some brilliant experiments.

For example, reduce a small piece of the metal antimony to a very fine powder in a mortar; place some of this on a bent card, then loosen the stopper of the bottle of chlorine, and throw in the antimony; it will take fire spontaneously, and burn with much splendor, thus exhibiting a cold metal spontaneously bursting into flame.

If, however, a lump of antimony be dropped into the chlorine, there will be no spontaneous combustion, nor immediate change; but, in the course of time, the antimony will become incrusted with a white powder, and no chlorine will be found in the bottle.

Or, provide copper in fine leaves, known as "Dutch metal;" slightly breathe on one end of a glass rod, about ten inches long, and cause one or two leaves of the metal to adhere to the damp end; then open a bottle of chlorine, quickly plunge in the leaves, when they will instantly take fire, and burn with a fine red light, leaving in the bottle a greenish-yellow solid substance.

A small *lump* of copper, or "Dutch metal," will not burn as above, but will be slowly acted upon, like the antimony.

Immerse gold leaf in a jar of chlorine gas, and combustion with a beautiful green flame will take place.

### PHOSPHORUS IN CHLORINE.

Put into a deflagrating spoon about four grains of phosphorus, and let it down into a bottle of chlorine, when the phosphorus will ignite instantaneously.

Or, fold a slip of blotting-paper into a match five inches long; dip it into oil of turpentine, drain it an instant, drop it into another bottle of chlorine, when it will burst into a flame, and deposit much carbon.

### MAGIC VAPOR.

Provide a glass tube, about three feet long and half an inch in diameter; nearly fill it with water, upon the surface of which pour a little colored ether; then close the open end of the tube carefully with the palm of the hand, invert it in a basin of water, and rest the tube against the wall: the ether will rise through the water to the upper end of the tube; pour a little hot water over the tube, and it will soon cause the ether to boil within, and its vapor may thus be made to drive nearly all the water out of the tube into the basin; if, however, you then cool the tube by pouring cold water over it, the vaporized ether will again become a liquid, and float upon the water as before.

### GAS FROM THE UNION OF METAL.

Nearly fill a wine-glass with diluted sulphuric acid, and place in it a wire of silver and another of zinc, taking care that they do not touch each other; when the zinc will be changed by the acid, but the silver will remain inert. But cause the upper ends of the wires to touch each other, and a stream of gas will issue from them.

### CAMPHOR SUBLIMED BY FLAME.

Set a metallic plate over the flame of a spirit lamp; place upon it a small portion of camphor under a glass funnel; and the camphor will be beautifully sublimed by the heat of the lamp, in an efflorescent crust on the sides of the funnel

### GREEN FIRE.

A beautiful green fire may be thus made. Take of flour of sulphur thirteen parts, nitrate of baryta seventy-seven, oxymuriate of potassa five, metallic arsenic two, and charcoal three. Let the nitrate of baryta be well dried and powdered; then add to it the other ingredients, all finely pulverized, and exceedingly well mixed and rubbed together. Place a portion of the composition in a small tin pan, having a polished reflector fitted to one side, and set light to it; when a splendid green illumination will be the result. By adding a little calamine, it will burn more slowly.

### BRILLIANT RED FIRE.

Weigh five ounces of dry nitrate of strontia, one ounce and a half of finely powdered sulphur, five drams of chlorate of potash, and four drams of sulphuret of antimony. Powder the chlorate of potash and the sulphuret of antimony separately in a mortar, and mix them on paper; after which add them to the other ingredients, previously powdered and mixed. No other kind of mixture than rubbing together on paper is required. For use, mix with a portion of the powder a small quantity of spirits of wine, in a tin pan resembling a cheese toaster, light the mixture, and it will shed a rich crimson hue. When the fire burns dim and badly, a very small quantity of finely powdered charcoal or lamp black will revive it.

### PURPLE FIRE.

Dissolve chloride of lithium in spirit of wine, and when lighted, it will burn with a purplish flame.

### SILVER FIRE.

Place upon a piece of burning charcoal a morsel of the dried crystals of nitrate of silver (not the lunar caustic), and it will immediately throw out the most beautiful sparks that can be imagined, whilst the surface of the charcoal will be coated with silver.

### THE FIERY FOUNTAIN.

Put into a glass tumbler fifteen grains of finely granulated zinc, and six grains of phosphorus, cut into very small pieces beneath water. Mix in another glass, gradually, a dram of sulphuric acid, with two drams of water. Remove both glasses into a dark room, and there pour the diluted acid over the zinc and phosphorus in the glass; in a short time beautiful jets of bluish flame will dart from all parts of the surface of the mixture; it will become quite luminous, and beautiful luminous smoke will rise in a column from the glass, thus representing a fountain of fire.

### COMBUSTION WITHOUT FLAME.

Light a small *green* wax taper; in a minute or two, blow out the flame, and the wick will continue red hot for many hours; and if the taper were regularly and carefully uncoiled, and the room kept free from the current of air, the wick would burn on in this manner until the whole was consumed. The same effect is not produced when the color of the wax is red, on which account red wax tapers are safer than green, for the latter, if left imperfectly extinguished, may set fire to any object with which they are in contact.

### COMBUSTION OF THREE METALS.

Mix a grain or two of potassium with an equal quantity of sodium; add a globule of quicksilver, and the three metals, when shaken, will take fire, and burn vividly.

### TO MAKE PAPER APPARENTLY INCOMBUSTIBLE.

Take a smooth cylindrical piece of metal, about one inch and a half in diameter, and eight inches long; wrap very closely round it a piece of clean writing paper, then hold the paper in the flame of a spirit lamp, and it will not take fire; but it may be held there for a considerable time, without being in the least affected by the flame. If the paper be strained over a cylinder of wood, it is quickly scorched.

### HEAT NOT TO BE ESTIMATED BY TOUCH.

Hold both hands in water which causes the thermometer to rise to ninety degrees, and when the liquid has become still, you will be insensible to the heat, and that the hand is touching anything. Then remove one hand to water that causes the thermometer to rise to two hundred degrees, and the other in water at thirty-two degrees. After holding the hands thus for some time, remove them, and again immerse them in the water at ninety degrees; when you will find *warmth* in one hand and *cold* in the other. To the hand which had been immersed in the water at thirty-two degrees, the water at ninety degrees will feel hot; and to the hand which had been immersed in the water at two hundred degrees, the water at ninety degrees will feel cool. If, therefore, the touch in this case be trusted, the same water will be judged to be hot and cold at the *same* time

### FLAME UPON WATER.

Fill a wine glass with cold water, pour lightly upon its surface a little ether; light it by a slip of paper, and it will burn for some time.

### ROSE-COLORED FLAME UPON WATER.

Drop a globule of potassium, about the size of a large pea, into a small cup, nearly full of water, containing a drop or two of strong nitric acid; the moment that the metal touches the liquid, it will float upon its surface, enveloped with a beautiful rose-colored flame, and entirely dissolve.

### TO SET A MIXTURE ON FIRE WITH WATER.

Pour into a saucer a little sulphuric acid, and place upon it a chip of sodium, which will float and remain uninflamed; but the addition of a drop of water will set it on fire.

### WAVES OF FIRE ON WATER.

On a lump of refined sugar let fall a few drops of phosphuretted ether, and put the sugar into a glass of warm water, which will instantly appear on fire at the surface, and in waves, if gently blown with the breath. This experiment should be exhibited in the dark.

### WATER FROM THE FLAME OF A CANDLE.

Hold a cold and dry bell glass over a lighted candle, and watery vapor will be directly condensed on the cold surface; then close the mouth of the glass with a card or plate, and turn the mouth uppermost; remove the card, quickly pour in a little lime-water, a perfectly clear liquid, and it will instantly become turbid and milky, upon meeting with the contents of the glass, just as lime-water changes when dropped into a glass full of water.

### FORMATION OF WATER BY FIRE.

Put into a tea cup a little spirit of wine, set it on fire, and invert a large bell-glass over it. In a short time, a thick watery vapor will be seen upon the inside of the bell, which may be collected by a dry sponge.

### BOILING UPON COLD WATER.

Provide a tall glass jar, filled with cold water, and place in it an air thermometer, which will nearly reach the surface; upon the surface place a small copper basin, into which put a little live charcoal: the surface of the water will soon be made to boil, while the thermometer will show that the water beneath is scarcely warmer than it was at first.

### CURRENTS IN BOILING WATER.

Fill a large glass tube with water, and throw into it a few particles of bruised amber, then hold the tube by a handle for the purpose, upright in the flame of a lamp, and as the water becomes warm, it will be seen that currents, carrying with them the pieces of amber, will begin to ascend in the center, and to descend towards the circumference of the tube. These currents will soon become rapid in their motions, and continue till the water boils.

## HOT WATER LIGHTER THAN COLD.

Pour into a glass tube, about ten inches long, and one inch in diameter, a little water colored with pink or other dye; then fill it up gradually and carefully with colorless water, so as not to mix them; apply heat at the bottom of the tube, and the colored water will ascend and be diffused throughout the whole.

The circulation of warm water may be very pleasingly shown, by heating water in a tube similar to the foregoing; the water having diffused in it some particles of any light substance not soluble in water.

## EXPANSION OF WATER BY COLD.

All fluids, except water, diminish in bulk till they freeze. Thus, fill a large thermometer tube with water, say of the temperature of eighty degrees, and then plunge the bulb into pounded ice and salt, or any other freezing mixture: the water will go on shrinking in the tube till it has attained the temperature of about forty degrees; and then, instead of continuing to contract till it freezes, (as in the case with all other liquids,) it will be seen slowly to expand, and consequently to rise in the tube, until it congeals. In this case, the expansion below forty degrees, and above forty degrees, seem to be equal; so that the water will be of the same bulk at thirty-two degrees as at forty-eight degrees, that is, at eight degrees above or below forty degrees.

## THE CUP OF TANTALUS.

This pretty toy may be purchased at any optician's for two or three shillings. It consists of a cup, in which is placed a standing human figure, concealing a syphon, or bent tube with one end longer than the other. This rises in one leg of the figure to reach the chin, and descends through the other leg, through the bottom of the cup to a reservoir beneath. If you pour water in the cup, it will rise in the shorter leg by its upward pressure, driving out the air before it through the longer leg ; and when the cup is filled above the bend of the syphon, (that is, level with the chin of the figure,) the pressure of the water will force it over into the longer leg of the syphon, and the cup will be emptied: the toy thus imitating Tantalus of mythology, who is represented by the poets as punished in Erebus with an insatiable thirst, and placed up to the chin in a pool of water, which, however, flowed away as soon as he attempted to taste it.

### THE MAGIC WHIRLPOOL.

Fill a glass tumbler with water, throw upon its surface a few fragments or thin shavings of camphor, and they will instantly begin to move, and acquire a motion both progressive and rotary, which will continue for a considerable time. During these rotations, if the water be touched by any substance which is at all greasy, the floating particles will quickly dart back, and as if by a stroke of magic, be instantly deprived of their motion and vivacity.

In like manner, if thin slices of cork be steeped in sulphuric ether in a closed bottle for two or three days, and then placed upon the water, they will rotate for several minutes, like the camphor ; until the slices of cork having discharged all their ether, and become soaked with water, they will keep at rest.

If the water be made hot, the motion of the camphor will be more rapid than in cold water, but it will cease in proportionately less time. Thus, provide two glasses, one containing water at fifty-eight degrees, and the other at two hundred and ten degrees ; place raspings of camphor upon each at the same time ; the camphor in the first glass will rotate for about five hours, until all but a very minute portion has evaporated, while the rotation of the camphor in the hot water will last only nineteen minutes : about half the camphor will pass off, and the remaining pieces, instead of being dull, white, and opaque, will be vitreous and transparent, and evidently soaked with water. The gyrations, too, which at first will be very rapid, will gradually decline in velocity, until they become quite sluggish.

The stilling influence of oil upon waves has become proverbial : the extraordinary manner in which a small quantity of oil instantly spreads over a very large surface of troubled water, and the stealthy manner in which even a rough wind glides over it, must have excited the admiration of all who have witnessed it.

By the same principle a drop of oil may be made to stop the motion of the camphor, as follows: Throw some camphor, both in slices and in small particles, upon the surface of water, and while they are rotating, dip a glass rod into oil of turpentine, and allow a single drop thereof to trickle down the inner side of the glass to the surface of the water; the camphor will instantly dart to the opposite point of the liquid surface, and cease to rotate. If a piece of hard tallow or lard be employed, the motion of the camphor will be more slowly stopped than by oil or fluid grease, as the latter spreads over the surface of the water with greater rapidity.

If a few drops of sulphuric or muriatic acid be let fall into the water, they will gradually stop the motion of the camphor; but if camphor be dropped into nitric acid diluted with its own bulk of water, it will rotate rapidly for a few seconds, and then stop.

If a piece of the rotating camphor be attentively examined with a lens, the currents of the water can be well distinguished, jetting out, chiefly from the corners of the camphor, and bearing it round with irregular force.

The currents, as given out by the camphor, may also be seen by means of the microscope; a drop or two of pure water being placed upon a slip of glass, with a particle of camphor floating upon it. By this means the current may be detected, and it will be seen that they cause the rotations.

Or a flat watch-glass, called a *lunar*, may be employed, raised a few inches, and supported on a wire ring, kept steady by thrusting one end into an upright piece of wood, like a retort stand. Then put the camphor and water in the watch-glass, and place under the frame a sheet of white paper, so that it may receive the shadow of the glass, camphor, &c., to be cast by a steady light, placed above, and somewhat on one side of the watch glass. On observing the shadow, which may be considered a magnified representation of the object itself, the rotations and currents can be distinguished.

### ARTIFICIAL FIRE BALLS.

Put thirty grains of phosphorus into a bottle, which contains three or four ounces of water. Place the vessel over a lamp, and give it a boiling heat. Balls of fire will soon be seen to issue from the water, after the manner of an artificial fire-work, attended with the most beautiful coruscations.

### TO MELT STEEL AS EASILY AS LEAD.

Make a piece of steel red in the fire, then hold it with a pair of pincers or tongs; take in the other hand a stick of brimstone, and touch the piece of steel with it. Immediately after their contact, you will see the steel melt and drop like a liquid.

### TO TELL A LADY IF SHE IS IN LOVE.

Put into a phial some sulphuric ether, color it red with orchanet, then saturate the tincture with spermaceti. This preparation is solid ten degrees above freezing point, and melts and boils at twenty degrees. Place the phial which contains it in a lady's hand, and tell her that if in love, the solid mass will dissolve. In a few minutes the substance will become fluid.

### AN EGG PUT INTO A PHIAL.

To accomplish this seemingly incredible act, requires the following preparation: You must take an egg and soak it in strong vinegar; and in process of time its shell will become quite soft, so that it may be extended lengthways without breaking; then insert it into the neck of a small bottle, and by pouring cold water upon it, it will reassume its former figure and hardness. This is really a complete curiosity, and baffles those who are not in the secret to find out how it is accomplished. If the vinegar used to saturate the egg is not sufficiently strong to produce the required softness of shell, add one teaspoonful of strong acetic acid to every two tablespoonfuls of vinegar. This will render the egg perfectly flexible, and of easy insertion into the bottle, which must then be filled with cold water.

### TO ASTONISH A LARGE PARTY.

With some lycopodium, powder the surface of a large or small vessel of water; you may then challenge any one to drop a piece of money into the water, and that you will get it with the hand without wetting your skin. The lycopodium adheres to the hand, and prevents its contact with the water. A little shake of the hand, after the feat is over, will dislodge the powder.

## TEST PAPERS.

On the otherwise barren rocks which fringe the shore of the Cape de Verd Islands, grows the archil—a famous seaweed or lichen, renowned among dyers. By a particular process of manufacture, this archil yields a beautiful blue pigment, known in the chemical laboratory by the name of *litmus*. Few colors are more fugitive than litmus. Being a fine violet-blue, it is changed to red by so minute a portion of any acid, that it becomes, when properly applied, *a test* of the presence of the latter substance. As it is so frequently desirable to know whether a fluid be acid or alkaline, one of the first practical lessons to a student in chemistry, is to prepare litmus test paper, thus: Put into a flask half an ounce of litmus, and three ounces of water; let them remain together in a warm place for a few hours, then filter the dark blue liquid from its impurities, divide the solution obtained into two parts, pour one portion into a saucer, and soak strips of white writing paper in it until it has acquired a distinct blue color. If not colored enough by once dipping and drying, repeat the operation. When dry, preserve these strips in a box, labeled " Blue litmus test papers." These serve to *test* any fluid, to ascertain if it has an *acid* reaction. It is instructive to learn how very small a portion of any acid in water will be indicated by the reddening of the litmus. With the second portion of the fluid, mix, cautiously, a few drops of lemon juice, until it is red; then color paper as before. When dry, this "red litmus test paper" serves to indicate the presence of alkalies, a class of bodies opposed to acids. Red litmus test paper, on being put into any fluid that is *alkaline*, such as lime-water, is immediately restored to its original blue color. Put the ashes of a cigar into water, the liquid, when "tested," will indicate the presence of an alkali. Test some stale milk. If your blue paper becomes red, the milk is sour; it is acid.

## INFINITE DIVISIBILITY OF MATTER.

Dissolve a single grain of copper in about one dram of nitric acid, and dilute the solution with about one ounce of water, when it will be evident that a single drop of the mixture must contain an almost immeasurably small portion of copper. Yet, if the blade of a knife be dipped into it, it will become covered with a coat of copper; thus showing that the copper can be infinitely divided without any alteration in its properties

# AMUSEMENTS
### IN
# ELECTRICITY, GALVANISM AND MAGNETISM

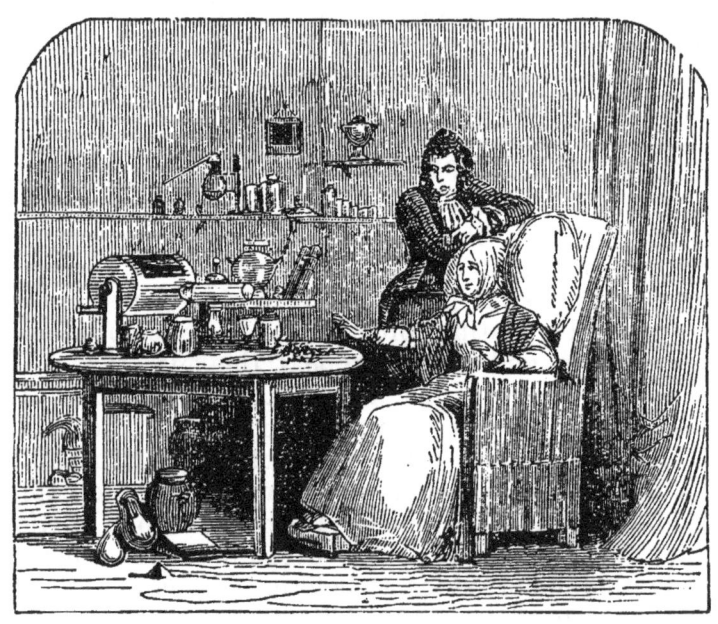

THE ORIGIN OF GALVANISM.

ELECTRICITY is one of the most active principles in nature. It exists in all bodies, and is exhibited by various means, one of which, and the most generally employed, is friction; but the bodies rubbed together must consist of different substances; for, if they are alike, electricity will not be evolved. Some substances, such as soot, charcoal, iron, gold, silver, copper, and other metals, water, &c., are called *good conductors*, because they transfer with great facility to other bodies the electric fluid, which glides over the surface with the velocity of light; while others, such as silk, wool, hair, feathers, dry paper, leather, glass, wax, &c., are called *non-conductors*, because they resist the progress of the fluid, which accumulates all the time the friction continues. It is from these media that are obtained the usual phenomena of electricity, as exhibited in the experiments which we shall hereafter describe. Its effects are felt in almost every part of nature; the awful lightning is the exhibition of the electric fluid, which accumulates in the clouds, and which is discharged when the heavy lurid masses come in contact with each other; the mysterious sweeping whirlwind, the terrific rising and rolling of the sand in the desert wilds of Africa, and the beautiful yet evanescent Aurora Borealis of the northern climes, are amongst a few of its effects.

The next branch of the science of Electricity is GALVANISM, or, as it is sometimes called, Voltaic Electricity; it is obtained through the simple contact of different conducting bodies with each other. It was first discovered at Bologna, in the year 1791, by the lady of Louis Galvani, an Italian philosopher of great merit, and professor of anatomy; from whom, indeed, the science received its name. His wife being possessed of a penetrating understanding, and passionately loving him, took a lively interest in the science which so much occupied his attention. At the time the incident we are about to narrate took place, she was in a declining state of health, and taking soup made of frogs, by way of restorative. Some of these animals, skinned for the purpose, happened to be lying on the table of Galvani's laboratory, where also stood an electrical machine, when the point of a knife was unintentionally brought into contact with the nerves of one of the frog's legs, which lay close to the conductor of the machine, and immediately the muscles of the limb were violently agitated. Madame Galvani having observed the phenomenon, instantly informed her husband of it, and this incident led to the experiments and interesting discoveries which will transmit his name to the latest posterity.

The uses of Galvanic Electricity for scientific purposes are incalculable; and its phenomena are so various and extraordinary, as to render the study of this science exceedingly interesting. Through means of a galvanic battery, substances are decomposed, colors changed, water is made inflammable, and motion is given to lifeless bodies.

The experiments we give on Galvanism show the effect of the combination which forms what is called a simple galvanic circle, by means of two metals, zinc and silver, or zinc and copper, and water.

Galvanic action is always accompanied by chemical action, and all that is necessary to disturb the galvanic fluid is to unite two metals together, and subject them to the action of a fluid, which will act chemically upon one of them, differently to what it does upon the other.

A galvanic circle may also be formed of one metal, and two different fluids, which have a different action upon the metal.

Magnetism is a modification of electricity: at least, there is sufficient evidence that these causes are intimately connected, if not identical ; but philosophers are as yet ignorant of its nature.

The property designated by the word magnetism is found in an iron ore of a certain composition, and of a dark gray color and peculiar luster. This ore alone is the local habitation of magnetism, whilst all others are subject to its influence, or to be attracted by it. Still, so little difference is there between the magnetic ore, or loadstone, and those which do not possess the property, that only practiced mineralogists can discern one from the other ; and an experienced eye may see two ores join each other by the principle of attraction, without knowing in which resides the power, until another ore, non-magnetic, is brought within the sphere of attraction, when it will adhere only to that which contains the principle.

This singular property of the loadstone is imparted to other metallic substances, by rubbing and keeping them close together for some length of time : if a metal be of a hard texture like steel, it retains the magnetic principle permanently ; but if soft, it loses the power as soon as seperated from the magnet. The metals thus prepared, acquire the same directive and attractive power as the loadstone or natural magnet, and are employed for purposes of the utmost importance.

We proceed to give the youthful amateur the opportunity of exemplifying the principles of electricity, galvanism, and magnetism, by several simple experiments.

## EXPERIMENTS IN ELECTRICITY.

1.—Lay a watch down upon a table, and on its face balance a tobacco-pipe very carefully. Next take a wine-glass, rub it quickly with a silk handkerchief, and hold it for half a minute 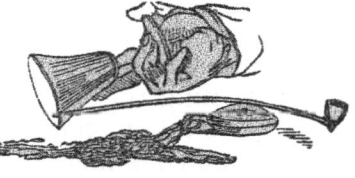 before the fire ; then apply it near to the end of the pipe, and the latter, attracted by the electricity evolved by the friction and warmth in the former, will immediately follow it ; and by carrying the glass around, always in front of the pipe, the latter will continue its rotatory motion ; the watch-glass being the center or pivot on which it acts.

2.—Warm a glass tube, rub it with a warm flannel, and then bring a downy feather near it. On the first moment of contact, the feather will adhere to the glass, but soon after will fly rapidly from it, and you may drive it about the room by holding the glass between it and the surrounding objects ; should it, however, come in contact with anything not under the influence of electricity, it will instantly fly back to the glass.

3.—A stick of sealing-wax rubbed against a warm piece of flannel or cloth, acquires the property of attracting light substances, such as small pieces of paper, lint, &c., if instantly applied at the distance of about an inch.

4.—Suspend two small pith balls, by fine silken threads of about six inches in length, in such a manner, that when at rest they may hang in contact with each other ; on applying a piece of sealing wax, excited as in the former experiment, they will repel each other.

5.—Take a piece of common brown paper, about the size of an octavo book, hold it before the fire till quite dry and hot, then draw it briskly under the arm several times, so as to rub it on both sides at once by the coat. The paper will be found so powerfully electrical, that if placed against a wainscoted or papered wall of a room, it will remain there for some minutes without falling.

6.—And if, while the paper adheres to the wall, a light fleecy feather be placed against it, it will be attracted to the paper, in the same way as the paper is attracted to the wall.

7.—If the paper be again warmed, and drawn under the arm as before, and hung up by a thread attached to one corner of it, it will hold up several feathers on each side ; should these fall off from different sides at the same time, they will cling together very strongly ; and if after a minute they be all shaken off, they will fly to one another in a very singular manner.

8.—Warm and excite the paper as before, lay it on a table, and place upon it a ball made of elder pith, about the size of a pea ; the ball will immediately run across the paper, and if a needle be pointed towards it, it will again run to another part, and so on for a considerable time

9.—Support a pane of glass, previously warmed, upon two books, one at each end, and place some bran underneath ; then rub the upper side of the glass with a black silk handkerchief, or a piece of flannel, and the bran will dance up and down under it with much rapidity.

10.—Place your left hand upon the throat of a cat, and with the middle finger and the thumb, press slightly the bones of the animal's shoulders ; then, if the right hand be gently passed along the back, perceptible shocks of electricity will be felt in the left hand. Shocks may also be obtained by touching the tips of the ears after rubbing the back. If the color of the cat be black, and the experiment be made in a dark room, the electric sparks may be very plainly seen. Very distinct charges of electricity may also be obtained by touching the tips of the ears after applying friction to the back, and the same may be obtained from the foot. Placing the cat on your knees, apply the right hand to the back; the left fore paw resting on the palm of your left hand, apply the thumb to the upper side of the paw, so as to extend the claws, and by this means, bring your fore finger into contact with one of the bones of the leg, where it joins the paw; when, from the knob or end of this bone, the finger slightly pressing on it, you may feel distinctly successive shocks, similar to those obtained from the ears. It is, perhaps, unnecessary to add, that, in order to this experiment being conveniently performed, the experimenter must be on good terms with the cat.

### ELECTRICAL SHOCK FROM A SHEET OF PAPER.

Place an iron japanned tea tray on a dry, clean, beaker glass; then take a sheet of foolscap writing paper, and hold it close to the fire until all its hygrometric moisture is dissipated, but not so as to scorch it; in this state it is one of the finest electrics we have. Hold one end down on a table with the finger and thumb, and give it about a dozen strokes with a large piece of India rubber from the left to the right, beginning at the top. Now take it up by two of the corners and bring it over the tray, and it will fall down on it like a stone; if one finger be now brought under the tray, a sensible shock will be felt. Now lay a needle on the tray with its point projecting outwards, remove the paper, and a star sign of the negative electricity will be seen: return the paper, and the positive brush will appear. In fact, it forms a very extemporaneous electrophorus, which will give a spark an inch long, and strong enough to set fire to some combustible bodies, and to exhibit all the electric phenomena not requiring coated surfaces. If four beaker glasses are placed on the floor, and a book laid on them, a person may stand on them insulated; if he then holds the tray vertically, the paper will adhere strongly to it, and sparks may be drawn from any part of his body; or he may draw sparks from any other person, as the case may be; or he may set fire to some inflammable bodies, by touching them with a piece of ice.

## LIGHT UNDER WATER.

Rub two pieces of fine lump sugar together in the dark, and a bright electric light will be produced. The same effect, but in a more intense degree, may be produced with two pieces of silex or quartz, the white quartz being best for this purpose. The same effect may also be witnessed by rubbing the pieces of quartz together, *under water.*

## SIMPLE MEANS OF PRODUCING ELECTRICITY.

To show the nature of electrical action, rub a piece of sealing-wax or amber upon the coat sleeve, and it will be found that while warm by the friction, it attracts light bodies, such as straws or small pieces of paper. In our experiments we have shown that if a clean glass tube be rubbed several times through a silken or leather cloth, and presented to any substance, it will immediately attract or repel them ; and if a poker suspended by a dry silk string be presented to its upper end, then the lower end of the poker will exhibit the same phenomena as the tube itself, which shows that the electrical fluid passes through the metal. But if for a metallic body a stick of glass or sealing wax be substituted, these phenomena will not occur, which proves that the electrical fluid does not pass through these substances.

By this it will be perceived that besides the class of bodies called electrics, there is another which we call conductors. These bodies cannot be excited themselves, but have the power of transmitting the electric fluid through them. These bodies comprise all the metals, some metal and metallic ores ; the fluids of animal bodies; water, and other fluids, except oil; ice, snow, earthy substances, smoke, steam, and even a vacuum.

When any electrified conductor is wholly surrounded by non-conductors, so that the electric fluid cannot pass from the conductor along conductors to the earth, it is said to be insulated. Thus the human body is a conductor of electricity ; but if a person standing on a glass stool (as represented in the drawing) be charged with electricity, the electric fluid cannot pass from him to the earth, and he is said to be *positively electrified,* because he has more than his natural share; he is also *insulated*, and if he be touched by another person standing on the ground, sparks will be exhibited at the point of contact, where also the person touching will feel a pricking sensation.

### ATTRACTION AND REPULSION EXHIBITED.

In order to illustrate certain remarkable facts in this science of an amusing character, attention must be directed to the figure A B, which is a metal stand; c is a small piece of cork or pith, which is suspended from the hook by a dry silken thread. Having rubbed an electron, as a dry rod of glass, and presented it to c, the ball will be instantaneously attracted to the glass, and will adhere to it. 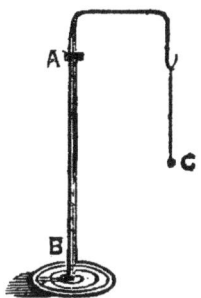 After they remain in contact for a few seconds, if the glass be withdrawn without being touched by the fingers, and again presented to the ball, the latter will be *repelled* instead of attracted, as in the first instance. By being touched with the finger, the ball can be deprived of its electricity, and if, after this has been done, we present a piece of sealing-wax in place of the glass formerly employed, the very same phenomena will take place. On the first application the ball will be *attracted*, and on the second *repelled*.

Before the young reader can perform any very important experiments with electricity, he must become possessed of an ELECTRICAL MACHINE, which is an instrument contrived for the purpose of rubbing together the surfaces of electrics and non-electrics. They generally consist of a cylinder, or plate of glass, and a piece of silk for it to rub against, covered with an amalgam, the method of preparing which we shall hereafter describe.

### HOW TO MAKE AN ELECTRICAL MACHINE.

It is very easy to make a glass machine of the cylindrical form, if the maker cannot afford to buy one. First procure

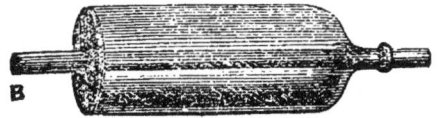

a common wine bottle of good dimensions, and thickish glass

Drill a hole through its bottom, by igniting a piece of worsted tied round round it, dipped in turpentine, which will do this. Through this hole and the mouth pass a spindle, as represented in the cut. The end of B should be squared to

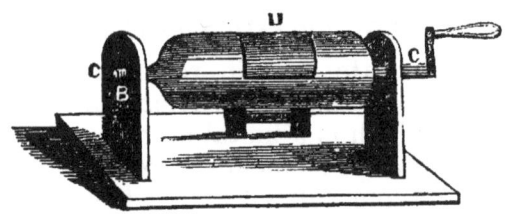

fix a handle on, and the spindle should be fixed firmly in the bottle. The bottle is then to be fixed in a frame, in the following manner: The end of the spindle c passes through a hole at B; and the other end at c has the handle for turning the machine.

Next make a cushion of wash-leather, stuffed with wool, and fastened to the top of a frame of the following figure.

CUSHION.

This frame is to be of such a height that the cushion shall press against the sides of the bottle, and a piece of black silk is sewn on to the top of the cushion, and hangs over the bottle D. The cushion should be smeared with an amalgam, formed by melting together in the bowl of a tobacco pipe, one part of tin with two of zinc; to which, while fluid, should be added six parts of mercury. These should be stirred about till quite cold, and then reduced to a fine powder in a mortar, and mixed with a sufficient quantity of lard to form a thickish paste. When all is done, the machine is complete.

### CONDUCTOR.

The electricity being generated by the friction produced between the rubber and the bottle from the motion imparted by the handle, it is necessary to draw it off for use. This is performed by what is called a conductor. This is made in the following manner: At right angles to one end of a cylinder of wood, about two inches and a half in diameter, and six inches long, fix a small wooden cylinder about three quarters of an inch in diameter, and three inches long, rounded at both ends—the other end of the larger cylinder is also to be rounded. Cover the whole with tinfoil, and mount it on a stand on a glass rod. When used, it is to be placed with the even piece in a line even with, and about half an inch from the bottle, and it should be of such a height as to come just below the silk apron. When it is wished to charge a Leyden jar, it is to be placed at the round end of the conductor. By these simple means a great variety of pleasing experiments may be performed; but to show the various phenomena connected with this interesting study, we shall now describe an electrical machine of the newest construction, and perform our experiments with it.

### THE PLATE ELECTRICAL MACHINE.

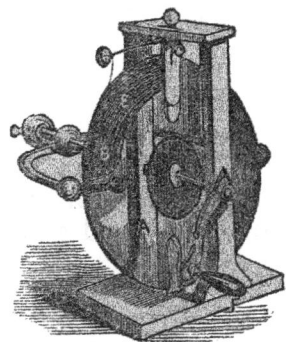

Formerly the electrical machine was made in the form of a cylinder, but now it consists of a plate A, as seen in the engraving. The plate is turned by the handle F, through the rubber B B, which diffuses the excitement over the glass. The points or balls at each side of the plate carry off a constant stream of positive electricity to the prime conductor C. Negative electricity is generated by insulating the conductor to which the cushion is attached, and continuing the prime conductor with the ground, so as to carry off the fluid collected from the plate.

### HOW TO DRAW SPARKS FROM THE TIP OF THE NOSE.

If the person who works the machine be supported on a stool having glass legs, and connected with the conductor by means of a glass rod, the electricity will pass from the conductor to him, and as it cannot get away, owing to the glass on which he stands being a non-conductor, any person on touching him can draw the electricity from him, which will exhibit itself in small sparks as it passes to the person who touches him. If touched on the nose, sparks of fire will issue from it.

### HOW TO GET A JAR FULL OF ELECTRICITY.

A most useful piece of electrical apparatus is called the Leyden jar, here represented. It is employed for the purpose of obtaining a quantity of electricity, which may be applied to any substance. It consists of a glass jar, coated

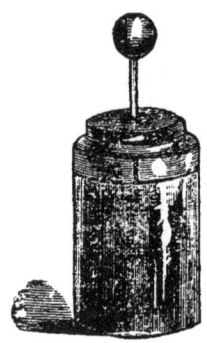
both inside and without, four fifths of the way up, with tinfoil. A knob rises through a wooden top, communicating with the inside of the jar. When it is wished to charge the jar, this knob is applied to the prime conductor of the electrical machine when in action, and a quantity of electricity being given off, the jar will remain charged with it till a connection is made, by some good conductor of electricity, between the knob and the outside tinfoil. A piece of brass chain must hang from the stem that carries the knob, and connect it with the interior of the ja

### THE ELECTRICAL BATTERY.

If several of these jars be united, an enormous quantity of electricity can be collected; but in arranging them, all the interior coatings must be made to communicate by metallic rods, and a similar union must be effected among the exterior coatings.

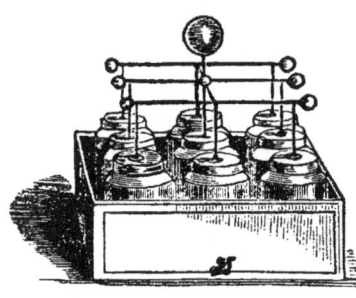

When thus arranged, the whole series may be charged as if they formed but one jar.

For the purpose of making a direct communication between the inner or outer coatings of a jar or battery, by which a discharge is effected, an instrument called a discharging rod is employed. It consists of two bent metallic rods, terminating at one end by brass balls, and connected at another by a joint which is fixed to the end of a glass handle, and which, acting like a pair of compasses, allows of the balls being separated at certain distances. When opened to the proper degree, one of the balls is made to touch the exterior coating, and the other ball is then brought into contact with the knob of the jar, when a discharge is effected; while the glass handle secures the person holding it from the effects of the shock.

### DANCING BALLS AND DOLLS.

Get two round pieces of wood, A B, and coat them with tin foil, or two pieces of metal plate; attach one of them to the prime conductor by a chain, and let it hang about two or three inches from the knob. Place some pith balls upon the bottom piece of wood B, and bring it under the other. Immediately this is done, and the upper piece is charged by electricity from the machine, the pith balls will jump up and down, and from one to the other with great rapidity. If some of the pith be formed into little figures, they will also dance and leap about in the most grotesque manner. The same may be made to dance by merely holding the inside of a dry glass tumbler to the prime conductor for a few minutes, while the machine is in action, and then whelming it over them, when they will jump about to the no 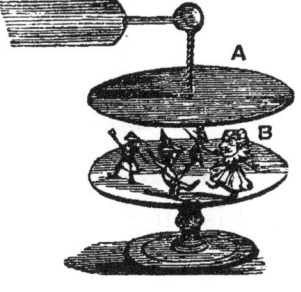  small astonishment of the spectators, as the cause of their motion is not quite so apparent.

### THE ELECTRICAL KISS.

This amusing experiment is performed by means of the electrical stool. Let any lady challenge a gentleman not acquainted with the experiment, to favor her with a salute. The lady thereupon mounts the glass stool, and takes hold of a chain connected with the prime conductor. The machine being then put in motion, the gentleman approaches the lady, and immediately he attempts to imprint the seal of soft affection upon her coral lips, a spark will fly in his face, which generally deters him from his rash and wicked intention.

### RINGING BELLS.

Bells may be made to ring by electricity in the following manner. Let three small bells be suspended from a brass wire D D, and supported by a glass pillar A, passing through bell B to the bell E. The electrical apparatus being attached to the knob F the electricity passes down the wires D D

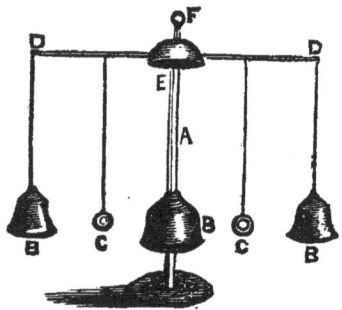

to the bells, which are then positively electrified, and attract the clappers c c, that are negatively so, in consequence of being insulated by the silken strings, which are not conductors. The bells therefore attract the clappers till they are charged, when they strike against the center bell to discharge themselves, and thus a peal is rung on the bells until the electricity is driven off.

### WORKING POWER OF ELECTRICITY.

This may be shown in a variety of ways. The subjoined machine will exhibit the principle upon which many ingenious toys may be made by the young philosopher. In the figure A is a wooden board or stand, B B B B, four pillars

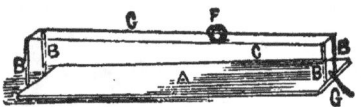

having fine wires, c c, stretched above. On these rest the rotatory wire or wheel F, having its points turned the reverse way. By means of a chain attached to the conductor, and to the instrument at B, the electricity passes over the pillar B, up the wire c into the wheel, and off at the points, which causes it to be turned round on an inclined plane till it reaches the top.

### THE ELECTRIFIED WIG.

While a person is on the electrical stool, if he be charged with much electricity,

Each hair will stand on end,
Like quills upon the fretful porcupine."

A wooden head, not your own, but a real wooden head, with a wig of streaming hair, and a handsome face to correspond, may be made in the following form, with a wire in the neck to support it by, and fixed in the conductor of an electrical machine. When this is put in motion, the hair will rise up as in figure 2, to astonish even "Whigs," who are seldom astonished by, or deterred from anything.

## IMITATION THUNDERCLOUDS,

To show the manner in which thunderclouds perform their operations in the air. A A is a wooden stand, on which are erected two uprights, B B ; C C are two small pulleys, over which a silken cord can pull easily; E is another silken line stretched across from one upright to another ; on these silken cords two pieces of thin cardboard, covered with tin foil, and cut so as to represent clouds, are to be fixed hori-

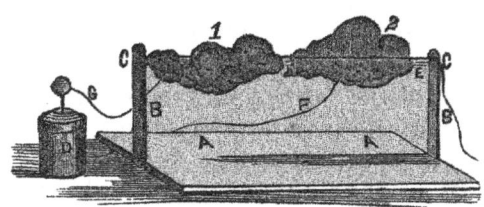

zontally, and made to communicate by means of thin wires, F and G, one with the *inside*, and the other with the outside of a charged jar, D. Now, by pulling the loop of the silk line E, the cloud 1 will be brought near the cloud 2 ; continue this slowly until the clouds (which are furnished with two small brass balls) are within an inch of each other, when a beautiful flash, strongly resembling lightning in miniature, will pass from one cloud to the other, restoring electrical equilibrium.

## THE LIGHTNING-STROKE IMITATED.

If the jar D be put behind the stand, and the cloud 2 removed, a vessel communicating by means of a wire with the outside of the jar, may be swum in water under the re-

maining cloud ; the mast being made of separate pieces, and but slightly joined together. When the cloud is passed over the vessel, the mast will be struck and shattered to pieces.

## THE SPORTSMAN.

This apparatus is capable of affording much amusement: A is a stand of wood, B is a common Leyden jar, out of which proceed the wires H H, one terminating in ball F, the other in the ball D, to which are attached a number of pith birds, by silken strings; E is a shelf for the birds to rest upon; C is the sportsman; G his gun.

To put this operation in motion, the Leyden jar is to be charged with electricity, by affixing a chain to the bottom part of it, and connecting it with an electrical machine in the usual manner, or by applying it to a prime conductor, when the birds will fly off the knob to which they are fixed, in consequence of their being repelled. If the sportsman and gun be then turned, so that the end of his gun shall touch the knob F, an electric spark will pass from one to

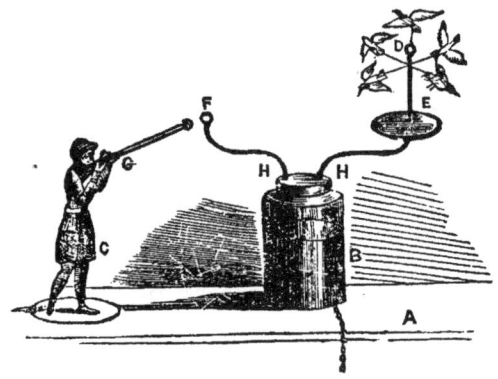

the other, a report will be heard, and the birds will fall down as if shot, in consequence of the electricity having been taken from the Leyden jar. There should be a communication between the sportsman and the jar, formed of tinfoil, or some metal, as shown by the dotted line on the stand.

Such are a few of many experiments which may be made by the young experimenter, who is fond of science and has any ingenuity; but should he possess little love of research, no ingenuity, and would like to amuse himself with an electrifying machine of little cost, he may sit himself down to a

### BLACK TOM CAT,

and be a Katterfelto at once.

## EXPERIMENTS IN GALVANISM.

1. Place a thin plate of zinc upon the upper surface of the tongue, and a half dollar or a piece of silver on the under surface. Allow the metals to remain for a little time in contact with the tongue before they are made to touch each other, that the taste of the metals themselves may not be confounded with the sensation produced by their contact. When the edges of the metals, which project beyond the tongue, are then suffered to touch, a galvanic sensation is produced, which it is difficult accurately to describe.

2. Place a silver teaspoon as high as possible between the gums and the upper lip, and a piece of zinc between the gums and the under lip. On bringing the extremities of the metals into contact, a very vivid sensation, and an effect like a flash of light across the eyes, will be perceived. It is singular that this light is equally vivid in the dark and in the strongest light, and whether the eyes be shut or open.

3. Put a silver cup or mug, filled with water, upon a plate of zinc on a table, and just touch the water with the tip of the tongue; it will be tasteless so long as the zinc plate is not handled, for the body does not form a voltaic circle with

the metals. Moisten your hand well, take hold of the plate of zinc, and touch the water with your tongue, when a very peculiar sensation, and an acid taste, will be experienced.

4. Take a piece of copper of about six inches in width, and put upon it a piece of zinc of rather smaller dimensions, inserting a piece of cloth, of the same size as the zinc, between them; place a leech upon the piece of zinc, and though there appear nothing to hinder it from crawling away, yet it will not pass from the zinc to the copper, because its damp body acting as a conductor to the fluid disturbed, as soon as it touches the copper it receives a galvanic shock, and of course retires to its resting-place.

5. Plunge an iron knife into a solution of sulphate of copper (blue-stone); by chemical action, only, it will become covered with metallic copper. Immerse in the same solution a piece of platinum, taking care not to let it touch the iron, and no deposition of copper will take place upon it; but if the upper ends of the metals be brought into contact with each other, a copious deposition of copper will soon settle upon the platinum likewise.

### WITH METAL PLATES IN WATER.

If we take two plates of different kinds of metal, platinum or copper, and zinc, for example, and immerse them in pure 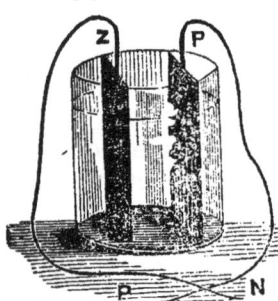 water, having wires attached to them above, then if the wire of each is brought into contact in another vessel of water, a galvanic circle will be formed, the water will be slowly decomposed, its oxygen will be fixed on the zinc wire, and at the same time a current of electricity will be transmitted through the liquid to the platinum or copper wire, on the end of which the other element of water, namely, the hydrogen, will make its appearance in the form of minute gas bubbles. The electrical current passes back again into the zinc at the points of its contact with the platinum, and thus a continued current is kept up, and hence it is called a galvanic circle. The moment the circuit is broken by separating the wires, the current ceases, but is again renewed by making them touch either in or out of the water. If a small quantity of sulphuric acid be added to the water, the phenomenon will be more apparent. The end of the wire attached to the piece of platinum or copper is called the positive pole of the battery, and that of the wire attached to the zinc is the negative pole.

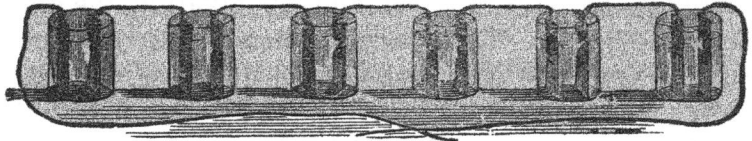

The current of electricity here generated will be extremely feeble, but this can be easily increased by multiplying the glasses and the number of the pieces of metal. If we take six such glasses instead of one, partially fill them with dilute sulphuric acid, and put a piece of zinc and copper into each, connecting them by means of copper wire from glass to glass through the whole series, a stronger current of electricity will be the result. The experimenter must be careful not to let the wire and zinc touch each other at the bottom of the tumblers, and must also remember that the copper of glass 1 is connected with the zinc of glass 2, and so on.

### TO MAKE A MAGNET BY GALVANISM.

To effect this, make a connection between the poles of the above or any excited battery with the two ends of a wire formed into a spiral coil, by bending common bonnet wire closely round a cylinder, or tube, of about an inch in diameter; into this coil introduce a needle, or piece of steel wire, laying it lengthways down the circles of the coil. In a few minutes after the electric fluid has passed through the spiral wire, and consequently round the needle or wire, the latter will be found to be strongly magnetized, and to possess all the properties of a magnet.

### EFFECTS OF GALVANISM ON A MAGNET.

If a galvanic current, or any electric current, be made to pass along a wire, under which and in a line with it a compass is placed, it will be found that the needle will no longer point north and south, but will take a direction nearly across the current, and point almost east and west.

### CHANGE OF COLOR BY GALVANISM.

Put a teaspoonful of sulphate of soda into a cup, and dissolve it in hot water; pour a little cabbage blue into the solution, and put a portion into two glasses, connecting them by a piece of linen or cotton cloth previously moistened in the same solution. On putting one of the wires of the galvanic pole into each glass, the acid accumulates in the one, turning the blue to a red, and the alkali in the other, rendering it green. If the wires be now reversed, the acid accumulates eventually in the glass where the alkali appeared, while the alkali passes to the glass where the acid was.

### THE GALVANIC SHOCK.

If the ends of the wires of a galvanic battery be placed in separate basins of water, then, on dipping the fingers of each hand in the basin, a smart shock will be felt, with a particular aching accompanied with trembling. With a strong battery this effect is felt as high as the shoulders. The shock will also be felt by simply holding the galvanic wires, one in each hand, provided the hands be moistened with salt and water. Several persons may receive the shock together by joining hands.

### FAMILIAR GALVANIC EFFECTS.

Coat the point of your tongue with tin-foil, and its middle part with gold or silver leaf, so that the two metals touch, when a sourish taste will be produced. This simple effect is termed "A Galvanic Tongue."

Ale and porter drink better out of a pewter or tin pot, than from glass or earthenware; because of the galvanic influence of the green copper as used to give the beer a frothy head.

Galvanic experiments may be made with the legs of a frog. A live flounder will answer nearly the same purpose. Lay the fish in a plate, upon a slip of zinc, to which is attached a piece of wire, and put a quarter dollar upon the flounder's back; then touch the quarter dollar with the wire, and at each contact strong muscular contractions will be produced.

## EXPERIMENTS IN MAGNETISM.

1. We have said that the agency of the magnet can be imparted to hard metallic bodies; this may be done in a very easy way. If you pass a magnet (which may be either natural or artificial) over a sewing-needle several times from the eye to the point, the needle will acquire the principle, and attract iron filings in the same manner as a natural magnet would do. But the part of the magnet which you apply to the needle must be the north pole; and you must not pass it over the needle backward and forward, but lift it always from the point and again begin from the eye. Suppose you wish to impart the principle to a small bar of tempered steel, tie the piece to be magnetized to a poker with a piece of silk, and hold the part of the poker to which it is attached in the left hand; take hold of the tongs, a little below the middle, with the right hand, and rub the steel bar with them, moving the tongs from the bottom to the top, and keeping them steadily in a vertical position all the time. About a dozen strokes on each side will im-

part sufficient magnetic power to the bar to enable the operator to lift up small pieces of iron and steel with it The lower end of the bar should be marked before it is fastened to the poker, so that the poles may be readily distinguished from each other when it is taken off; the upper end being the south pole, and the lower the north.

2. Scatter some iron filings upon a piece of paper, and hold a magnet underneath it. The instant the contact takes place, the filings will raise themselves upright, and fall down as soon as the magnet is withdrawn. The effect is singular, and indeed very amusing; the diminutive iron particles rising and falling, as if by supernatural agency.

### TEST OF MAGNETIC POWER.

To ascertain whether a piece of metal, or mineral, is magnetic, present it to one of the poles of a poised magnet. If it be attracted at both poles, you may then conclude that the substance so tested is not magnetic.

Dip a magnet into boiling water, and it will lose half of its magnetism; but as the magnet cools, its full power will return.

### TO MAKE ARTIFICIAL MAGNETS.

This may be done by stroking a piece of hard steel with a natural or artificial magnet. Take a common sewing-needle, and pass the north pole of a magnet from the eye to the point, pressing it gently in so doing. After reaching the end of the needle, the magnet must not be passed back again towards the eye, but must be lifted up and applied again to that end, the friction being always in the same direction. After repeating this for a few times, the needle will become magnetized, and attract iron filings, &c.

### HOW TO MAGNETIZE A POKER.

Hold it in the left hand in a position slightly inclined from the perpendicular, the lower end pointing to the north, and then strike it smartly several times with a large iron hammer, and it will be found to possess the powers of a magnet, although but slightly.

# EXPERIMENTS IN MAGNETISM.

### TO SHOW MAGNETIC REPULSION AND ATTRACTION.

Suspend two short pieces of iron wire, N S, N S, so that they will hang in contact in a vertical position. If the north pole of a magnet N be now brought to a moderate distance between the wires, they will recede from each other as in figure 1.

The ends s s being made south poles by induction from the north pole N, will repel each other, and so will the north poles N N. This separation of the wires will increase as the magnet approaches them, but there will be a particular distance at which the attractive force of N overcomes the repulsive force of the poles s s, and causes the wires to converge as in figure 2 ; the north poles N N still exhibiting their mutual repulsion.

### VARIATION OF THE NEEDLE.

The magnetic needle does not point exactly north and south, but the north pole of the needle takes a direction considerably to the west of the true north. It is constantly changing, and varies at different parts of the earth, and at different times of the day.

### DIP OF THE NEEDLE.

Another remarkable and evident manifestation of the influence of the magnetism of the earth upon the needle is the inclination or dip of the latter, which is a deviation from its horizontal place in a downward direction in northern regions of its north, and in southern regions of its south pole. The causes of the dipping of the needle are yet unexplained. In balancing the needle on the crd, aon account of this dipping, a small weight or moveable piece of brass is placed on one end of the needle, by the shifting of which either nearer to or further from the center, the needle will always be balanced.

### TO SUSPEND A NEEDLE IN THE AIR BY MAGNETISM.

Place a magnet on a stand to raise it a little above the table ; then bring a small sewing-needle containing a thread, within a little distance of the magnet, keeping hold of the thread to prevent the needle from attaching itself to the magnet. The needle in endeavoring to fly to the magnet, and being prevented by the thread, will remain curiously suspended in the air, like Mahommed's coffin.

### MAGNETISM BY HAMMERING.

Place a bar of iron in a vertical position, and give it a series of slight blows with a hammer or poker, when it will acquire a feeble degree of magnetism; hence it happens, thst the anvils and other tools employed in smithies are endowed with magnetism.

It is, however, a remarkable circumstance, that if you strike a magnet its magnetizing force will be either very much impaired, or altogether destroyed.

Percussion and friction in the required position would seem, from this and preceding experiments, to be the chief means of magnetizing iron and steel. These operations, as it were, waken up the inert particles of the metal to admit new magnetism, or to develop that which already resides in it, originally derived from the earth.

### POWER OF THE ELECTRO MAGNET.

The same influence which affects the magnetic needle already described, will also communicate magnetism to soft iron. If a bar of that metal, bent as in the drawing, be surrounded with a common bonnet wire, or a copper wire prevented from touching the iron by a winding of cotton or thread, and then if a current of voltaic electricity be sent through the wire, the bar becomes a powerful magnet, and will continue so as long as the connection with the battery is preserved. On breaking the contact, the magnetism disappears. This experiment may be easily made by the young reader with a horse-shoe magnet, surrounded by several coils of wire. P is the positive and N the negative pole.

### THE MARINER'S COMPASS.

The mariner's compass is an artificial magnet fitted in a proper box, and consists of three parts—1, the box; 2, the card or fly; and 3, the needle. The box is suspended in a square wooden case, by means of two concentric brass circles called gimbals, so fixed by brazen axes to the two boxes, that the inner one, or compass-box, retains a horizon-

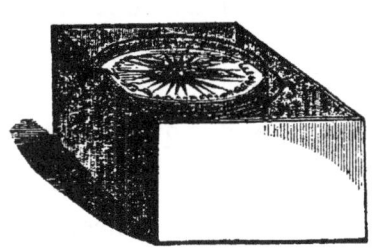 

tal position in all motions of the ship. The card is a circular piece of paper which is fastened upon the needle, and moves with it. The outer edge of the card is divided into thirty-two points, as shown in the engraving, called points of the compass. The needle is a slender bar of hardened steel, having a hollow agate cup in the center, which moves upon the point of a pivot made of brass.

### TO MAKE ARTIFICIAL MAGNETS WITHOUT THE AID EITHER OF NATURAL LOADSTONES OR ARTIFICIAL MAGNETS.

Take an iron poker and tongs, or two bars of iron, the larger and the older the better, and fixing the poker upright, hold to it with the left hand near the top P by a silk thread, a bar of soft steel about three inches long, one fourth of an inch broad, and one twentieth thick; mark one end, and let this end be downwards. Then grasping the tongs T with the right hand a little below the middle, and keeping them nearly in a vertical line, let the bar B be rubbed with the lower end L of the tongs, from the marked end of the bar to its upper end, about ten times on each side of it. By this means the bar B will receive as much magnetism as will enable it to lift a small key at the marked end; and this end, the bar being suspended by its middle or made to rest on a joint, will turn to the north, and is called its north pole, the unmarked end being

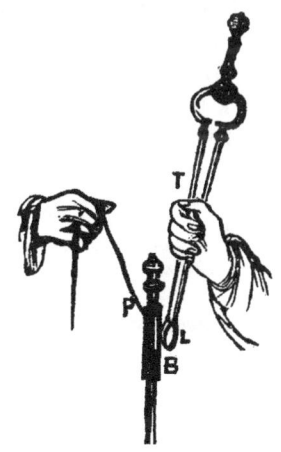

the south pole. This is the method recommended by **Mr. Cax-ton**, in his process, which he regarded superior to those in former use, and of which a more detailed account will be found in his interesting volume.

### THE WATCH MAGNETIZED.

Borrow a watch from the company, and inquire if it will go when laid on the table. Then place it just over the point at which a magnet is fixed underneath the top of the table, and the magnet will attract the balance-wheel of the watch, and cause it to stop.

### NORTH AND SOUTH POLES OF THE MAGNET.

Each magnet has its poles, north and south, the north or south poles of one magnet, repel the north and south pole of another. If a magnet, as in the following figure, be dipped in some iron filings, they will be immediately attracted to one end. Supposing this to be the north pole, each of the ends of the filings, not in contact with the magnet, will become north poles, while the ends in contact will by induction become south poles. Both will have a tendency to repel each other, and the filings will stand on the magnet as in the figure.

### POLARITY OF THE MAGNET.

The best method of proving this is to take a magnet or a piece of steel rendered magnetic, and to place it on a piece of cork by laying it in a groove cut to receive it. If the cork be placed in the center of a basin of water, and allowed to swim freely on its surface, so that it is not attracted by

the sides of the basin, it will be found to turn its north pole to the north, and its south pole to the south, the same as the mariner's compass. If you fix two magnets in two pieces of cork, and place them also in a basin of water, and they are in a parallel position with the same poles together, that is, north to north, and south to south, they will mutually repel each other; but if the contrary poles point to one another, as north to south, they will be attracted.

## MAGNETIC ACTION AND REACTION.

A magnet and a piece of iron attract each other equally, whatever disproportion there is between their sizes. If either be balanced in a scale, and the other be brought within a certain distance beneath it, the very same counterpoise will be required to prevent their approach, whichever be in the scale. If the two were hanging near each other, as pendulums, they would approach and meet, but the little one would perform more of the journey in proportion to its littleness.

## TO PASS MAGNETISM THROUGH A BOARD.

Place a common sewing-needle on a smooth horizontal board, and move a strong magnet underneath the board, when the needle will revolve along the board, according to the peculiar motion given to the magnet.

## THE MAGNETIC TABLE.

Under the top of a common table, place a magnet that turns on a pivot, and fix a board under it that nothing may appear. There may also be a drawer under the table, which you pull out, to show that there is nothing concealed. At one end of the table there must be a pin that communicates with a magnet, and by which it may be placed in different positions; this pin must be so placed as not to be visible to the spectators. Strew some steel filings, or very small nails, over that part of the table where the magnet is. Then ask any one to lend a knife, or a key, which will then attract part of the nails or filings. Then placing your hand, in a careless manner, on the pin at the end of the table, you alter the position of the magnet; and giving the key to any person, you desire him to make the experiment, which he will then not be able to perform. You then give the key to another person, at the same time placing the magnet, by means of the pin, in the first position, when that person will immediately perform the experiment.

## INTERESTING PARTICULARS CONCERNING THE MAGNET.

Fire-irons which have rested in one position in a room during the summer months are often highly magnetic.

Iron bars standing erect, such as the gratings of a prison cell, or the iron railings before houses, are often magnetic.

The uppermost of the iron tires round a carriage wheel

attracts the north end of a magnet, and has hence south polarity, while the lower end attracting the south end of the same, has north polarity.

### CONCLUSION.

The preceding experiments in Electricity, Galvanism, and Magnetism, we have selected for the simple yet clear expositions which they offer of the fundamental principles of those branches of philosophy; more elaborate experiments we have refrained from inserting, as although, perhaps, more astonishing and impressive in their effects, the costly and cumbrous apparatus which they require, raise them far above the means of most boys, for whose instruction and amusement we cater.

### EXAGGERATED MAGNETISM.

Our readers will, doubtless, recollect several stories, in which the powers of the magnet are greatly exaggerated. Other accounts of its virtues, though true in fact, yet really appear, without some consideration, to be fictitious.

In a German collection of fairy tales, in which the ancient chivalry of the court of the famous Charlemagne, the faithful squires who attended on his heroic knights, the damsels in distress whom they relieved, the dwarfs who were their friends, and the giants and magicians who "worked their earthly woe," are the principal characters, we remember a passage to the effect following: "The knight, who volunteered to adventure forward from the body of cavalry that were bent on this exploit, to reconnoitre the position of this gigantic enchanter's castle, had scarcely approached within sight of it, when he beheld the enormous bulk of the giant himself leaning against the outward wall. Pursuant to the instructions he had received, the knight, forthwith, turned his gallant steed's head towards his companions in arms, and, at a swift pace, came pricking o'er the plain. He now heard the giant in pursuit, and struck his spurs into his good steed's flank; but, alas! he had scarcely approached within view of the chivalric troop, when the mighty hand of the giant magician was stretched forth, armed only with one of his horse's shoes, which was made of loadstone, and, by its attractive powers on his steel armor, his grieved associates had the mortification of seeing the knight unhorsed."

# THE MAGIC OF
# PNEUMATICS AND AËROSTATICS.

"There is a tricksey spirit in the air
That plays sad gambols."—BEN JONSON

THE branch of the physical sciences which relates to the air and its various phenomena is called Pneumatics. By it we learn many curious particulars. By it we find that the air has weight and pressure, color, density, elasticity, compressibility, and some other properties with which we shall endeavor to make the young reader acquainted by many pleasing experiments, earnestly impressing upon him to lose no opportunity of making physical science his study.

To show that the air has weight and pressure, the common leather sucker by which boys raise stones will show the pressure of the atmosphere. It consists of a piece of soft but firm leather, having a piece of string drawn through its center. The leather is made quite wet and pliable, and then its under part is placed on the stone and stamped down by the foot. This pressing of the leather excludes the air from between the leather and the stone, and by pulling the string a vacuum is left underneath its center; consequently the weight of the air about the edges of the leather, not being counterbalanced by any air between it and the stone, enables the boy to lift it.

### WEIGHT OF THE AIR PROVED BY A PAIR OF BELLOWS.

Shut the nozzle and valve-hole of a pair of bellows, and after having squeezed the air out of them, if they are perfectly air-tight, we shall find that a very great force, even some hundreds of pounds, is necessary for separating the boards. They are kept together by the weight of the heavy air which surrounds them in the same manner as if they were surrounded by water.

### THE PRESSURE OF THE AIR SHOWN BY A WINE-GLASS.

Place a card on a wine-glass filled with water, then invert the glass, the water will not escape, the pressure of the atmosphere on the outside of the card being sufficient to support the water.

### ANOTHER.

Invert a tall glass jar in a dish of water, and place a lighted taper under it; as the taper consumes the air in the jar, the water from the pressure without  *rises up* to supply the place of the air removed by the combustion. In the operation of cupping, the operator holds the flame of a lamp under a bell-shaped glass. The air within this being rarefied and expanded, a considerable portion is given off. In this state the glass is placed upon the flesh, and as the air within it cools, it contracts, and the glass adheres to the flesh by the difference of the pressure of the internal and external air.

### ELASTICITY OF THE AIR.

This can be shown by a beautiful philosophical toy which may easily be constructed. Procure a glass jar, such as is here represented. Then mould three or four little figures in wax, and make them hollow within, and having each a minute opening at the heel, by which water may pass in and out. Place them in the jar, as seen in the figure, and adjust them by the quantity of water admitted to them, so that in specific gravity they differ a little from each other. The mouth of the jar should now be covered with a piece of skin or India-rubber, and then, if the hand be pressed upon the top or mouth of the jar, the figures will be seen to rise or descend as the pressure is gentle or heavy, rising and falling, or standing still, according to the pressure made.

### REASON FOR THIS.

The reason of this is, that the pressure on the top of the jar condenses the air between the cover and the water surface; this condensation then presses on the water below, and influences it through its whole extent, compressing also the air in the figures, forcing as much more water into them as to render them heavier than water, and therefore heavy enough to sink.

### THE AIR-PUMP.

The time was, and that not very long ago, when the air pump was only obtainable by the philosophical professor, or by persons of enlarged means. But now, owing to our "cheap way of doing things," a small air-pump may be obtained for about five or six dollars, and we would strongly advise our young friend to procure one, as it will be a source of endless amusement to him ; and, supposing that he takes our advice, we give him the following experiments.

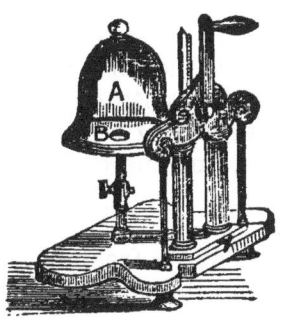

The air-pump consists of a bell glass, called the receiver, A, and a stand, upon which is a perforated plate B. The hole in this plate is connected with two pistons, the rods of which are moved by a wheel handle backwards and forwards, and thus pump the air out of the receiver. When the air is taken out, a stop-cock is turned, and then the experiments may be performed.

Under the receiver of an air-pump, when the air has been thoroughly exhausted, light and heavy bodies fall with the same swiftness, Animals quickly die for want of air, combustion ceases, gunpowder will not explode, a bell sounds faint, magnets are powerless, and waters and other fluids turn to vapor.

### TO PROVE THAT AIR HAS WEIGHT.

Take a florence flask, fitted up with a screw and fine oiled silk valve. Screw the flask on the plate of the air-pump, exhaust the air, take it off the plate and weigh it. Then let in the air, and again weigh the whole, and it will be found to have increased by several grains.

### TO PROVE AIR ELASTIC.

Place a bladder, out of which all the air has apparently been squeezed, under the receiver, upon it lay a weight, exhaust the air, and it will be seen that the small quantity of air left within the bladder will so expand itself as to lift the weight. Put a corked bottle into the receiver, exhaust the air, and the cork will fly out.

### AIR IN THE EGG.

Take a fresh egg and cut off a little of the shell and film from its smaller end, then put the egg under a receiver and pump out the air, upon which all the contents of the egg will be forced out by the expansion of the small bubble of air contained in the great end between the shell and the film.

AIR IN THE EGG.

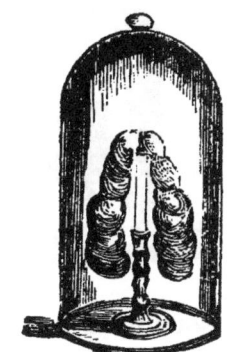

DESCENDING SMOKE.

### THE DESCENDING SMOKE.

Set a lighted candle on a plate, and cover it with a tall receiver. The candle will continue to burn while the air remains, but when exhausted, will go out, and the smoke from the wick, instead of rising, will descend in dense clouds towards the bottom of the glass, because the air which would have supported it has been withdrawn.

### HALF EAGLE AND FEATHER.

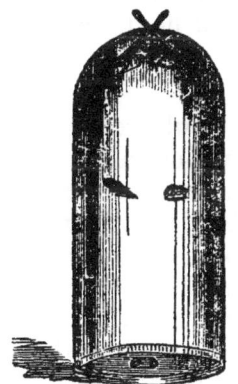

Place a nicely-adjusted pair of forceps at the top of the receiver, communicating with the top at the outside through a hole, so that they may be opened by the fingers. Then place on each of the little plates a *half-eagle* and a *feather*. Exhaust the air from the receiver, and having done so, detach the objects, so that they may fall. In the open air the half-eagle will fall long before the feather, but in vacuo, as in the receiver now exhausted of its air, they will fall both together, and reach the bottom of the glass at same instant.

### THE SOUNDLESS BELL.

Set a bell on the pump-plate, having a contrivance so as to ring it at pleasure, and cover it with a receiver, then make the clapper sound against the bell, and it will be

SOUNDLESS BELL.

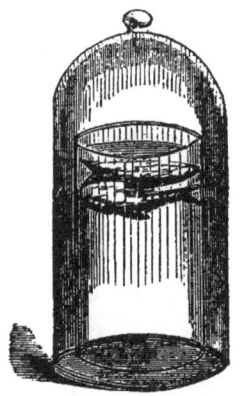
FLOATING FISH.

heard to sound very well; now exhaust the receiver of air, and then, when the clapper strikes against the sides of the bell, the sound can be scarcely heard.

### THE FLOATING FISH.

If a glass vessel, containing water, in which a couple of fish are put be placed under the receiver, upon exhausting the air, the fish will be unable to keep at the bottom of the glass, owing to the expansion of the air within their bodies, contained in the air bladder. They will consequently rise and float, belly upwards, upon the surface of the water.

### THE MYSTERIOUS CIRCLES.

Cut from a card two discs or circular pieces, about two inches in diameter. In the center of one of them make a hole, into which put the tube of a common quill, one end being even with the surface of the card. Make the other piece a little convex, and lay its center over the end of the quill, with the concave side of the card downwards, the center of the upper card being from one eighth to one fourth of an inch above the end of the quill—attempt to blow off the upper card by blowing through the quill, and *it will be found impossible.*

If, however, the edges of the two cards be made to fit each other very accurately, the upper card will move, and sometimes it will be thrown off; but when the edges of the cards are, on two sides, sufficiently far apart to permit the air to escape, the loose card will retain its position, even when the current of air sent against it be strong. The experiment will succeed equally well, whether the current of air be made from the mouth or from a pair of bellows. When the quill fits the card rather loosely, a comparatively light puff will throw both cards three or four feet in height. When, from the humidity of the breath, the upper surface of the perforated card has a little expanded, and the two opposite sides are somewhat depressed, those depressed sides may be seen distinctly to rise and approach the upper card, directly in proportion to the force of the current of air.

Another fact to be shown with this simple apparatus appears equally inexplicable with the former. Lay the loose card upon the hand with the concave side up ; blow forcibly through the tube, and, at the same time, bring the two cards towards each other ; when within three eighths of an inch, if the current of air be strong, the loose card will suddenly rise, and adhere to the perforated card. If the card through which the quill passes has several holes made in it, the loose card may be instantly thrown off with the least puff of air.

For the explanation of the above phenomenon, a gold medal and one hundred guineas were offered, some years since, by the Royal Society. Such explanation has been given by Dr. Robert Hare, late of the University of Pennsylvania, and is as follows :

Supposing the diameters of the discs of card to be to that of the hole as 8 to 1, the area of the former to the latter must be as 64 to 1. Hence, if the discs were to be separated (their surfaces remaining parallel) with a velocity as great as that of the air blast, a column of air must, meantime, be interposed, 64 times greater than that which would escape from the tube during the interim ; consequently, if all the air necessary to preserve the balance be supplied from the tube, the discs must be separated with a velocity as much less than that of the blast, as the column required between them is greater than that yielded by the tube ; and yet the air cannot be supplied from any other source, unless a deficit of pressure be created between the discs, unfavorable to their separation.

It follows, then, that, under the circumstances in question, the discs cannot be made to move asunder with a velocity greater than one sixty-fourth of that of the blast. Of course all the force of the current of air through the tube will be expended on the moveable disc, and the thin ring of air, which exists round the orifice between the discs; and since the moveable discs can only move with one sixty-fourth the velocity of the blast, the ring of air in the interstice must experience nearly all the force of the jet, and must be driven outwards, the blast following it, in various currents radiating from the common center of the tube and discs.

### THE DIVING BELL.

The diving-bell is a pneumatic engine, by means of which persons can descend to great depths in the sea, and recover from it valuable portions of wrecks and other matters. Its principle may be well illustrated by the following experiment. Take a glass tumbler, and plunge it into the water with the mouth downwards, and it will be found that the water will not rise much more than half way in the tumbler. This may be made very evident if a piece of cork be suffered to float inside of

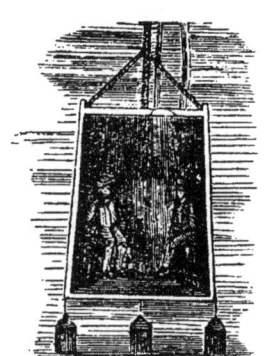

the glass on the surface of the water. The air within the tumbler does not entirely exclude the water, because air is elastic, and consequently compressible, and hence the air in the tumbler is what is called condensed. The diving-bell is formed upon the above principle, but instead of being of glass, it is a wooden or metal vessel, of very large dimensions, so as to hold three or four persons, who are supplied with air from above by means of a tube, having a corresponding tube to let off the breathed air, the circulation of which is kept up by pumps, which pump the air in and draw it out of the bell.

### THE AIR BALLOON.

The art of sailing or navigating a body through the air is called aëronautics. In remote ages, Icarus is said to have risen so high in the air that the sun melted his wings, and he fell into the Ægean sea, and was drowned; and there is reason to believe, from some figures that have recently been discovered on Egyptian and Assyrian monuments, that the ancients possessed means of rising in the air with which we are not now acquainted.

The air-balloon, as now constructed, is a bag of silk of large dimensions, usually cut in gores, and is, when expanded by gas, of a pear shape. It ascends in the atmosphere because its whole bulk is much lighter than the air would be in the space it occupies. It is, in fact, a vessel filled with a fluid which will float on another fluid lighter than itself.

### HOW TO MAKE AN AIR-BALLOON.

The best shape for an air-balloon, or rather a gas-balloon, is that of a peg-top. And in preparing the gores proceed as follows : Get some close texture silk, and cut it into a form resembling a narrow pear with a very thin stalk. Fourteen of these pieces will be found to be the best number ; and, of course, the breadths of each piece must be measured accordingly. When sewing them together, it will be of advantage to coat the parts that overlap with a layer of varnish, as this will save much trouble afterwards, and hold the silk firmer in its place during the stitching. The threads must be placed very regularly, or the balloon will be drawn out of shape, and it will be found useful if the gores are covered with an interior coating of varnish before they are finally sewn together. Take care not to have the varnish too thick. To the upper part of the balloon there should be a valve opening inwards, to which a string should

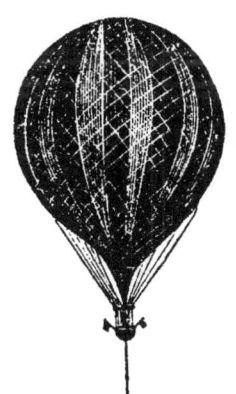

be fastened, passing through a hole made in a small piece of wood fixed in the lower part of the balloon, so that the aëronaut may open the valve when he wishes to descend ; and this should be imitated on a small scale, so that the young aëronaut may be perfectly familiar with the construction of a balloon. The gores are to be covered with a varnish of India rubber dissolved in a mixture of turpentine and naphtha. Over the whole of the upper part should be a net-work, which should come down to the middle, with various cords, proceeding from it to the circumference of a circle about two feet below the balloon. The circle may be made of wood, or of several pieces of slender cane bound together. The meshes should be small at the top, against which part of the balloon the inflammable air exerts the greatest force, and increase in size as they recede from the top.

The car is made of wicker work; it is usually covered with leather, and is well varnished or painted. It is suspended by ropes proceeding from the net which goes over the balloon. Balloons of this kind cannot be made smaller than six feet in diameter, of oiled silk, as the weight of the material is too great for the air to buoy it up. They may be made smaller of thin slips of bladder, or other membrane glued together, or of thin gutta-percha cloth, which is now extensively used for this purpose; with this they may be made a foot in diameter, and will rise beautifully.

### HOW TO FILL A BALLOON.

Procure a large stone bottle which will hold a gallon of water, into this put a pound of iron filings, or granulated zinc, with two quarts of water, and add to this by degrees one pint of sulphuric acid. Then take a tube, either of glass or metal, and introduce one end of it through a cork, which place in the bottle, then put the other end into the neck of the balloon, and the gas will rise into the body of it. When quite full withdraw the tube, and tie the neck of the balloon with strong cord very tightly. If freed it will now rise in the air.

### TO MAKE FIRE-BALLOONS.

Cut the gores, according to the form already given, from well woven tissue paper, paste the gores nicely together,

and look well over the surface of the paper for any small hole or slit, over which paste a piece of paper, and let it dry. Pass a wire round the neck of the balloon, and have two cross pieces at its diameter a little bent, so that a piece of soft cotton dipped in spirits of wine may be laid on them. When all is prepared let some one hold the balloon from its top by means of a stick, while you dip the cotton in spirits of wine till it is thoroughly saturated, place it under the balloon, and set fire to it, but be

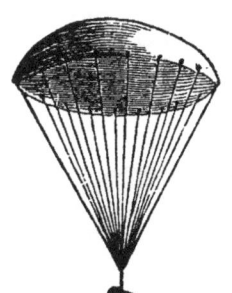

very careful you do not set fire to the balloon. When the air is sufficiently heated within, the balloon will indicate a desire to rise, and when it pulls very hard, let it go, and it will ascend to a great height in the air, and at night present a very beautiful appearance.

### PARACHUTES.

These are easily made by cutting a piece of paper in a circular form, and placing threads round the edges, which may be made to converge to a point, at which a cork may be placed as a balance. They ascend by the air getting under them, and are frequently blown to a great distance.

### THE MYSTERIOUS BOTTLE.

Pierce a few holes with a glazier's diamond in a common black bottle; place it in a vase or jug of water, so that the neck only is above the surface. Then, with a funnel, fill the bottle and cork it well, and while it is in the jug or vase. Take it out, notwithstanding the holes in the bottom, it will not leak; wipe it dry, and give it to some person to uncork. The moment the cork is drawn, to the party's astonishment, the water will begin to run out of the bottom of the bottle.

### CAOUTCHOUC BALLOONS.

Put a little ether into a bottle of caoutchouc, close it tightly, soak it in hot water, and it will become inflated to a considerable size. These globes may be made so thin as to be transparent.

A piece of caoutchouc, the size of a walnut, has thus been extended to a ball fifteen inches in diameter; and a few years since a caoutchouc balloon, thus made, escaped from Philadelphia, and was found one hundred and thirty miles from that city.

# THE MAGIC OF
# OPTICS AND OPTICAL AMUSEMENTS.

"'Seeing is believing,' so the sages say,
To prove this false, hear me, my friends, I pray,
And very soon you all will be agreeing,
That nought is so deceptive as our *seeing*.—MARTIN.

OPTICS is the science of *light* and *vision*. Concerning the nature of light, two theories are at present very ably maintained by their respective advocates. One is termed the Newtonian theory, and the other the Huygenean. The Newtonian theory considers light to consist of inconceivably small bodies emanating from the sun, or any other luminous

## OPTICS AND OPTICAL AMUSEMENTS. 159

body. The Huygenean conceives it to consist in the undulations of a highly elastic and subtle fluid, propagated round luminous centers in spherical waves, like those arising in a placid lake when a stone is dropped into the water.

### LIGHT AS AN EFFECT.

Light follows the same laws as gravity, and its intensity or degree decreases as the square of the distance from the luminous body increases. Thus, at the distance of two yards from a candle we shall have four times less light than we should have, were we only one yard from it, and so on in the same proportion.

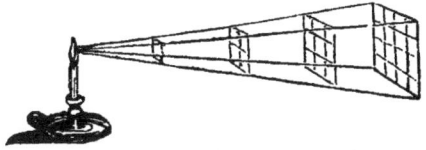

### REFRACTION.

Bodies which suffer the rays of light to pass through them, such as water or glass, are called refracting media. When rays of light enter these, they do not proceed in straight lines, but are said to be refracted, or bent out of their course, as seen in the drawing. The ray of light proceeding from B through the glass L G is bent from the point c, instead of passing in the direction of the dotted line. But if the ray F c falls perpendicularly on the glass, there is no refraction, and it proceeds in a direct line to K; hence refraction only takes place when rays fall obliquely or aslant on the media.

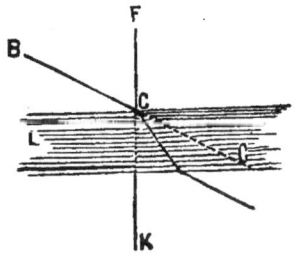

### THE INVISIBLE COIN MADE VISIBLE.

If a coin be placed in a basin, so that on standing at a

certain distance it be just hid from the eye of an observer

by the rim or edge of the basin, and then water be poured in by a second person, the first keeping his position; as the water rises the coin will become visible, and will appear to have moved from the side to the middle of the basin.

## THE MULTIPLYING GLASS.

The multiplying glass is a semicircular piece of glass cut into facets or distinct surfaces; and in looking through it we have an illustration of the laws of refraction, for if a small object, such as a fly, be placed at D, an eye at 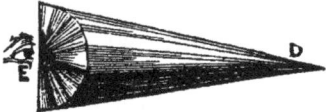 E will see as many flies as there are surfaces or facets on the glass.

## TRANSPARENT BODIES.

Transparent bodies, such as glass, may be made of such form as to cause all the rays which pass through them from any given point to meet in any other given point beyond them, or which will disperse them from the given point. These are are called lenses, and have different names according to their form. 1 is called the plano-convex lens; 2, plano-concave; 3, double convex; 4, double concave; 5, a meniscus, so called from its resembling the crescent moon.

## THE PRISM.

The prism is a triangular solid of glass, and by it the young optician may decompose a ray of light into its primitive and supplementary colors, for a ray of light is of a compound nature. 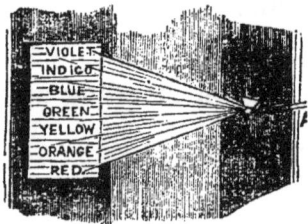 By the prism the ray A is divided into its three primitive colors, blue, red, and yellow; and their four supplementary ones, violet, indigo, green, and orange. The best way to perform this experiment is to cut a small slit in a window-shutter, on which the sun shines at some period of the day, and directly opposite the hole place a prism P; a beam of light in passing through it will then be decomposed, and if let fall upon a sheet of white paper, or

## OPTICS AND OPTICAL AMUSEMENTS.

against a white wall, the seven colors of the rainbow will be observed

### TO MAKE A PRISM.

Provide two small pieces of window-glass and a lump of wax; soften and mould the wax, stick the two pieces of glass upon it, so that they meet, as in the cut, where $w$ is the wax, $g$ and $g$ the glasses stuck to it (Fig. 1). The end view (Fig. 2) will show the angle, $a$, at which the pieces of glass meet; into which angle put a drop of water.

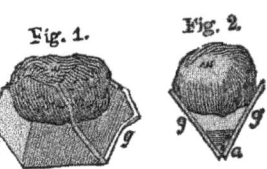

Fig. 1. Fig. 2.

To use the instrument thus made, make a small hole, or a narrow horizontal slit, so that you can see the sky through it, when you stand at some distance from it in the room; or a piece of pasteboard placed in the upper part of the window-sash, with a slit cut in it, will serve the purpose of the hole in the shutter. The slit should be about one tenth of an inch wide, and an inch or two long, with even edges. Then hold the prism in your hand, place it close to your eye, and look through the drop of water, when you will see a beautiful train of colors, called a spectrum; at one end red, at the other violet, and in the middle yellowish green.

The annexed figure 3 will better explain the direction in which we look: here, $e$ is the eye of the spectator, $p$ is the prism, $h$ the hole in the shutter or pasteboard, $s$ the spectrum. By a little practice, you will soon become accustomed to look in the right direction, and will see the colors very bright and distinct.

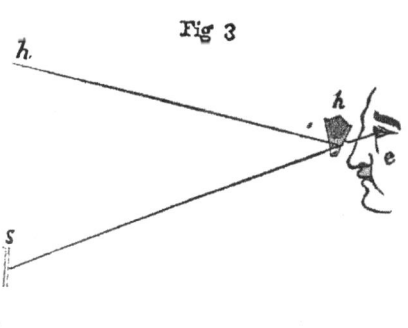

Fig 3

By means of this simple contrivance white light may be analyzed, and proved to consist of colored rays, and several of its properties be beautifully illustrated.

### COMPOSITION OF LIGHT.

The beam of light passing through the prism is decomposed, and the spaces occupied by the colors are in the following proportions: red, 6; orange, 4; yellow, 7; green,

8; blue, 8; indigo, 6; violet, 11. Now, if you paste a sheet of white paper on a circular piece of board about six inches in diameter, and divide it with 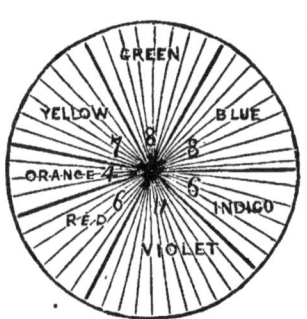 a pencil into fifty parts, and paint colors in them in the proportions given above, painting them dark in the center parts, and gradually fainter at the edges, till they blend with the one adjoining; and if the board be then fixed to an axle, and made to revolve quickly, the colors will no longer appear separate and distinct, but becoming gradually less visible, they will ultimately appear *white*, giving this appearance to the whole surface of the paper.

### A NATURAL CAMERA OBSCURA.

The human eye is a camera obscura, for on the back of it, on the retina, every object in a landscape is beautifully depicted in miniature. This may be proved by the

### BULLOCK'S EYE EXPERIMENT.

Procure a fresh bullock's eye from the butcher, and carefully thin the outer coat of it behind; take care not to cut it, for if this should be done the vitreous humor will escape, and the experiment cannot be performed. Having so prepared the eye, if the pupil of it be directed to any bright objects, they will appear distinctly delineated on the back part precisely as objects appear in the instrument we are about to describe. The effect will be heightened if the eye is viewed in a dark room with a small hole in the shutter, but in every case the appearance will be very striking.

### THE CAMERA OBSCURA.

This is a very pleasing and instructive optical apparatus, and may be purchased for four or five shillings. But it may 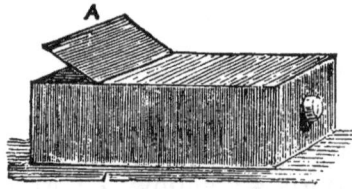 be easily made by the young optician. Procure an oblong box, about two feet long, twelve inches wide, and eight high. In one end of this a tube must be fitted containing a lens, and be made to slide backwards

# OPTICS AND OPTICAL AMUSEMENTS.

and forwards so as to suit the focus. Within the box should be a plane mirror, reclining backwards from the tube at an angle of forty-five degrees. At the top of the box is a square of unpolished glass, upon which from beneath the picture will be thrown, and may be seen by raising the lid A. To use the camera, place the tube with the lens on it opposite to the object, and having adjusted the focus, the image will be thrown upon the ground-glass as above stated, where it may be easily copied by a pencil or in colors.

The form of a camera obscura used in a public exhibition is as follows: D D is a large wooden box stained black in the inside, and capable of containing from one to eight persons. A B is a sliding piece, having a sloping mirror C, and a double convex lens F, which may, with the mirror C, be slid up or down so as to accommodate the lens to near and distant objects. When the rays proceeding from an object without fall upon the mirror, they are reflected upon the lens F, and brought to fall on the bottom of the box, or upon a table placed horizontally to receive them, which may be seen by the spectator whose eye is at E.

## THE MAGIC LANTERN.

This is one of the most pleasing of all optical instruments, and it is used to produce enlarged pictures of objects, which being painted on a glass in various colors are thrown

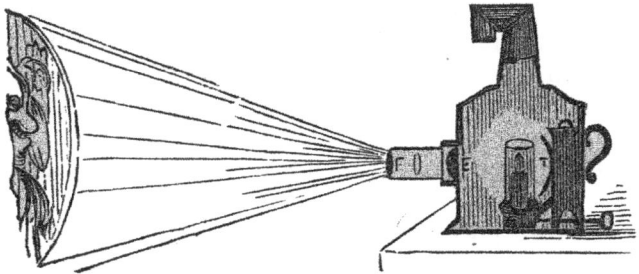

upon a screen or white sheet placed against the wall of a large room. It consists of a sort of tin box, within which is a lamp, the light of which (strongly reflected by the reflector T,) passes through a great plano-convex lens E fixed in the front. This strongly illuminates the objects which are painted on the slides or slips of glass, and placed before the lens in an inverted position, and the rays passing through them and the lens F, fall on a sheet, or other white surface, placed to receive the image. The glasses on which the figures are drawn are inverted, in order that the images of them may be erect.

### THE CAMERA LUCIDA.

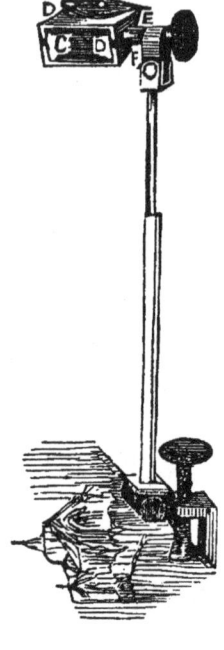

This instrument consists of a glass prism, C, D, D, E, having four sides covered. The sides C. D, being exposed to the object to be delineated, rays pass through the glass and fall on the sloping side D, E; from this they are reflected to the top, and finally pass out of the prism to the eye;* now from the direction at which the rays enter the eye, it receives them as if coming from an image at A, B, and if a sheet of paper be placed below the instrument, a perfect delineation of the object may be traced with a pencil. This is a very useful instrument to young draughtsmen.

### PAINTING THE SLIDES.

The slides containing the objects usually shown in a magic lantern, are to be bought of opticians with the lantern, and can be procured cheaper and better in this way than by any attempt at manufacturing them. Should, however, the young optician wish to make a few slides of objects of particular interest to himself, he may proceed as follows:

Draw first on paper the figures you wish to paint, lay it

* The eye is to be applied to the little circular hole seen on the upper surface.

on the table, and cover it over with a piece of glass of this shape; now draw the outlines with a fine camel's

hair pencil in black paint mixed with varnish, and when this is dry, fill up the other parts with the proper colors, shading with bistre also mixed with varnish. The transparent colors are alone to be used in this kind of painting.

### TO EXHIBIT THE MAGIC LANTERN.

The room for the exhibition ought to be large, and of an oblong shape. At one end of it suspend a large sheet so as to cover the whole of the wall. The company being all seated, darken the room, and placing the lantern with its tube in the direction of the sheet, introduce one of the slides into the slit, taking care to invert the figures; then adjust the focus of the glasses in the tube by drawing it in or out as required, and a perfect representation of the object will appear.

### EFFECTS OF THE MAGIC LANTERN.

Most extraordinary effects may be produced by means of the magic lantern; one of the most effective of which is a

#### TEMPEST AT SEA.

This is effected by having two slides painted, one with the tempest as approaching on one side, and continuing in

intensity till it reaches the other. Another slide has ships painted on it, and while the lantern is in use, that containing the ships is dexterously drawn before the other, and represents *ships in the storm.*

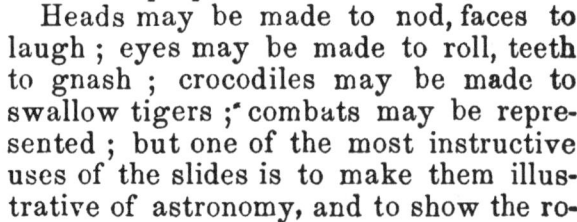

The effects of sunrise, moonlight, starlight, &c., may be imitated, also by means of double sliders; and figures may be introduced sometimes of fearful proportions.

Heads may be made to nod, faces to laugh; eyes may be made to roll, teeth to gnash; crocodiles may be made to swallow tigers; combats may be represented; but one of the most instructive uses of the slides is to make them illustrative of astronomy, and to show the rotation of the seasons, the cause of eclipses, the mountains in the moon, spots on the sun, and the various motions of the planetary bodies, and their satellites.

### THE PHANTASMAGORIA.

Between the phantasmagoria and the magic lantern there is this difference; in common magic lanterns the figures are painted on transparent glass, consequently the image on the screen is a circle of light having figures upon it; but in the phantasmagoria all the glass is made opaque, except the figures, which, being painted in transparent colors, the light shines through them, and no light can come upon the screen except that which passes through the figure, as is here represented.

There is no sheet to receive the picture, but the representation is thrown on a thin screen of silk or muslin placed between *the spectators and the lantern.* The images are made to appear approaching and receding by removing the lantern further from the screen, or bringing it nearer to it. This is a great advantage over the arrangements of the magic lantern, and by it the most astonishing effects are often produced.

## DISSOLVING VIEWS.

The dissolving views, by which one landscape or scene appears to pass into the other while the scene is changing, are produced by using two magic lanterns placed side by side, and that can be a little inclined towards each other when necessary, so as to mix the rays of light proceeding from the lenses of each together, which produces that confusion of images, in which one view melts as it were into the other, which gradually becomes clear and distinct.

## HOW TO RAISE A GHOST.

The magic lantern or phantasmagoria, may be used in a number of marvelous ways, but in none more striking than in raising an apparent specter. Let an open box, A B, about three feet long, a foot and half broad, and two feet high, be prepared. At one end of this place a small swing dressing glass, and at the other let a magic lantern be fixed with its lenses in a direction towards the glass. A glass should now be made to slide up and down in the groove C D, to which a cord and pulley should be attached, the end of the cord coming to the part of the box marked A. On this glass the most hideous specter that can be imagined may be painted, but in a squat or contracted position, and when all is done, the lid of the box must be prepared by raising a kind of gable at the end of the box B, and in its lower part at E, an oval hole should be cut sufficiently large to suffer the rays

reflected from the glass to pass through them. On the top of the box F place a chafing dish, upon which put some burning charcoal. Now light the lamp G in the lantern, sprinke some powdered camphor or white incense on the charcoal, adjust the slide on which the specter is painted, and the image will be thrown upon the smoke. In performing this feat the room must be darkened, and the box should be placed on a high table, that the hole through which the light comes may not be noticed.

### THE THAUMATROPE.

This word is derived from two Greek words, one of which signifies *wonder*, and the other *to turn*. It is a very pretty philosophical toy, and is founded upon the principle in optics, that an impression made upon the retina of the eye lasts for a short interval after the object which produced it has been withdrawn. The impression which the mind receives lasts for about the eighth part of a second, as may be easily shown by whirling round a lighted stick, which if made to complete the circle within that period, will exhibit not a fiery point, but a fiery circle in the air.

### THE BIRD IN THE CAGE.

Cut a piece of cardboard of the size of a penny piece, and paint on one side a bird, and on the other a cage; fasten two pieces of thread, one on each side, at opposite points of the card, so that the card can be made to revolve by twirling the threads with the finger and thumb; while the toy is in its revolution, the bird will be seen within the cage. A bat may in the same manner be painted on one side of the

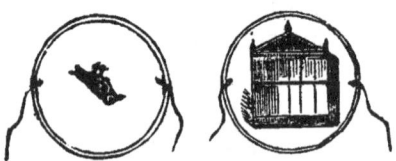

card, and a cricketer upon the other, which will exhibit the same phenomenon, arising from the same principle.

### CONSTRUCTION OF THE PHANTASMASCOPE.

The above-named figure is a Thaumatrope, as much as the one we are about to describe, although the term Phantasmascope is generally applied to the latter instrument; which consists of a disc of darkened tin-plate, with a slit or narrow opening in it, about two inches in length. It is fixed upon a stand, and the slit placed upwards, so that it may easily be looked through. Another disc of pasteboard, about a foot in diameter, is now prepared and fixed on a similar stand, but with this difference, that it is made to revolve round an axis in the center. On this pasteboard disc, paint in colors a number of frogs in relative and progressive positions of leaping; make between each figure a slit of about a quarter of an inch deep; and when this second disc is made to revolve at a foot distance behind the first, and the eye is placed near the slit, the whole of the figures, instead of appearing to revolve with the disc, will all appear in the attitudes of leaping up and down, increasing in agility as the velocity of the motion is increased. It is necessary, when trying the effect of this instrument, to stand before a looking-glass, and to present the painted face of the machine towards the glass.

A very great number of figures may be prepared to preduce similar effects—horses with riders in various attitudes of leaping, toads crawling, snakes twisting and writhing, faces laughing and crying, men dancing, jugglers throwing up balls, &c.; all of which, by the peculiar arrangement above detailed, will seem to be in motion. A little ingenuity displayed in the construction and painting of the figures upon the pasteboard disc will afford a great fund of amusement.

### CURIOUS OPTICAL ILLUSION.

One of the most curious facts relating to the science of vision is the absolute insensibility of a certain portion of the retina to the impression of light, so that the image of any object falling on that point would be invisible. When we look with the right eye, this point will be about fifteen degrees to the right of the object observed, or to the right of the axis of the eye, or the point of most distinct vision. When looking with the left eye, the point will be as far to the left. The point in question is the basis of the optic nerve, and its insensibility to light was first observed by the French philosopher, Mariotte. This remarkable phenomenon may be experimentally proved in the following manner:

Place on a sheet of writing-paper, at the distance of about three inches apart, two colored wafers; then, on looking at the left-hand wafer with the right eye, at the distance of about a foot, keeping the eye straight above the wafer, and both eyes parallel with the line which forms the wafers, the left eye being closed, the right-hand wafer will become invisible; and a similar effect will take place if we close the right eye, and look with the left.

### ANOTHER.

Cut a circular piece of white paper, about two inches in diameter, which affix to a dark wall. At the distance of two feet on each side, but a little lower, make two marks; then place yourself directly opposite the paper, and hold the end of your finger before your face, so that when the right eye is open it shall conceal the mark on your left, and when the left eye is open the mark on your right. If you then look with both eyes at the end of your finger, the paper disc will be invisible.

### ANOTHER.

Fix a similar disc of paper, two inches in diameter, at the height of your eye on a dark wall; a little lower than this, at the distance of two feet on the right hand, fix another of about three inches in diameter; now place yourself opposite the first sheet of paper, and, shutting the left eye, keep the right eye still fixed on the first object, and when at the distance of about ten feet, the second piece of paper will be invisible.

Or, fix three pieces of paper against the wall of a room, at equal distances, at the height of the eye. Place yourself directly before them, at a few yards distance, close your right eye, and look at them with your left, when you will see only two of them, suppose the first and second; alter your position a second time, and you will see the second and third, but never the whole three pieces together.

On a sheet of black paper, or other dark ground, place two white wafers, having their centers three inches distant. Vertically above the paper, and to the left, look with the right eye, at twelve inches from it, and so, that when looking down on it, the line joining the two eyes shall be parallel to that joining the center of the wafers. In this situation close the left eye, and look full with the right perpendicularly at the wafer below it, when this wafer only will be seen, the other being completely invisible. But if it be removed ever so little from its place, either to the right or left, above or below, it will become immediately visible, and start, as it were, into existence. "It will cease to be thought singular," says Sir John Herschel, " that this fact of the absolute invisibility of objects in a certain point of the field of view of each eye should be one of which not one person in ten thousand is apprized, when we learn that it is not extremely uncommon to find persons who have for some time been totally blind with one eye without being aware of the fact.

### THE PICTURE IN THE AIR.

One of the numerous optical illusions which have, from time to time, been evolved by scientific minds, is that of making an image or picture appear in the air. This is produced by means of a mirror, and an object in relief, upon which a strong light is thrown—the mirror being set at such an angle as to throw up the reflection of the image to a certain point, in the view of the spectator. This illusion is produced as follows : Let a screen be constructed in which is an arched aperture, the center of which may be five feet from the floor ; behind the screen is placed a large mirror of an elliptical form. An object is now placed behind the screen, upon which the light of a strong lamp is thrown from a point above the mirror, and is received by the mirror and reflected to the center of the arched cavity in the screen, where it will appear to the spectator. Care should be taken to place the image in an inverted position, and the light should be so placed that none of it may reach the opening : the light must also be very powerful.

### BREATHING LIGHT AND DARKNESS.

The following experiment, if performed with care, is exceedingly striking. Let s be a candle, whose light falls at an angle of 56° 45′ upon two plate glasses, A B, placed close to each other ; and let the reflected rays, A C, B D, fall at the same angle upon two similar plates, C D, but so placed that the plane of reflection from the latter is at right angles to the plane of reflection from the former. An eye placed at E, and looking at the same time on the two plates, C and D, will see very faint images 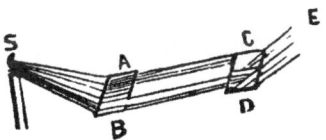 of the candle s ; which by a slight adjustment of the plates, may be made to disappear almost wholly, allowing the plate C to remain where it is. Change the position of D till its inclination to the ray B D is diminished about 3°, or made nearly 53° 11′. The distance may be easily found by a little practice. When this is done, the image that had disappeared on looking into D, will be restored, so that the spectator at E, upon looking into the two mirrors, C D, will see no light in C, because the candle has nearly disappeared, while the candle is distinctly seen in D. If, while the spectator is looking into these two mirrors, either he or another person breathes upon them gently and quickly, the breath will revive the extinguished image in C, and will extinguish the visible image in D.

EXPLANATION.—The light A, C, B, D is polarized by reflection from the plates A B, because it is incident at the polarizing angle 56° 45' for glass. When we breathe upon the plates C D, we form upon their surface a thin film of water, whose polarizing angle is 53° 11', so that if the polarized rays A C, B D, fall upon the plates C D, at an angle of 53° 11', the candle from which they proceed would not be visible, or they would not suffer reflection from the plates C D. At all the other angles the light would be reflected, and the candle visible. Now the plate D is placed at an angle of 53° 11', and C at an angle of 56° 45', so that when a film of water is breathed upon them, the light will be reflected from the latter, and none from the former; that is, the act of breathing upon the glass plates will restore the invisible, and extinguish the visible image.

TO SHOW WHAT RAYS OF LIGHT DO NOT OBSTRUCT EACH OTHER.

Make a small hole in a sheet of pasteboard A, and placing it upright before three candles B, placed closely together, it

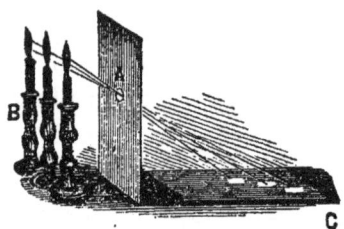

will be found that the images of all the candle flames will be formed separately on a piece of paper C, laid on the table to receive them. This proves that the rays of light do not obstruct each other in their progress, although all cross in passing through the hole

HOW TO SEE THROUGH A PHILADELPHIA BRICK.

Construct a hollow box or case, like the figure in the margin. One side is purposely removed in the engraving, to enable you to see the arrangement of the interior. A, B C, and D, are four small pieces of looking-glass, all placed at an angle of 45°, with respect to those sides of the box on which they are fixed; at E and G, two flat pieces of glass are inserted, as in the eye-glass of a telescope. Supposing you look through the opening E, in the direction of an object placed at o, you would see it in the same manner as if there was an uninterrupted view between E and G, which

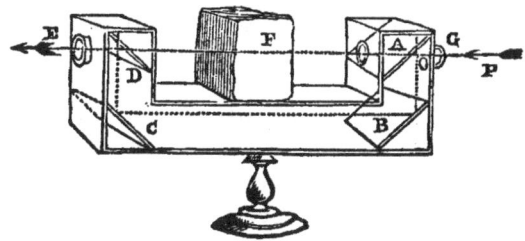

is evidently not the case. The cause of this is readily explained. The image of the object at o is received on the looking-glass A, by which it is reflected to B, as it is again from B to C, and afterwards to D; and this last image in D is seen by the eye of the spectator placed at E, in the same direction as if in reality he was looking at the real object itself, in the direction of the dotted line from o to E. From this it is evident that the placing an opaque body at F, cannot prevent the object at o being seen. Of course all this arrangement of the instrument is concealed, and you place it in the hands of a companion, that he may look through E or G, it matters not which, at any object placed beyond. You may then safely lay a wager that your instrument is of so magical a nature that it will enable you to see through a brick wall; but as a single brick will be more convenient, and equally wonderful, you are willing to satisfy his doubts at once. Of course, the hand or the hat, or any other opaque object, will answer the same purpose.

## THE STEREOSCOPE.

This is one of the newest and most interesting optical surprises invented, but, like many other instruments, it is indulged with a very hard name, which means, "Solids I see." For mere amusement, the instrument supplied with the necessary pictures may suffice, and they are now sold like the kaleidoscope at all optical instrument makers, toyshops, &c. The effect consists in obtaining the perfect solidity of a geometric object from two ordinary drawings, pictures of columns, statuary, figures, flowers, &c., &c., having a rounded appearance, "breadth," and keeping, which induce the spectator to believe he is gazing at the natural figure. Our limits preclude a lengthened description of the philosophy of this instrument, the invention of Professor Wheatstone. We may, however, first recommend our readers to study the structure of the eye, in Brewster's Treatise on Optics, which may be thoroughly impressed on the mind by dissecting carefully the eye of a sheep or bullock. Now, if we cut open a portion of the eye of a recently killed animal, and look in upon the retina, which is a delicate network of nerves, and is considered the "mind of the eye," we shall behold all images inverted. How then, do we see them upright? Again, as we have two eyes at a distance from each other, the images formed on the two retinæ cannot be precisely alike : how is it that confusion is not the result, instead of perfect images, in which we can appreciate the geometric niceties of length, breadth, and thickness? Now the stereoscope assists us in understanding these difficult questions; and, quoting Professor Wheatstone, we find he states "that the theory which has obtained the greatest currency is that which assumes that an object is seen single because its pictures fall on corresponding points of the two retinæ; that is, on points which are similarly situated with respect to the two centers, both in distance and position. This theory supposes that the pictures projected on the retinæ, are exactly similar to each other corresponding points of the two pictures falling on corresponding points of the two retinæ."

Now, the fact is, that an object presents an entirely different appearance to each eye. Sir D. Brewster remarks, "That were a painter called upon to take drawings of a statue, as seen by each eye, he would fix at the height of his eyes a metallic plate, with two small holes in it, and he would then draw the statue as seen through the holes by each eye." With the utmost care, however, he could not reproduce the statue by their union. In order to do this, a camera with *two lenses* of the same aperture and focal length, placed at the same distance as the *two eyes*, must be constructed and used.

The stereoscope is, consequently, an imitation of the powers of the eyes, giving solidity and a perfect relievo appearance to any two pictures which might be drawn separately from the two lenses in the camera obscura mentioned. That is to say, if it were possible to be behind the retina of each eye, and draw the two pictures of any object seen by our eyes, those pictures put into the stereoscope, would reproduce the solidity from which they were drawn.

Two instruments are sold, and may be obtained with the photographic pictures, almost at any optician's, viz.: the reflecting and the refracting stereoscope, of which we give drawings.

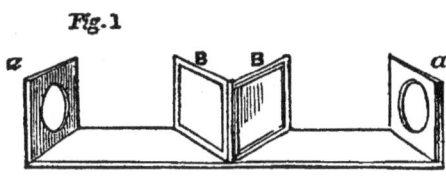

THE REFLECTING STEREOSCOPE.

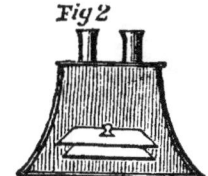

REFRACTING STERESCOPE.

*a a*, the two pictures. B B, the two mirrors, so adjusted that their backs form an angle of ninety degrees with each other, i. e., the quarter of a circle.

### OCULAR SPECTRA.

One of the most curious affections of the eye is that in virtue of which it sees what are called *ocular spectra*, or accidental colors. If we place a red wafer on a sheet of white paper, and, closing one eye, keep the other directed for some time to the center of the wafer, then, if we turn the same eye to another part of the paper, we shall see a green wafer, the color of which will continue to grow fainter and fainter, as we continue to look at it.

By using differently-colored wafers, we obtain the following results:

| WAFER. | SPECIMEN. |
|---|---|
| Black, | White. |
| White, | Black. |
| Red, | Bluish Green. |
| Orange, | Blue. |
| Yellow, | Indigo. |
| Green, | Violet, with a little Red. |
| Blue, | Orange Red. |
| Indigo, | Orange Yellow. |
| Violet, | Bluish Green. |

### BRILLIANT WATER MIRROR.

Nearly fill a glass tumbler with water, and hold it, with

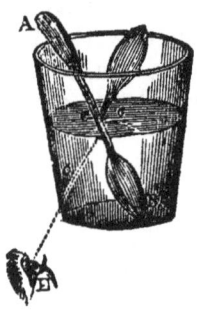
your back to the window, above the level of the eye, as in the engraving. Then look obliquely, as in the direction E, *a, c,* and you will see the whole surface shining like burnished silver, with a strong metallic reflection; and any object, as a spoon, A, C, B, immersed in the water, will have its immersed part, C B, reflected on the surface, as in a mirror, but with a brilliancy far surpassing that which can be obtained from quicksilver, or from the most highly-polished metals, by any means whatever.

### OPTICS OF A SOAP BUBBLE.

If a soap-bubble be blown up, and set under a glass, so that the motion of air may not affect it, as the water glides down the sides and the top grows thinner, several colors will successively appear at the top, and spread themselves from thence down the sides of the bubble, till they vanish in the same order in which they appear. At length, a black spot appears at the top, and spreads till the bubble bursts.*

### THE KALEIDOSCOPE.

If any object be placed between two plane mirrors, inclined towards each other at an angle of thirty degrees, three several images will be perceived in the circumference of a circle. On this principle is formed the kaleidoscope, invented by Sir David Brewster, and by means of which the reflected images viewed from a particular point exhibit symmetrical figures, under an infinite arrangement of beautiful

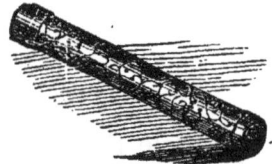
forms and colors. The kaleidoscope may be bought at any toy-shop, but it is requisite that every young person should be able to construct one for himself. He must, therefore, procure a tube of tin or paper, of about ten

---

* The thinnest substance ever observed is the aqueous film of the soap-bubble previous to bursting; yet it is capable of reflecting the faint image of a candle, or the sun. Hence its thickness must correspond with what Sir Isaac Newton calls the beginning of black, which appears in water at the thickness of the seven hundred and fifty thousandth part of an inch

inches in length, and two and a half or three inches in diameter. One end of this should be stopped up with tin or paper, securely fastened, in which is to be made a hole, about the size of a small pea, for the eye to look through. Two pieces of well-silvered looking-glass, B B, are now to be procured; they must be not quite so long as the tube, and they should be placed in the tube lengthwise, at an angle of 60 degrees, meeting together in a point at A, and separating to the points c c, the polished surfaces looking inwards. A circular piece of glass is now to be laid on the top of the edges of the reflectors, B B; which, by their not being quite so long as the tube, will allow room for its falling in, and it will be supported by the edges of the tube, which may be slightly bent over, to prevent the glass from falling out.  This having been done, now proceed to make the "cap" of the instrument. A rim of tin or pasteboard must be cut, so as to fit over the glass end of the tube; and in this, on the outer side, a piece of ground glass must be fastened, so that the whole may fit on the tube like the lid of a pill-box. Then, before putting it on, obtain some small pieces of broken glass of various colors, beads, little strips of wire, or any other object, and place them in the cap; and by passing it over the end, so that the broken glass, &c. has free motion, the instrument is complete. To use it, apply the eye to the small hole, and, on turning it, the most beautiful forms will appear, in the most wonderful combinations.

The following curious calculation has been made of the number of changes this instrument will admit of. Supposing it to contain 20 small pieces of glass, and that you make 10 changes in a minute, it will take an inconceivable space of time, *i. e.* 462,880,899,576 years, and 360 days, to go through the immense number of changes of which it is capable.

### SIMPLE SOLAR MICROSCOPE.

Having made a circular hole in a window-shutter, about three inches in diameter, place in it a glass lens of about twelve inches focal distance. To the inside of the hole adapt a tube, having at a small distance from the lens a slit, capable of receiving one or two very thin plates of glass, to which the object to be viewed must be affixed by means of a little gum water exceedingly transparent. Into this tube fit another, furnished at its extremity with a lens of half an inch focal distance. Place a mirror before the hole of the window-shutter on the outside, in such a manner as to throw the light of the sun into the tube, and you will have a solar magic lantern.

The method of employing this arrangement of lenses for microscopic purposes is as follows : Having darkened the room, and by means of the mirror reflected the sun's rays on the glasses in a direction parallel to the axis, place some small object between the two moveable plates of glass, or affix it to one of them with very transparent gum water, and bring it exactly into the axis of the tube ; if the moveable tube be then pushed out or drawn in, till the object be a little beyond the focus, it will be seen painted very distinctly on a card, or piece of white paper, held at a proper distance, and will appear to be greatly magnified. A small insect will appear as a large animal, a hair as big as a walking-stick, and the almost invisible eels in paste or vinegar as large as common eels.

### ANAMORPHOSES.

This is a very curious optical effect, producing a distorted and grotesque figure from a regular one. The term is derived from two Greek words, signifying a distortion of figure, and by its means many optical puzzles may be produced geometrically.

Take any subject, such as the portrait of a head ; divide it vertically and horizontally with parallel lines, of which the outer sides shall form the boundary, A, B, C, D, and the whole shall be equi-distant. Then, on a separate piece of paper, or cardboard, prepare a drawing similar to Fig. 2 by the following means :

1. Draw a horizontal line, *a b*, equal to A B, and divide it into as many equal parts as the latter is divided.

2. Let fall a perpendicular line, *e v*, from the middle of *a b*, and then draw *s v* parallel to *a b*.

3. Both *e v* and *s v* may be any length at pleasure, but the longer the first is, and the shorter the other, so will the anamorphoses be more and more deformed. The proportions in our figures are sufficiently different.

4 After having drawn from the point *v* right lines, *v* 1, *v* 2, *v* 3, *v* 4, to the divisions of *a b*, draw the line *s b*, and

through each point where *s b* intersects the divergent lines, draw other horizontal lines parallel to *a b*. We now have a *trapezium, a b c d*, divided into as many cells as the square in Fig. 1.

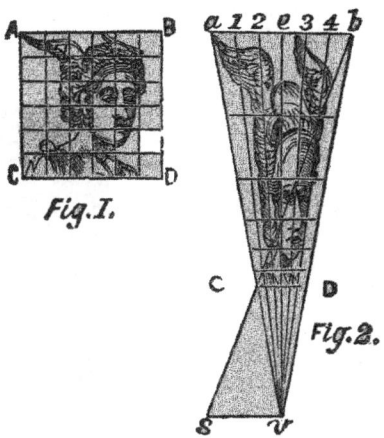

The next step is to fill up all the cells of Fig. 2 with portions of the device, proportionate to their position in Fig. 1. For instance, in Fig. 1 the nose is in the second vertical division from the left, and in the third and fourth horizontal divisions from the top, and that portion of the face must accordingly be placed in a corresponding part of Fig. 2.

By these means we procure the anamorphosis seen in Fig. 2, which, when viewed from a particular position, will lose all its distortion, and assume an appearance resembling that in Fig. 1. This position lies immediately over the point *v*, and at a height above it equal to the length of the line *s v;* and the means of determining it are as follow :

Place the drawing horizontally before a window ; take a slip of card, and rest its lower edge on the line *s v*, the card being accurately vertical ; pierce a small hole in the card vertically over the point *v*, and at a height from it equal to the length of the line *s v*, then, with the eye placed immediately behind the card, look through the orifice at the anamorphosis, and it will be found that as soon as the eye has become accustomed to the novelty of the experiment the anamorphosis will lose its distortion, and appear almost exactly like the symmetrical figure.

It would be very difficult, and would require geometrical reasoning of a lengthened kind, to show why this particular form of construction should lead to such results.

### THE COSMORAMA.

The principle upon which the cosmorama is formed is so simple, that any person may easily fit up one in a small summer house, &c. Nothing more is necessary than to fix in a hole a double convex lens of about three feet focus, A, and at rather less than this distance a picture, B, is to be hung.

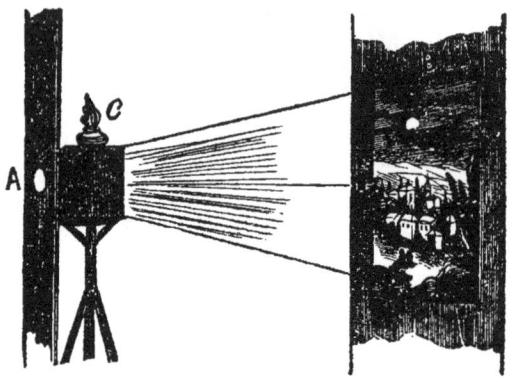

To absorb all the rays of light but those necessary for seeing the picture, a squared frame of wood blackened on the inside is placed between the lens and the picture. The picture may be hung in a large box having a light coming in upon it from above, or in a small closet illuminated in the same manner. Should it be wished to show the picture by candle-light, a lamp, c, may be placed on the top of the wooden frame, and if the light of this be converged by a lens to a moderate radius, it will be more effective.

### DISTORTED LANDSCAPES.

Landscapes or other matters may be drawn so as to produce curious optical illusions by the following method. Take a piece of smooth white pasteboard, and sketch the design upon it. Prick the outlines in every part with a fine pin or needle, then place the pricked drawing in a perpendicular position, and put a lighted candle behind it. Place before it another piece of pasteboard, and follow with a pencil the lines given by the light, and you have produced a distorted landscape. Now take away the candle and the pricked drawing, and place your eye where the light was, and the drawing will assume the regular form. To get your eye in the proper position, it will be advisable to cut out a piece of card according to the preceding pattern, and raising it on its base, B, look through the hole at A, when the object will appear in its proper proportions.

THE MAGIC COIN.

Among the numerous experiments with which science astonishes and sometimes even strikes terror into the ignorant, there is none more calculated to produce this effect than that of displaying to the eye in absolute darkness the legend or inscription upon a coin. To do this, take a silver coin (I have always used an old one), and after polishing the surface as much as possible, make the parts of it which are raised rough by the action of an acid, the parts not raised, or those which are to be rendered darkest, retaining their polish. If the coin thus prepared is placed upon a mass of red-hot iron, and removed into a dark room, the inscription upon it will become less luminous than the rest, so that it may be distinctly read by the spectator. The mass of red-hot iron should be concealed from the observer's eye, both for the purpose of rendering the eye fitter for observing the effect, and of removing all doubt that the inscription is really read in the dark, that is, without receiving any light, direct or reflected, from any other body. If, in place of polishing the depressed parts, and roughening its raised parts, we make the raised parts polished, and roughen the depressed parts, the inscription will now be less luminous than the depressed parts.

# TRICKS IN MECHANICS.

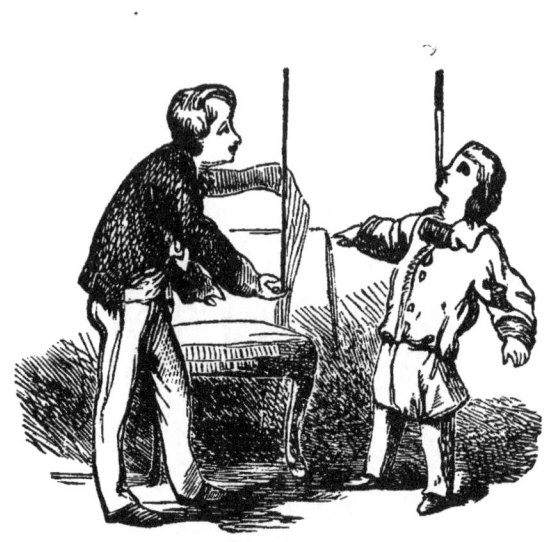

"These are machinations comical."—FORD.

There is no subject of such importance as Mechanics, as its principles are founded upon the properties of matter and the laws of motion; and in knowing something of these, the tyro will lay the foundation of all substantial knowledge.

The properties of matter are the following: Solidity (or Impenetrability), Divisibility, Mobility, Elasticity, Brittleness, Malleability, Ductility, and Tenacity.

The laws of motion are as follow:

1. Every body continues in a state of rest or of uniform rectilineal motion, unless affected by some extraneous force.

2. The change of motion is always proportionate to the impelling force.

3. Action and reaction are always equal and contrary.

### EXPERIMENT OF THE LAW OF MOTION.

In shooting at "taw," if the marble be struck "plump," as it is called, it moves forward exactly in the same line of direction; but if struck sideways, it will move in an oblique direction, and its course will be in a line situated between the direction of its former motion and that of the force impressed. This is called the resolution of forces.

## BALANCING

The center of gravity in a body is that part about which all the other parts equally balance each other. In balancing a stick upon the finger, or upon the chin, it is necessary only to keep the chin or finger exactly under the point which is called the center of gravity.

## THE PRANCING HORSE.

Cut out the figure of a horse, and having fixed a curved iron wire to the under part of its body, place a small ball of lead upon it. Place the hind legs of the horse on the table, and it will rock to and fro. If the ball be removed, the horse would immediately tumble, because unsupported, the center of gravity being in the front of the prop; but upon the ball being replaced, the center of gravity immediately changes its position, and is brought under the prop, and the horse is again in equilibrio.

TO CONSTRUCT A FIGURE, WHICH, BEING PLACED UPON A CURVED SURFACE, AND INCLINED IN ANY POSITION, SHALL, WHEN LEFT TO ITSELF, RETURN TO ITS FORMER POSITION.

The feet of the figure rest on a curved pivot, which is sustained by two loaded balls below; for the weight of these balls being much greater than that of the figure, their effect is to bring the center of gravity of the whole beneath the point on which it rests; consequently the equilibrium will resist any slight force to disturb it.

TO MAKE A CARRIAGE RUN IN AN INVERTED POSITION WITHOUT FALLING.

It is pretty well known to most boys, that if a tumbler of water be placed within a broad wooden hoop, the whole may be whirled round without falling, owing to the centrifugal force. On the same principle, if a small carriage be placed on an iron band or rail, it will ascend the

curve, become inverted, and descend again, without falling.

## TO CAUSE A CYLINDER TO ROLL BY ITS OWN WEIGHT UP HILL

Procure a coffee canister, and loading it at F with a piece of lead, which may be fixed in with solder, the position of the center of gravity is thus altered. If a cylinder so constructed be placed on an inclined plane, and the loaded part above, it will roll up hill without assistance.

## THE BALANCED STICK.

Procure a piece of wood, about nine incnes in length and about half an inch in thickness, and thrust into its upper end the blades of two penknives, on either side one. Place the other end upon the tip of the fore-finger, and it will keep its place without falling.

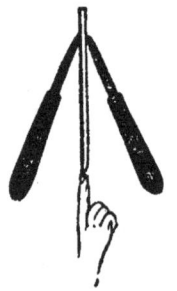 

## THE CHINESE MANDARIN.

Construct out of the pith of elder a little mandarin; then provide a base for it to sit in, like a kettle-drum. Into this put some heavy substance, such as half a leaden bullet; fasten the figure to this, and in whatever position it may be placed, it will, when left to itself, immediately return to its upright position.

## TO MAKE A QUARTER DOLLAR TURN ON ITS EDGE ON THE POINT OF A NEEDLE.

Take a bottle, with a cork in its neck, and in it, in a perpendicular position, a middle-sized needle. Fix a quarter dollar into another cork, by cutting a nick in it; and stick into the same cork two small table-forks, opposite each other, with the handles inclining downwards. If the rim of the quarter dollar be now poised on the point of the needle, it may easily be made to spin round without falling, as the center of gravity is below the the center of suspension.

### THE SELF-BALANCED PAIL.

You lay a stick across the table, letting one third of it project over the edge; and you undertake to hang a pail of water on it, without either fastening the stick on the table, or letting the pail rest on any support; and this feat the laws of gravitation will enable you literally to accomplish.

You take the pail of water, and hang it by the handle upon the projecting end of the stick, in such a manner that the handle may rest on it in an inclined position, with the middle of the pail within the edge of the table. That it may be fixed in this situation, place another

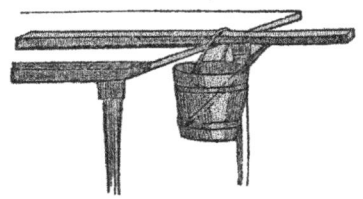

stick with one of its ends resting against the side at the bottom of the pail, and its other end against the first stick, where there should be a notch to retain it. By these means, the pail will remain fixed in that situation, without being able to incline to either side; nor can the stick slide along the table, or move along its edge, without raising the center of gravity of the pail, and the water it contains.

### TO LIFT A BOTTLE WITH A STRAW.

Take a straw, and having bent the thicker end of it in a sharp angle, as in figure subjoined, put this hooked end into the bottle, so that the bent part may rest against its side; you may then take the other end, and lift up the bottle by it, without breaking the straw, and this will be the more readily accomplished as the angular part of the straw ap-

proaches nearer to that which comes out of the bottle. It is necessary, in order to succeed in this feat, to be particularly careful in choosing a stout straw, which is neither broken nor bruised; if it have been previously bent or damaged, it is unfit for the purpose of performing this trick, as it will be too weak in the part so bent, or damaged, to support the bottle.

### THE DANCING PEA.

If you stick through a pea, or small ball of pith, two pins* at right angles, and defend the points with pieces of seal-

ing wax, it may be kept in equilibrio at a short distance from the end of a straight tube by means of a current of breath from the mouth, which imparts a rotary motion to the pea.

### THE TOPER'S TRIPOD.

Place three tobacco pipes in the position shown in the engraving, the mouth of the bowls downwards, and the lower end of the stems upon the stem just by the bowls. This tripod, if carefully put together, will support considerably more than a pot of ale.

* The pins are only used to hold the pea steady before it is blown from the pipe, as the pea alone will dance quite as well.

## TRICKS IN MECHANICS. 187

### OBLIQUITY OF MOTION.

Cut a piece of pasteboard into the following shape, and describe on it a spiral line; cut this out with a penknife,

and then suspend it on a large skewer or pin, as seen in the engraving. If the whole be now placed on a warm stove, or over the flame of a candle or lamp, it will revolve with considerable velocity. The card, after being cut into the spiral, may be made to represent a snake or dragon, and when in motion will produce a very pleasing effect.

### THE BRIDGE OF KNIVES

Place three glasses, A A A, in the form of a triangle, and arrange three knives upon them, as shown in the figure,

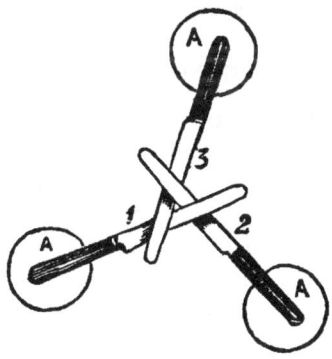

the blade of No. 1 over that of No. 2, and that over No. 3, which rests on No. 1. The bridge so made will be self-supported

## SAND IN THE HOUR-GLASS.

It is a remarkable fact, that the flow of sand in the hour-glass is perfectly equable, whatever may be the quantity in the glass; that is, the sand runs no faster when the upper half of the glass is quite full than when it is nearly empty. It would, however, be natural enough to conclude that, when full of sand, it would be more swiftly urged through the aperture, than when the glass was only a quarter full, and near the close of the hour.

The fact of the even flow of sand may be proved by a very simple experiment. Provide some silver sand, dry it over or before the fire, and pass it through a tolerably fine sieve. Then take a tube, of any length or diameter, closed at one end, in which make a small hole, say the eighth of an inch; stop this with a peg, and fill up the tube with the sifted sand. Hold the tube steadily, or fix it to a wall, or frame, at any height from a table; remove the peg, and permit the sand to flow in any measure for any given time, and note the quantity. Then, let the tube be emptied, and only half or a quarter filled with the sand; measure again, for a like time, and the same quantity of sand will flow: even if you press the sand in the tube with a ruler or stick, the flow of the sand through the hole will not be increased.

The above is explained by the fact, that when the sand is poured into the tube, it fills it with a succession of conical heaps, and that all the weight which the bottom of the tube sustains is only that of the heap which *first* falls upon it; as the succeeding heaps do not press downwards, but only against the sides or walls of the tube.

## RESISTANCE OF SAND.

From the above experiment it may be concluded, that it is extremely difficult to thrust sand out of a tube by means of a fitting plug or piston; and this, upon trial, is found to be the case. Fit a piston to a tube (exactly like a boy's pop-gun,) pour some sand in, and try with the utmost strength of the arm to push out the sand. It will be found impossible to do this: rather than the sand should be shot out, the tube will burst at the sides.

# TRICKS IN HYDRAULICS.

The science of Hydraulics comprehends the laws which regulate non-elastic fluids in motion, and especially water, &c.

Water can only be set in motion by two causes—the pressure of the atmosphere, or its own gravity. The principal law concerning fluids is, that they always preserve their own level. Hence water can be distributed over a town from any reservoir that is higher than the houses to be supplied; and the same principle will enable us to form fountains in a garden, or other place. Should any of our young

friends wish to form a fountain, or jet-d'-eau, they may, by bringing a pipe from T, a water-tank, which should be at the upper part of the house, convey the water down to the garden. Then by leading it through the earth, underneath the path or grass plot, and turning it to a perpendicular position, the water will spring out, and rise nearly as high as the level of that in the tank. The part of the pipe at B should have a turnkey, so that the water may be let on or shut off at pleasure.

## THE PUMP.

The action of the common pump is as follows: When the handle A is raised, the piston-rod B descends, and brings the piston-valve, called the sucker, or bucket, to another valve, c, which is fixed, and opens inwards towards the piston. When the handle is drawn down, the piston is raised, and, as it is air-tight, a vacuum is produced between

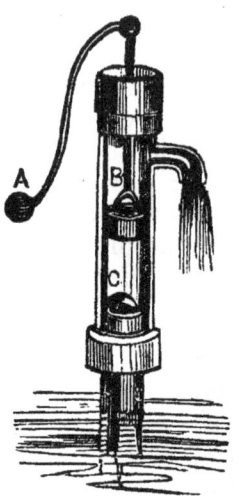

the two valves; the air in the valve of the pump, betwixt the lower valve and the water, then forces open the lower valve, and rushes through to fill up this vacuum; and the air in the pump being less dense than the external atmosphere, the water is forced a short way up the barrel. When the piston again descends to the lower valve, the air between them is again forced out by forcing open the upper valve; and when the piston is raised, a vacuum is again produced, and the air below the lower valve rushes up, and the water in consequence is again raised a little further. This operation continues until the water rises above the lower valve; at every stroke afterwards, the water passes through the valve of the descending piston, and is raised by it, on its ascent, until it issues out of the spout.

THE HYDRAULIC DANCER.

Make a little figure of cork, in the shape of a dancing mountebank, sailor, &c. In this figure place a small hollow cone, made of thin leaf brass. When

## TRICKS IN HYDRAULICS.

this figure is placed upon any jet-d'-eau, such as that of the fountain recommended to be constructed, it will be suspended on the top of the water, and perform a great variety of amusing motions. If a hollow ball of very thin copper, about an inch in diameter, be placed on a similar cone, it will remain suspended, turning round and spreading the water all about it.

### THE SYPHON.

The syphon is a bent tube, having one leg shorter than the other. It acts by the pressure of the atmosphere being removed from the surface of a fluid, which makes it to rise above its common level at B. In order to make a syphon act, it is necessary first to fill both legs quite full of the fluid; and then the shorter leg must be placed in the vessel to be emptied.
Immediately upon withdrawing the finger from the longer leg, the liquor will flow. Any young person may form a syphon by a small piece of leaden pipe, bent into the form above.

### THE WATER SNAIL, OR ARCHIMEDIAN SCREW

may easily be constructed. Purchase a yard of small leaden pipe, and twist it round a pole, as in the following figure, A; place a handle at its upper end, B, and let its lower end rest in the water. Between the last turn of the pipe and

the orifice place a paddle-wheel, C. Now, should the water be that of a running stream, the force of the stream will turn the pipe, and the water will rise in it till it empties itself into the trough at D. Should the water have no motion, the turning of the handle at B will elevate the water from the lower to the higher level.

### THE BOTTLE EJECTMENT.

Fill a small white glass bottle, with a very narrow neck, full of wine; place it in a glass vase, which must previously have sufficient water in it to rise above the mouth of the bottle. Immediately you will perceive the wine rise, in the form of a little column, toward the surface of the water, and the water will, in the mean time, begin to take the place of the wine at the bottom of the bottle. The cause of this is, that the water is heavier than the wine, which it displaces, and forces it to rise toward the surface.

### THE MAGIC OF HYDROSTATICS WITH THE ANCIENTS.

The principles of *Hydrostatics* were available in the work of magical deception. The marvelous fountain which Pliny describes in the island of Andros as discharging wine for seven days, and water during the rest of the year,—the spring of oil which broke out in Rome to welcome the return of Augustus from the Sicilian war,—the three empty urns which filled themselves with wine at the annual feast of Bacchus in the city of Elis,—the glass tomb of Belus, which was full of oil, and which, when once emptied by Xerxes, could not again be filled,—the weeping statues, and the perpetual lamps of the ancients,—were all the obvious effect of the equilibrium and pressure of fluids.

### TO EMPTY A GLASS UNDER WATER.

Fill a wine-glass with water, place over its mouth a card, so as to prevent the water from escaping, and put the glass, mouth downwards, into a basin of water. Next, remove the card, and raise the glass partly above the surface, but keep its mouth below the surface, so that the glass still remains completely filled with water. Then insert one end of a quill or reed in the water below the mouth of the glass, and blow gently at the other end, when air will ascend in bubbles to the highest part of the glass, and expel the water from it; and, if you continue to blow throw the quill, all the water will be emptied from the glass, which will be filled with air.

# TRICKS IN ACOUSTICS.

ACOUSTICS is the science relating to sound and hearing. Sound is heard when any shock or impulse is given to the air, or to any other body which is in contact directly or indirectly with the ear.

### DIFFERENCE BETWEEN SOUND AND NOISE.

Noises are made by the cracks of whips, the beating of hammers, the creak of a file or saw, or the hubbub of a multitude. But when a bell is struck, the bow of a violin drawn across the strings, or the wetted finger turned round a musical glass, we have what are properly called sounds.

### SOUNDS, HOW PROPAGATED.

Sounds are propagated on all bodies much after the manner that waves are in water, with a velocity of 1,142 feet in a second. Sounds in liquids and in solids are more rapid than in air. Two stones rubbed together may be heard in water at half a mile; solid bodies convey sounds to great distances, and pipes may be made to convey the voice over every part of the house.

### VISIBLE VIBRATION.

Provide a glass goblet about two thirds filled with colored water, draw a fiddle bow against its edge, and the surface of the water will exhibit a pleasing figure, composed of fans, four, six, or eight in number, dependent on the dimensions of the vessel, but chiefly on the pitch of the note produced.

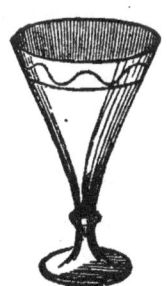

Or, nearly fill a glass with water, draw the bow strongly against its edge, the water will be elevated and depressed; and when the vibration has ceased, and the surface of the water has become tranquil, these elevations will be exhibited in the form of a curved line, passing round the interior surface of the glass, and above the surface of the water. If the action of the bow be strong, the water will be sprinkled on the inside of the glass, above the liquid surface, and this sprinkling will show the curved line very perfectly, as in the engraving. The water should be carefully poured, so that the glass above the liquid be preserved dry; the portion of the glass between the edge and curved line will then be seen partially sprinkled; but, between the level of the water and the curved line, it will have become wholly wetted, thereby indicating the height to which the fluid has been thrown.

### TRANSMITTED VIBRATION.

Provide a long, flat glass ruler or rod, as in the engraving, and cement it with mastic to the edge of a drinking glass, fixed into a wooden stand; support the other end of the rod

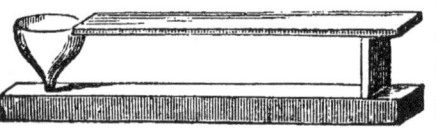

very lightly on a piece of cork, and strew its upper surface with sand; set the glass in vibration by a bow, at a point opposite where the rod meets it, and the motions will be communicated to the rod without any change in their direction. If the apparatus be inverted, and sand be strewed on the under side of the rod, the figures will be seen to correspond with those produced on the upper surface.

### DOUBLE VIBRATION.

Provide two disks of metal or glass, precisely of the same dimensions, and a glass or metal rod; cement the two disks

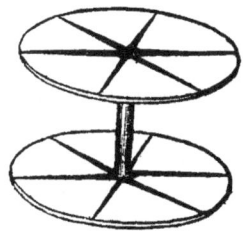

at their centers to the ends of the rod, as in the engraving, and strew their upper surfaces with sand. Cause one of the disks, viz., the upper one, to vibrate by a bow, and its vibration will be exactly imitated by the lower disk, and the sand strewed over both will arrange itself in precisely the same forms on both disks.

### CHAMPAGNE AND SOUND.

Pour sparkling champagne into a glass, until it is half full, when the glass will lose its power of ringing by a stroke upon its edge, and will emit only a disagreeable and puffy sound. Nor will a glass ring while the wine is brisk, and filled with air-bubbles; but as the effervescence subsides, the sound will become clearer and clearer, and when the air-bubbles have entirely disappeared, the glass will ring as usual. If a crumb of bread be thrown into the champagne, and effervescence be reproduced, the glass will again cease to ring. The same experiment will also succeed with soda water, ginger wine, or any other effervescing liquid.

### MUSIC OF THE SNAIL.

Place a garden snail upon a pane of glass, and in drawing itself along, it will frequently produce sounds similar to those of musical glasses.

### THE TUNING-FORK A FLUTE PLAYER.

Take a common tuning-fork, and on one of its branches fasten with sealing-wax a circular piece of card, of the size of a small wafer, or sufficient nearly to cover the aperture of a pipe, as the sliding 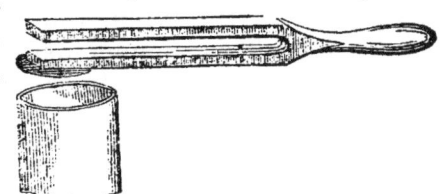 of the upper end of a flute with the mouth stopped: it may be tuned in unison with the loaded tuning-fork (a C fork), by means of the moveable stopper or card, or the fork may be loaded till the unison is perfect. Then set the fork in vibration by a blow on the unloaded branch, and hold the card closely over the mouth of the pipe, as in the engraving, when a note of surprising clearness and strength will be heard. Indeed, a flute may be made to "speak" perfectly well, by holding close to the opening a vibrating tuning-fork, while the fingering proper to the note of the fork is at the same time performed.

### MUSICAL BOTTLES.

Provide two glass bottles, and tune them by pouring water into them, so that each corresponds to the sound of a different tuning-fork. Then apply both tuning-forks to the mouth of each bottle alternately, when that sound only will be heard, in each case, which is reciprocated by the unisonant bottle; or, in other words, by that bottle which contains a column of air, susceptible of vibrating in unison with the fork.

### THEORY OF WHISPERING.

Apartments of a circular or elliptical form are best calculated for the exhibition of this phenomenon. If a person stand near the wall, with his face turned to it, and whisper a few words, they may be more distinctly heard at nearly the opposite side of the apartment, than if the listener was situated near to the speaker.

### THEORY OF THE VOICE.

Provide a species of whistle, common as a child's toy or a sportsman's call, in the form of a hollow cylinder, about three fourths of an inch in diameter, closed at both ends by flat circular plates, with holes in their centers. Hold this toy between the teeth and lips; blow through it, and you may produce sounds varying in pitch with the force with which you blow. If the air be cautiously graduated, all the sounds within the compass of a double octave may be produced from it; and, if great precaution be taken in the management of the wind, tones even yet graver may be brought out. This simple instrument, or toy, has indeed the greatest resemblance to the larynx, which is the organ of voice.

### TO TUNE A GUITAR WITHOUT THE ASSISTANCE OF THE EAR.

Make one string to sound, and its vibrations will, with much force, be transferred to the next string: this transference may be seen, by placing a saddle of paper (like an inverted $\Lambda$) upon the string, at first in a state of rest. When this string *hears* the other, the saddle will be shaken, or fall off; when both strings are in harmony, the paper will be very little, or not at all shaken.

### PROGRESS OF SOUND.

When a bow is drawn across the strings of a violin, the impulses produced may be rendered evident by fixing a small steel bead upon the bow; when looked at by light, or in sunshine, the bead will seem to form a series of dots during the passage of the bow.

### TO MAKE AN ÆOLIAN HARP.

This instrument consists of a long narrow box of very thin pine, about six inches deep, with a circle in the middle of the upper side, of an inch and half in diameter, in which are to be drilled small holes. On this side seven, ten, or more strings of very fine catgut are stretched over bridges at each end like the bridge of a fiddle, and screwed up or relaxed with screw pins. The strings must all be tuned to one and the same note,* and the instrument should be placed in a window partly open, in which the width is exactly equal to the length of the harp, with the sash just raised to give the air admission. When the air blows upon these strings with different degrees of force it will excite different tones of sound. Sometimes the blast brings out all the tones in full concert, and sometimes it sinks them to the softest murmurs.

A colossal imitation of the instrument just described was invented at Milan in 1786, by the Abbate Gattoni. He stretched seven strong iron wires, tuned to the notes of the gamut, from the top of a tower sixty feet high, to the house of a Signor Moscate, who was interested in the success of the experiment, and this apparatus, called the "giant's harp," in blowing weather yielded lengthened peals of harmonious music. In a storm this music was sometimes heard at the distance of several miles.

### THE INVISIBLE GIRL.

The facility with which the voice circulates through tubes was known to the ancients, and no doubt has afforded the priests of all religions means of deception to the ignorant and credulous. But of late days the light of science dispels all such wicked deceptions. A very clever machine was produced at Paris several years ago, and afterwards exhibited in New York and other cities in the United States, under the name of the "Invisible Girl," since

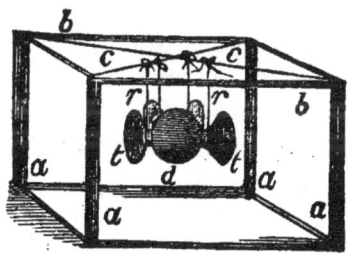

the apparatus was so constructed that the voice of a female at a distance was heard as if it originated from a hollow globe, not more than a foot in diameter. It consisted of a wooden frame something like a tent bedstead, formed

---

* D is a good note for it. The upper string may be tuned to the upper D, and the two lower to the lower D, and D D. The "harmonics," are the sounds produced.

by four pillars *a a a a*, connected by upper cross rails *b b*, and similar rails below, while it terminated above in four bent wires *c c*, proceeding at right angles of the frame, and meeting in a central point. The hollow copper ball *d*, with four trumpets, *t t*, crossing from it at right angles, hung in the center of the frame, being connected with the wires alone by four narrow ribbons *r r*. The questions were proposed close to the open mouth of one of these trumpets, and the reply was returned from the same orifice. The means used in the deception were as follows: a pipe or tube was attached to one of the hollow pillars, and carried into another apartment, in which a female was placed; and this tube having been carried up the leg or pillar of the instrument to the cross-rails, had apertures exactly opposite two of the trumpet mouths; so that what was spoken was immediately answered through a very simple mode of communication.

### THE MAGIC OF ACOUSTICS.

The science of *Acoustics* furnished the ancient sorcerers with some of their best deceptions. The imitation of thunder in their subterranean temples could not fail to indicate the presence of a supernatural agent. The golden virgins whose ravishing voices resounded through the temple of Delphos,—the stone from the river Pactolus, whose trumpet notes scared the robber from the treasure which it guarded,—the speaking head which uttered its oracular responses at Lesbos,—and the vocal statue of Memnon, which began at the break of day to accost the rising sun,—were all deceptions derived from science, and from a diligent observation of the phemomena of nature.

### TO SHOW HOW SOUND TRAVELS THROUGH A SOLID.

Take a long piece of wood, such as the handle of a hair broom, and placing a watch at one end, apply your ear to the other, and the tickings will be distinctly heard.

### TO SHOW THAT SOUND DEPENDS ON VIBRATION.

Touch a bell when it is sounding, and the noise ceases; the same may be done to a musical string with the same results. Hold a musical pitchfork to the lips, when it is made to sound, and a quivering motion will be felt from its vibrations. These experiments show that sound is produced by the quick motions and vibrations of different bodies.

# THE MAGIC OF NUMBERS
## OR, CURIOUS PROBLEMS IN ARITHMETIC.

As the principal object of this volume is to enable the young reader to learn something in his sports, and to understand what he is doing, we shall, before proceeding to the curious tricks and feats connected with the science of numbers, present him with some arithmetical aphorisms, upon which most of the following examples are founded.

### APHORISMS OF NUMBER.

1. If two even numbers be added together, or subtracted from each other, their sum or difference will be an even number.

2. If two uneven numbers be added or subtracted, their sum or difference will be an even number.

3. The sum or difference of an even and an uneven number added or subtracted, will be an uneven number.

4. The product of two even numbers will be an even number, and the product of two uneven numbers will be an uneven number.

5. The product of an even and uneven number will be an even number.

6. If two different numbers be divisible by any one num-

ber, their sum and their difference will also be divisible by that number.

7. If several different numbers, divided by 3, be added or multiplied together, their sum and their product will also be divisible by 3.

8. If two numbers, divisible by 9, be added together, the sum of the figures in the amount will be either 9, or a number divisible by 9.

9. If any number be multiplied by 9, or by any other number divisible by 9, the amount of the figures of the product will be either 9, or a number divisible by 9.

10. In every arithmetical progression, if the first and last term be each multiplied by the number of terms, and the sum of the two products be divided by 2, the quotient will be the sum of the series.

11. In every geometric progression, if any two terms be multiplied together, their product will be equal to that term, which answers to the sum of these two indices. Thus, in the series—

$$\begin{array}{ccccc} 1 & 2 & 3 & 4 & 5 \\ 2 & 4 & 8 & 16 & 32 \end{array}$$

If the third and fourth terms 8 and 16 be multiplied together, the product 128 will be the seventh term of the series. In like manner, if the fifth term be multiplied into itself, the product will be the tenth term, and if that sum be multiplied into itself, the product will be the twentieth term. Therefore, to find the last, or any other term of a geometric series, it is not necessary to continue the series beyond a few of the first terms.

Previous to the numerical recreations, we shall here describe certain mechanical methods of performing arithmetical calculations, such as are not only in themselves entertaining, but will be found more or less useful to the young reader

### PALPABLE ARITHMETIC.

The blind mathematician, Dr. Saunderson, adopted a very ingenious device for performing arithmetical operations by the sense of touch.

Small cubes of wood were provided, and in one face of each, nine holes were pierced, thus:

$$\begin{array}{ccc} 1 & 2 & 3 \\ 4 & 5 & 6 \\ 7 & 8 & 9 \end{array} \qquad \begin{array}{ccc} \circ & \circ & \circ \\ \circ & \circ & \circ \\ \circ & \circ & \circ \end{array}$$

These holes represented the nine digits, as in the figure, and to denote any figure, a small peg was inserted into the hole corresponding to it. If the number consisted of several figures, more cubes were used, one for each. A cipher was represented by a peg of different shape from that of the others, and inserted in the central hole.

To perform any arithmetical process, a square board was provided, divided by ridges into recesses of the same width as the cubes, and by this the cubes were retained in the required horizontal and perpindicular lines. Suppose it was necessary to add together the numbers 763, 124, 859, the cubes and pegs would be arranged thus:

```
  o c o    o o o    o o ●
  o o o    o o ●    o o o
  ● o o    o o o    ● o o

  ● o o    o ● o    o o o
  o o o    o o o    ● o o
  o o o    o o o    o o o

  o o o    o o o    o o o
  o o o    o ● o    o o o
  o ● o    o o o    o o ●

● o o    o o o    o o o    o o o
o o o    o o o    ● o o    o o ●
o o o    ● o o    o o o    o o o
```

## THE ABACUS.

This instrument is used for teaching numeration, and the first principles of arithmetic.

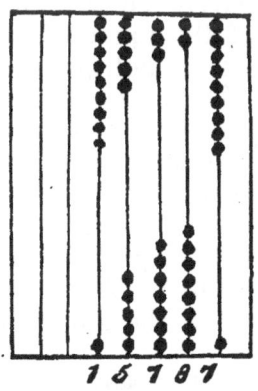

Mount Blanc.

Upon a frame are placed wires, parallel to one another, and at equal distances. Ten small balls are strung upon each wire, being placed as in the margin. The right wire denotes units, the next tens, and so on, the 7th wire being the place of millions. In using the abacus, all the balls are first ranged at one end, and a number of them are then moved to the other end of each wire, to correspond to the figures required. The example given in the margin is 15,781, **the height of**

## NAPIER'S RODS.

The object of this contrivance is to render arithmetical multiplication more easy, and to secure its correctness; it was much used by astronomers before the invention of logarithms.

To appreciate the merits of this invention, we must consider the process of multiplication as usually performed. Suppose we had to multiply 8,679 by 8:

$$\begin{array}{r} 8,679 \\ 8 \\ \hline 69,432 \end{array}$$

We first multiply 9 by 8 = 72, and putting down 2 as the first figure in the product, carry the 7 to add to the next product of 7 by 8 = 56; this gives us 63, the 3 being put down as the second figure; 6 is carried to add to the product of 6 by 8, and so on.

A blunder may be made in each part of this process; for 1st, we might reckon 8 times 9 as some other number than 72; 2d, after multiplying the 7 by the 8, we might add to the resulting 56 some other figure than the 7, which we carried; 3d, we may add 56 to 7 inaccurately, making some other sum of it than the right one, 63. Errors in a long multiplication problem are usually made in one of these three ways, and to prevent such errors, Lord Napier* introduced this useful contrivance. Thin strips of card, wood, or bone, 9 times as long as they are broad, are each divided into 9 equal squares, a figure is printed or written on the top square, and in each of the squares underneath is the product of multiplying that figure by 2, 3, 4, &c., up to 9.

To use these in multiplication, select the strips, the top figures of which make the number to be multiplied. For example:

To multiply 8,679 by 8, look at the eighth line of squares from the top, and on that line will be found the product of each of the integers 8, 6, 7, 9, when multiplied by 8. We have then to write down the 2 as the first figure of the product,

---

* Ancestor of the fighting and writing Napiers of our day.

add 7 and 6 together = 13; write 3 as the next figure, carry 1 to add to the sum of 8 and 5, and so on.

The reason for dividing the figures in each square by a diagonal line, and for placing the left-hand figure higher than the right is, that the eye may be thus assisted in adding the carried figure of one slip to the unit of the next.

To provide for the occurrence of more than one of the same figures in the multiplicand, there should be several slips or rods for each of the digits.

In practice the rods are placed on a flat piece of wood, with two ridges at right angles, by which they are preserved in a proper position.

This instrument can be made useful in "divisions," by making by means of it a table of the product of the divisor, multiplied by each of the numbers 1 to 9.

### THE ARITHMETICAL BOOMERANG.

The boomerang is an instrument of peculiar form, used by the natives of New South Wales, for the purpose of killing wild fowl and other small animals. If projected forwards, it at first proceeds in a straight line, but afterwards rises in the air, and after performing sundry peculiar gyrations, returns in the direction of the place where it was thrown.

The term is applied to those arithmetical processes by which you can divine a number thought of by another. You throw forwards the number by means of addition and multiplication, and then, by means of subtraction and division, you bring it back to the original starting point, making it proceed in a track so circuitous as to evade the superficial notice of the tyro.

### TO FIND A NUMBER THOUGHT OF.
#### *First Method.*

This is an arithmetical trick which, to those who are unacquainted with it, seems very surprising; but, when explained, it is very simple. For instance, ask a person to *think* of any number under 10. When he says he has done so, desire him to treble that number. Then ask him whether the sum of the number he has thought of (now multiplied by 3) be odd or even; if odd, tell him to add 1 to make the sum even. He is next to halve the sum, and then treble that half. Again ask whether the amount be odd or even.

If odd, add 1 (as before) to make it even, and then halve it. Now ask how many nines are contained in the remainder. The secret is, to bear in mind whether the first sum be odd or even; if odd, retain 1 in the memory; if odd a second time, retain 2 more (making in all 3 to be retained in the memory;) to which add 4 for every nine contained in the remainder.

For example, No. 7 is odd the first and also the second time; and the remainder (17) contains one nine; so that 1, added to 2, make 3, and 3, added to 4, make 7, the number thought of. No. 1 is odd the first time (retain 1), and even the second (of which no notice is taken), but the remainder is not equal to nine. No. 2 is even the first and odd the second time (retain 2), but the remainder contains no nine. No. 3 is odd the first and the second time, still there is no nine in the remainder. No. 4 is even both times, and contains one nine. No. 5 is odd the first time and the remainder contains one nine. No. 6 is odd the second time, and contains one nine in the remainder. No. 8 is even both times, and the remainder contains two nines. No notice need be taken of any overplus of a remainder, after being divided by nine.

The following are illustrations of the result with each number:

```
   1        2        3        4       5        6       7        8       9
   3        3        3        3       3        3       3        3       3
  ───      ───      ───      ───     ───      ───     ───      ───     ───
   3      2)6        9     2)12      15     2)18      21     2)24      27
 Add 1     —      Add 1      —     Add 1      —     Add 1      —     Add 1
   —       3        —        6       —        9       —       12       —
 2)4       3     2)10        3     2)16       3     2)22        3    2)28
 ───      ───     ───       ───    ───       ───    ───        ───    ───
   2       9        5     2)18       8       27      11     2)36      14
 3 Add 1            3        —     3 Add 1            3       —        3
  ───     ───      ───      9)9     ───      ───     ───     9)18     ───
 2)6    2)10       15       —     2)24    2)28       33       —     2)42
   —      —      Add 1       1       —      — Add 1             2      —
   3       5       —              9)12    9)14       —              9)21
                 2)16              —       —      2)34              ───
                 ───                1       1       —                 2
                   8                              9)17
                                                  ───
                                                    1
```

## Second Method.

**EXAMPLE.**

Let a person think of a number, say - - 6
1. Let him multiply it by 3 - - - - 18
2. Add 1 - - - - - - - 19
3. Multiply by 3 - - - - - 57
4. Add to this the number thought of - - 63

Let him inform you what is the number produced; it will always end with 3. Strike off the 3, and inform him that he thought of 6.

## Third Method.

**EXAMPLE.**

Suppose the number thought of to be - - 6
1. Let him double it - - - - - 12
2. Add 4 - - - - - - - 16
3. Multiply by 6 - - - - - - 80
4. Add 12 - - - - - - - 92
5. Multiply by 10 - - - - - - 920

Let him inform you what is the number produced. You must in every case subtract 320; the remainder is, in this example, 600; strike off the two ciphers, and announce 6 as the number thought of.

## Fourth Method.

Desire a person to think of a number, say 6. He must then proceed—

**EXAMPLE.**

1. To multiply this number by itself - - 36
2. So take 1 from the number thought of - 5
3. To multiply this by itself - - - 25
4. To tell you the difference between this product and the former - - - - 11
You must then add 1 to it - - - - 12
And halve this number - - - - - 6
Which will be the number thought of.

## Fifth Method.

Desire a person to think of a number, say 6. He must then proceed as follows:

**EXAMPLE.**

1. Add 1 to it - - - - - - 7
2. Multiply by 3 - - - - 21
3. Add 1 again - - - - - - 22
4. Add the number thought of - - - 28

Let him tell you the figures produced (28):

5. You then subtract 4 from it - - - 24
6. And divide by 4 - - - - - - 6

Which you can say is the number thought of.

*Sixth Method.*

**EXAMPLE.**

Suppose the number thought of - - - - 6
1. Let him double it - - - - - 12
2. Desire him to add to this any number you tell him, say 4 - - - - - 16
3. To halve it - - - - - - 8

You can then tell him that if he will subtract from this the number he thought of, the remainder will be, in the case supposed, 2.

*Note.*—The remainder is always half of the number you tell him to add.

TO DISCOVER TWO OR MORE NUMBERS THAT A PERSON HAS THOUGHT OF

*1st Case.*—Where each of the numbers is less than 10. Suppose the numbers thought of were 2, 3, 5.

**EXAMPLE.**

1. Desire him to double the first number making - - - - - - 4
2. To add 1 to it - - - - - - 5
3. To multiply by 5 - - - - - - 25
4. To add the second number - - - 28

There being a third number, repeat this process—

5. To double it - - - - - - - 56
6. To add 1 to it - - - - - - 57
7. To multiply by 5 - - - - - 285
8. To add the third number - - - 290

And to proceed in the same manner for as many numbers as were thought of. Let him tell you the last sum produced (in this case 290). Then, if there were two numbers thought of, you must subtract 5; if three, 55; if four, 555. You must here subtract 55, leaving a remainder of 235, which are the numbers thought of, 2, 3 and 5

# THE MAGIC OF NUMBERS.

*2d Case.*—Where one or more of the numbers are 10, or more than 10, and where there is an *odd* number of numbers thought of.

Suppose he fixes upon five numbers, viz. 4, 6, 9, 15, 16.

He must add together the numbers as follows, and tell you the various sums:

 1. The sum of the 1st and 2d - - 10
 2. The sum of the 2d and 3d - - - 15
 3. The sum of the 3d and 4th - - 24
 4. The sum of the 4th and 5th - - - 31
 5. The sum of the 1st and last - - 20

You must then add together the 1st, 3d and 5th sums, viz. $10+24+20=54$, and the 2d and 4th, $15+31=46$; take one from the other, leaving 8. The half of this is the 1st number, 4; if you take this from the sum of the 1st and 2d you will have the 2d number, 6; this taken from the sum of the 2d and 3d will give you the 3d, 9; and so on for the other numbers.

*3d Case.*—Where one or more of the numbers are 10, or more than 10, and where an *even* number of numbers has been thought of.

Suppose he fixes on six numbers, viz. 2, 6, 7, 15, 16, 18. He must add together the numbers as follows, and tell you the sum in each case:—

 1. The sum of the 1st and 2d - - 8
 2. The sum of the 2d and 3d - - - 13
 3. The sum of the 3d and 4th - - 22
 4. The sum of the 4th and 5th - - 31
 5. The sum of the 5th and 6th - - 34
 6. The sum of the 2d and last - - - 24

You must then add together the 2d, 4th and 6th sums, $13+31+24=68$, and the 3d and 5th sums, $22+34=56$. Subtract one from the other, leaving 12; the 2d number will be 6, the half of this; take the 2d from the sum of the 1st and 2d you will get the 1st; take the 2nd from the sum of the 2d and 3d, and you will have the 3d, and so on.

### HOW MANY COUNTERS HAVE I IN MY HANDS?

A person having an equal number of counters in each hand, it is required to find how many he has altogether.

Suppose he has 16 counters, or 8 in each hand. Desire him to transfer from one hand to the other a certain number of them, and to tell you the number so transferred. Suppose it be 4, the hands now contain 4 and 12. Ask him how many times the smaller number is contained in the larger ; in this case it is 3 times. You must then multiply the number transferred, 4, by the 3, making 12, and add the 4, making 16 ; then divide 16 by the 3 *minus* 1 ; this will bring 8, the number in each hand.

In most cases fractions will occur in the process : when 10 counters are in each hand, and if 4 be transferred, the hands will contain 6 and 14.

He will divide 14 by 6 and inform you that the quotient is $2\frac{2}{6}$ or $2\frac{1}{3}$.

You multiply 4 by $2\frac{1}{3}$, which is $9\frac{1}{3}$.
Add 4 to this, making $13\frac{1}{3}$, equal to $\frac{40}{3}$.
Subtract 1 from $2\frac{1}{3}$, leaving $1\frac{1}{3}$ or $\frac{4}{3}$.
Divide $\frac{40}{3}$ by $\frac{4}{3}$, giving 10, the number in each hand.

### THE MYSTERIOUS HALVINGS.
*To tell the number a person has thought of.*

One of the company must fix upon any one of the numbers from 1 to 15 ; this he keeps secret, as well as the numbers produced by the succeeding operations :

| | |
|---|---:|
| Suppose he fixes on | 8 |
| He must add 1 to it, making | 9 |
| Triple it | 27 |
| Halve it*—1st *halving*—(*larger half*) | 14 |
| Triple it | 42 |
| Halve it—2d *halving* | 21 |
| Triple it | 63 |
| Halve it—3d *halving*—(*larger half*) | 32 |
| Triple it | 96 |
| Halve it—4th *halving*. | 48 |

He need not inform you that 48 is the figure produced, but he must let you know in which of the four halvings he was obliged to take a "larger half ;" having ascertained this point, you discover the number fixed upon in the following manner. Carry in your mind, or on a slip of paper, the following list of names in which the letter A occurs in one or more of the three syllables of all except the last.

* When an *exact half* cannot be taken without a fraction, he must take the *larger half*—you must tell him this before he commences. Here it is the *larger half*.

# THE MAGIC OF NUMBERS.

The three syllables are intended to represent the 1st, 2d, and 3d halvings, and the occurrence of the letter A corresponds to the occurrence of a "larger half" in one or more of these three halvings. Having been informed where the *larger half* was taken, refer to the word which has A in the corresponding syllable, and against it stand two numbers, one of which was the number thought of; and of these two, the right hand number is the correct one *if a larger half was taken in the 4th stage*, and the left hand one *if the 4th halving was exact*.

In the example given, a *larger half* occurred in the 1st and 3d stage; this points us to *Car-ro-way*, and the halving in the 4th stage being exact, shows us that 8 was the number fixed upon.

|  | If the 4th halving is *exact*. | If a *larger half* occurs in the 4th halving. |
|---|---|---|
| WAsh-ing-ton | 4 | 12 |
| LA-fAy-ette | 2 | 10 |
| CAr-row-wAy | 8 | 0 |
| MAn-hAt-tAn | 6 | 14 |
| Ger-mA-ny | 13 | 5 |
| Tel-e-grAph | 3 | 11 |
| Bo-nA-pArte | 1 | 9 |
| Long-fel-low | 15 | 7 |

It will be observed that there is always a difference of 8 between the numbers of the columns, so that it is necessary to recollect only one of them. Perhaps some of our readers who wish to be adepts in this game, would prefer recollecting the above table if put in this form:

| 2-3 | 1-2 | 3 | 1-2-3 | 1-3 | 2 | none |
|---|---|---|---|---|---|---|
| 1 | 2 | 3 | 4 | 8 | 13 | 15 |

where the upper line denotes the cases in which the "larger half" was taken, and the lower line the numbers of the left hand column above given.

### *Another Method.*

The person having chosen any number from one to fifteen, he is to add twenty-one to that number, and triple the amount. Then,

1st. He is to take half of that triple, and triple that half.

2nd. To take the half of the last triple, and triple that half.

3rd To take the half of the last triple.

14

4th, To take the half of the last half.

In this operation there are four distinct cases or stages where the half is to be taken. The three first are denoted by one of the eight following Latin words, each word being composed of three syllables, and the syllables containing the letter $i$ corresponding in numerical order with the cases where the half cannot be taken without a fraction; consequently, in those cases the person who makes the deduction is to add one to the number to be divided. The fourth case shows which of the two numbers corresponding to each word has been chosen. For if the fourth half can be taken without adding one, the number chosen is in the first, or left-hand column; but if not, it is in the second column to the right.

| The words. | The numbers denoted. | |
| --- | --- | --- |
| Mi-ser-is | 8 | 0 |
| Ob-tin-git | 1 | 9 |
| Ni-mi-um | 2 | 10 |
| No-tar-i | 3 | 11 |
| In-fer-nos | 4 | 12 |
| Or-di-nes | 13 | 5 |
| Ti-mi-di | 6 | 14 |
| Te-ne-ant | 15 | 7 |

*Example.*—Suppose the number chosen to be nine, to which is to be added one, making ten, and which last, being tripled, gives thirty. Then:

| | | |
| --- | --- | --- |
| 1st case. | The half of the triple is | 15 |
| | which tripled, makes | 45 |
| 2nd case | The half of tha triple, 1 being added to make an even number, is | 23 |
| | and that tripled, makes | 69 |
| 3rd case, | The half of the last triple, 1 being added, is | 35 |
| 4th case. | The half of the last half, 1 being again added, is | 18 |

Here we see, that in the second and third case, one had to be added, and, looking at the table, we find that the only corresponding word having an $i$ in its second and third syllables is *Ob-tin-git*, which represents the figures one and nine. Then, as one had to be added in the fourth case, we know by the rule, that the figure in the second column, 9,

# THE MAGIC OF NUMBERS. 211

is the one required. Observe, that if no addition be required at any of the four stages, the number thought of will be fifteen; and if one addition only be required at the fourth stage, the number will be seven.

## WHO WEARS THE RING?

This is an elegant application of the principles involved in discovering a number fixed upon. The number of persons participating in the game should not exceed nine. One of them puts a ring on one of his fingers, and it is your object to discover—1st. The wearer of the ring. 2d. The hand. 3d. The finger. 4th. The joint.

The company being seated in order the persons must be numbered 1, 2, 3, &c.; the thumb must be termed the first finger, the fore finger being the second; the joint nearest the extremity must be called the first joint; the right hand is one, and the left hand two.

These preliminaries having been arranged, leave the room in order that the ring may be placed unobserved by you. We will suppose that the third person has the ring on the right hand, third finger, and first joint; your object is to discover the figures 3131.

Desire one of the company to perform secretly the following arithmetical operations:

1. Double the number of the person who has the ring; in the case supposed, this will produce   6
2. Add 5   -   -   -   -   -   -   -   11
3. Multiply by 5   -   -   -   -   -   -   55
4. Add 10   -   -   -   -   -   -   -   65
5. Add the number denoting the hand   -   -   66
6. Multiply by 10   -   -   -   -   -   -   660
7. Add the number of the finger   -   -   -   663
8. Multiply by 10   -   -   -   -   -   -   6630
9. Add the number of the joint   -   -   -   6631
10. Add 35   -   -   -   -   -   -   -   6666

He must apprise you of the figures now produced, 6666; you will then in all cases subtract from it 3535; in the present instance there will remain 3131, denoting the person No. 3, the hand No. 1, the finger No. 3, and the joint No 1.

## PROBABILITIES.*

When we look around us at results happening daily, of the causes of which we are ignorant, we are led to regard them as isolated incidents subject to no law or rule; but could we see and understand the secret workings and connection existing between cause and effect, we might frequently discover that all works by rule. As it is, we may readily mark the boundaries, within which events must happen in very many instances; and do much to estimate their probability. We speak of *Chance* as something without plan or design, but taking in a large range, our calculations will approximate closely to the truth. When we throw a copper into the air, the chances of "heads or tails," as the boys say, are equal, and though one or the other may occur most frequently for a few throws, in a large number, say a thousand, the results will be about equally divided. In this case the sides of the coin must be equal in weight, else it will be like the grumbler's bread and butter:

"I never had a piece of bread,
    Particularly good and wide,
  But fell upon the sanded floor,
    And always on the buttered side."

Had he put on less butter, perhaps the sides would have been more equal in weight, and the probability of the buttered side being uppermost would have been increased. Disturbing causes unknown to us, may often shape the result; but in the absence of these, we may pretty accurately estimate our chances.

We see accidents from fire and flood, happening at times and points least expected; but the insurer has learned by observation to estimate probabilities, and by taking a wide range of country and a period of years, he does a comparatively safe business. Death takes the young and the old; but the life insurer has conned the bills of mortality, and studied the ages of those who have died, until he can estimate at once the probability of duration of life, and determine what he can afford to pay for an annuity contingent on life, or engage for a present sum, or an annual sum paid for life, to pay the heirs at the death of the insured. In one instance his estimate may fall short, and in another exceed, but the average will be about right.

* From Parkes' Philosophy of Arithmetic, a capital work published by Moss & Bro. Philadelphia.

So, too, the man who deals in lotteries and games of chance, knows the data and calculates carefully the probabilities, and though "luck" may sometimes be against him, his estimates of probabilities are based on mathematical principles, and he is secure in being ultimately the gaining party.

How these chances are calculated, depends on the data in each case, and it is not within the range of our present plan to attempt more than giving a general idea of the subject; and this with any one of ordinary prudence, will be sufficient to prevent all intermeddling with lotteries and every other species of gambling. The probabilities are always against the casual operator, even if all be conducted fairly; what then must they be when fraud and dishonesty are superadded? It is downright swindling!

In lottery schemes generally, fifteen per cent. is reserved as profit, but this is a small part of what may be secured; yet even this amounts to a great deal. If a man were to draw a prize nominally of $100,000, fifteen thousand would be deducted at once, and he would be entitled to only $85,000. It is true that in his good fortune he would not probably regard the abatement, but that does not change the principle.

## VARIATIONS.

It is obvious that if we have a number of single things arranged in any order, we may change the arrangement into a variety of forms, and in doing so, we may take all together, or we may take only part at once. For instance, we may arrange the six vowels, a e, i, o, u, y, in a great number of ways, as a, e i o u y, a i e o u y, e a i o u y, &c., &c.; or we may form them into groups, as ae, io, uy, ai, eu, oy, &c.; or, we may take three, four, five, or, as above, all at a time; and it is reasonable to suppose that the number of possible changes may, in all cases, be calculated.

When all are taken together, the operation is called *Permutation*; but if a part only be taken, it is called either a *Variation* or a *Combination;* a e, i o, u y, are distinct combinations, and are also considered one of the variations of two of which those six letters are susceptible; e a, o i, y u, are three other variations, but they are the same combinations; for a change of order will constitute a new variation but not a new combination; hence the number of variations will always exceed the number of combinations.

The doctrine of variations and combinations forms the

basis of many forms of lotteries, and of other calculations used in practical life.

## COMBINATIONS AND PERMUTATIONS.

"Combinations are the different ways in which a certain number of things can be selected out of a larger number, when taken 1 at a time, 2 at a time, or any other number each time, but without regard to the order in which the selected numbers can be arranged among themselves. The latter is the province of "Permutation," which refers to the different ways in which a number can be selected out of one that is larger, and, *in addition to this*, to the different ways of *grouping* these selected numbers.

Thus 4 things can be taken 2 at a time in 6 different ways; for instance, the letters a, b, c, d, can be taken 2 at a time thus, a and b, a and c, a and d, b and c, b and d, c and d; if we regard the *order* of the selected letters we shall find that these 4 letters are capable of 12 different permutations, as ab, ba, ac, ca, ad, da, bc, cb, bd, db, cd, dc.

If we selected 3 letters at a time we could make 4 different selections, and 24 different changes of grouping.

The rule to compute the number of these different ways is very simple, but sometimes involves a multitude of figures.

To determine the number of permutations, commence with unity, and multiply by the successive terms of the natural series 1, 2, 3, &c., until the highest multiplier shall express the number of individual things. The last product will indicate the number of possible changes.

*Example* 1. How many changes can be made in the arrangement of 5 grains of corn, all of different colors, laid in a row? *Solution.* $1 \times 2 \times 3 \times 4 \times 5 = 120$, *Ans.*

This may seem improbable, the number being so great, but if there were but a single grain more, the possible changes would be 720; and another would extend the limit to 5040; and so onward in a constantly increasing ratio. The reason, however, will be obvious on a little scrunity. If there were but one thing, as *a*, it would admit of but one position; but if two, as *a b*, it would admit of two positions, *ab, ba*. If three things, as *a b c*, then they will admit of $1 \times 2 \times 3 = 6$ changes, for the last two will admit of two variations, as *a b c, a c b*, and each of the three may successively be placed first, and two changes made to each of the others, so that 3×2=6, the number of possible changes. In the same way we may show that if there be four individual things, each one will be first in each of the six changes which the other three will undergo, and consequently, there will be 24 changes in all. In this way we might show that when there are 5 individual things, there will be 5 times as many changes as when there were but 4; and when 6, there will be 6 times as many changes as when there are only 5; and so on *ad infinitum*, according to the same law.

*Example* 2. In how many ways may a family of 10 persons seat themselves differently at dinner? *Ans.* 3,628,800.

When we consider that this would require a period of $9935\frac{55}{487}$ years, the mind is lost in astonishment. The story of the man who bought a horse at a farthing for the first nail in his shoe, a penny for the second, &c., is thrown into the shade; and we incline to doubt whether there is not some mistake; and yet on just such chances as one to all these, do gamblers constantly risk their money!

*Example* 3. I have written the letters contained in the word N I M R O D on 6 cards; being one letter on each, and having thrown them confusedly into a hat, I am offered $10 to draw the cards successively, so as to spell the name correctly. What is my chance of success worth? *Ans.* $1\frac{7}{18}$ cents.

*Example* 4. In order to form a lottery scheme, I have put into the wheel as many cards as I can put 4 letters of the word Charleston on, without having the same letters in the same order upon any two cards. I offer $100 to him who draws the card having on it the first four letters of the said word in their natural order (Char). What is the chance of drawing a prize worth?

There are 10 letters in the word, and the combination is of the 4th class; and, according to the mode of determining combinations with repetitions, we find the whole number of combinations of the 4th class which the word admits of is 210. Then he has one chance in 210 of drawing the letters Char, in *some* order. The number of permutations of four individual things is 1×2×3×4=24, and 210×24=5040 his chance of drawing them in the right order, and $100 divided by 5040 gives *Ans.* $1\frac{62}{63}$ cents.

Suppose that the numbers from 1 to 78, inclusive, be placed upon 78 cards, and the cards placed in a wheel by which they are thoroughly mixed; and then 13 cards be successively drawn out, by a person who has no means of choosing, and the numbers on them registered. Suppose also that tickets have been issued, containing each three of the 78 numbers, but no two having *all* the same numbers, and that he who holds the ticket having on it the first three drawn numbers in their regular order, shall be entitled to $100,000; what would the probability of drawing such a ticket be worth? *Ans.* 21 $\frac{5183}{5938}$ cents.

*Note.*—It is usual also, to give smaller prizes to the holders of tickets having the numbers in any order, or having any two or one of the drawn numbers. Lotteries may be arranged on a great diversity of plans, and in each the probability of drawing prizes will vary.

A speaks the truth 3 times in 4; B 4 times in 5, and C 6 times in 7. What is the probability of an event which A and B assert, and C denies? *Ans* $\frac{140}{143}$

Suppose a coin be thrown up, having two faces; what is the probability that the obverse (heads) side will fall upward, and what the reverse?

Here there are only two possible cases, and one favors each of the contingencies the probability of each will be $\frac{1}{1+1} = \frac{1}{2}$; there being no reason why one side should fall uppermost rather than the other.

What would be the probability of either side presenting upwards twice in two throws?

Here we have 4 possible cases, viz.:

   Obverse and reversé;
   Obverse both times;
   Reverse and obverse;
   Reverse both times.

Of the 4 possibilities there is only one which favors the turning up of the obverse twice in successsion, and the same is true of the reverse, hence the probability of either is only $\frac{1}{4}$.

In like manner we might show that the probability of the obverse presenting upwards three times in succession will be $\frac{1}{8}$, or $\frac{1}{2} \times \frac{1}{2} \times \frac{1}{2}$; the general principle being to multiply successively together the independent probabilities of an event for the fraction expressing the chance of all the events happening.

### THE VISITORS TO THE CRYSTAL PALACE.

In a family consisting of 8 young people, it was agreed that 3 at a time should visit the Crystal Palace, and that the visit should be repeated each day as long as a different trio could be selected. In how many days were the possible combinations of 3 out of 8 completed?

We must multiply $8 \times 7 \times 6$, and also $3 \times 2 \times 1$, and divide the product of the former, 336, by the product of the latter, 6; the result is 56, the number of visits, a different three going each time. So much gratified were they with the results of their agreement, that they wished to be allowed another series of visits, to be continued as many days as they could group 3 together in different order when starting. If Paterfamilias had granted such permission he would have had to wait 56 multiplied by $3 \times 2 \times 1$, or 336 days, before this "new series" of visits would have come to a *finis*.

### HOW MANY CHANGES CAN BE GIVEN TO 7 NOTES OF A PIANO?

That is to say, in how many ways can 7 keys be struck in succession, so that there shall be some difference in the order of the notes each time?

The result of multiplying
$$7 \times 6 \times 5 \times 4 \times 3 \times 2 \times 1$$
is 5,040, the number of changes.

### THE ARITHMETICAL TRIANGLE.

This name has been given to a contrivance said to have originated with the famous Pascal, or to have been perfected by him.

```
1
2   1
3   3    1
4   6    4    1
5  10   10    5    1
6  15   20   15    6    1
7  21   35   35   21    7    1
8  28   56   70   56   28    8    1
&c.                 &c.
```

This peculiar series of numbers is thus formed: Write down the numbers 1, 2, 3, &c., as far as you please, in a vertical row. On the right hand of 2 place 1, add them together, and place 3 under the 1; then 3 added to 3=6, which place under the 3; 4 and 6 are 10, which place under the 6, and so on as far as you wish. This is the second vertical row, and the third is formed from the second in a similar way.

This triangle has the property of informing us, without the trouble of calculation, how many combinations can be made, taking any number at a time out of a larger number.

Suppose the question were that just given; how many selections can be made of 3 at a time out of 8? On the horizontal row commencing with 8, look for the third number; this is 56, which is the answer.

### HOW MANY DIFFERENT DEALS CAN BE MADE WITH 13 CARDS OUT OF 52?

To discover this we must make a continued multiplication of $52 \times 51 \times 50 \times 49 \times 48 \times 47 \times 46 \times 45 \times 44 \times 43 \times 42 \times 41 \times 40$, being 13 terms for the 13 cards, also a continued multiplication of $13 \times 12 \times 11 \times 10 \times 9 \times 8 \times 7 \times 6 \times 5 \times 4 \times 3 \times 2 \times 1$; and having found the two products, we must divide one by the other, and the quotient is the number of different deals out of 52 cards. This "sum," that looks so formidable with natural figures, is a very short one by logarithms.

### THE THREE GRACES.

Three articles, or three names inscribed on cards, having been distributed between three persons, you are to tell which article or card each person has.

Designate the three persons in your own mind, as 1st, 2d, and 3d, and the three articles, A, E, I. Provide 24 counters, and give 1 to the first person, 2 to the 2d, 3 to the 3d. Place the remaining 18 on the table. Request that the three persons will distribute among themselves the three articles, and that, having done so, the person who has the one which you have secretly denoted by A, will take as many counters as he may have already; the holder of E must take twice as many as he may have; and the holder of I must take four times as many. Then leave the room, in order that the distribution of articles and of counters may be made unobserved by you. We will suppose that the three articles are three cards, on which are the words Clara, Rosa, Emily, which you will yourself secretly denote by the letters A, E, I. Suppose also that in the division the first person has Emily (I), the second has Clara (A), and the third has Rosa (E), then the 1st will take four times as many counters as he has (1), and will therefore take 4; the 2d will take as many as

THE MAGIC OF NUMBERS.  219

he has (2), and will therefore take 2 ; the 3d will take 6, being twice as many as he has (3). On the table will be left 6 counters. The distribution having been made, you will return and observe the number of counters on the table, from which you can find who is the holder of each card by the following method.

It is plain that if the cards held by the 1st and 2d can be told, that held by the 3d will be known. It will be found that only six numbers can remain, viz. 1, 2, 3, 5, 6, 7 ; never 4, and never more than 7. Now the 6 combinations of a, e, and i, here given, represent the articles held by the 1st and 2d persons.

| 1 | 2 | 3 | 4 | 5 | 6 | 7 |
|---|---|---|---|---|---|---|
| ae | ea | ai | — | ei | ia | ie |

In the case supposed, 6 counters being on the table, the combination *ia* indicates that the first person has the card you have called I (Emily), the 2d has A (Clara), so that the 3d has E (Rosa).

In order to recollect the combinations of A, E, and I, it will be best to keep in memory some 7 words which form a sentence, and which contain these vowels in the order just given.

Our young friends can amuse themselves in forming a sentence for themselves, but as examples we supply three.

| 1 | 2 | 3 | 4 | 5 | 6 | 7 |
|---|---|---|---|---|---|---|
| *a e* | *e a* | *a i* | — | *e i* | *i a* | *i e* |
| James | easy | admires | now | reigning | with a | bride. |
| Anger, | fear, | pain | | may | be hid | with a | smile. |
| Graceful | Emma, | charming | she | reigns | in all | circles. |

Or, if they prefer Latin, they can use the pentameter made up by the inventor of this beautiful pastime :

| 1 | 2 | 3 | 5 | 6 | 7 |
|---|---|---|---|---|---|
| Salve | certa | animæ | semita | vita | quies. |

### ANOTHER METHOD.

The performer must mentally distinguish the articles by the letters A, B, C, and the persons as 1st, 2d, and 3d. The persons having made their choice, give 12 counters to the 1st, 24 to the 2d, and 36 to the 3d. Then request the 1st person to add together the half of the counters of the person who has chosen A, the 3d of the person who has chosen B, and the 4th of those of the person who has chosen c, and then ask the sum, which must be either 23, 24, 25, 27, 28, or 29, as in the following table:

| First. | Second. | Third. | |
|---|---|---|---|
| 12 | 24 | 36 | |
| A | B | C | 23 |
| A | C | B | 24 |
| B | A | C | 25 |
| C | A | B | 27 |
| B | C | A | 28 |
| C | B | A | 29 |

This table shows that if the sum be 25, for example, the 1st person must have chosen B, the 2d A, and the 3d C; or if it be 28, the 1st must have chosen B, the 2d C, and the 3d A.

### ANOTHER METHOD.

Three things having been divided between three persons, you are to determine the holder of each.

Call the persons in your own mind 1st, 2d, 3d.

Give to the 1st a card on which you have written the number 12; to the 2d the number 24; to the 3d 36.

The three things you must denote as A, E, I.

To simplify it you may have three cards with a name upon each, of which the initial letters are A, E, I, as Anna, Emma, Isabel.

Request your friends to divide between them the three articles, and then to add together certain parts of the numbers on their cards, as follows:

Whoever has A must supply one half of the number on his card;

Whoever has E must supply one third;

Whoever has I must supply one fourth;

This half, third and fourth having been added together, the sum must be announced to you on your return; and from this number you can tell who has A, who has E, and who has I.

| If the No. is | the 1st has | the 2d has | the 3d has |
|---|---|---|---|
| 23 | A | E | I |
| 24 | A | I | E |
| 25 | E | A | I |
| 27 | I | A | E |
| 28 | E | I | A |
| 29 | I | E | A |

# THE MAGIC OF NUMBERS.

The sum which will be given to you can be one of six only. There are only six ways in which the articles can be divided, and there is a definite number for each of them.

The number 26 can never occur, and to recollect the six which do occur, and which you perceive are consecutive, you need take note only of what the 1st and 2d persons have.

        23    24    25    26    27    28    29
        ae    ai ·   ea    —    ia    ei    ie

If you make up a line of good (or bad) English, having the vowels in the order here given, you will find it will aid you in their recollection. We give one as a specimen:

        ae    ai    ea    —    ia    ei    ie
Brave dashing sea, like a giant revives itself.

## THE FORTUNATE NINTH.

A sharp youth, fresh from school, having gone to visit a good-natured uncle, the latter placed on a table fifteen fine oranges and fifteen apples, and desired his young friend to take half. He, not liking the apples, was about to take the fifteen oranges; but this monopoly of the best fruit being objected to, the old gentleman told him to range all the fruit in a circle, and to take every ninth. The clever fellow ranged them in such a way as that, by taking away every ninth, all the apples were left on the table, and all the oranges were transferred to his capacious pockets. How did he arrange them?

He placed them as in the margin, A representing apples, and O oranges; and it will be found that, by commencing at the four apples, and going round and round the circle, taking away every ninth, all the oranges will be removed, and all the apples will remain.

    If we let the vowels a e i o u
      denote the figures  1 2 3 4 5,

the arrangement of the figures 4, 5, 2, 1, &c., can be easily recollected by the following line:

    Our earth's final fate—enigma ever dark
    45  21     31  12    23   122   1

or,    Our dear Richard's tale begins at the sea.
        45   21    31     12   23    1  2  21

Our young friends may find amusement in forming lines for themselves as much superior to these as possible.

## THE TEN TENS.

Take ten pieces of card, and upon each write any ten words; there is no restriction as to the initial letter of nine of the words, but the last word on each card must commence with certain letters which you must in your own mind associate with the numbers 1 to 10, so that by knowing the initial letter of the last word on each card, you can determine its number.

Here are ten cards, (call these the *Selecting Cards*,) which we give by way of example, though our readers will perhaps prefer having words of their own selection.

| Jane. | Ellen. | George. | James. | Newton. |
|---|---|---|---|---|
| Mary. | Fanny. | William. | Clement. | Davy. |
| Matilda. | Caroline. | Frederick. | Edward. | Morse. |
| Sarah. | Isabel. | Robert. | Ralph. | Fulton. |
| Rosa. | Flora. | Edmund. | Francis. | Franklin. |
| Elizabeth. | Laura. | John. | Edwin. | Arago. |
| Harriet. | Maria. | Alfred. | Walter. | Spurzheim. |
| Ann. | Frances. | Albert. | Charles. | Laplace. |
| Emily. | Edith. | Henry. | Samuel. | Steers. |
| **E**mma. | **D**orothea. | **I**saac. | **T**heodore. | **H**erschel. |

| Sister. | Rose. | Friendship. | Putnam. | Clay. |
|---|---|---|---|---|
| Brother. | Violet. | Happiness. | Lafayette. | Webster. |
| Uncle. | Lupin. | Industry. | Steuben. | Calhoun. |
| Aunt. | Daisy. | Ambition. | Scott. | Benton. |
| Grandmother. | Tulip. | Energy. | Taylor. | Jefferson. |
| Grandfather. | Peony. | Fidelity. | Green. | Adams. |
| Nephew. | Hyacinth. | Affection. | Harrison. | Madison. |
| Niece. | Pink. | Hope. | Hamilton. | Jackson. |
| Cousin. | Snowdrop. | Justice. | Wayne. | Monroe. |
| **F**ather. | **L**ily. | **O**rder. | **W**ashington. | **N**apoleon. |

For these the key words are, "Edith Flown," so that the letters

                E D I T H F L O W N
Stand for     1 2 3 4 5 6 7 8 9 10

For the success of the game, the key words and the numbers denoted by their letters, must be carefully concealed.

Take ten other cards, which call the "*grouped cards*," and

upon one write down the first word from each of the selecting cards, being careful to write them in the same order. Let another card contain all the words which are second from the top, and so on till all the words have been grouped together. As an example, we give the 1st and 4th grouped cards.

| 1st. | 4th. |
|---|---|
| Jane. | Sarah. |
| Ellen. | Isabel. |
| George. | Robert. |
| James. | Ralph. |
| Newton. | Fulton. |
| Sister. | Aunt. |
| Rose. | Daisy. |
| Friendship. | Ambition |
| Putnam. | Scott. |
| Clay. | Benton. |

The object of the game is to guess which of the words from any of the *selecting cards* any person may have fixed upon.

Let any one choose a card out of the *selecting cards*, and after he has fixed upon a word, give it back to you; when receiving it, carefully note the last word upon it, which will give you, by the aid of the key word, the number of the card; this you must keep secret, and you then give him all the *grouped cards*, and request him to show you the cards which contain the words he fixed upon.

You can then announce the word; for the number of the word from the top on the grouped card is the same as the number of the selecting card, from which he made his choice.

Suppose he made his choice from the card which has Theodore for its last word—this is No. 4; when he shows you the grouped card, which he says contains the selected word, you will know that Ralph, the fourth from the top, is the name he fixed upon.

### DIVIDING THE BEER.

During the siege of Sebastopol, when the troops were on "short allowance," a can of eight pints of porter was ordered to be equally divided between two messes; but having only a five pint can, and one which held three pints, it was found impossible to make this division, till one of the clever sappers suggested the following method; and, to understand it, we will put down the contents of each of the three cans at each stage of the process; commencing with

|  | 8-pt. | 5-pt. | 3-pt. |
|---|---|---|---|
| The 8-pint can full, and the others empty, | 8 | 0 | 0 |
| 1. Filled the 5-pint can | 3 | 5 | 0 |
| 2. Filled the 3-pint can from the 5-pint | 3 | 2 | 3 |
| 3. Pour the contents of the 3-pint into the 8-pint | 6 | 2 | 0 |
| 4. Transfer the 2 pints from the 5-pint to the 3-pint | 6 | 0 | 2 |
| 5. Filled the 5-pint from the 8-pint | 1 | 5 | 2 |
| 6. Fill up the 3-pint from the 5-pint | 1 | 4 | 3 |
| 7. Poured the 3 pints into the 8-pint; completing the feat | 4 | 4 | 0 |

This was a dexterous expedient of the worthy sapper, the only objections to it being the time the thirty men had to wait, and the resulting flat condition of the beer.

### THE DIFFICULT CASE OF WINE.

A gentleman had a bottle containing 12 pints of wine, 6 of which he was desirous of giving to a friend; but he had nothing to measure it, except two other bottles, one of 7 pints, and the other of 5. How did he contrive to put 6 pints into the 7-pint bottle?

|  | 12-pt. | 7-pt. | 5-pt. |
|---|---|---|---|
| Before he commenced, the contents of the bottles were | 12 | 0 | 0 |
| 1. He filled the 5-pint | 7 | 0 | 5 |
| 2. Emptied the 5-pint into the 7-pint | 7 | 5 | 0 |
| 3. Filled again the 5-pint from the 12-pint | 2 | 5 | 5 |
| 4. Filled up the 7-pint from the 5 | 2 | 7 | 3 |
| 5. Emptied the 7-pint into the 12-pint | 9 | 0 | 3 |
| 6. Poured the 3 pints from the 5 into the 7 | 9 | 3 | 0 |
| 7. Filled the 5-pint from the 12-pint | 4 | 3 | 5 |
| 8. Filled up the 7-pint from the 5-pint | 4 | 7 | 1 |
| 9. Emptied the 7-pint into the 12-pint | 11 | 0 | 1 |
| 10. Poured 1 pint from the 5-pint into the 7-pint | 11 | 1 | 0 |
| 11. Filled the 5-pint from the 12-pint | 6 | 1 | 5 |
| 12. Poured the contents of the 5-pint into the 7-pint | 6 | 6 | 0 |

### ANOTHER DECIMATION OF FRUIT.

On the next visit of the youth to his uncle, the latter produced thirty apples and ten oranges, and offered him the

# THE MAGIC OF NUMBERS.

favorite oranges, if his nephew could arrange them in an oval, so that by taking every twelfth the apples should remain. But this he could not accomplish, and the old gentleman, being well versed in the "Recreations in Science," proceded to arrange them thus:

The places which the oranges here occupy can be easily remembered, being Nos. 7, 8, 11, 12, 21, 22, 24, 34, 36, 37.

### THE WINE AND THE TABLES.

A certain hotel-keeper was dexterous in contrivances to produce a large appearance with small means. In the dining-room were three tables, between which he could divide 21 bottles, of which 7 only were full, 7 half full, and 7 apparently just emptied, and in such a manner that each table had the same number of bottles, and the same quantity of wine. He did this in two ways:

| Table. | Full | Hf. full. | Empty. | Table. | Full. | Hf. full. | Empty |
|---|---|---|---|---|---|---|---|
| 1 . | 2 | 3 | 2 | 1 . | 3 | 1 | 3 |
| 2 . | 2 | 3 | 2 | 2 . | 3 | 1 | 3 |
| 3 . | 3 | 1 | 3 | 3 . | 1 | 5 | 1 |

He also performed a similar exploit with 24 bottles, 8 full, 8 half-full, and 8 empty:

| Table. | Full. | Hf. full. | Empty. | Table. | Full. | Hf. full. | Empty. |
|---|---|---|---|---|---|---|---|
| 1 . | 3 | 2 | 3 | 1 . | 2 | 4 | 2 |
| 2 . | 3 | 2 | 2 | 2 . | 2 | 4 | 2 |
| 3 . | 2 | 4 | 2 | 3 . | 4 | 0 | 4 |

Also with 27 bottles, 9 full, 9 half-full, and 9 empty:

| Table. | Full. | Hf. full. | Empty. | Table. | Full. | Hf. full. | Empty. |
|---|---|---|---|---|---|---|---|
| 1 . | 2 | 5 | 2 | 1 . | 1 | 7 | 1 |
| 2 . | 3 | 3 | 3 | 2 . | 4 | 1 | 4 |
| 3 . | 4 | 1 | 4 | 3 . | 4 | 1 | 4 |

### THE THREE TRAVELERS.

Three men met at a caravansary or inn, in Persia; and two of them brought their provision along with them, according to the custom of the country; but the third not having provided any, proposed to the others that they should eat together, and he would pay the value of his proportion. This being agreed to, A produced 5 loaves, and B 3 loaves, all of which the travelers ate together, and C paid 8 pieces of money as the value of his share, with which the others were satisfied, but quarreled about the division of it. Upon this the matter was referred to the judge, who decided impartially. What was his decision?

At first sight it would seem that the money should be divided according to the bread furnished; but we must consider that, as the 3 ate 8 loaves, each one ate $2\frac{2}{3}$ loaves of the bread he furnished. This from 5 would leave $2\frac{1}{3}$ loaves furnished the stranger by A; and $3-2\frac{2}{3}=\frac{1}{3}$ furnished by B, hence $2\frac{1}{3}$ to $\frac{1}{3}=7$ to 1, is the ratio in which the money is to be divided. If you imagine A and B to furnish, and C to consume all, then the division will be according to amounts furnished.

### WHICH COUNTER HAS BEEN THOUGHT OF OUT OF SIXTEEN?

Take sixteen pieces of card, and number them 1 to 16 Arrange them in two rows, as at A B.

| A | B | C | B | D | M | E | B | F | N | G | B | H |
|---|---|---|---|---|---|---|---|---|---|---|---|---|
| 1 | 9 | 1 | 9 | 2 | 2 | 2 | 9 | 4 | 2 | 2 | 9 | 6 |
| 2 | 10 | 3 | 10 | 4 | 4 | 6 | 10 | 8 | 6 | 1 | 10 | 5 |
| 3 | 11 | 5 | 11 | 6 | 6 | 1 | 11 | 3 | 1 | 4 | 11 | 8 |
| 4 | 12 | 7 | 12 | 8 | 8 | 5 | 12 | 7 | 5 | 3 | 12 | 7 |
| 5 | 13 | | 13 | | 1 | | 13 | | 4 | | 13 | |
| 6 | 14 | | 14 | | 3 | | 14 | | 8 | | 14 | |
| 7 | 15 | | 15 | | 5 | | 15 | | 3 | | 15 | |
| 8 | 16 | | 16 | | 7 | | 16 | | 7 | | 16 | |

Desire a person to think of one of the numbers, and to tell you in which row it is. Suppose he fixes on 6; he will tell you that the row A contains the number he thought of.

Take up the row A, and arrange the numbers on each side of the row B, as shown at C D, so that the first number of the row A may be the first of the row C; the second of A be the first of D, the third of A be the second of C, and so on.

Ask in which of the rows, C or D, is the number thought of: in the case supposed it is in D.

Take up the rows C D, and put one underneath the other, as at M, taking care that the half-row in which is the number thought of, shall be above the other.

Divide it again into two rows, as at E F, on each side of B, in the same way as before. Ask again in which row it is: it is now in E.

Place one row under the other, as at N, and divide again into two rows, which will now be as G H.

You will be informed that the number is in row H, and you may then announce it to be the top number of that row.

The number thought of will always be *at the top of one of the rows after three transpositions.* If there were 32 counters it would be at the top after four transpositions.

### MAGIC SQUARES.

The name "Magic Square" is given to a square divided into several smaller squares, in which numbers are placed in such a manner that every column of numbers, whether vertical, horizontal, or from corner to corner, shall amount to the same sum.

They are divided into three principal classes: 1st, Those which have an odd number of squares in each band; 2d, Those which have an even number of squares in each band, this even number being divisible exactly by 4; 3d, Where the even number of squares in each band cannot be divided by 4 without a fraction.

### ODD MAGIC SQUARES.

Squares of this kind are formed thus. Imagine an exterior line of squares above the magic square you wish to form, and another exterior line on the right hand of it These two imaginary lines are shown in the figure.

Then attend to the two following rules:

1st. In placing the numbers in the squares we must go in an ascending oblique direction from left to right; any number which, by pursuing this direction, would fall into the exterior line, must be carried along that line of squares, whether vertical or horizontal, to the last square. Thus, 1 having been placed in the center of the top line, (see the first table on p. 228,) 2 would fall into the exterior square above the fourth vertical line; it must be therefore carried down to the lowest square of that line; then, ascending obliquely 3 falls into the square, but four falls out of it, to the end of a horizontal line, and it must be carried along that line to the extreme left, and there placed. Resuming our oblique ascension to the right, we place 5, where the reader sees it, and would place 6 in the middle of the top band, but finding it occupied by 1, we look for direction to the

|    |    |    |    |    |
|----|----|----|----|----|
| 17 | 24 | 1  | 8  | 15 |
| 23 | 5  | 7  | 14 | 16 |
| 4  | 6  | 13 | 20 | 22 |
| 10 | 12 | 19 | 21 | 3  |
| 11 | 18 | 25 | 2  | 9  |

| 30 | 39 | 48 | 1  | 10 | 19 | 28 |
|----|----|----|----|----|----|----|
| 38 | 47 | 7  | 9  | 18 | 27 | 29 |
| 46 | 6  | 8  | 17 | 26 | 35 | 37 |
| 5  | 14 | 16 | 25 | 34 | 36 | 45 |
| 13 | 15 | 24 | 33 | 42 | 44 | 4  |
| 21 | 23 | 32 | 41 | 43 | 3  | 12 |
| 22 | 31 | 40 | 49 | 2  | 11 | 20 |

2d Rule, which prescribes that, when in ascending obliquely, we come to a square already occupied, we must place the number, which according to the first rule should go into that occupied square, directly under the last number placed Thus, in ascending with 4, 5, 6, the 6 must be placed directly under the 5, because the square next to 5 in an oblique direction is "engaged."

Magic squares of this class, however large in the number of compartments, can be easily filled up by attending to these two rules.

We give opposite, a seven-placed square.

There are various other kinds of magic squares; but explanations of them would be too lengthy for our work.

The invention of these contrivances has been traced back to the early ages of science, and talismanic properties were attributed to them. Modern philosophers have amused themselves in bringing them to perfection, and none has contributed so much as "the model of practical wisdom," Dr. Franklin.

### THE SQUARE OF GOTHAM.

The wise men of Gotham, famous for their eccentric blunders, once undertook the management of a school; they arranged their establishment in the form of a square divided into 9 rooms. The playground occupied the center, and 24 scholars the rooms around it, 3 being in each. In spite of the strictness of discipline, it was suspected that the boys were in the habit of playing truant, and it was determined to set a strict watch. To assure themselves that all the boys were on the premises, they visited the rooms, and found three in each, or 9 in each row. Four boys then went out, and the wise men soon after visited the rooms, and finding 9 in each row, thought all was right. The four boys then came back, accompanied by four strangers; and the Gothamites, on their third round, finding still 9 in each row, entertained no suspicion of what had taken place. Then 4 more "chums" were admitted; but the clever men, on examining the establishment a fourth time, still found 9 in each row, and so came to an opinion that their previous suspicions had been unfounded. How was all this possible?

The following figures represent the contents of each room at the four different visits; the first, at the commencement of the watch; the second, when four had gone out; the third, when these 4 accompanied by another 4, had returned; and the fourth, when 4 more had joined them.

|     | I.  |     |     | II. |     |     | III.|     |     | IV. |     |
| --- | --- | --- | --- | --- | --- | --- | --- | --- | --- | --- | --- |
| 3   | 3   | 3   | 4   | 1   | 4   | 2   | 5   | 2   | 1   | 7   | 1   |
| 3   |     | 3   | 1   |     | 1   | 5   |     | 5   | 7   |     | 7   |
| 3   | 3   | 3   | 4   | 1   | 4   | 2   | 5   | 2   | 1   | 7   | 1   |

On each change the boys arranged themselves in the rooms in such a manner that, when the corner rooms were counted as a part of two rows, each entire row of three rooms contained the same number of boys. The illusion of the wise men was due to their mistake in counting each corner room twice.

### THE MATHEMATICAL BLACKSMITH.

A blacksmith had a stone weighing 40 lbs. A mason coming into the shop, hammer in hand, struck it and broke it into four pieces. "There," says the smith, "you have ruined my weight." "No," says the mason, "I have made it better, for whereas you could before weigh but 40 lbs. with it, now you can weigh every pound from 1 to 40." Required size of the pieces?

*Ans.* 1, 3, 9, 27; for in any geometrical series proceeding in a triple ratio, each term is 1 more than twice the sum of all the preceding, and the above series might proceed to any extent. In using the weights, they must be put in one or both scales as may be necessary: as to weigh 2, put 1 in one scale, and 3 in the other.

### CURIOUS PROPERTIES OF SOME FIGURES.

Select any two numbers you please, and you will find that one of the two, their amount when added together, or their difference, is always 3, or a number divisible by 3.

Thus, if the numbers are 3 and 8, the first number is 3; let the numbers be 1 and 2, their sum is 3; let them be 4 and 7, the difference is 3. Again, 15 and 22, the first number is divisible by 3: 17 and 26, their difference is divisible by 3, &c.

All the odd numbers above 3, that can only be divided by 1, can be divided by 6, by the addition or subtraction of a unit. For instance, 13 can only be divided by 1; but after deducting 1, the remainder can be divided by 6; for example, $5+1=6$; $7-1=6$; $17+1=18$; $19-1=18$; $25-1=24$, and so on.

If you multiply 5 by itself, and the quotient again by itself, and the second quotient by itself, the last figure of each quotient will always be 5. Thus $5\times 5=25$; $25\times 25=125$; $125\times 125=625$, &c. Again, if you proceed in the same manner with the figure 6, the last figure will constantly be 6; thus, $6\times 6=36$; $36\times 36=216$; $216\times 216=1,296$, and so on.

To multiply by 2 is the same as to multiply by 10 and divide by 5.

Any number of figures you may wish to multiply by 5, will give the same result if divided by 2—a much quicker operation than the former; but you must remember to annex a cipher to the answer where there is no remainder, and where there is a remainder, annex a 5 to the answer. Thus, multiply 464 by 5, the answer will be 2320; divide the same number by 2, and you have 232, and as there is no remainder you add a cipher. Now, take 357, and multiply by 5—the answer is 1785. On dividing 357 by 2, there is 178, and a remainder; you therefore place 5 at the right of the line, and the result is again 1785.

There is something more curious in the properties of the number 9. Any number multiplied by 9 produces a sum of figures which, added together, continually makes 9. For example, all the first multiples of 9, as 18, 27, 36, 45, 54, 63, 72, 81, sum up 9 each. Each of them multiplied by any number whatever produces a similar result; as 8 times 81 are 648, these added together make 18, 1 and 8 are 9. Multiply 648 by itself, the product is 419,904—the sum of these digits is 27, 2 and 7 are 9. The rule is invariable. Take any number whatever and multiply it by 9; or any multiple of 9, and the sum will consist of figures which, added together, continually number 9. As $17\times 18=306$, 6 and 3 are 9; $117\times 27=3,159$, the figures sum up 18, 8 and 1 are 9; $4591\times 72=330,552$, the figures sum up 18, 8 and 1 are 9. Again, $87,363\times 54=4,717,422$; added together the product is 27, or 2 and 7 are 9, and so always. If any row of two or more figures be reversed and subtracted from itself, the figures composing the remainder, will, when added horizontally, be a multiple of nine:

```
    42            886           326
    24            688          1623
   ———          ———          ————
 18–9×2.       198–9×2.      1638–9×2.
```

If a multiplicand be formed of the digits in their regular order, omitting the 8, a multiplier may be found by a rule, which will give a product, each figure of which shall be the same. Thus if 12345679 be given, and it be required to find a multiplier which shall give the product all in 2, that multiplier will be 18 : if in 3, the multiplier will be 27 : if all 4, it will be 36—and so forth.

```
   12345679       12345679       12345679
         18             27             36
   ————         ————         ————
   98765432       86419753       74074074
   12345679       24691358       37037037
   ————         ————         ————
  222222222      333333333      444444444
```

The rule by which the multiplier is discovered (but which we do not attempt to explain) is this : Multiply the last figure (the 9) of the multiplicand by the figure of which you wish the product to be composed, and that number will be the required multiplier. Thus, when it was required to have the product composed of 2, the 2 multiplied by 9 gives 18, the multiplier : 3 multiplied by 9 gives 27, the multiplier to give the product in 3 ; &c.

If a figure, with a number of ciphers attached to it, be divided by 9, the quotient will be composed of one figure only, namely, the first figure of the dividend, as—

```
   9)600,000              9)40,000
   ————                 ————
    66,666–6               4,444–4
```

If any sum of figures can be divided by 9 as, $\begin{cases} 9)549 \\ \overline{\phantom{00}61\phantom{00}} \end{cases}$

the amount of these figures, when added together, can be divided by 9 :—thus, 5, 4, 9, added together, make 18, which is divisible by 9. If the sum 549 is multiplied by any figure, the product can also be divided by 9, as—

## THE MAGIC OF NUMBERS.

```
    549 ⎫                                       ⎧  3
      6 ⎪                                       ⎪  2
 ────── ⎪   And the amount of the figures of    ⎨  9
 9)3294 ⎬   the product can also be divided by  ⎪  4
 ────── ⎪   9 ; thus,                           ⎪ ──
    366 ⎪                                       ⎪ 2)18
        ⎭                                       ⎩  9
```

To multiply by 9, add a cipher, and deduct the sum that is to be multiplied : thus,

```
 43,260 ⎫                            ⎧  4,326
  4,326 ⎬ Produces the same result as⎨      9
 ────── ⎪                            ⎪ ──────
 38,934 ⎭                            ⎩ 38,934
```

In the same manner, to multiply by 99, add two ciphers; by 999, three ciphers, &c. These properties of the figure 9 will enable the young arithmetician to perform an amusing trick, quite sufficient to excite the wonder of the uninitiated.

Any series of numbers that can be divided by 9, as 365, 472,821,754, &c., being shown, a person may be requested to multiply secretly either of these series by any figure he pleases, to strike out one number of the quotient, and to let you know the figures which remain, in any order he likes; you will then, by the assistance of the knowledge of the above properties of 9, easily declare the number which has been erased. Thus, suppose 365,472 are the numbers chosen, and the multiplier is six; if then, 8 is stuck out, the numbers returned to you will be

```
           ⎧ 2
           ⎪ 1
 365472    ⎪ 9
      6    ⎨ 2
 ──────    ⎪ 3
 219232    ⎪ 2
           ⎪ ──
           ⎩ 19
```

The amount of these numbers is 19; but 19, divided by 9, leaves a remainder of 1; you, therefore, want 8 to complete another 9 : 8, then, is the number erased.

The component figures of the product made by the multiplication of every digit into the number 9, when added together, make NINE.

The order of these component figures is reversed after the said number has been multiplied by 5.

The component figures of the amount of the multipliers (viz. 45,) when added together, make NINE.

The amount by the several products, or multiples of 9 (viz. 405) when divided by 9, gives for a quotient, 45; that is, 4+5=NINE.

The amount of the first product (viz. 9,) when added to the other product, whose respective component figures make 9, is 81; which is the square of NINE.

The said number 81, when added to the above mentioned amount of the several products, or multiples of 9 (viz. 405) makes 486, which, if divided by 9, gives for a quotient 54; that is, 5+4=NINE.

It is also observable, that the number of changes that may be rung on nine bells is 362,880; which figures, added together, make 27; that is, 2+7=NINE.

And the quotient of 362,880, divided by 9, will be 40,320; that is 4+0+3+2+0=NINE.

If number 37 be multiplied by any of the progressive numbers arising from the multiplication of 3 with any of the units, the figures in the quotient will be similar, and the result may be known beforehand by merely inspecting the progressive numbers, thus, 3, 6, 9, 12, 15, 18, 21, 24, 27, &c., are the progressive numbers formed by 3 multiplied by the units 1 to 9; and the result of the multiplication of any of these numbers with 37 may be seen in the following examples :—$37\times3=111$; $37\times6=222$; $37\times12=444$; $37\times24=888$; by which it appears that the numbers of which the quotient is formed are the same as the units by which number 3 was multiplied to obtain the respective progressive numbers. Thus—3 multiplied by 2 is equal to 6, and 37 multiplied by 9 is equal to 222; so, again, 4 multiplied by 3 produces 12, and 37 multiplied by 12 is equal to 444, and so on.

### THE INDUSTRIOUS FROG

There was a well 30 feet deep, and at the bottom a frog anxious to get out. He got up 3 feet per day, but regularly fell back 2 feet at night. Required the number of days necessary to enable him to get out?

The frog appears to have cleared one foot per day, and at the end of 27 days, he would be 27 feet up, or within 3 feet of the top, and the next day he would get out. He would therefore be 28 days getting out.

## THE COUNCIL OF TEN.

Ten cards or counters, numbered from one to ten, or the first ten playing cards of any suit disposed in a circular form may be employed with great convenience for performing this feat. The accompanying figure shows the cards thus arranged, number one, or the ace, designated by A, and the ten by K.

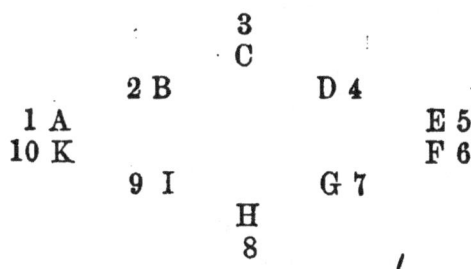

Having placed the cards in the above order, desire a bystander to think of a card or number, and when he has done so, to touch any other card or number. Request him then to add to the number of the card touched the number of the cards employed, which in this case is ten. Then desire him to count the sum in an order contrary to that of the natural numbers, beginning at the card he touched, and assigning it the number of the card he thought of. By counting in this manner, he will end at the number or card he thought of, and consequently you will immediately know it.

Thus, for example, suppose the person had thought of 3 C, and touched 6 F; then, if 10 be added to 6, the sum will be 16; and if that number be counted from F, the number touched, towards E D B C A, and so on, in the retrograde order, counting F three, the number thought of, E five, D six, and so round to sixteen, that number will terminate at C, showing that the person thought of 3, the number which corresponds to C.

A greater or less number of cards or counters may be employed at pleasure; but in every instance the whole number of cards must be added to the number of the card touched.

## THE TWO TRAVELERS.

Two travelers trudged along the road together,
Talking, as Yankees do, about the weather;

When, lo! beside their path the foremost spies
Three casks, and loud exclaims "A prize, a prize!"
One large, two small, but all of various size.
This way and that they gazed, and all around,
Each wondering if an owner might be found:
But not a soul was there—the coast was clear,
So to the barrels they at once drew near,
And both agree whatever may be there
In friendly partnership they'll fairly share.
Two they find empty, but the other full,
And straightway from his pocket one doth pull
A large clasp-knife. A heavy stone lay handy,
And thus in time they found their prize was brandy.
'Tis tasted and approved: their lips they smack,
And each pronounces 't is the famed Cognac.
"Won't we have many a jolly night, my boy!
May no ill luck our present hopes destroy!"
'T was fortunate one knew the mathematics,
And had a smattering of hydrostatics;
Then measured he the casks, and said, "I see
This is eight gallons, those are five and three."
The question then was how they might divide
The brandy, so that each should be supplied
With just four gallons, neither less nor more.
With eight, and five, and three they puzzle sore,
Filled up the five—filled up the three, in vain;
At length a happy thought came o'er the brain
Of one: 'twas done, and each went home content,
And their good dames declared 'twas excellent.
With those three casks they made division true;
I found the puzzle out, say, friend, can you?

The five-gallon barrel was filled first, and from that the three-gallon barrel, thus leaving two gallons in the five-gallon barrel; the three-gallon barrel was then emptied into the eight-gallon barrel, and the two gallons poured from the five-gallon barrel into the empty three-gallon barrel; the five-gallon barrel was then filled, and one gallon poured into the three-gallon barrel, therefore leaving four gallons in the five-gallon barrel, one gallon in the eight-gallon barrel, and three gallons in the three-gallon barrel, which was then emptied into the eight-gallon barrel. Thus each person had four gallons of brandy in the eight and five-gallon barrels respectively.

## ARITHMETICAL PUZZLE.

If from 6 you take 9, and from 9 you take 10; and if 50 from 40 be taken, there will just half a dozen remain.

### ANSWER.

| From SIX | From IX | From XL |
| Take IX | Take X | Take L |
| ——— | ——— | ——— |
| S | I | X Remains. |

## THE MONEY GAME.

A person having in one hand a piece of gold, and in the other a piece of silver, you may tell in which hand he has the gold, and in which the silver, by the following method: Some value, represented by an even number, such as 8, must be assigned to the gold; and a value represented by an odd number, such as three, must be assigned to the silver; after which, desire the person to multiply the number in the right hand by any even number whatever, such as 2, and that in the left by an odd number, as 3; then bid him add together the two products, and if the whole sum be odd, the gold will be in the right hand, and the silver in the left; if the sum be even, the contrary will be the case.

To conceal the artifice better, it will be sufficient to ask whether the sum of the two products can be halved without a remainder; for in that case the total will be even, and in the contrary case odd.

It may be readily seen, that the pieces, instead of being in the two hands of the same person, may be supposed to be in the hands of two persons, one of whom has the even number, or piece of gold, and the other the odd number, or piece of silver. The same operations may then be performed in regard to these two persons, as are performed in regard to the two hands of the same person, calling the one privately the right, and the other the left.

## THE PHILOSOPHER'S PUPILS.

To find a number of which the half, fourth, and seventh added to three shall be equal to itself.

This was a favorite problem among the ancient Grecian arithmeticians, who stated the question in the following manner: "Tell us, illustrious Pythagoras, how many pupils frequent thy school?" "One half," replied the philosopher, "study mathematics, one fourth natural philosophy, one seventh observe silence, and there are three females besides."

The answer is, 28 : 14+7+4+3=28.

### TO DISCOVER A SQUARE NUMBER.

A square number is a number produced by the multiplication of any number into itself; thus, 4 multiplied by 4 is equal to 16, and 16 is consequently a square number, 4 being the square root from which it springs. The extraction of the square root of any number takes some time; and after all your labor you may perhaps find that the number is not a square number. To save this trouble, it is worth knowing that every square number ends either with a 1, 4, 5, 6, or 9, or with two cyphers, preceded by one of these numbers.

Another property of a square number is, that if it be divided by 4, the remainder, if any, will be 1—thus, the square of 5 is 25, and 25 divided by 4 leaves a remainder of 1; and again, 16, being a square number, can be divided by 4 without leaving a remainder.

### THE SHEEP-FOLD.

A farmer had a pen made of 50 hurdles, capable of holding 100 sheep only; supposing he wanted to make it sufficiently large to hold double that number, how many additional hurdles would he have occasion for?

*Answer.*—Two. There were 24 hurdles on each side of the pen; a hurdle at the top, and another at the bottom; so that, by moving one of the sides a little back, and placing an additional hurdle at the top and bottom, the size of the pen would be exactly doubled.

### COUNTRYWOMAN AND EGGS.

A countrywoman carried eggs to a garrison, where she had three guards to pass, sold to the first guard half the number she had, and half an egg more; to the second, the half of what remained, and half an egg besides; and to the third guard she sold the half of the remainder, and half another egg. When she arrived at the market-place, she had three dozen still to sell; how was this possible, without breaking any of the eggs? It would seem at the first view that this is impossible, for how can half an egg be sold without breaking any of the eggs? The possibility of this seeming

## THE MAGIC OF NUMBERS. 239

impossibility will be evident, when it is considered, that by taking the greater half of an odd number, we take the exact half $+\frac{1}{2}$. When the countrywoman passed the first guard, she had 295 eggs; by selling to that guard 148, which is the half $+\frac{1}{2}$, she had 147 remaining; to the second guard she disposed of 74, which is the major half of 147; and, of of course, after selling 37 out of 74 to the last guard, she had still three dozen remaining.

### HOW TO RUB OUT TWENTY CHALKS AT FIVE TIMES, RUBBING OUT EVERY TIME AN ODD ONE.

To do this trick, you must make twenty chalks, or long strokes, upon a board, as in the margin:

Then begin and count backwards, as 20, 19, 18, 17, rub out these four; then proceed saying, 16, 15, 14, 13, rub out these four; and begin again, 12, 11, 10, 9, and rub out these; and proceed again, 8, 7, 6, 5, then rub out these; and lastly say, 4, 3, 2, 1, when these four are rubbed out. The whole twenty are rubbed out at five times, and every time an odd one, that is, 17th, 13th, 9th, 5th, and 1st.

This is a trick which, if once seen, may be easily retained; and the puzzle at first is, it not occurring immediately to the mind to begin to rub them out backwards. It is as simple as any thing possibly can be.

### THE IMPOSSIBLE TRIANGLE

The longest side of a triangle is 100 rods; and each of the other sides 50. Required the value of the grass at $5 per acre.

This is a catch question, as a triangle cannot be formed unless any two of the lines are longer than the third.

### ODD OR EVEN

Every odd number multiplied by an odd number produces an odd number; every odd number multiplied by an even number produces an even number; and every even number multiplied by an even number also produces an even number. So, again, an even number added to an even number, and an odd number added to an odd number, produce an even number; while an odd and even number added together produce an odd number.

If any one holds an odd number of counters in one hand, and an even number in the other, it is not difficult to discover in which hand the odd or even number is. Desire the party to multiply the number in the right hand by an even number, and that in the left hand by an odd number, then to add the two sums together, and tell you the last figure of the product; if it is even, the odd number will be in the right hand; and if odd, in the left hand; thus, supposing there are 5 counters in the right hand, and 4 in the left hand, multiply 5 by 2, and 4 by 3, thus: $5 \times 2 = 10$, $4 \times 3 = 12$, and then adding 10 to 12, you have $10 + 12 = 22$, the last figure of which, 2, is even, and the odd number will consequently be in the right hand.

THE FIGURES, UP TO 100, ARRANGED SO AS TO MAKE 505 IN EACH COLUMN, WHEN COUNTED IN TEN COLUMNS PERPENDICULARLY, AND THE SAME WHEN COUNTED IN TEN FILES HORIZONTALLY.

| 10  | 92 | 93 | 7  | 5  | 96 | 4  | 98 | 99 | 1  |
|-----|----|----|----|----|----|----|----|----|----|
| 11  | 19 | 18 | 84 | 85 | 86 | 87 | 13 | 12 | 90 |
| 71  | 29 | 28 | 77 | 76 | 75 | 24 | 23 | 22 | 80 |
| 70  | 62 | 63 | 37 | 36 | 35 | 34 | 68 | 69 | 31 |
| 41  | 52 | 53 | 44 | 46 | 45 | 47 | 58 | 59 | 60 |
| 51  | 42 | 43 | 54 | 56 | 55 | 57 | 48 | 49 | 50 |
| 40  | 32 | 33 | 67 | 65 | 66 | 64 | 38 | 39 | 61 |
| 30  | 79 | 78 | 27 | 26 | 25 | 74 | 73 | 72 | 21 |
| 81  | 89 | 88 | 14 | 15 | 16 | 17 | 83 | 82 | 20 |
| 100 | 9  | 8  | 94 | 95 | 6  | 97 | 3  | 2  | 91 |

Each of these files, when added up, makes 505.

Each of these ten columns, when added up, makes 505.

### THE OLD WOMAN AND HER EGGS.

At a time when eggs were scarce, an old woman who possessed some remarkably good-laying hens, wishing to oblige her neighbors, sent her daughter round with a basket of eggs to three of them; at the first house, which was the squire's, she left half the number of eggs she had and half a one over; at the second she left half of what remained and half an egg over; and at the third she again left half of the remainder, and half a one over; she returned with one egg in her basket, not having broken any. Required— the number she set out with. *Ans.* 15 eggs.

## THE MATHEMATICAL FORTUNE TELLER.

Procure six cards, and having ruled them the same as the following diagrams, write in the figures neatly and legibly.

It is required to tell the number thought by any person, the numbers being contained in the cards, and such numbers not to exceed 60. How is this done?

| 3 | 5 | 7 | 9 | 11 | 1 |
|---|---|---|---|----|---|
| 13 | 15 | 17 | 19 | 21 | 23 |
| 25 | 27 | 29 | 31 | 33 | 35 |
| 37 | 39 | 41 | 43 | 45 | 47 |
| 49 | 51 | 53 | 55 | 57 | 59 |

| 5 | 6 | 7 | 13 | 12 | 4 |
|---|---|---|----|----|---|
| 14 | 15 | 20 | 21 | 22 | 23 |
| 28 | 29 | 30 | 31 | 36 | 37 |
| 52 | 38 | 39 | 44 | 45 | 46 |
| 47 | 53 | 54 | 55 | 60 | 13 |

| 9 | 10 | 11 | 12 | 13 | 8 |
|---|----|----|----|----|---|
| 14 | 15 | 24 | 25 | 26 | 27 |
| 28 | 29 | 30 | 31 | 40 | 41 |
| 42 | 43 | 44 | 45 | 46 | 47 |
| 56 | 57 | 58 | 59 | 60 | 13 |

| 3 | 6 | 7 | 10 | 11 | 2 |
|---|---|---|----|----|---|
| 14 | 15 | 18 | 19 | 22 | 23 |
| 26 | 27 | 30 | 31 | 34 | 35 |
| 38 | 39 | 42 | 43 | 46 | 47 |
| 50 | 51 | 54 | 55 | 58 | 59 |

| 17 | 18 | 19 | 20 | 21 | 16 |
|----|----|----|----|----|----|
| 22 | 23 | 24 | 25 | 26 | 27 |
| 28 | 29 | 30 | 31 | 48 | 49 |
| 50 | 51 | 52 | 53 | 54 | 55 |
| 56 | 57 | 58 | 59 | 30 | 60 |

| 33 | 34 | 35 | 36 | 37 | 32 |
|----|----|----|----|----|----|
| 38 | 39 | 40 | 41 | 42 | 43 |
| 44 | 45 | 46 | 47 | 48 | 49 |
| 50 | 51 | 52 | 53 | 54 | 55 |
| 56 | 57 | 58 | 59 | 60 | 41 |

Request the person to give you the cards containing the number, and then add the right hand upper corner figures together, which will give the correct answer. For example: suppose 10 is the number thought of, the cards with 2 and 8 in the corners will be given, which makes the answer 10, and so on with the others.

### THE DICE GUESSED UNSEEN.

A pair of dice being thrown, to find the number of points on each die without seeing them. Tell the person who cast the dice to double the number of points upon one of them, and add 5 to it; then to multiply the sum produced by 5, and to add to the product the number of points upon the other die. This being done, desire him to tell you the amount, and, having thrown out 25, the remainder will be a number consisting of two figures, the first of which, to the left, is the number of points on the first die, and the second figure, to the right, the number on the other. Thus:

Suppose the number of points of the first die which comes up to be 2, and that of the other 3; then, if to four, the double of the points of the first, there be added 5, and the sum produced, 9, be multiplied by 5, the product will be 45; to which, if 3, the number of points on the other die, be added, 48 will be produced, from which, if 25 be subtracted, 23 will remain; the first figure of which is 2, the number of points on the first die, and the second figure 3, the number on the other.

### THE SOVEREIGN AND THE SAGE.

A sovereign being desirous to confer a liberal reward on one of his courtiers, who had performed some very important service, desired him to ask whatever he thought proper, assuring him it should be granted. The courtier, who was well acquainted with the science of numbers, only requested that the monarch would give him a quantity of wheat equal to that which would arise from one grain doubled sixty-three times successively. The value of the reward was immense; for it will be found by calculation that the sixty-fourth term of the double progression divided by 1, 2, 4, 8, 16, 32, &c., is 9223372036854775808. But the sum of all the terms of a double progression, beginning with 1, may be obtained by doubling the last term, and subtracting from it 1. The number of the grains of wheat, therefore, in the present case, will be 18446744073709551615. Now, if a pint contain 9216 grains of wheat, a gallon will contain 73728; and, as eight gallons make one bushel, if we divide the above result by eight times 73728 we shall have 31274997411295 for the number of the bushels of wheat equal to the above number of grains, a quantity greater than what the whole surface of the earth could produce in several years, and which in value would exceed all the riches, perhaps, on the globe.

### THE KNOWING SHEPHERD.

A shepherd was going to market with some sheep, when he met a man who said to him, "Good morning, friend, with your score." "No," said the shepherd, "I have not a score; but if I had as many more, half as many more, and two sheep and a half, I should have just a score." How many sheep had he?

He had 7 sheep: as many more 7; half as many more, $3\frac{1}{2}$; and $2\frac{1}{2}$; making in all 20.

### THE CERTAIN GAME.

Two persons agree to take, alternately, numbers less than a given number, for example, 11, and to add them together till one of them has reached a certain sum, such as 100. By what means can one of them infallibly attain to that number before the other?

The whole artifice in this consists in immediately making choice of the numbers 1, 12, 23, 34, and so on, or of a series which continually increases by 11, up to 100. Let us suppose that the first person, who knows the game, makes choice of 1; it is evident that his adversary, as he must count less than 11, can at most reach 11, by adding 10 to it. The first will then take 1, which will make 12; and whatever number the second may add the first will certainly win, provided he continually add the number which forms the complement of that of his adversary to 11; that is to say, if the latter take 8, he must take 3; if 9, he must take 2; and so on. By following this method he will infallibly attain to 89, and it will then be impossible for the second to prevent him from getting first to 100; for whatever number the second takes he can attain only to 99; after which the first may say—" and 1 makes 100." If the second take 1 after 89, it would make 90, and his adversary would finish by saying—" and 10 make 100." Between two persons who are equally acquainted with the game, he who begins must necessarily win.

## THE ASTONISHED FARMER.

A and B took each 30 pigs to market, A sold his at 3 for a dollar, B at 2 for a dollar, and together they received $25. A afterwards took 60 alone, which he sold *as before*, at 5 for $2, and received but $24; what became of the other dollar?

This is rather a catch question, the insinuation that the first lot were sold at the rate of five for $2, being only true in part. They commence selling at that rate, but after making ten sales, A's pigs are exhausted, and they have received $20: B still has 10 which he sells at "2 for a dollar" and of course receives $5; whereas had he sold them at the rate of 5 for $2, he would have received but $4. Hence the difficulty is easily settled.

## MAGICAL CENTURY.

If the number 11 be multiplied by any one of the nine digits, the two figures of the product will always be alike, as appears in the following example:—

| 11 | 11 | 11 | 11 | 11 | 11 | 11 | 11 | 11 |
|----|----|----|----|----|----|----|----|----|
| 1  | 2  | 3  | 4  | 5  | 6  | 7  | 8  | 9  |
| 11 | 22 | 33 | 44 | 55 | 66 | 77 | 88 | 99 |

Now, if another person and yourself have fifty counters a-piece, and agree never to stake more than ten at a time, you may tell him that if he permit you to stake first, you always complete the even century before him.

In order to succeed, you must first stake 1, and remembering the order of the above series, constantly add to what he stakes as many as will make one more than the numbers 11, 22, 33, &c., of which it is composed, till you come to 89, after which your opponent cannot possibly reach the even century himself, or prevent you from reaching it.

If your opponent has no knowledge of numbers, you may stake any other number first, under 10, provided you subsequently take care to secure one of the last terms, 56, 67, 78, &c.; or you may even let him stake first, if you take care afterward to secure one of these numbers.

This exercise may be performed with other numbers; but, in order to succeed, you must divide the number to be attained by a number which is a unit greater than what you can stake each time, and the remainder will then be the number you must first stake. Suppose, for example, the number to be attained be 52 (making use of a pack of cards instead of counters), and that you are never to add more than 6; then, dividing 52 by 7, the remainder, which is 3, will be the number which you must first stake; and whatever your opponent stakes, you must add as much to it as will make it equal to 7, the number by which you divided, and so in continuation.

### THE UNLUCKY HATTER.

A blackleg passing through a town in Ohio, bought a hat for $8 and gave in payment a $50 bill. The hatter called on a merchant near by, who changed the note for him, and the blackleg having received his $42 change went his way. The next day the merchant discovered the note to be a counterfeit, and called upon the hatter, who was compelled forthwith to borrow $50 of another friend to redeem it with; but on turning to search for the blackleg he had left town, so that the note was useless on the hatter's hands. The question is, what did he lose—was it $50 besides the hat, or was it $50 including the hat?

This question is generally given with names and circumstances as a real transaction, and if the company knows such persons so much the better, as it serves to withdraw attention from the question; and in almost every case the first impression is, that the hatter lost $50 besides the hat, though it is evident he was paid for the hat, and had he kept the $8 he needed only to have borrowed $42 additional to redeem the note.

### THE BASKET OF NUTS.

A person remarked that when he counted over his basket of nuts, two by two, three by three, four by four, five by five, or six by six, there was one remaining; but when he counted them by sevens, there was no remainder. How many had he?

The least common multiple of 2, 3, 4, 5, and 6 being 60, it is evident, that if 61 were divisible by 7, it would answer the conditions of the question. This not being the case, however, let $60 \times 2 + 1$, $60 \times 3 + 1$, $60 \times 4 + 1$, &c., be tried successively, and it will be found that $301 = 60 \times 5 + 1$, is divisible by 7; and consequently this number answers the conditions of the question. If to this we add 420, the least common multiple of 2, 3, 4, 5, 6 and 7, the sum 721 will be another answer; and by adding perpetually 420, we may find as many answers as we please.

### THE UNITED DIGITS.

Arrange the figures 1 to 9 in such order that, by adding them together, they amount to 100.

```
   15
   36
   47
   ──
   98
    2
   ──
  100
```

### DECEMBER AND MAY.

An old man married a young woman; their united ages amounted to C. The man's age multiplied by 4 and divided by 9, gives the woman's age. What were their respective ages?

ANSWER.—The man's age, 60 years 12 weeks; the woman's age, 30 years 40 weeks.

### THE TWO DROVERS.

Two drovers, A and B, meeting on the road, began discoursing about the number of sheep they each had. Says B to A, "Pray give me one of your sheep and I will have as many as you." "Nay," replied A, "but give me one of your sheep and I will have as many again as you." Required to know the number of sheep they each had?

A had seven and B had five sheep.

### THE BASKET AND STONES.

If a hundred stones be placed in a straight line, at the distance of a yard from each other, the first being at the same distance from a basket, how many yards must the person walk who engages to pick them up, one by one, and put them into the basket? It is evident that, to pick up the first stone, and put it into the basket, the person must walk two yards; for the second, he must walk four; for the third, six: and so on increasing by two, to the hundredth.

The number of yards, therefore, which the person must walk will be equal to the sum of the progression, 2, 4, 6, &c., the last term of which is 200 (22). But the sum of the progression is equal to 202, the sum of the two extremes, multiplied by 50, or half the number of terms: that is to say, 10,100 yards, which makes more than 5½ miles.

### THE FAMOUS FORTY-FIVE.

How can number 45 be divided into four such parts that, if to the first part you add 2, from the second part you subtract 2, the third part you multiply by 2, and the fourth part you divide by 2, the sum of the addition, the remainder of the subtraction, the product of the multiplication, and the quotient of the division be all equal?

The 1st is  8; to which add 2, the sum is       10
The 2nd is 12; subtract     2, the remainder is 10
The 3rd is  5; multiplied by 2, the product is  10
The 4th is 20; divided by   2, the quotient is  10
—
45

Required to subtract 45 from 45, and leave 45 as a remainder?

SOLUTION.—$9+8+7+6+5+4+3+2+1=45$
$1+2+3+4+5+6+7+8+9=45$
—————————————
$8+6+4+1+9+7+5+3+2=45$

### SUBTRACTION.

From 1 mile subtract 7 furlongs, 39 rods, 5 yards, 1 foot, 5 inches.

|      | miles, | furlongs, | rods, | yards, | feet, | inches. |
|------|---|----|----|---|---|---|
| From | 1 | 0  | 0  | 0 | 0 | 0 |
| Take | 0 | 7  | 39 | 5 | 1 | 5 |
|      | 0 | 0  | 0  | 0 | 0 | 1 |

In this problem, instead of borrowing 1 foot, we borrow ½ a foot = 6 inches, from which we take 5 inches, and 1 remains; we then carry ½ to 1, and borrowing ½ a yard = 1½ feet, we have 1½ from 1½ = 0, and afterwards proceed as usual.

### THE EXPUNGED FIGURE.

In the first place desire a person to write down secretly, in a line, any number of figures he may choose, and add them together as units; having done this, tell him to subtract that sum from the line of figures originally set down; then desire him to strike out any figure he pleases, and add the remaining figures in the line together as units, (as in the first instance,) and inform you of the result, when you will tell him the figure he has struck out.

```
76542-24
    24
―――――
 76518
```

Suppose, for example, the figures put down are 76542; these, added together, as units, make a total of 24: deduct 24 from the first line, and 76518 remain; if 5, the center figure be struck out, the total will be 22. If 8, the first figure be struck out, 19 will be the total.

In order to ascertain which figure has been struck out, you make a mental sum one multiple of 9 higher than the total given. If 22 be given as the total, then 3 times 9 are 27, and 22 from 27 show that 5 was struck out. If 19 be given, that sum deducted from 27 shows 8.

Should the total be equal multiplies of 9, as 18, 27, 36, then 9 has been expunged.

With very little practice any person may perform this with rapidity, it is therefore needless to give any further examples. The only way in which a person can fail in solving this riddle is, when either the number 9 or a cipher is struck out, as it then becomes impossible to tell which of the two it is, the sum of the figure in the line being an even number of nines in both cases.

### THE MYSTERIOUS ADDITION.

It is required to name the quotient of five or three lines of figures—each line consisting of five or more figures—only seeing the first line before the other lines are even put down. Any person may write down the first line of figures for you. How do you find the quotient?

EXAMPLE.—When the first line of figures is set down, subtract 2 from the last right-hand figure, and place it before the first figure of the line, and that is the quotient for five lines. For example, suppose the figures given are 86,214, the quotient will be 286,212. You may allow any person to put down the two first and the fourth lines, but you must always set down the third and fifth lines, and in doing so, always make up 9 with the line above, as in the following example:

## THE MAGIC OF NUMBERS.   249

```
      86,214
      42,680
      57,319
      62,854
      37,145
      ------
Qt.  268,212

      67,856
      47,218
      52,781
      ------
Qt.  167,855
```

Therefore in the annexed diagram you will see that you have made 9 in the third and fifth lines with the lines above them. If the person desire to put down the figures should set down a 1 or 0 for the last figure, you must say we will have another figure, and another, and so on until he sets down something above 1 or 2.

In solving the puzzle with three lines, you subtract 1 from the last figure, and place it before the first figure, and make up the third line yourself to 9. For example: 67,856 is given, and the quotient will be 167,855, as shown in the above diagram.

### TO TELL AT WHAT HOUR A PERSON INTENDS TO RISE.

Let the person set the hand of the dial of a watch at any hour he pleases, and tell you what hour that is; and to the number of that hour you add in your mind 12; then tell him to count privately the number of that amount upon the dial, beginning with the next hour to that on which he proposes to rise, and counting backwards, first reckoning the number of the hour at which he has placed the hand. For example:

Suppose the hour at which he intends to rise be 8, and that he has placed the hand at 5; you will add 12 to 5, and tell him to count 17 on the dial, first reckoning 5, the hour at which the index stands, and counting backwards from the hour at which he intends to rise; and the number 17 will necessarily end at 8, which shows that to be the hour he chose.

### TO FIND THE DIFFERENCE BETWEEN TWO NUMBERS, THE GREATEST OF WHICH IS UNKNOWN.

Take as many nines as there are figures in the smallest number, and subtract that sum from the number of nines. Let another person add the difference to the largest number, and taking away the first figure of the amount add it to the last figure, and that sum will be the difference of the two numbers.

For example: John, who is 22, tells Thomas, who is older, that he can discover the difference of their ages; he therefore privately deducts 22 from 99 (his age consisting of two figures, he of course takes two nines); the difference, which is 77, he tells Thomas to add to his age, and to take away the first figure from the amount, and add it to the last figure and that will be the difference of their ages; thus,

The difference between John's age and 99 is......77
To which Thomas adding his age..................35
                                                 ———
The sum is........................., 112
Then by taking away the first figure 1, and adding it to the figure 2, the sum is............ .13
Which add to John's age................... ..22
                                                 ———
Gives the age of Thomas......................35

### THE REMAINDER.

A very pleasing way to arrive at an arithmetical sum, without the use of either slate or pencil, is to ask a person to think of a figure, then to double it, then add a certain figure to it, now halve the whole sum, and finally to subtract from that the figure first thought of. You are then to tell the thinker what is the remainder.

The key to this lock of figures is, that HALF of whatever sum you request to be added during the working of the sum IS THE REMAINDER. In the example given, five is the half of ten, the number requested to be added. Any amount may be added, but the operation is simplified by giving only even numbers, as they will divide without fractions.

*Example.*

Think of.................................. 7
Double it.................................14
Add 10 to it..............................10
                                          ———
Halve it.............................2)24

Which will leave..........................12
Subtract the number thought of.............7
                                          ———
THE REMAINDER will be......................5

A PERSON HAVING AN EQUAL NUMBER OF COUNTERS, OR PIECES OF MONEY, IN EACH HAND, TO FIND HOW MANY HE HAS ALTOGETHER.

Request the person to convey any number, as 4, for example, from the one hand to the other, and then ask how many times the less number is contained in the greater. Let us

# THE MAGIC OF NUMBERS.

suppose that he says the one is the triple of the other; and, in this case, multiply 4, the number of the counters conveyed, by 3, and add to the product the same number, which will make 16. Lastly, take 1 from 3, and if 16 be divided by the remainder 2, the quotient will be the number contained in each hand, and consequently the whole number is 16.

This curious problem deserves another example. Let us again suppose that 4 counters are passed from one hand to the other, and the less number is contained in the greater $2\frac{1}{3}$ times. In this case, we must, as before, multiply 4 by $2\frac{1}{3}$, which will give $9\frac{1}{3}$; to which, if 4 be added, we shall have $13\frac{1}{3}$, or $\frac{40}{3}$; if 1, then, be taken from $2\frac{1}{3}$, the remainder will be $1\frac{1}{3}$, or $\frac{4}{3}$, by which, if $\frac{40}{3}$ be divided, the quotient 10 will be the number of counters in each hand.

### THE THREE JEALOUS HUSBANDS.

Three jealous husbands, A, B, and C, with their wives, being ready to pass by night over a river, find at the water side a boat which can carry but two at a time, and for want of a waterman they are compelled to row themselves over the river at several times. The question is how those six persons shall pass, two at a time, so that none of the three wives may be found in the company of one or two men, unless her husband be present?

This may be effected in two or three ways; the following may be as good as any: Let A and wife go over—let A return—let B's and C's wives go over—A's wife returns—B and C go over—B and wife return, A and B go over—C's wife returns, and A's and B's wives go over—then C comes back for his wife. Simple as this question may appear, it is found in the works of Alcuin, who flourished a thousand years ago, hundreds of years before the art of printing was invented.

### THE FALSE SCALES.

A cheese being put into one of the scales of a false balance, was found to weigh 16 lbs., and when put into the other only 9 lbs. What is the true weight?

The true weight is a mean proportional between the two false ones, and is found by extracting the square root of their product. Thus $16 \times 9 = 144$; and square root $144 = 12$ lbs., the weight required

## THE APPLE WOMAN.

A poor woman, carrying a basket of apples, was met by three boys, the first of whom bought half of what she had, and then gave her back 10; the second boy bought a third of what remained, and gave her back 2; and the third bought half of what she had now left, and returned her 1; after which she found she had 12 apples remaining. What number had she at first?

From the 12 remaining, deduct 1, and 11 is the number she sold the last boy, which was half she had; her number at that time, therefore, was 22. From 22 deduct two, and the remaining 20 was $\frac{2}{3}$ of her prior stock, which was therefore 30. From 30 deduct 10, and the remainder 20 is half her original stock; consequently she had at first 40 apples.

## THE GRACES AND MUSES.

The three Graces, carrying each an equal number of oranges, were met by the nine Muses, who asked for some of them; and each Grace having given to each Muse the same number, it was then found that they had all equal shares. How many had the Graces at first?

The least number that will answer this question is twelve; for if we suppose that each Grace gave one to each Muse, the latter would each have three, and there would remain three for each Grace. (Any multiple of 12 will answer the conditions of the question.)

## THE JESUITICAL TEACHER.

A teacher, having fifteen young ladies under her care, wished them to take a walk each day of the week. They were to walk in five divisions of three ladies each, but no two ladies were to be allowed to walk together twice during the week. How could they be arranged to suit the above conditions?

| SUN. | MON. | TUES. | WEDN. | THURS. | FRID. | SAT. |
|---|---|---|---|---|---|---|
| a b c | a d g | a k n | a e l | a h o | a f p | a i m |
| d e f | b e h | b l o | b f m | b i p | b d n | b g k |
| g h i | c m p | c f i | c g n | c d k | c h l | c e o |
| k l m | f k o | d h m | d i o | e m n | e i k | d l p |
| n o p | i l n | e g p | h k p | f g l | g m o | h f n |

# THE MAGIC OF NUMBERS. 253

## QUAINT QUESTIONS.

What is the difference between twenty four quart bottles, and four and twenty quart bottles?
*Ans.*—56 quarts difference.

What three figures, multiplied by 4, will make precisely 5 ?
*Ans.*—$1\frac{1}{4}$, or 1·25.

What is the difference between six dozen dozen, and half-a-dozen dozen?
*Ans.*—792: Six dozen dozen being 864, and half-a-dozen dozen, 72.

Place three sixes together, so as to make seven.
*Ans.*—$6\frac{6}{6}$.

Add one to nine and make it twenty.
*Ans.* IX—cross the *I*, it makes XX.

Place four fives so as to make six and a half. *Ans.* $5\frac{5}{5}$ ·5

A room with eight corners had a cat in each corner, seven cats before each cat, and a cat on every cat's tail. What was the total number of cats? *Ans.* Eight cats.

Prove that seven is the half of twelve. *Ans.*—Place the Roman figures on a piece of paper, and draw a line through the middle of it, the upper will be VII.

## THE FOX, GOOSE AND CORN.

A countryman having a Fox, a Goose, and a peck of Corn, came to a river, where it so happened that he could carry but one over at a time. Now as no two were to be left together that might destroy each other, he was at his wit's end, for says he "Though the corn can't eat the goose, nor the goose eat the fox; yet the fox can eat the goose, and the goose eat the corn" How shall he carry them over, that they shall not destroy each other?

Let him first take over the Goose, leaving the Fox and Corn; then let him take over the Fox and bring the Goose back; then take over the Corn; and lastly take over the Goose again.

## MULTIPLYING MONEY BY MONEY.

Amongst the various questions that are given for the purpose of puzzling the unwary arithmetician, the multiplication of money by money is one of the most curious : take for instance the following problems :

Multiply £99 19s. 11¾d. by £99 19s. 11¾d.
Multiply £11 11s. 11d. by £11 11s. 11d.

To the uninitiated they usually appear easy of solution but the various modes of working them out, and the different results obtained, prove that there is something absurd and wrong in the questions themselves. Some reduce all to farthings, and after multiplying one term by the other, return the product into pounds, shillings, and pence. Others convert them into decimals; whilst some work the problem in the style of duodecimals.

Having sufficiently puzzled the tyros, the querist remarks: "The problem itself is absurd, it is incapable of solution; for what is the nature of the product of pounds, shillings, and pence multiplied by pounds, shillings and pence? We know that a yard multiplied by a yard is a square yard, but who can tell what is a penny multiplied by a penny, or a penny by a pound?"

Now all this is quite correct, provided the question is limited, as above to the product of pounds, shillings, and pence, into pounds, shillings, and pence; put suppose the problem were put in this form—If a capital of £1 produces by compound interest, in a certain time, £99 19s. 11¾d., how much would be produced by a capital of £99 19s. 11¾d? It is evident that, to answer this, we must multiply £99 19s. 11¾d. by £99 19s. 11¾d.: these are in fact the second and, third terms of an ordinary "rule of three;" and though one of the terms is a "concrete" quantity of pounds, shillings, and pence, the other must be regarded as an "abstract" mathematical quantity, being 99 and a fraction, of which the number of farthings in a pound is the denominator, 960, and the number of farthings in the third term is the numerator, 959; or, instead of this, the shillings and pence might be converted into decimals of a pound, or into aliquot parts. The product of multiplying £99 19s. 11¾d. by $99\frac{959}{960}$ is £9,999 15s. $10\frac{1}{3840}d.$; the quickest way of doing this, is to multiply by 100, and to subtract from the product the 960th part of the multiplicand.

In the other question proposed, the product of £11 11s. 11d. into £11 11s. 11d., or $11\frac{143}{240}$, is £134 9s. $3\frac{49}{140}d.$

Number and value are distinct abstract ideas, and cannot, without committing a logical absurdity, be confused. To multiply is to repeat a certain number of *times*, and it is ob-

# THE MAGIC OF NUMBERS.

viously impossible to bring *value* into the question. Value is arbitrary; number is fixed. Put it in this way, and the absurdity is evident: One pound is equivalent to 20 shillings, or 240 pence, or 960 farthings. In value there is no difference whatever; but what an enormous difference between multiplying by 1, 20, 240, or 960 !

## THE UNFAIR DIVISION.

A gentleman rented a farm, and contracted to give to his landlord $\frac{2}{5}$ of the produce; put prior to the time of dividing the corn, the tenant used 45 bushels. When the general division was made, it was proposed to give to the landlord 18 bushels from the heap, in lieu of his share of the 45 bushels which the tenant had used, and then to begin and divide the remainder as though none had been used. Would this method have been correct ?

The landlord would lose $7\frac{1}{5}$ bushels by such an arrangement, as the rent would entitle him to $\frac{2}{5}$ of the 18. The tenant should give him 18 bushels from his own share after the division is completed, otherwise the landlord would receive but $\frac{2}{5}$ of the first 63 bushels.

## A POPULAR FALLACY.

It is often suggested from the pulpit and elsewhere, that enough persons have lived and died in the world to cover its whole surface with bodies; and even two or three strata deep. Is this probable?

Say the earth has existed 6000 years, the population always having been 800,000,000, and the average life of man 30 years; this being the utmost that could be claimed. Allow then the State of Virginia to contain 70,000 square miles, and each grave to occupy a space of 6 feet by 2; the territory of the State would contain 162,624,000,000; while the mighty army of the dead would number only 160,000,000,000; leaving 2,624,000,000 graves yet unoccupied. How wide of truth then is the position often set forth so positively !

# TRICKS IN GEOMETRY.

> "Let young beginners come and try
> Their hands at our geometry."

The word Geometry is derived from the Greek, and signifies the art of measuring land. The invention of it is ascribed by some to the Chaldeans and Babylonians, by others to the Egyptians, who were obliged to determine the boundaries of their fields after the inundation of the Nile, by geometrical measurements. According to Cassiodorus, the Egyptians either derived the art from the Babylonians, or invented it after it was known to them. Thales, a Phœnician, who died 548 years B. C., and Pythagoras of Samos, who flourished about 520 B. C., introduced it from Egypt into Greece. In elementary geometry, Euclid of Alexandria, as everybody knows, is particularly distinguished. Archimedes measured the sphere, and after him other philosophers prosecuted the science with the utmost assiduity. In Italy, where the sciences first revived after the dark ages, several mathematicians were distinguished in the 16th century. The French, and after them the Germans, followed; while in England, Hook, Newton, and others, carried the science to the highest pitch of usefulness, and through its aid made the most prodigious discoveries. It is not, however, our province to enter into a long disquisition on the subject, but simply to set before the young reader some of the more curious properties of the science, that he may be excited to study it for himself; and we will promise him that should he devote his mind to its study, he will be amply repaid for any amount of labor he may bestow upon it.

## GEOMETRICAL DEFINITIONS.

In geometry a *point* is said to have neither breadth, length, nor thickness. A *line* is the distance between two points; parallel lines always keep at the same distance from each other. A *right* line is what is commonly called a straight

# TRICKS IN GEOMETRY.

line. A *curve* is a line which continually changes its direction. An *angle* is the inclination or opening of two lines meeting in a point. A *figure* is a bounded space, and is either a superficies or a solid. A *triangle* is a figure with three sides and three angles. A *square* has four equal sides, and four right angles. A *circle* is a plane figure bounded by a curved line running into itself. Its diameter is a straight line drawn from one extremity of its circumference to the other, and its center is equally distant from every part of the circumference. A *solid* is any body which has length, breadth, and thickness; and a sphere is a solid, terminated by a convex surface, every part of which is at an equal distance from a point within, called its center.

## THE FIVE GEOMETRICAL SOLIDS.

The following figures will show how the five geometrical solids may be cut out of a piece of cardboard. Where the lines are drawn the board is to be partly cut through with a penknife, so as to render the angles of the models as sharp and as straight as possible. The edges which require

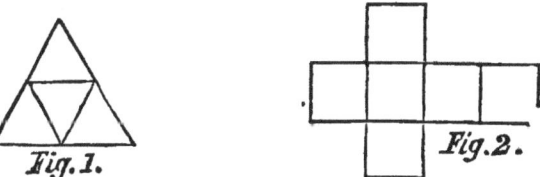

joining are to be fastened together with a slip of thin paper and gum dissolved in just sufficient water to bring it to the consistence of treacle. Fig. 1 will form a tetrahedron, a

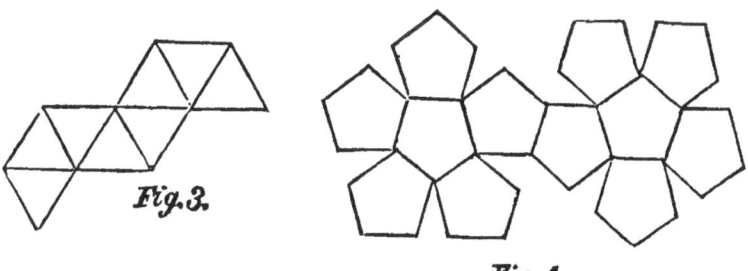

figure with four sides, each shaped like an equilateral triangle. Fig. 2 forms a cube or hexahedron. Fig. 3 an octohedron, with eight triangular sides. Fig. 4, a dodecahedron, with twelve sides shaped like pentagons, with five equal

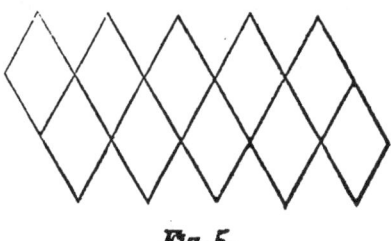

*Fig. 5.*

sides. Fig. 5, an isocahedron, with twenty sides, formed of equilateral triangles

HOW TO MAKE FIVE SQUARES INTO A LARGE ONE WITHOUT ANY WASTE OF STUFF.

Suppose you have five squares of cloth, or anything else, as in Fig. 7; find the center of one side of four of these

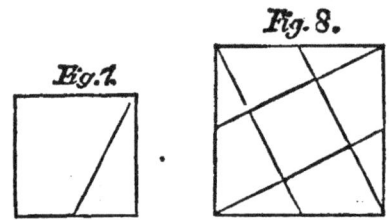

squares, and cut them from that point to the opposite corner, then place the perfect square in the centre, and the other pieces round, as seen in Fig. 8.

DECEPTIVE VISION.

The following sleight shows how easily the eye may be deceived. Take a piece of pasteboard, an inch and a half in width, and five inches in length, and divide it by inked

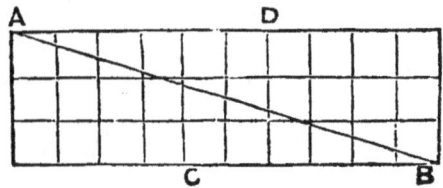

lines into thirty squares, then cut it from corner to corner, so as to form two triangles. After this cut off the top of these triangles at C and D,* and arrange the pieces in this manner:—

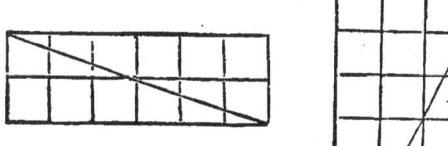

On counting the squares in the first figure, there appear to be thirty, but the other arrangement of the same card seems to contain thirty-two. It does so, however, only in appearance, but it is only a very correct eye that can detect the imperfection.

### THE CARPENTER PUZZLED.

A carpenter having a piece of mahogany of a triangular form, (see Fig.) wished to know how he could make it up to the best advantage. His first idea was to make an oblong square table of it, but he found that if he did so the waste of the wood would be very great. After consideration he discovered that the most economical method of using the wood would be to form it into an oval. To make this oval contain as much wood as possible, he proceeded in the following manner: Let B G D be the triangular piece of wood; take G H one half of the base, and divide the triangle by drawing a line from H to B. Take G H in the compasses, and set it off on one of the sides from G to E, draw 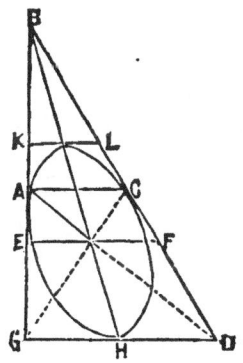 the line E F, and the point I will be the center of the oval; draw K L parallel to E F, and at the same distance from the center as the base G. The points A and C are found by dividing the line from E to K and drawing A C, or by drawing the dotted lines D A and G C through the center at I. These points being found, the oval must be completed by the eye of the draughtsman.

---

* I. e., at the fourth square from the right angle.

### THE BRICKLAYER PUZZLED

A bricklayer had to construct a wall, whose length in the direction A B C was twenty-four feet. The one half of this wall, namely from B to C, had to be built over a piece of

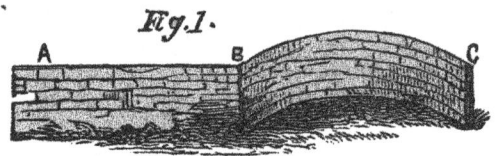

Fig. 1.

rising ground, so that the base of this part of the wall would necessarily be more than twelve feet. In making out his account he charged more for this half of the wall than for that which was built on level ground from A to B. A geometrician assured him that the square contents of both portions of the wall were exactly alike; which may be proved in the following manner:—

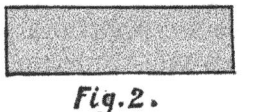
Fig. 2.

Fig. 3.

Cut two pieces of cardboard, in the form shown in Figs. 2 and 3, to represent the two parts of the wall; lay the piece representing the straight wall on the curved piece,

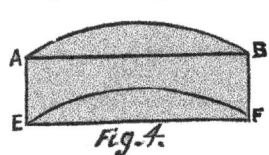
Fig. 4.

and it will be found that the angles which project at A and B will exactly fill up the spaces at E and F. The piece of board representing the straight wall may thus be found to be exactly sufficient to form a piece equal to that representing the curved wall. You may then lay the curved piece upon the straight one, and reversing the experiment prove that the curved piece is capable of forming a rectangular piece equal to the other.

### TRIANGULAR PROBLEM.

Take four square pieces of pasteboard of the same dimensions, and divide them diagonally, that is, by drawing a line from two opposite angles, as in the figures, into eight triangles. Paint seven of these triangles with the prismatic colors, red, orange, yellow, green, blue, indigo, violet, and let the eighth be white. To find how many chequers or regular four-sided figures, different either in form or color, may be made out of these eight triangles.

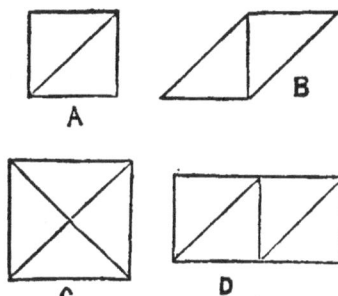

First, by combining two of these triangles there may be formed, either the triangular square A, or the inclined square B, called a Rhomb. Secondly, by combining four of the triangles the large square C may be formed, or the long square D, called a parallelogram. Now the first two squares, consisting of two parts out of eight, may each of them by the eighth rank of the triangle be taken twenty-eight different ways, which makes fifty-six. And the last two squares, consisting of four parts, may each be taken by the same rank of the triangle seventy times, which makes 140.

### TO FORM A SQUARE.

Take a piece of card of the shape and size or proportions of the subjoined, and cut it into three parts, and with these three form a perfect square.

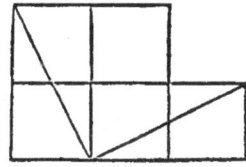

To do this, cut it in the direction of the dotted lines, and it will then be easy to lay down the pieces to form a perfect square.

### SQUARING THE CIRCLE.

"Squaring the circle," as it is called, is the puzzle of puzzles, and there are many persons who fancy this can be accomplished, as there are also many who believe that they can discover "perpetual motion."

The meaning of this phrase *squaring* is scientifically expressed by the term finding the quadrature of the circle; that is, the act of producing a square equal to a given circle : and many persons but slightly acquainted with mathematics have puzzled their brains to effect this object. The Cardinal de Cusa rolled a cylinder over a plane, till the point which was first in contact with the plane touched it again ; and then, by a train of reasoning very unmathematical, he endeavored to determine the length of the line thus described. Oliver de Serras worked a circle, and also a triangle equal to an equilateral triangle, inscribed within the circle, and imagined that the former was exactly equal to two of the latter, forgetting that the double of this triangle is equal to the hexagon inscribed within the circle, and therefore smaller than the circle itself. A Frenchman challenged the world, and deposited 10,000 livres as a stake, that he could accomplish the feat. He reduced the problem to the mechanical process of dividing a circle into four quarters, and then turning these with their angles outwards, so as to form a square, which he asserted to be equal to the circle; this however was soon proved to be ridiculous.

Some persons have taken a piece of pasteboard, and cutting it out into a circular form, and by cutting that circular disc into pieces of a square form and definite dimensions, and fitting the same turned pieces one into the other, have come *near* to a notion of the superficial area of a circle. But this kind of demonstration is purely mechanical, and is neither geometrical nor scientific, and, is in fact, no demonstration according to mathematics. For if we take the pieces of card, however exactly they may appear to be formed, and examine them with a microscope, we shall soon find that none of them are geometrically true, nor of the same length or breadth, and therefore the conclusion arrived at is a false one.

The early mathematicians, in their attempts to solve this problem, generally proceeded on the following plan. If we

  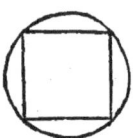 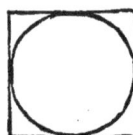

draw a square exterior to a circle, that is, touching the square in four points, each side of the square being equal to the diameter of the circle, we can soon convince ourselves that the boundary of the square will be greater than the circumference of the circle, and the area of the former greater than that of the latter. But if the square be drawn within the circle, so that only the four corners touch it, then it is equally evident that the circle is larger, both in boundary and area, than the square. By this proceeding, we arrive at the conclusion that a circle is *smaller* than a square

## TRICKS IN GEOMETRY. 263

*external* to it, and *larger* than one *internal* to it. Let us next suppose that we draw a regular pentagon, that is, a figure of five equal sides, exterior to the circle, and touching it on five points; then it is evident that as the circle is wholly contained within the pentagon, it must be smaller than that which contains it. But if the pentagon be described within the circle, touching it at the five angular points, then of course the circle is larger than the pentagon which it contains.

Now, in geometry, my young readers must bear in mind, the exact periphery or circumference, and the exact area of any figure bounded by straight lines, may be determined with rigorous accuracy; and if we draw two polygons—say of one hundred sides, one within and one without the circle—we can ascertain the exact area of those polygons, and affirm that the area of a circle is greater than a certain amount, and less than another certain amount. These two amounts, if the number of the sides of the polygon be so

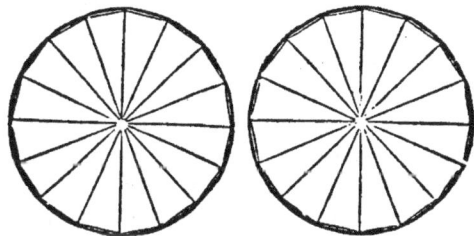

large as we here suppose, may be so very nearly alike, that either one will give the area of the circle with great closeness.

By some such means as these Archimedes found that if the diameter of a circle be called 7, then the circumference will be nearly 22; and that if the square of the diameter be 14, then the area of the circle will be equal to about 11; but this computation was slightly in error, and gave to the area of the circle too great a measure by about one three-thousandth part of the whole. At a later period, however, a European mathematician, named Metius, discovered a method which makes an extraordinary approach to accuracy, and is at the same time easily remembered. He found that if the diameter be considered equal to 113, then the circumference would equal 355; or if we multiply the square of the radius by 355, and divide it by 113, the area will be given. Now this method is so very nearly correct, that the area of a circle one foot in diameter is given within the fifty-thousandth part of a square inch.

Other mathematicians have carried the approximation still further. Ludolph Van Ceulen worked it out to 36 places of figures, showing that if the diameter be 1, the circumference will be

3.14,159,265,358,979,323,846,264,338,327,950,288.

or that if the last figure be 8, the result will be a little below the truth, and if 9, a little above it.

Since this, Mr. Sharp, an English mathematician, carried the approximation to 72 places of figures; Mr. John Machin to 100 figures, and eclipsed all others. M. de Lagny worked it out to 128 places of figures, and of the degree of *nearness* to which this computation brings the proportion, Montucla says, "If we suppose a circle, the *diameter* of which is a thousand million times greater than the distance between the sun and the earth, the error in the proportion of the circumference would be a thousand million times less than the thickness of a hair."

But after all, none of these computations are quite correct; they all deviate from the truth, and bring us to the conclusion that there are no numbers or collection of numbers which will give the exact ratio of the circumference, or of the area of a circle to its diameter. We offer this explanation on the subject to our young friends that they may not be puzzled by the question; and that should they be asked to square the circle, or hear any one assert that he can do so, they may be able to show that they are "awake" to the question, and know how to explain it.

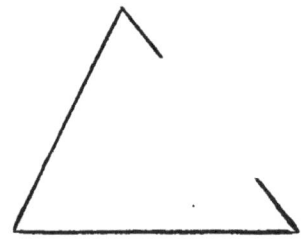

# PRACTICAL PARADOXES AND PUZZLES.

A puzzle is not solved, impatient sirs,
By peeping at its answer. in a trice—
When Gordius, the plow-boy, king of Phrygia,
Tied up his implements of husbandry
In the far-famed knot, rash Alexander
Did not undo, by cutting it in twain.

PARADOXES and Puzzles, although by many persons looked upon as mere trifles, have, in numerous instances, cost their inventors considerable time, and exhibit a great degree of ingenuity. We can readily imagine that some of the complicated puzzles in the ensuing pages may have been originally constructed by captives, to pass away the hours of a long and dreary imprisonment; thus does the misery of a few frequently conduce to the amusement of many. We look upon a Paradox as a sort of superior riddle, and a tolerable Puzzle, in our opinion, takes precedence of a first-rate rebus. There is often considerable thought, calculation, patience, and management, required to solve some of these strange enigmas; and we have, ere now, followed the mazes of a Puzzle so ardently, as to be entirely absorbed in devising means to extricate ourself from its bewildering difficulties; and felt almost as much pleasure in eventually achieving victory over it, as we have in conquering an adversary at some superior game of skill. It is "in good sooth, a right dainty and pleasant pastime," to watch the stray wanderings of another person attempting to elucidate a Paradox, or perform a Puzzle, with which one is previously acquainted. It is laughable to see him elated with hope at the apparent speedy end of his troubles, when you know that, at that moment, he is actually farther from his object than he was when he began; and it is no less amusing to watch his increasing despair, as he conceives himself to be getting more and more involved, when you are well aware that he is within a single turn of a happy termination of his toils; but what a mirthful moment is that, when there being only two ways to turn, the one right and the other wrong, as is usually the case, he takes the latter, and becomes more than ever

"Pozed, puzzled, and perplexed."

Puzzles are by no means of modern origin; the Sphynx puzzled the brains of some of the heroes of antiquity, and even Alexander the Great, as it is written, made several essays to untie the knot with which Gordius, the Phrygian king, who had been raised from the plow to the throne, tied up his implements of husbandry in the temple, in so intricate a manner, that universal monarchy was promised to the man who could undo it: after having been repeatedly baffled, he, at length, drew his sword, considering that he was entitled to the fulfillment of the promise, by cutting the Gordian knot.

### 1. THE CHINESE CROSS.

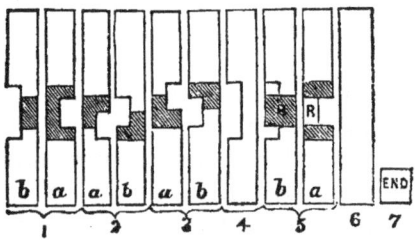

Have six pieces of wood, bone, or metal, made of the same length as No. 6, in the above figures, and each piece of the same size as No. 7. It is required to construct a cross, with six arms, from these pieces, and in such a manner that it shall not be displaced when thrown upon the floor.

The shaded parts of each figure represent the parts that are cut *out* of the wood, and each piece marked *a* is supposed to be facing the reader, while the pieces marked *b* are the *right* side of each piece turned over *towards* the left, so as to face the reader. No. 7 represents the end of each piece of wood, &c., and is given to show the dimensions.

## 2. THE PARALLELOGRAM.

A parallelogram, as in the illustration, fig. 1, may be cut into two pieces, so that by shifting the position of the pieces, two other figures may be formed, as shown by figs. 2 and 3.

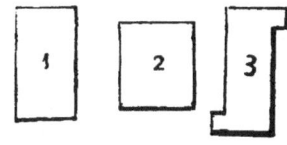

## 3. THE DIVIDED GARDEN.

A person let his house to several inmates, who occupied different floors, and having a garden attached to the house, he was desirous of dividing it among them. There were ten trees in the garden, and he was desirous of dividing it so that each of the five inmates should have an equal share of garden and two trees. How did he do it?

## 4. THE ENDLESS STRING.

Now, sir, your coat is off!
And see—
Your right-hand pocketed!
So let it be:
While o'er your arm
An endless string—
Some three yards round—
Hangs like a sling.
Take the string off—
But, just for fun,
It must be done
Keeping your right-hand in its place,
And not a smile must stir your face.
Until you find this puzzle out,
No coat shall wrap your back about.

## 5. CHINESE MAZE THE WILLOW-PATTERN PLATE.

Ye fair ones who, in continent or isle,
  Long for delights which love alone can bring;
Whilst ruby lips display affection's smile,
  Haste through the maze, and reach the "wedding ring!"
The sweet Koong-see, whose spirit hovers near,
  Shall watch thee wand'ring through the doubtful way;
And when thou showest aught of hope or fear,
  Shall whisper to thee, as thy footsteps stray!

## 6. THE VERTICAL LINE PUZZLE.

Draw six vertical lines, as below, and, by adding **five** other lines to them, let the whole form nine.

## PRACTICAL PARADOXES AND PUZZLES.

#### 7. THE THREE RABBITS.

Draw three rabbits, so that each shall appear to have two ears, while, in fact, they have only three ears between them.

#### 8. THE ACCOMMODATING SQUARE.

Make eight squares of card, then divide four of them from corner to corner, so that you will now have twelve pieces. Form a square with them.

#### 9. THE CIRCLE PUZZLE.

Draw a circle upon a piece of paper, and thrust a pin through it without crossing the circle, or thrusting it downward through the center.

#### 10. THE CARDBOARD PUZZLE.

Take a piece of cardboard or leather, of the shape and measurement indicated by the diagram, cut it in such a manner that you yourself may pass through it, still keeping it in one piece.

#### 11. THE BUTTON PUZZLE.

In the center of a piece of leather make two parallel cuts with a penknife, and just below a small hole of the same width; then pass a piece of string under the slit and through the hole, as in the figure, and tie two buttons much larger than the hole to the ends of the string. The puzzle is, to get the string out again without taking off the buttons.

#### 12. THE QUARTO PUZZLE.

Divide this figure into four equal parts, each of the same figure.

270   THE MAGICIAN'S OWN BOOK.

### 13. THE PUZZLE OF FOURTEEN.

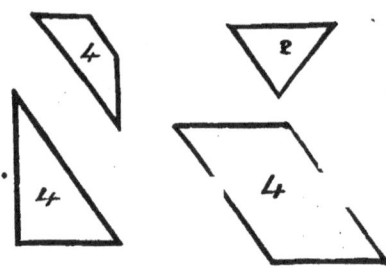

Cut out fourteen pieces of paper, card, or wood, of the same size and shape as those shown in the diagram, and then form an oblong with them.

### 14. THE SQUARE AND CIRCLE PUZZLE.

Get a piece of cardboard, the size and shape of the diagram, and punch in it twelve circles or holes in the position

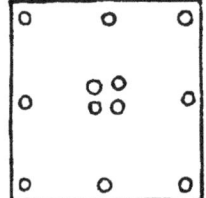

shown. The puzzle is, to cut the cardboard into four pieces of equal size, each piece to be of the same shape, and to contain three circles, without cutting into any of them.

### 15. THE SCALE AND RING PUZZLE.

Provide a thin piece of wood of about two inches and a half square; make a round hole at each corner, sufficiently large to admit three or four times the thickness of the cord you will afterwards use, and in the middle of the board make four smaller round holes in the form of a square, and about half an inch between each. Then take four pieces of thin silken cord, each about six inches long, pass one through each of the four corner holes, tying a knot underneath at the end, or affixing a little ball or bead to prevent its drawing through; take another cord, which, when doubled, will be about seven inches long, and pass the two ends through the middle holes *a a*, from the front to the back of the board, (one cord through each hole,) and again from back to front through the other holes *b b*; tie the six ends together in a knot, so as to form a small scale, and proportioning the length of the cords, so that when you hold the scale suspended, the middle cord, besides passing through the four center holes, will admit of being drawn up into a loop of about half an inch from the surface of the scale; provide a ring of metal or bone, of about three quarters of an inch in diameter, and place it on the scale, bringing the loop through its middle; then, drawing the loop a little through the scale toward you, pass it, double as it is, through the hole at the corner A, over the knot underneath, and draw it back; then pass it in the same way through the hole at corner B, over the knot, and draw it back; then, drawing up the loop a little more, pass it over the knot at top, and afterward through the holes C and D in succession, like the others, and the ring will be fixed.

### 16. THE HEART PUZZLE.

Cut a piece of thin wood the shape indicated by the diagram, and having perforated it as above, draw a piece of

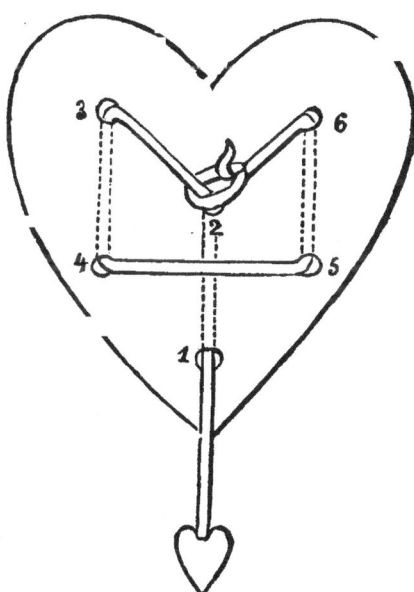

string, with a smaller heart attached at the end, through

No. 1, pass it behind, and bring it through 2 before, and through 3, and so on to 6, when a loop must be made so as to enclose that part of the string which runs from 2 to 3. The puzzle is to remove the string from the large heart altogether, without unfastening the loop.

Care should be taken to avoid twisting or entangling the string. The length of the string should be proportioned to the size of the heart; if you make the heart two inches and a half high, the string when doubled should be about nine inches long.

### 17. THE CROSS PUZZLE.

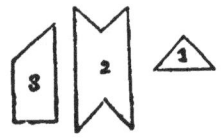

Cut three pieces of paper to the shape of No. 1, one to the shape of No. 2, and one to that of No. 3. Let them be of proportional sizes. Then place the pieces together so as to form a cross.

### 18. THE YANKEE SQUARE.

Cut as many pieces of each figure in cardboard as they

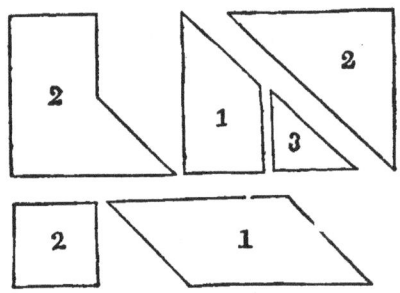

have numbers marked on each; then form the pride of the American army.

### 19. THE CARD PUZZLE.

One of the best puzzles hitherto made is represented in the annexed cut. A is a piece of card; $bb$ a narrow slip divided from its bottom edge, the whole breadth of the card, except just sufficient to hold it on at  each side; $cc$ is another small slip of card with two large square ends, $ee$; $d$ is a bit of tobacco-pipe, through which $cc$ is passed, and which is kept on by the two ends $ee$. The puzzle consists in getting the pipe off without breaking it or injuring any other part of the puzzle. This, which appears to be impossible, is done in the most simple manner. On a moment's consideration it will appear plainly that there must be as much difficulty in getting the pipe in its present situation, as there can be in taking it away. The way to put the puzzle together is as follows: The slip *c c e e* is cut out of a piece of card in the shape delineated in Fig. 3. The card in the first figure must then be gently bent at A, so as to allow of the slip at the bottom of it being also bent sufficiently to pass double through the pipe, as in Fig. 2. The detached slip with the square ends (Fig. 3) is then to be passed half way through the loop *f* at the bottom of the pipe; it is next to be doubled in the center at *a*, and pulled through the pipe, double; by means of the loop of the slip to the card. Upon unbending the card the puzzle will be complete, and appear as represented in Fig. 1.

### 20. THREE SQUARE PUZZLE.

Cut seventeen slips of cardboard of equal lengths, and place them on a table to form six squares, as in the diagram. It is now required to take away five of the pieces, yet to leave but three perfect squares.

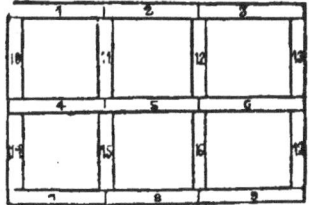

### 21. THE CYLINDER PUZZLE.

Cut a piece of cardboard about four inches long, of the shape of the diagram, and make three holes in it, as represented. The puzzle is, to make one piece of wood to pass through, and also exactly to fill, each of the three holes

### 22. PUZZLE OF THE FOUR TENANTS.

I have a square plot of ground, in one quarter of which I have built a house, which I have let to four tenants. I tell them that if they can divide the remaining ground into four equal plots, alike in shape, and each containing one of the four apple trees I have planted, they shall have it without any increase of rent. How may they succeed?

### 23. THE PUZZLE WALL.

Suppose there was a pond, around which four poor men built their houses, thus:

Suppose four evil-disposed rich men afterwards built houses around the poor people, thus:

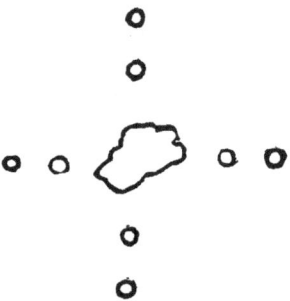

and wished to have all the water of the pond to themselves. How could they build a high wall, so as to shut out the poor people from the pond?

### 24. THE NUNS.

Twenty-four nuns were arranged in a convent by night, by a sister, to count nine each way, as in the diagram. Four of them went out for a walk by moonlight. How were the remainder placed in the square so as still to count nine each way? The four who went out returned, bringing with them four friends; how were they all placed still to count nine each way, and thus to deceive the sister, as to whether there were 20, 24, 28, or 32, in the square?

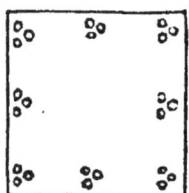

### 25. THE HORSE SHOE PUZZLE.

Cut a piece of apple or turnip into the shape of a horse shoe, stick six pins in it for nails, and then, by two cuts, divide it into six parts, each to contain one pin.

PRACTICAL PARADOXES AND PUZZLES. 275

### 26. THE CARD SQUARE.

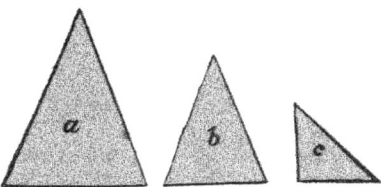

With eight pieces of card or paper, of the shape of Fig. *a*, four of Fig. *b*, and four of Fig. *c*, and of proportionate sizes, form a perfect square.

### 27. THE DOG PUZZLE.

The dogs are, by placing two lines upon them, to be suddenly aroused to life and made to run. Query, How and where should these lines be placed, and what should be the forms of them?

### 28. PUZZLE OF THE TWO FATHERS.

Two fathers have each a square of land. One father divides his so as to reserve to himself one fourth; thus—

The other father divides his so as to reserve to himself one fourth in the form of a triangle; thus—

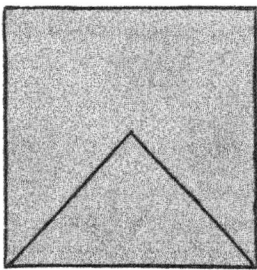

They each have four sons, and each divides the remainder

among his sons in such a way that each son will share equally with his brother, and in similar shape. How were the two farms divided?

### 29. THE TRIANGLE PUZZLE.

Cut twenty triangles out of ten square pieces of wood; mix them together, and request a person to make an exact square with them.

### 30. CUTTING OUT A CROSS.

How can be cut out of a single piece of paper, and with

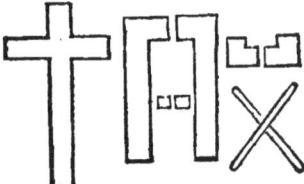

one cut of the scissors, a perfect cross, and all the other forms as shown in the cuts?

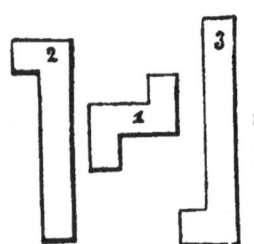

### 31. ANOTHER CROSS PUZZLE.

With three pieces of cardboard of the shape and size of No. 1, and one each of No. 2 and 3, to form a cross.

### 32. THE FOUNTAIN PUZZLE.

A is a wall, B C D three houses, and E F G three fountains or canals.

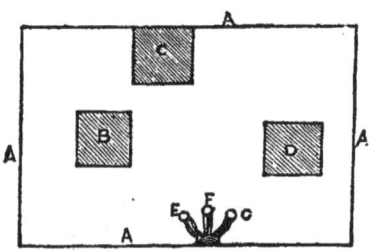

It is required to bring the water from E to D, from G to B,

and from F to C, without one crossing the other, or passing outside of the wall A.

### 33. THE PUZZLE OF THE STARS.

Friends one and all, I pray you show
How you *nine stars* would so bestow,
*Ten* rows to form—in each row *three*—
Tell me, ye wits, how this can be?

### 34. THE COUNTER PUZZLE.

Place eight counters or coins, as in the diagram; it is then required to lay them in four couples, removing only one at a time, and in each removal passing the one in the hand over *two* on the table.

### 35. THE JAPAN SQUARE PUZZLE.

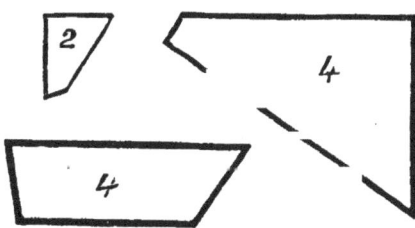

Cut out ten pieces of card or wood of the same sizes and shapes as in the diagram, and then form a square with them

### 36. THE CABINET MAKER'S PUZZLE.

A cabinet-maker has a circular piece of veneering with which he has to veneer the tops of two oval stools; but it so happens that the area of the stools, exclusive of the hand-holes in the center, and that of the circular piece, are the same. How must he cut his stuff so as to be exactly sufficient for his purpose?

### 37. THE STRING AND BALLS PUZZLE.

Get an oblong strip of wood or ivory, and bore three holes in it, as shown in the cut. Then take a piece of twine, passing the two ends through the holes at the extremities, fastening them with a knot, and thread upon it two beads or rings, as depicted above. The puzzle is to get both beads

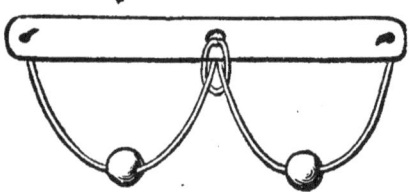

on the same side, without removing the string from the holes, or untying the knots.

### 38. THE DOUBLE-HEADED PUZZLE.

Cut a circular piece of wood as in the cut No. 1, and

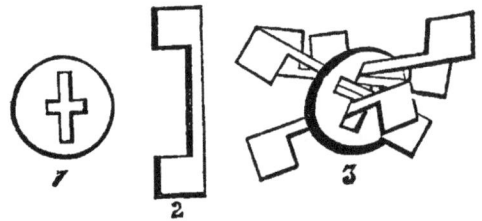

four others, like No. 2. The puzzle consists in getting them all into the cross-shaped slit, until they look like Fig. 3.

### 39. ARITHMETICAL PUZZLE.

The sum of four figures in value will be.
Above seven thousand nine hundred and three;
But when they are halved, you'll find very fair
The sum will be nothing, in truth I declare.

### 40. GRAMMATICAL PUZZLE.

Let the rich, great, and noble, banquet in the festal halls,
And pass the hours away, as the most thoughtless revel;
Then seek the poor man's dreary home, whose very dingy walls
Proclaim full well to all how low his rank and level.

Take away one letter from a word in the above stanza, and substitute another, leaving the word so metamorphosed still a word of the English language ; and, by that change, totally after the syntactical construction of the whole sentence, changing the moods and tenses of verbs, turning verbs into nouns, nouns into adjectives, and adjectives into adverbs, &c., and so make the entire stanza bear quite a different meaning from that which it has as it stands above

### 41. THE TREE PUZZLE.

Plant an orchard of twenty-one trees, so that there shall be nine straight rows, with five trees in each row, the *outline* a regular geometrical figure, and the trees all at unequal distances from each other.

### 42. AN EPITAPH ON ELLINOR BACHELLOR, AN OLD PYE WOMAN.

Bene A. Thin Thed Ustt HEMO. Uld yo
L.D.C. RUSTO! Fnel L.B.
Ach El Lor. Lat. ELY,
Wa. S. shove N. W. How—Ass! kill'd I. N. T. H.
Ear T. Sofp, I, Escu Star.
D. San D T Art. San D K. N E. W. E
Ver——Yus E.—Oft He ove N W. Hens He
'Dli V'DL. on geno
Ug H S hem A.D.E. he R. la Stp. Uf——fap
Uf. F. B Y he. R hu
S. Ban D. M.
Uch pra is 'D. No. Wheres Hedot
HL. i. e. Tom. A kead I.R.T.P. Yein hop Esthathe
R. C. RUSTWI,
L L B. Era is '——D!

### 43. A CURIOUS LETTER.

Friends      Sir,      friends,
stand your disposition;
I bearing
a man      the world
is      whilst the
contempt,
ridicule.
are
ambitious.

### 44. A PUZZLING INSCRIPTION.

P R S V R Y P R F C T M N
V R K P T H S P R C P T S T N.

The two lines above were affixed to the communion table of a small church in Wales, and continued to puzzle the learned congregation for several centuries, but at length the inscription was deciphered. What was it?

### 45. THE PUZZLING RINGS.

This perplexing invention is of great antiquity, and was treated on by Cardan, the mathematician, at the beginning of the sixteenth century It consists of a flat piece of thin metal or bone, with ten holes in it; in each hole a wire is loosely fixed, beaten out into a head at one end, to prevent its slipping through, and the other fastened to a ring, also loose. Each wire has been passed through the ring of the next wire, previously to its own ring being fastened on; and through the whole of the rings runs a wire loop or bow, which also contains, within its oblong space, all the wires to which the rings are fastened; the whole presenting so complicated an appearance, as to make the releasing the rings from the bow appear an impossibility. The construction of it would be found rather troublesome to the amateur, but it may be purchased at most of the toy shops very lightly and elegantly made. It also exists in various parts of the country, forged in iron, perhaps by some ingenious village mechanic, and aptly named "The Tiring Irons." The following instructions will show the principle on which the puzzle is constructed, and will prove a key to its solution.

Take the loop in your left hand, holding it at the end, B, and consider the rings as being numbered 1st to 10th. The 1st will be the extreme ring to the right, and the 10th the nearest your left hand.

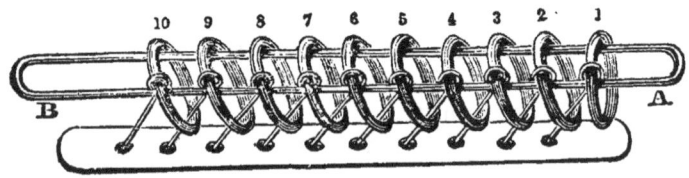

It will be seen that the difficulty arises from each ring passing round the wire of its right-hand neighbor. The extreme ring at the right hand, of course, being unconnected with any other wire than its own, may at any time be drawn off the end of the bow at A, raised up, dropped through the bow, and finally released. After you have done this, try to pass the second ring in the same way, and you will not succeed, as it is obstructed by the wire of the first ring; but if you bring the first ring on again, by reversing the process by which you took it off, viz., by putting it up through the bow, and on to the end of it, you will then find that by taking the first and second rings together, they will both draw off, lift up, and drop through the bow. Having done this, try to pass the third ring off, and you will not be able;

because it is fastened on one side to its own wire, which is within the bow, and on the other side to the second ring, which is without the bow. Therefore, leaving the third ring for the present, try the fourth ring, which is now at the end all but one, and both of the wires which affect it being within the bow, you will draw it off without obstruction; and, in doing this, you will have to slip the third ring off, which will not drop through for the reasons before given; so, having dropped the fourth ring through, you can only slip the third ring on again. You will now comprehend that (with the exception of the first ring) the only ring which can at any time be released is that which happens to be second on the bow, at the right-hand end; because both the wires which affect it being within the bow, there will be no impediment to its dropping through. You have now the first and second rings released, and the fourth also—the third still fixed; to release which we must make it last but one on the bow, and to effect which pass the first and second rings together through the bow, and on to it; then release the first ring again by slipping it off and dropping it through, and the third ring will stand as second on the bow, in its proper position for releasing, by drawing the second and third off together, dropping the third through, and slipping the second on again. Now to release the second, put the first up, through and on the bow; then slip the two together off, raise them up, and drop them through. The sixth will now stand second, consequently in its proper place for releasing; therefore draw it toward the end, A, slip the fifth off, then the sixth, and drop it through; after which replace the fifth, as you cannot release it until it stands in the position of a second ring; in order to effect this you must bring the first and second rings together, through and on to the bow; then in order to get the third on, slip the first off and down through the bow; then bring the third up, through and on to the bow; then bring the first ring up and on again, and, releasing the first and second together, bring the fourth through and on to the bow, replacing the third; then bring the first and second together on, drop the first off and through, then the third the same, replace the first on the bow, take off the first and second together, and the fifth will then stand second, as you desired; draw it toward the end, slip it off and through, replace the fourth, bring the first and second together up and on again, release the first, bring on the third, passing the second ring on to the bow again, replace the first, in order to release the first and second together; then bring the fourth toward the end, slipping it off and through, replace the third, bring the first and second together up and on again, release the first, then the third, replacing the second, bring the first up and on, in order to release the first and second together, which having done, your eighth ring will then stand second, consequently you can release it, slipping the seventh on again. Then to release the seventh, you must begin by putting the first and second up and on together, and going through the movements in the same succession as before, until you find you have only the tenth and ninth on the bow; then slip the tenth off and through the bow, and replace the ninth. This dropping of the tenth ring is the first effectual movement toward getting the rings off, as all the changes you have gone through were only to enable you to get at the tenth ring. You will then find that you have only the ninth left on the bow, and you must not be discouraged on learning, that in order to get that ring off, all the others to the right hand must be put on again, beginning by putting the first and second together, and working as before, until you find that the ninth stands as second on the bow, at which time you can release it. You will then have only the eighth left on the bow; you must again put on all the rings to the right hand, beginning by putting up the first and second together, till you find the eighth standing as second on the bow, or in its proper position for releasing; and so you proceed until you find all the rings finally released. As you commence your operations with all the rings ready fixed on the bow, you will release the tenth ring in one hundred and seventy moves; but as you then have only the ninth on, and as it is necessary to bring on again all the rings up to the ninth, in order to release the ninth, and which requires fifteen moves more, you will, consequently, release the ninth ring in two hundred and fifty-six moves; and, for your encouragement, your labor will diminish, by one half, with each following ring which is finally released. The eighth comes off in one hundred and twenty-eight moves, the seventh in sixty-four moves, and so on, until you arrive at the second and first rings, which come off together, making six hundred and eighty-one moves, which are necessary to take off all the rings

With the experience you will by this time have acquired, it is only necessary to say, that to replace the rings, you begin by putting up the first and second together, and follow precisely the same system as before.

### 46. MOVING THE KNIGHT OVER ALL THE SQUARES ALTERNATELY.

The problem respecting the placing the knight on any given square, and moving him from that square to any house on the board, has not been thought unworthy the attention of the first mathematicians. Euler, Ozanam, De Montmart, De Moivre, De Majron, and others, have all given methods by which this feat might be accomplished. It was reserved, however, for the present century to lay this down on a general plan; and the only English writer who has noticed this is Mr. George Walker, in his *Treatise on Chess*. The plan is this: Let the knight be placed on any square, and move him from square to square, on the principle of always playing him to that point, from which, in actual play, he would command the fewest other squares; observing, that in reckoning the squares commanded by him you must omit such as he has already covered. If, too, there are two squares, on both of which his powers would be equal, you may move him to

EULER'S METHOD.

either. Try this on the board, with some counters or wafers, placing one on every square; and, when you clearly understand it, you may astonish your friends by inviting them to station the knight on any square they like, and engaging to play him, from that square, over the remaining sixty-three in sixty-three moves. When the automaton Chessplayer was last exhibited in England, this was made part of the wonders he accomplished, though as the above plan was not then known here, he could not adopt it, but used something like the method laid down by Euler, and which we subjoin.

Our young Chess-players must remember that it does not matter on which square the knight is placed at starting; as, by acquiring the plan by heart, which is soon done, he can play him over all the squares from any given point, his last square being at the distance of a knight's move from his first. It is obvious that this route may be varied many ways, and we have often amused ourselves by trying to work it on a slate.

### ANOTHER METHOD.

The problem of the knight's covering successively each square of the board, has, in all ages, attracted the attention of the first mathematicians; it is only lately, however, that this very ingenious system for performing the feat without seeing the board, has been invented by an Edinburgh gentleman. We well recollect the surprise occasioned among chess-amateurs when it was first performed; indeed it was generally considered a greater mental effort than that of playing three games of chess at the same time, without seeing the board.

The general rule for moving the Knight upon all the squares of the board, is to commence by moving him to that square which commands the fewest points of attack, and by continuing this principle he will occupy all the squares in rotation, observing, that if on any two or more squares his power would be equal, he may be placed indifferently on either of such squares. Thus we see, that there are different routes which the Knight-errant may take in his progress over all the board; still, whichever of these routes for covering the sixty-four squares may be adapted, each move forms, if we may so express ourselves, a link in an endless chain, so that whatever square we start from, by taking one known route, we are sure to arrive at a square, the last link of the chain, a Knight's move distant from the square of our departure. Consequently, if any person could commit to memory the consecutive moves of any one route over the board, he would be able to start from any one square in that route, in the same manner that any of us, if required to mention the numerals up to sixty-four, could as easily start at thirty and end at twenty-nine, as if we started at one and ended at sixty-four.

These considerations greatly reduce the apparent impossibility of performing the feat; but the reader will exclaim, "What an immense undertaking it would be, to commit to memory the moves forming a Knight's route over the sixty-four squares!" and we reply, "Certainly it would be, if we used the language of Chess to designate the squares;" and herein lies the beauty of the invention. A set of names, whose application can be understood at a glance, are in-

| Met. | Let. | Ket. | Het. | Get. | Fet. | Det. | Bet. |
| --- | --- | --- | --- | --- | --- | --- | --- |
| Men. | Len. | Ken. | Hen. | Gen. | Fen. | Den. | Ben. |
| Mix. | Lix. | Kix. | Hix. | Gix. | Fix. | Dix. | Bix. |
| Miv. | Liv. | Kiv. | Hiv. | Giv. | Fiv. | Div. | Biv. |
| Mor. | Lor. | Kor. | Hor. | Gor. | For. | Dor. | Bor. |
| Mee. | Lee. | Kee. | Hee. | Gee. | Fee. | Dee. | Bee. |
| Moo. | Loo. | Koo. | Hoo. | Goo. | Foo. | Doo. | Boo. |
| Mun. | Lun. | Kun. | Hun. | Gun. | Fun. | Dun. | Bun. |
| M | L | K | H | G | F | D | B |

vented for the squares, and the performer of the feat, having learned a route of the Knight, expressed by these invented names, thinks in the new language which he directs the moves in the terms of chess—just as many of us *think* in English, when we are writing or speaking French.

The diagram given above represents the chess-board; the distinction of white and black squares is not necessary for our purpose. The files, commencing from the right hand are distinguished by the consonants in alphabetical succession (C and J are, for obvious reasons, omitted.) Thus, the King's rook's file is known as B, the King's Knight's as D, the King's Bishops as F, the King's as G, the Queen's as H, the Queen's Bishop's as K, the Queen's Knight's as L, and the Queen's Rook's as M. This is all that has to be learned, in this system of Chess notation; for the lines of squares tell their own numbers—one being *un*, two *oo*, three *ee*, four *or*, six *ix*, seven *en*, eight *et*—being, in fact, the terminal sounds of the first eight numerals. Bun being B *one*, or King's Rook's square; Gix, G *six*, or King's sixth square. We consider it quite unnecessary to say another word in explanation of this system; its ingenious simplicity causes it to be understood and learned at a glance. All that is required now is, to select a Knight's route over all the squares of the board, and commit it to memory, not in the complicated terms of Chess, but in these simple equivalents. Suppose we start from the Queen's Knights seventh square, *len*, the route will be as follows:

| Len | het | fen | bet. | Dix | bor | doo | gun |
|-----|-----|-----|------|-----|-----|-----|-----|
| Koo | mun | lee | kun. | Moo | kee | goo | dun. |
| Bee | div | ben | fet. | Hen | let | mix | lor. |
| Hee | kiv | gor | hix. | Liv | men | ket | gen. |
| Kix | giv | fee | hor. | Gix | for | hiv | gee. |
| Fiv | den | biv | dee. | Bun | foo | hun | loo. |
| Mor | lix | met | ken. | Get | fix | det | bix. |
| Dor | boo | fun | hoo. | Lun | mee | kor | miv |

The only trouble is to commit this cabalistical-looking table to memory, which may be all accomplished in half an hour; the process will be greatly facilitated by the learner frequently playing the route over on the chess-board. He will be amply rewarded by the astonishment he will cause to the *natives* of his locality, who may have the great misfortune of being unacquainted with our book's entightening pages; and, if not quite a first-rate player, he will acquire an intimate knowledge of the peculiar powers and perplexing peregrinations of the eccentric *Caballeros*, who

" —— fiery coursers guide
With headlong speed throng war's empurpled tide;
Alert and brave they spring amidst the fight,
From white to black, from black to candid white."

|  1 |  2 |  3 |  4 |  5 |  6 |  7 |  8 |
|----|----|----|----|----|----|----|----|
|  9 | 10 | 11 | 12 | 13 | 14 | 15 | 16 |
| 17 | 18 | 19 | 20 | 21 | 22 | 23 | 24 |
| 25 | 26 | 27 | 28 | 29 | 30 | 31 | 32 |
| 33 | 34 | 35 | 36 | 37 | 38 | 39 | 40 |
| 41 | 42 | 43 | 44 | 45 | 46 | 47 | 48 |
| 49 | 50 | 51 | 52 | 53 | 54 | 55 | 56 |
| 57 | 58 | 59 | 60 | 61 | 62 | 63 | 64 |

### ANOTHER METHOD.

Let Black Queen's Rook's Square count 1, (as in the diagram,) Black King's Rook 8, and count all the other Squares in the same way from 9 to 64. Place the Knight upon Black King's Rook's Square, 8, and move as follows: 23, 40, 55, 61, 51, 57, 42, 25, 10, 4, 14, 24, 39, 56, 62, 52, 58, 41, 26, 9, 3, 13, 7, 22, 32, 47, 64, 54, 60, 50, 33, 18, 1, 11, 5, 15, 21, 6, 16, 31, 48, 63, 53, 59, 49, 34, 17, 2, 12, 27, 44, 38, 28, 43, 37, 20, 35, 45, 30, 36, 18, 29, and 46. It may be well to chalk the figures on the board, as a guide, until the feat is well understood.

### 47. ROSAMOND'S BOWER.

The subjoined cut represents, it is said, the Maze at Woodstock, in which King Henry placed Fair Rosamond to protect her from the Queen. It certainly is a most ingenious contrivance, and may be made productive of much amusement. The puzzle consists in getting, from one of the numerous outlets, to the bower in the center, without crossing any of the lines.

ROSAMOND'S BOWER.

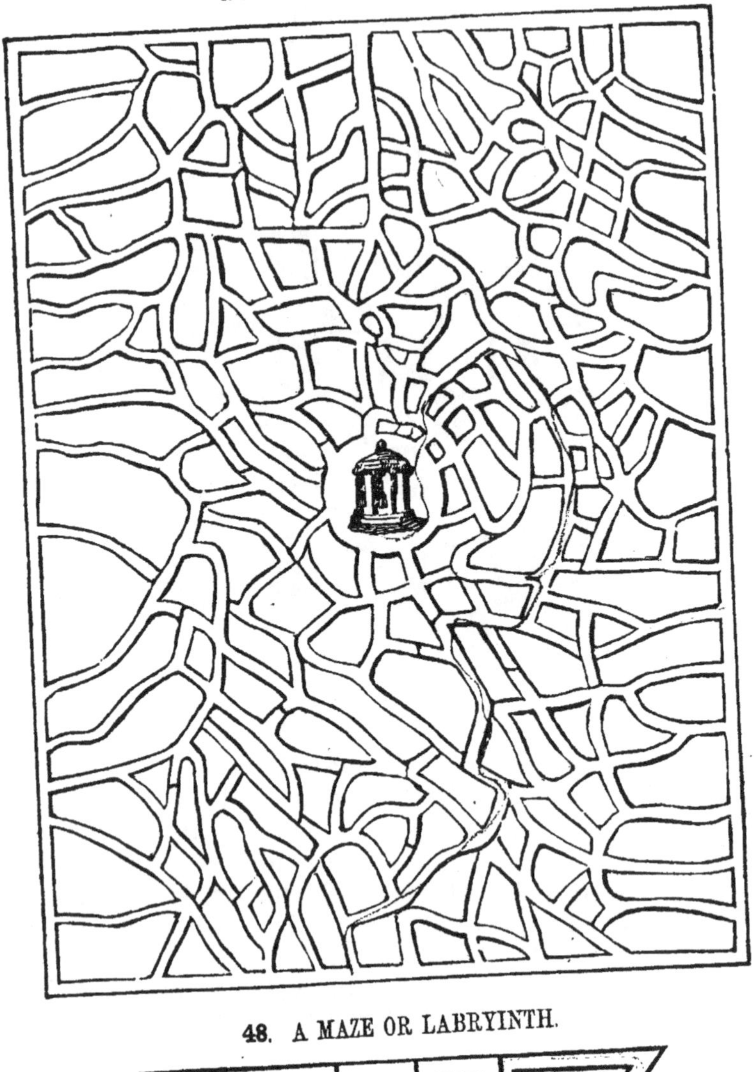

48. A MAZE OR LABRYINTH.

This maze is a correct ground-plan of one in the gardens of the Palace of Hampton Court. No legendary tale is attached to it, of which we are aware, but its labyrinthine walks occasion much amusement to the numerous holiday parties who frequent the palace grounds. The puzzle is to get into the center, where seats are placed under two lofty trees ; and many are the disappointments experienced before the end is attained ; and even then, the trouble is not over, it being quite as difficult to get *out* as to get *in*.

### 49. THE CHINESE PUZZLE.

This puzzle, being one for the purpose of constructing different figures by arranging variously-shaped pieces of card

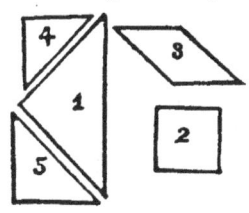

or wood in certain ways, requires no separate explanation. Cut out of very stiff cardboard, or thin mahogany, which is decidedly preferable, seven pieces, in shape like the annexed figures and bearing the same proportion to each other ; one piece must be made in the shape of figure 1, one of figure 2, and one of figure 3, and two of each of the other figures. The combinations of which

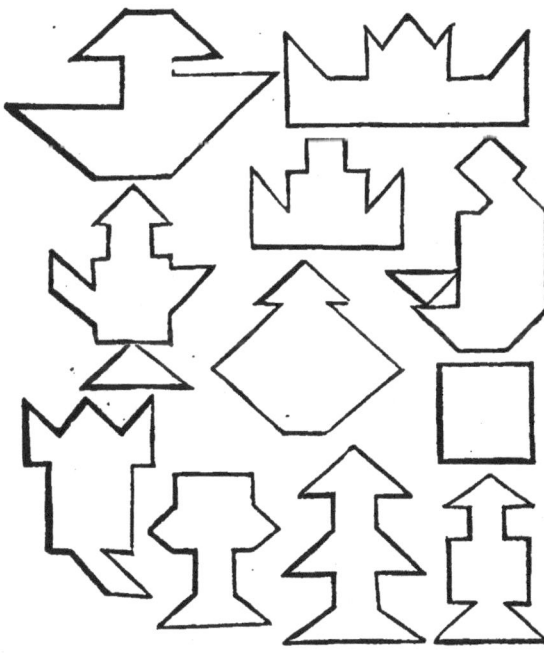

these figures are susceptible, are almost infinite; and we subjoin a representation of a few of the most curious. It is to be borne in mind, that all the pieces of which the puzzle consists, must be employed to form each figure.

### 50. TROUBLE-WIT.

Take a sheet of stiff paper, fold it down the middle of the sheet, longways; then turn down the edge of each fold outward, the breadth of a penny; measure it as it is folded, into three equal parts, with compasses, which make six divisions in the sheet; let each third part be turned outward, and the other, of course, will fall right; then pinch it a quarter of an inch deep, in plaits, like a ruff, so that, when the paper lies pinched in its form, it is in the fashion represented by A; when closed together, it will be like B; unclose it again, shuffle it with each hand, and it will resemble the shuffling of a pack of cards; close it and turn each corner inward with your fore finger and thumb, it will appear as a rosette for a lady's shoe, as C; stretch it forth, and it will resemble a cover for an Italian couch, as D; let go your fore finger at the lower end, and it will resemble a wicket, as E; close it again, and pinch it at the bottom, spreading the top, and it will represent a fan, as F; pinch it half way, and open the top, and it will appear in the form shown by G; hold it in that form, and with the thumb of your left hand turn out the next fold, and it will be as H.

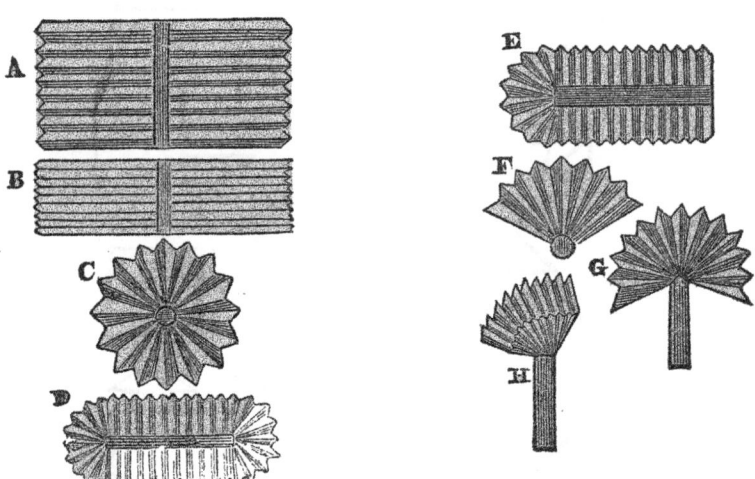

In fact, by a little ingenuity and practice, Trouble-wit may be made to assume an infinite variety of forms, and be productive of very considerable amusement.

# ANSWERS TO PRACTICAL PUZZLES.

### 1. THE CHINESE CROSS ANSWER.

Place Nos. 1 and 2 close together, as in Fig. 1; then hold them together with the finger and thumb of the left hand horizontally and with the square hole to the right. Push No. 3—placed in the same position *facing you* (*a*) in No. 4—through the opening at K, and slide it to the left at A, so that the profile of the pieces should be as in Fig. 2. Now

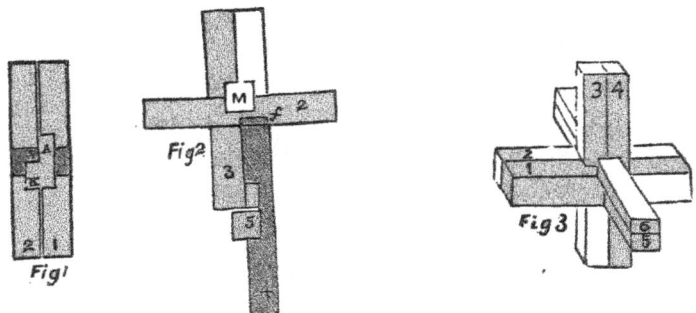

push No. 4 *partially* through the space from below upwards, as seen in f, Fig. 2. Place No. 5 cross-ways upon the part Y, so that the point R is directed upwards to the right hand side; then push No. 4 quite through, and it will be in the position shown by the dotted lines in Fig. 2. All that now remains is to push No. 6—which is the key—through the opening M and the cross is completed as in Fig. 3.

### 2. ANSWER TO THE "PARALLELOGRAM."

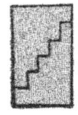  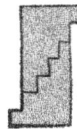

Divide the piece of card into five steps, and by shifting the position of the pieces, the desired figures may be obtained.

### 3. THE DIVIDED GARDEN ANSWER

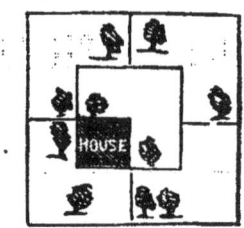

### 4. ANSWER TO THE ENDLESS STRING.

The string must be put through the armhole, and over the head, then through the opposite armhole; then the hand must be put up underneath the waistcoat, and the string drawn down around the body until the former drops down about the waist, when the experimenter may jump out of it and claim his coat.

### 5. ANSWER TO THE CHINESE MAZE.

#### KOONG-SEE'S WHISPERS.

A Why linger near the fence? a word or two
  Would kindle up a flame for ever true.
B Beware of rivals—mischief hovers near;
  Or, worse mischance, parental frowns appear.
C Favored indeed, the open door to gain—
  Let no dishonor now your conduct stain.
E The ground is rough, and difficult the road;
  But, faint not, thou shalt reach thy love's abode!
F Against thy course runs the opposing tide,
  And waves of trouble cast thy hopes aside.
G A modest competence thy lot will be;
  But richer joys than wealth are stored for thee.
A Take heed! take heed! a strange transforming **doom**
  May fix thy love, but never let it bloom.
J Be not too rash—nor leap the Bridge of Love,
  Leaving fond eyelids, moist with tears, above.
K What dost thou on the house top? do not steal
  Thy love, but win by dutiful appeal!
L A barren path this way thy footsteps tread;
  Thy heart will soon grow cold, thy love be fled.
M Thou hast a friend can help thy onward way—
  And such a friend will ne'er thy trust betray.

D Joy! thou hast reached, at length, the wedding ring;
Let white-robed maidens orange blossoms bring;
Oh may your years of happy wedlock be
Bright as your hopes, and from misgiving free.

### 6. ANSWER TO VERTICAL LINE PUZZLE.

# NINE

### 7. THE THREE RABBITS, ANSWER

### 8. THE ACCOMMODATING SQUARE.

### 9. ANSWER TO THE CIRCLE PUZZLE.

**Thrust** it upwards from the other side.

## 10. ANSWER TO THE CUT CARD PUZZLE.

Double the cardboard or leather lengthways down the middle, and then cut first to the right, nearly to the end, (the narrow way,) and then to the left, and so on to the end of the card; then open it and cut down the middle, except the two ends. The diagram shows the proper cuttings. By opening the card or leather, a person may pass through it. A laurel leaf may be treated in the same manner.

## 11. ANSWER TO THE BUTTON PUZZLE.

Draw the narrow slip of the leather through the hole, and the string and buttons may be easily released.

## 12. ANSWER TO THE QUARTO PUZZLE.

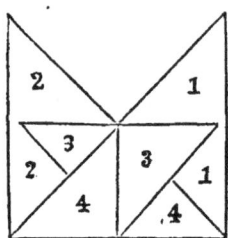

Divide the figure in the direction shown by the lines, and you will have four pieces of the same size and shape.

## 13. ANSWER TO THE PUZZLE OF FOURTEEN.

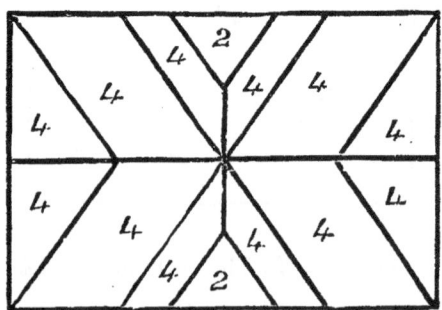

## ANSWERS TO PRACTICAL PUZZLES. 295

**14. ANSWER TO THE SQUARE AND CIRCLE PUZZLE.**

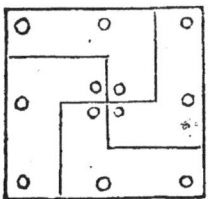

**15. THE SCALE AND RING PUZZLE.**

The puzzle consists in releasing the ring; to effect which, you have only to reverse the former process, by passing the loop through the holes D, C, B, and A, in the manner before described.

**16. ANSWER TO THE HEART PUZZLE.**

Loosen the string, and draw the loop through the hole No. 2; pass it behind, and bring it through No. 1, and slip it over the smaller heart; then the string may be easily drawn out.

**17. ANSWER TO THE CROSS PUZZLE.**

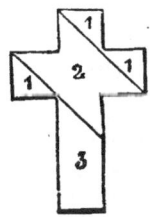

**18. ANSWER TO THE YANKEE SQUARE**

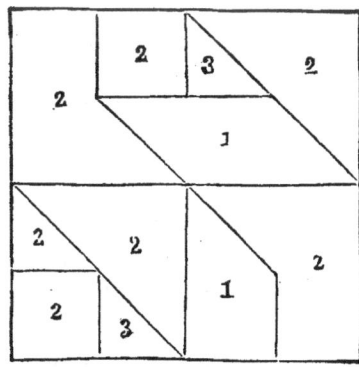

Arrange the pieces as shown in the figure above.

## 19. ANSWER TO THE CARD PUZZLE.

In order to take the pipe off, the card must be doubled (as in Fig. 2), the slip passed through it, until there is sufficient of the loop below the pipe to allow one of the square ends of the slip (Fig. 3) being passed through it. Fig. 3 is then to be taken away, and the pipe slipped off. The card for this puzzle must be cut very neatly, the puzzle handled gently, and great care taken that, in doubling the card to put on the pipe no creases are made in it, as they would in all probability spoil your puzzle, by betraying to an acute spectator the mode of operation.

## 20. ANSWER TO THE THREE SQUARE PUZZLE.

**Take** away the pieces numbered 8, 10, 1, 3, 13, and three squares only will remain.

## 21. ANSWER TO THE CYLINDER PUZZLE.

Take a round cylinder of the diameter of the circular hole, and of the height of the square hole. Having drawn a straight line across the end, dividing it into two equal parts, cut an equal section from either side to the edge of the circular base, a figure like that represented by the woodcut in the margin would then be produced, which would fulfill the required conditions.

## 22. ANSWER TO THE FOUR TENANTS.

My ground is divided,
  My tenants at work,
And he'll profit most
  Who does not labor shirk
So let them toil on
  Till cabbages rise,
And carrots and turnips
  To gladden their eyes.
Gooseberries and currants,
  And raspberries too,
Shall amply repay
  The work they may do.

### 23. THE PUZZLE WALL.

### 24. ANSWER TO THE NUN'S PUZZLE.

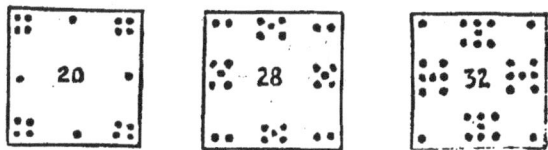

### 25. HORSE SHOE PUZZLE.

By cutting off the upper circular part containing two of the pins, and by changing the position of the pieces, another cut will divide the horse shoe into six portions, each containing one pin.

### 26. ANSWER TO CARD SQUARE PUZZLE.

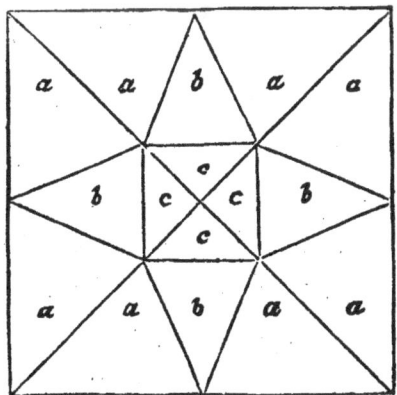

298        THE MAGICIAN'S OWN BOOK.

### 27. THE DOGS PUZZLE ANSWERED SEE DOTTED LINES.

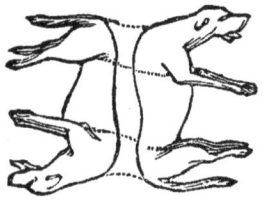

### 28. PUZZLE OF THE TWO FATHERS.

The first father divided the land in this way:

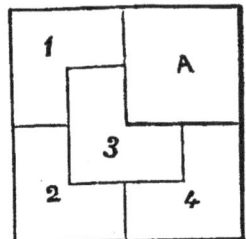

The second father divided the land in the following manner:

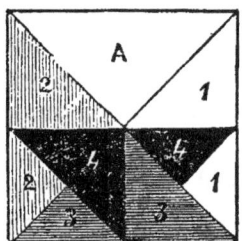

The different colors represent the several sons' portions.

### 29. THE TRIANGLE PUZZLE.

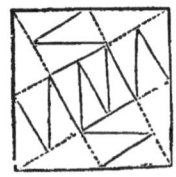

The solution of this puzzle may be easily acquired by observing the dotted lines in the engraving; by which it will be seen that four triangles are to be placed at the corners, and a small square made in the center. When this is done, the rest of the square may be quickly formed.

# ANSWERS TO PRACTICAL PUZZLES. 299

### 30. ANSWER TO CUTTING OUT A CROSS PUZZLE.

Take a piece of writing paper about three times as long as it is broad, say six inches long and two wide. Fold the upper corner down, as shown in Fig. 1; then fold the other upper corner over the first, and it will appear as in Fig. 2; you next fold the paper in half lengthwise, and it will appear as in Fig. 3. Then the last fold is made lengthwise

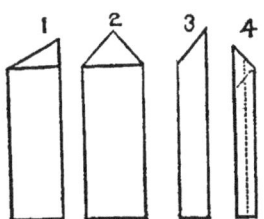

also, in the middle of the paper, and it will exhibit the form of Fig. 4, which, when cut through with the scissors in the direction of the dotted line, will give all the forms mentioned.

### 31. ANSWER TO ANOTHER CROSS PUZZLE.

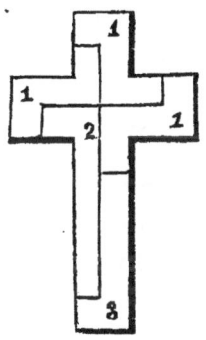

### 32. ANSWER TO THE FOUNTAIN PUZZLE

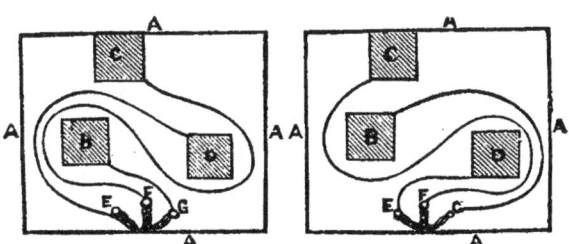

## 33. ANSWER TO THE STAR PUZZLE.

Good-tempered friends! here *nine* stars see:
*Ten* rows there are, in each row *three!*

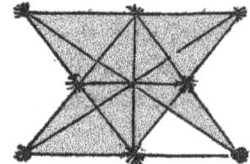

## 34. THE COUNTER PUZZLE ANSWER.

Place 4 on 7, 6 on 2, 1 on 3, and 8 on 5; *or*, 5 on 2, 3 on 7, 8 on 6, 4 on 1, &c.

## 35. ANSWER TO THE JAPAN SQUARE.

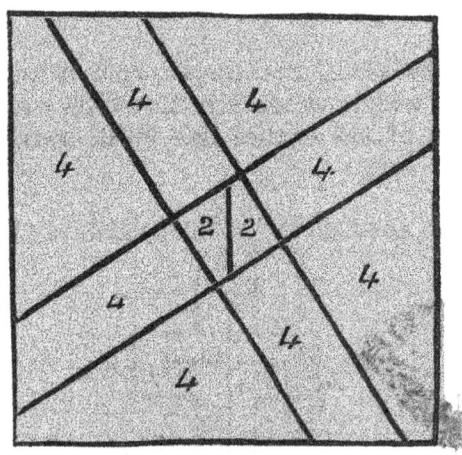

## 36. ANSWER TO THE CABINET MAKERS' PUZZLE.

The cabinet-maker must find the center of the circle, and strike another circle, half the diameter of the first, and hav-

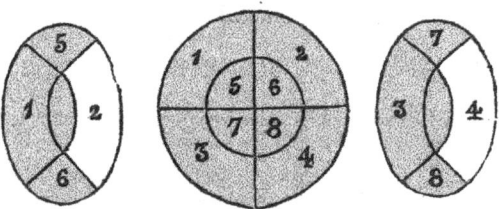

ing the same center. Then cut the whole into four parts, by means of two lines drawn at right angles to each other, then cut along the inner circle, and put the pieces **together** as in the above diagram.

### 37. ANSWER TO THE STRING AND BALLS PUZZLE.

Draw the loop well down, slipping either ball through it. Push it through the hole at the extremities, pass it over the knot, and draw it through again. The same process must be repeated with the other ball; the loop can then be drawn through the hole in the center, and the ball will slide along the cord until it reaches the other side. The string is then replaced, having both balls on the same side.

There is another and perhaps a neater way of performing this trick. Draw the loop through the central hole, and bring it through far enough to pass one of the balls through. Having done this, draw the string back, and both balls will be found on the same side.

### 38. ANSWER TO THE DOUBLE-HEADED PUZZLE.

Arrange them side by side in the short arms of the cross, draw out the center piece, and the rest will follow easily. The reversal of the same process will put them back again.

### 39. ARITHMETICAL PUZZLE.

The four figures are 8888, which being divided by a line drawn through the middle, become $\frac{0000}{0000}$, the sum of which is eight 0s, or nothing.

### 40. GRAMMATICAL PUZZLE.

Take away L in the subjunctive "Let" at the beginning of the first line, and substitute S, and so turn it into the imperative "Set," when the changes which necessarily follow will be immediately apparent.

### 41. ANSWER TO THE TREE PUZZLE.

## 42. ANSWER TO AN EPITAPH ON ELLINOR BACHELLOR, AN OLD PIE WOMAN.

BENEATH in the dust
The mouldy old crust
Of Nell Bachellor lately was shoven:
Who was skilled in the arts
Of pies, custards, and tarts,
And knew every use of the oven.
When she'd liv'd long enough,
She made her last puff,
A puff by her husband much prais'd:
Now here she doth lie,
To make a dirt pie,
In hopes that her crust will be rais'd.

## 43. ANSWER TO A CURIOUS LETTER.

"Sir, between friends, I understand your overbearing disposition; a man even with the world is above contempt, whilst the ambitious are beneath ridicule."

## 44. ANSWER TO THE PUZZLE INSCRIPTION

By the use of the single vowel E, the following couplet was formed,

PERSEVERE YE PERFECT MEN,
EVER KEEP THESE PRECEPTS TEN.

# THE MAGIC OF ART.

"Tired at first sight with what the Muse imparts,
In fearless youth we tempt the height of arts."

An almost endless source of amusement, combining at the same time a considerable amount of instruction, may be obtained in the following manner. Take a card or piece of pasteboard, or even stiff paper, and draw upon it the form of an egg—an oval in outline. The dimensions of the oval are immaterial, and the experimenter may suit his own fancy in this respect. With a stout needle, or tracing point, prick quite through the outline, for the purposes of tracing. Some of our readers may be unacquainted with the mode of tracing an outline, and it may be advisable to particularize one method among many. Having pricked out the oval upon the card, get a little red or black lead, powdered, and placing the card upon a piece of drawing paper—any white paper will however do—rub it over the pricked-out oval, which will be found to be transferred to the white paper beneath, thus:

The powder may be applied either with a piece of wool or wadding, or by means of a dry camel's-hair pencil; care should be taken not to let the tracing-powder get beyond the edge of the pricked card, as in that case a soiled, dirty appearance is given to the tracing. The pierced card will serve, if carefully done, for hundreds of tracings, and it is obviously the best plan to take a little extra pains with that in the first instance.

With this traced oval for a basis, (a little further on we shall speak of other figures, to be used singly or in combination with each other) any one with a very little skill will be able to form an infinite number of objects.

The best drawing tool will be found to be an ordinary black lead pencil.

Figs. 1, 2, 3, 4, 5, 6 are very easy results, suggestive also of others. The rules of procedure are the same in all. Leaving the traced-out oval at first in its dotted form, with the pencil you draw a horizontal line as the basis of your figure. Let this and the other lines, which serve merely as the scaffolding of your figure, be done faintly or in dots. Next, draw a line through the center of the oval and perpendicular to the first. These will ensure your making the object square and properly balanced. After this you may draw lines parallel to the others: but these are not so material, although they serve as guides.

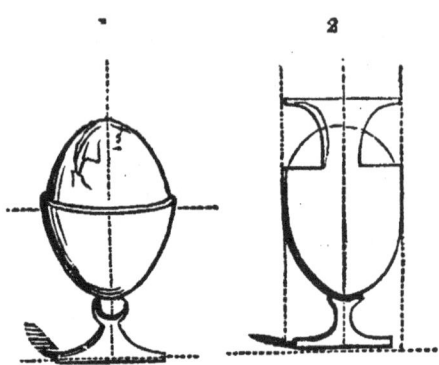

Now the imagination and fancy may step in to produce forms having the oval for a foundation; and not only is a very rational source of amusement opened out, but the

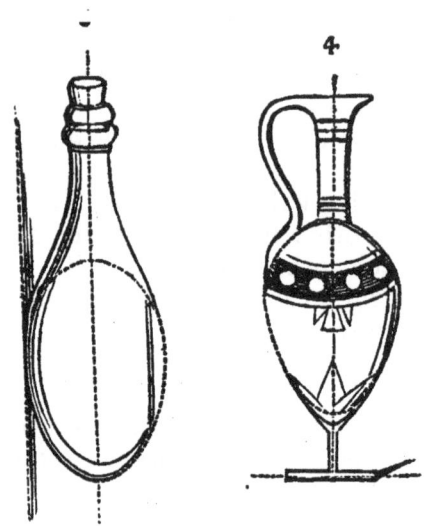

opportunity is given to a cultivation of the noble art of design, whether as applied to utility or ornament.

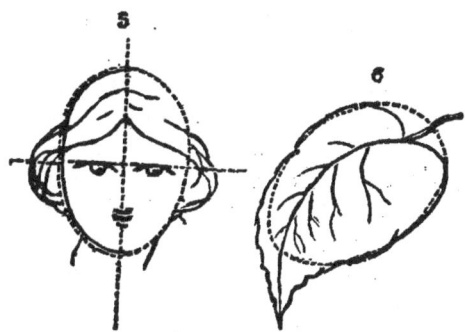

It is obvious to remark that the hand of many an amateur artist will readly be able to form the oval without having recourse to the pierced card ; but as this portion of our work is intended for *all*, we have suggested the above mode as sure to succeed under every circumstance.

Following the same plan in every particular, we subjoin some examples of what may be done with the square.

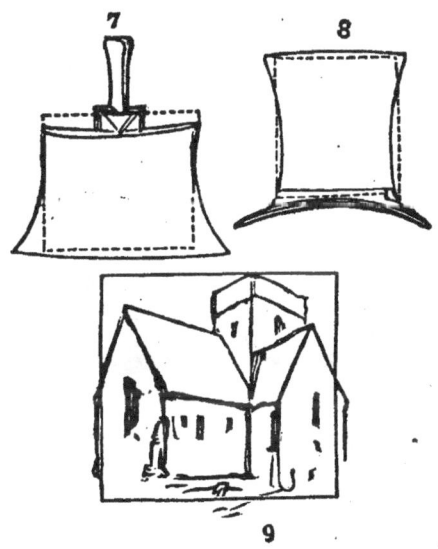

The dotted lines (*figs.* 7, 8) represent the traced or sketched square and plan lines ; the firmer lines suggest objects formed upon that figure. In the same way the thin square outline (*fig.* 9) suggests the inner sketch of a church.

I stated before that the size of the fundamental oval or square made little difference,; but I would recommend my younger readers to get these as large as possible, or convenient. If a large black board, such as is used in most schools, could be obtained, and the tracings prepared proportionably large (pounded chalk being used instead of the black or red powder in transferring the forms therto), and the designs made upon these with a piece of chalk, so much the better. However, this matters little; and each one will suit his or her own taste in that respect. I now proceed to submit some examples of what may be done with other rudimentary forms.

Following the instructions previously given, in place of the square suggested in Figs. 7, 8, 9, describe a circle

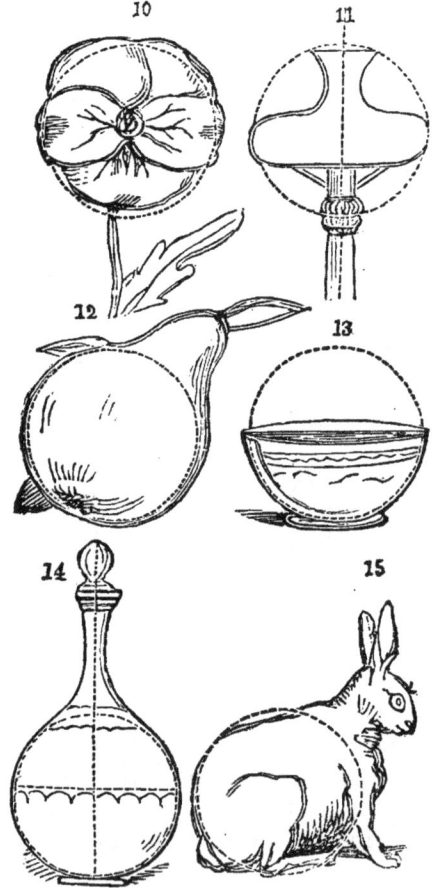

This may be done with a pair of compasses, or simply

## THE MAGIC OF ART.

sketched or traced by means of any round object, such as a coin laid flat upon the paper. Fig 10, 11, 12, 13, 14, 15, are given merely as suggestions, the circle forming an important part of their figure. The mind of the experimenter will immediately revert to other objects —thousands such are to be met with around us—having the circle or the sphere for their basis. And it will be no mean result of my labors, if any number of my younger readers are led thereby to a habit of observation, whereby they will not fail to notice that nearly all natural objects have the curved line for a basis, if they are not actually distinguishable thereby from those that are artificial.

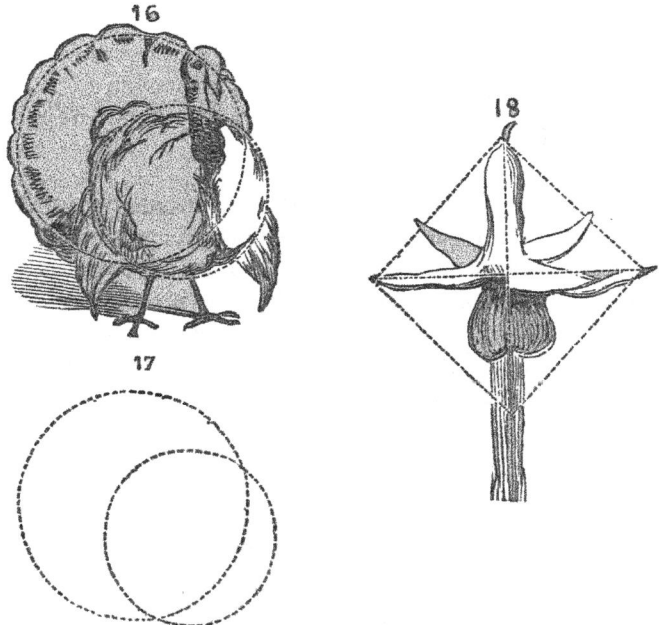

Fig. 16 is drawn upon two circles in combination with each other. The dotted lines of the plan will be readily perceived; but lest there should be any difficulty, they have been drawn separately in Fig. 17. With this uplex figure little skill will be required to present the lord of the farm yard. The three outlines, Figs. 18, 19, 20, are based upon the square turned diamond-wise, and will need no further remark : examples upon this plan may be multiplied easily. Those given will serve as hints in the several directions of flowers, foliage, and landscapes generally.

308    THE MAGICIAN'S OWN BOOK.

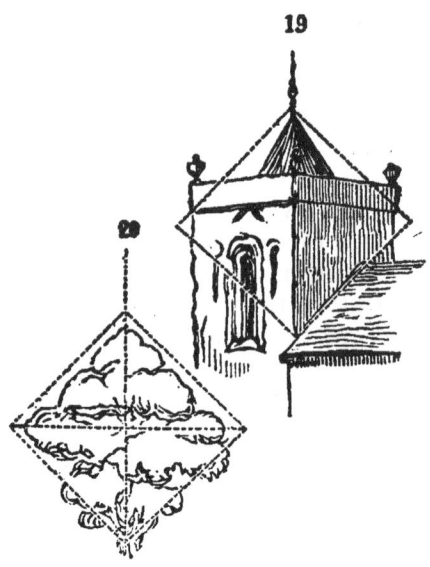

Before proceeding to show what may easily be done by a simple combination of the figures we have constructed, *i. e.*, the oval, square, and circle, let me introduce another, which enters, by a kind of natural law, into almost all forms or groups of forms, namely, the triangle. Observe in the annexed cut, Fig. 21, how naturally, although unconsciously, the girl seats herself within one.

A moment's reflection will show, that from the little nymph in the cut to the great pyramid, everything that rests solidly upon the earth must take the form, more or less, of this broad-based tapering figure. Roofs of houses, churches, and

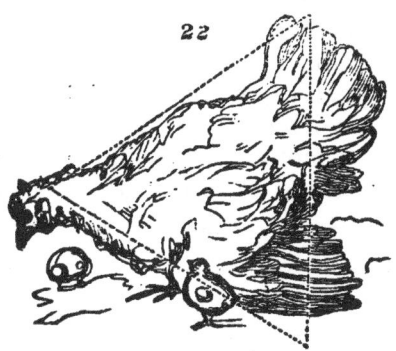

towers, are all triangular in their form, as are all great trees, differing from each other only in the width of their angles.

Construct a triangle,* and trace it according to former directions, and from the examples, Figs. 22, 23, 24, look

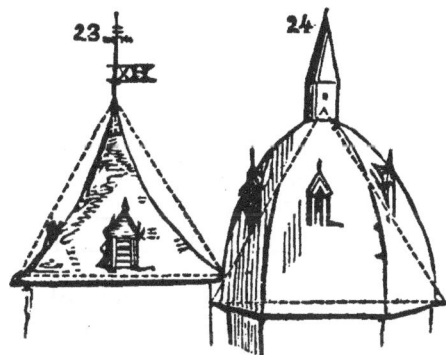

around you for others, and make various exercises upon this foundation.

Now, to proceed to something more complicated. Suppose you had either in your mind, or sketched out upon pa-

---

* This is done easily enough, but the following directions may not be needless for some. Draw a straight line for a base of any length. If you wish to form a equilateral triangle, *i. e.* one of which the three sides are equal, divide this base line by two, and at the point of division set up an upright line; then from each end of the base line slant against the central upright line one the length of the base. These, of course, will meet at the top, and the triangle is formed. Any other triangle may be formed in a similar manner, the length of the sides being at the choice of the artist.

per, the plan of a garden; that is to say, suppose you had the dimensions of a piece of ground, and intended to lay it out as a garden, allotting so much space to this and that bed, so much to gravel walks, and wanted to see how such an arrangement would look in perspective,—in other words, in reality, for perspective, however alarming it may look in books, with its net-work of lines, cross and across, like an insoluble riddle or a monster cobweb, is nothing more than the actual representation of things as they meet the eye.

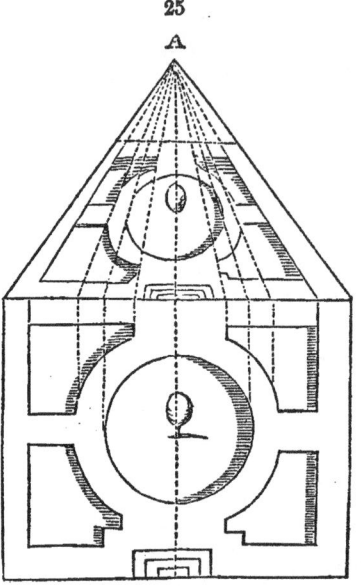

25

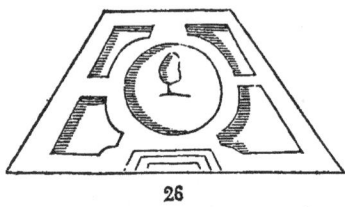

26

Let your plan be what is shown in the square portion of Fig. 25; at the top of this plan place your triangle, draw a line through the center of the square upwards, until it meets the top A of the triangle. Next draw lines from the corner of the beds parallel to the center line until they meet the base line of the triangle. From thence continue all these lines to the point A. These give you the width of the beds *in perspective*. The other sides of their figure may be easily enough found. Fig. 26 is the perspective view sought, and is what your experimental drawing would be if, having done the plan and guide-lines in pencil and the rest in pen and ink, you had erased the former with a piece of india rubber.

I do not know whether my readers regard the matter in the same light, but it appears to the present writer that this little figure—the triangle—is capable of working wonders in the hands of an amateur draughtsman, if only properly used. Of course, those regularly educated, or submitted to a long course of training as artists, are not referred to, but only the general public, which by the by, means nineteen out of every twenty individuals. I ask whether the preceding cut is any exaggeration on the average sort of result attained, not only amongst very juvenile experimenters, but those of maturer age?

Everybody possessed of vision can tell, ordinarily, whether

a building or other object is upright, or in the position proper to it, or necessary to its stability. By accustoming the hand to form lines, ovals, circles, squares, and triangles, and by habituating the mind to form comparisons between objects, and these and other figures, a person is put imperceptibly, as it were, in the way of depicting them with accuracy.

To proceed—let us take the above misrepresented country residence, and applying to it the previously given rules, see what we can make of it. We would first draw or trace the parallelogram shown in dotted lines; over this, we place a triangle; then drawing an upright line through the center of both, make that the base of another and lengthened triangle, as shown (see Fig. 28). Thus we get the three lines of the side and roofs; and if we knew the proportionate height of the side window, by marking the same at a, b, and carrying the lines from those points to the apex of the triangle, we get its true perspective dimensions.

The difference between the two results is as great as possible.

In Fig. 29 the triangle placed at the side of the soldier in front gives the perspective of the whole line.

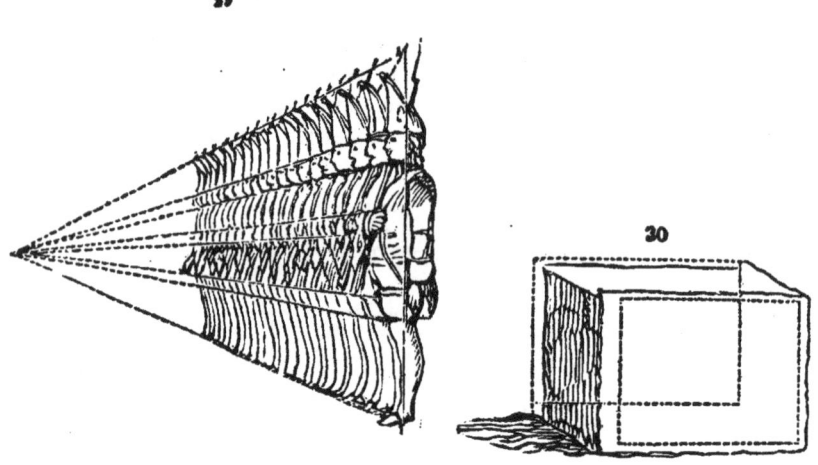

Fig. 30 shows how two parallelograms in combination assist in giving the perspective of a block of stone or bale of goods.

Fig. 31 exhibits the parallelogram and triangle in combination.

Perhaps nothing is more puzzling to the tyro in sketching

THE MAGIC OF ART.    813

than the interior of rooms and halls. In Fig. 32 a very easy method is given. Trace the outer parallelogram, and with-

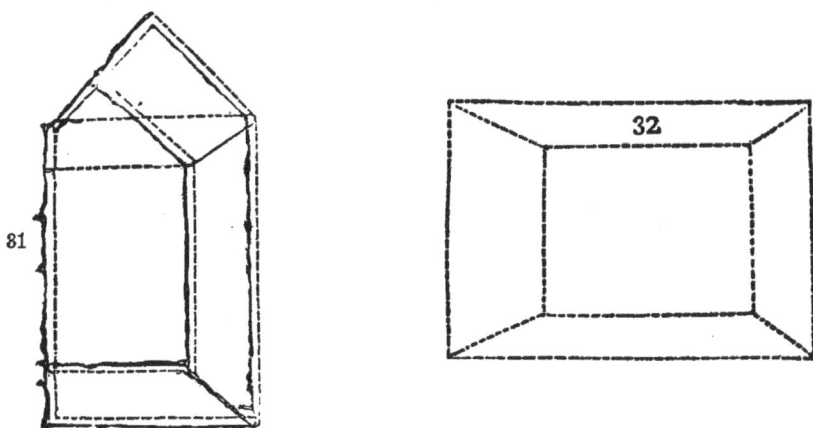

in it, a smaller one; then connect the corners of the two as shown in the cut.

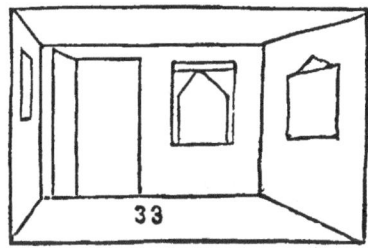

Fig. 33 is the application of the preceding.

By the present paper I intend to let you into a great secret, the secret, namely, of Comic or "Funny" Drawing—a method, in fact, which is at the bottom of all humorous, or

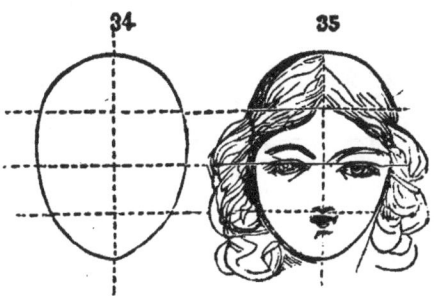

caricature sketching. Don't let any one be alarmed, and

14

suppose that it is intended to set you quizzing and caricaturing your friends. Far from it.

Draw the oval, Fig. 34. Divide it by transverse lines into about equal portions. You have now the basis for a face. Let the central line (across) mark the position of the eyes, the line above that the top of the forehead, the one below

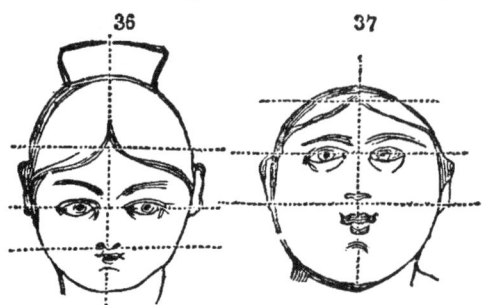

the bottom of the nose. By Fig. 35 you will see this worked out, and have what is considered a well proportioned face.

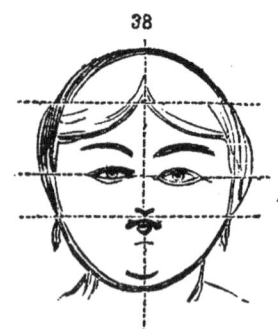

Now oddity of feature or expression is simply the result of a deviation from this regularity; and if, as you will perceive by the other Figs., 36, 37 and 38, these lines are placed higher or lower, or out of their, strictly speaking, *proper places*, you have, as a necessary result of such disarrangement, oddity, or comicality, which is founded upon irregularity or incongruity in things.

I shall carry out this hint more fully, at present merely pointing out, in reference to the next two figures, how the

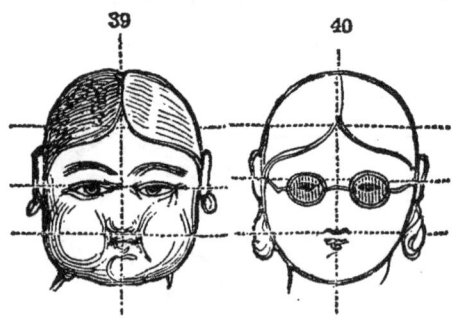

end is attained by placing a pair of dark spectacles upon a

regularly-featured face, or adding a little flesh to the lower portion of that at Fig. 39.

But not to forget the "Art" in the "Sport," let me add, that by sketching the plain oval, and remarking whereabout the lines of their features would cut it, you may, without difficulty, attempt likenesses of your friends and companions.

Now fill your slates or sketch-books with ovals, and try the effects of which the above are but indications. Your imaginations will furnish an endless variety of subjects. The omission of one eye, or its being covered by a shade, or closed while the other stares; the nose slightly on one side, the mouth a little wider than usual- these are all sources of the humorous, which, however, is far from being heightened by *ugliness*. Indeed, it should be borne in mind, that great distortion or hideousness, so far from contributing to humor, destroys it by raising painful images in the mind. True humor is closely allied to kindness.

Now let us take the simplest elements of the profile or side face. This is also formed upon the oval, with a slight variation. And here we must go a little more into the "Art" than at first sight the "Sport" seems to warrant. You will perceive by Fig. 41 that the oval used for profile purposes is divided as before into four about equal portions, which are appropriated in the same manner. That is to say, the central line across is for the eye, and the other two for the limit of the hair and the bottom of the nose.

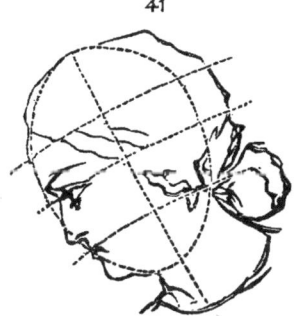

But take notice that portions are cut off—*e. g.*, at the back where the neck is inserted; a little has to be added for forehead, chin, and hair; and some modification takes place about the region of the eye.

Suffice it that the oval forms essentially the basis of the structure of a well proportioned face, such as is shown in the Fig. (41). Draw for yourself, or trace from Fig. 41, a figure for your basis. Next make a number of these tracings upon a clean sheet of drawing paper, and marking them in very lightly, in pencil, proceed as directed in the case of the front face in the last lesson; altering the feature lines, lengthening or shortening the chin, nose, and forehead according to your fancy. This will be a sufficient guide for you, and illustrations of this are accordingly omitted here.

Let us proceed a step further. The last hint only dealt with the depth relatively of the several parts of the face

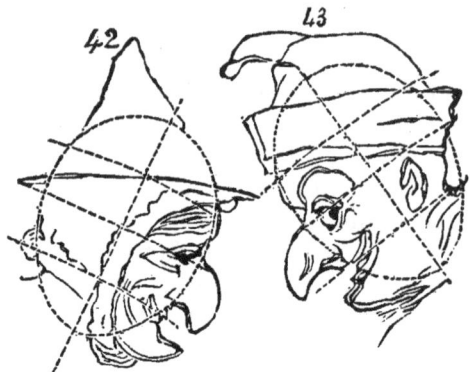

Now, as to their prominence. How very easily, by means of a few magic touches, which, by this time, you are magi-

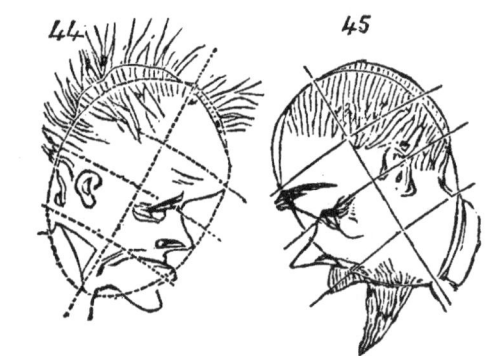

cians enough to impart, may you summon up our ancient acquaintance Mother Hubbard, or the modern hero Punch. (See Figs. 42, 43.)

Observe that the peculiarity of these comic physiognomies consists merely in their deviation from the regularly formed head of Fig. 41. They are constructed upon that figure, which may be seen underneath in dotted lines. The variety of ways in which this exercise may be worked is infinite. Subjoined are a few. In Figs. 44 and 45, beards, mustaches, eyebrows, the hair cut absurdly short, or left redundant, joined to the sinking in of the facial angle, produce the effect of comicality. In Figs. 46, 47, the same end is attained by the simplest means, and with even less exaggeration. And here I again repeat, that the less deviation there is from the proper proportions the better.

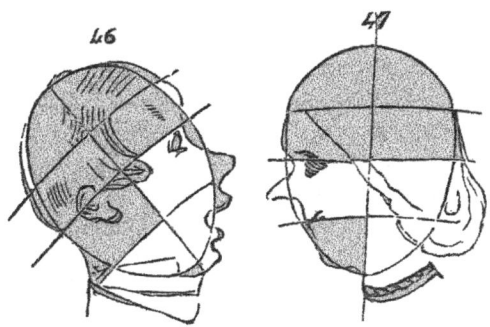

As a pendant to the comical landscape given No. 27 I give you the annexed (Fig. 48).

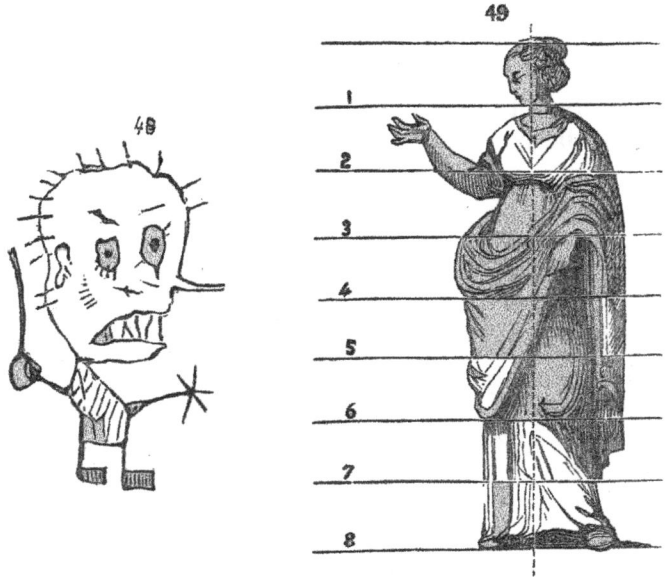

Every one will recognize it as a model drawing—such as is to be found upon walls, and occasionally upon the margins of school-books. This the artist (!) intends from a comic drawing. Of course it is no such thing.

We will new take up the grandest object of art the Human Figure. In desigining the human figure, there are three principal rules to be observed :

First, the standard height of the human body may be reckoned as eight times the length of the face. Dividing the entire length by eight, as shown in the annexed diagram (Fig. 49), it will be perceived that the face comprises one of the spaces: the second reaching to the chest: the third, to above the hips; the fourth cuts the entire length into two equal parts; the fifth extends to the center of the thigh: the sixth, to the knee joint; the seventh to half way down the leg; and the eighth, to the sole of the foot.

The second rule is, that no part of the body, viewed laterally, is more than twice the thickness of the head. In very young children, however, the rule is, that where the head will go, any part of the body will follow, as the experience of most people has tested.

The third rule concerns the center of gravity. By reference to the fig. (49), a vertical line will be perceived, drawn through the center of the figure. Whenever the body is at rest upon its legs, standing at ease, as one may say, this imaginary line must always pass through its center.

We shall see more about this hereafter, at present confining ourselves to the consideration of the first two rules. These must be considered as only generally true.

They have, however, to be well considered in connection

# THE MAGIC OF ART.

with our present subject; for as we said with the face, any great deviation from them leads to oddity, and is at the root of caricature drawing.

Trace out, or sketch out any size, the figures (Fig. 49 and 50), or any others for yourselves : or taking any well drawn figure in a print which may not be too costly to use so, draw with a black lead pencil upon the print similar lines to those in the figures, that is to say, divide its length into eight parts, first dropping a central line perpendicular to the ground.

You will thus test the accuracy of the rule, and familiarize yourself with the proportions of the figure. Then, for the purpose of comic drawing, you will vary these proportions. A face too long or too short, a body too large or too small for the legs, or legs otherwise disproportionate to the rest of the body, will yield the desired results. It will be seen by the Figs. 51 and 52 that their oddity has been arrived

at simply by this rule, or by the deviation from the strict rule of proportion.

Fig. 53 is given in illustration of the remarks upon the second rule. The form is correct enough as regards height, and deviates in the matter of lateral proportion.

We now come to consider the third principle—that of the center of gravity.

Observe in the annexed figures how the first (Fig. being at rest, commends itself to the reason like a mathematical demonstration. The next diagram shows a partial deviation from the center of gravity, is in a false posi-

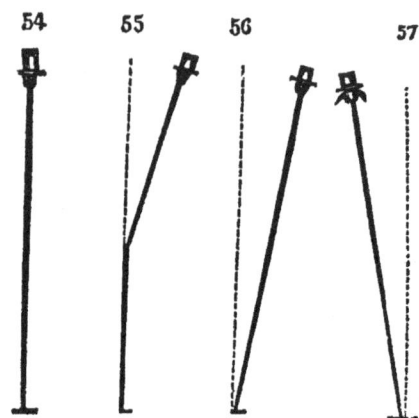

tion, and we begin either to pity or to laugh—poor diagram! The two following figures are other cases of the same sort —we feel instinctively for them—they are very far gone.

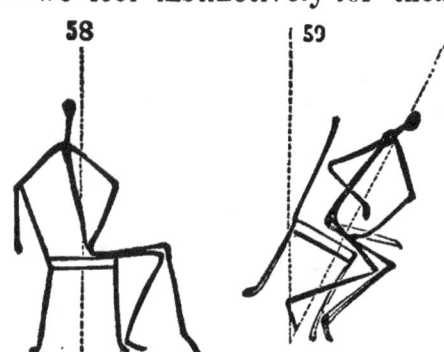

Try this rule upon your slates or sketching blocks; and after that we will go on to the next subject. In the diagrams (Figs. 58, 59), the same principle is enforced. The first is at rest, because the line passing through the center of the figure is a vertical line. In the next figure, that line being out of the vertical, the balance is disturbed, and the figure topples; so with the next. This is so plain that argument is not needed to demonstrate it.

Try this also for yourselves as before. Nor need we confine our experiments to figures comparatively at rest: forms in every variety of action come under the same rule—it is a law of nature There is a central line drawn through

# THE MAGIC OF ART.

the whole system of the universe, through every tree, and plant, and stone, and every upright thing, could we but see it.

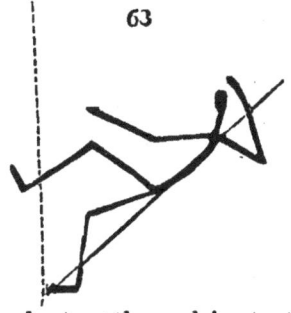

The first of the following figures is in full action, but it may go on for ever, as its balance is not in any way disturbed. The second is fast hastening to its fall. The third is much nearer still to that consummation.

It will suggest itself to every reader to apply the rule to other objects than the human figure. Trees in the positions of Figs. 64 and 65 are never seen unless through some violent accident; they may bend, and twist, and meander, but taking the objects as a whole, a central line, vertical to the horizon, will be detected, as shown in Fig. 65.

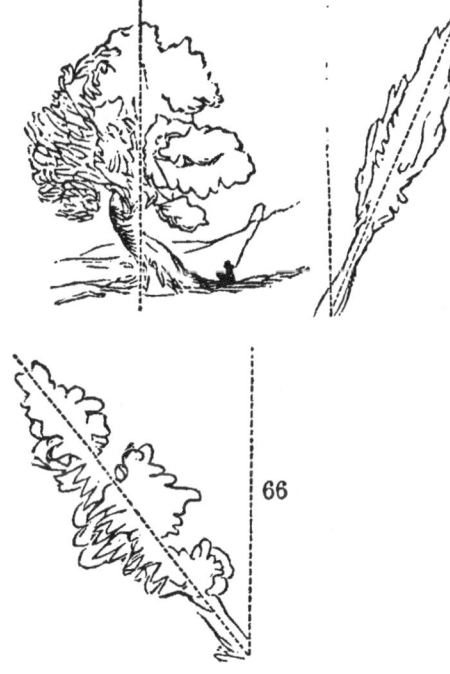

If we turn our attention in any direction upon natural objects, the clouds, the earth, the sea, flowers, trees, or animal bodies, we cannot fail to see that *a curved line* is always to be made out in their forms. Indeed, just so far as they are graceful and pleasing objects to the eye, this curved line is distinguishable. On the contrary, square lines offend the eye when met with under such circumstances. It is almost impossible indeed to imagine a square cloud, a square flower, or a square horse. When we see a square headed man, we are not impressed in his favor. We may have met with representations of natural objects, such as rocks, hill tops, mountain precipices, and the like, which had a square or nearly square appearance; but such things are almost always presented to our view as phenomena—*i. e.* things violating the regular order or general rule of nature. This curved line, which is the line of beauty, *must* pervade all nature; it is the natural law; and we cannot sufficiently admire the truth that that which is most necessary is also most beautiful.

Does any one ask what particular reference these observations have to "Art in Sport?" Let us say that they alone can properly understand what *is* comic who have learned to appreciate what is *not* comic. The distance between the sublime and the ridiculous is said to be very small—only one step. At any rate, the student who best understands the first will best appreciate the second. Socrates did not disdain to write an essay upon this subject, insisting that the very same qualities were essential in the comic and the tragic artist. But this is digressive.

Let us resume: In the annexed figure (67) you perceive the curved line. In proportion as you are able to make this perfectly, you will succeed in drawing gracefully. I must presume that very many of my readers will have no difficulty in copying the few natural objects suggested below. Practice upon your slate or board the figure (67) until you can do it easily. Then, for the purposes of "sport," proceed as follows. You wish to produce a droll "bit" of landscape Take any simple view, such as submitted in Fig. 68.

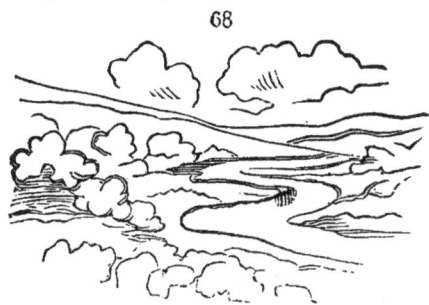

In this you will readily discover, as I said above, the curved, graceful lines of beauty—in the clouds, the outline of the distant hills, the foliage, the meandering stream. Let me advise you to practice this lesson somewhat perseveringly; apart from the new source of amusement which it is the object of these papers to open up, a beautiful lesson could be impressed upon the mind. Nothing is more calculated to refine the mind, to ennoble the thoughts, than to withdraw one's self from the artificial world, and to gaze upon the fresh face of nature.

And if we are able to do this intelligently—in other words, if, having learned the alphabet, we are able to peruse as it were the book of nature—the delight and the advantage is proportionably increased. Now turn to the example shown in Fig. 69. What do we see? The lines of beauty have given place to others less pleasing to the eye, and (except as a source of merriment) less acceptable to the mind. Fig. 69 is a comic landscape; how it has become so must be clearly apparent.

In Fig. 70, the same process is carried out, and the result is similar.

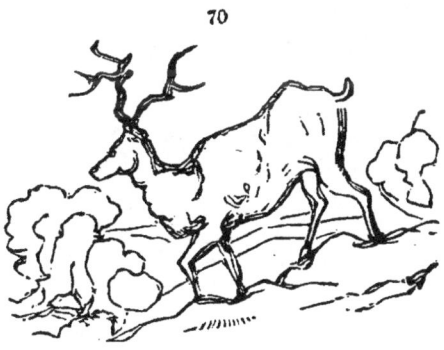

I hope that I shall not be understood to mean, that in order to be graceful everything must be round, or that everything round is graceful, or that every square object is ungraceful; or, again, that by making any curved line into a square or straight one the end we propose is to be obtained. Doubtless many round things are ungraceful, as many others composed entirely of straight lines at various angles to each other are exceedingly graceful. But what is meant is this: that natural objects, in which, left to themselves, the curved line predominates, are made odd and comic-looking when drawn upon the square.

In Fig. 71, not only the lines of the shepherd's form are

curved lines, and, therefore, conducive in a degree to its general pleasing character, but the *attitude* is formed upon a curved line. This will be perceived clearer by reference to the next figure, (72,) in which, without using a single

straight line in the parts of the form, the oddity is attained by making the whole attitude stiff and angular.

The student will find no difficulty in multiplying examples for himself: those given will suffice as hints. We must now proceed to show how comic designs may be made and applied to the slides of magic lanterns. The proper course of procedure is as follows:

Procure a piece of clear common window glass, without specks or scratches; let this be made perfectly clean. Prepare your design, which should be made the exact size you intend it to be painted upon the glass; color it; and when quite dry, place it beneath your slide of glass, to which it might be fastened at the corners by means of a little gum or varnish. Now commence to paint upon the glass an exact fac simile of the design, which, of course, you see clearly enough through the glass.

Common camel's hair brushes will do; those made of sable are, however, much better; but the first will suffice for ordinary purposes.

The colors necessary are what are called silica colors, and are procurable of most artist's color makers.

It will be necessary to let your first colors dry before putting on your shades; and it is desirable not to work in too hot a room, as the nature of the varnish with which you work is to dry very rapidly.

Bear in mind too, that upon glass you cannot wash in a tint. Broad surfaces, such as skies, must be stippled in, as in painting upon ivory.

In originating this paper on "The Magic of Art," the author did not propose to himself to give a complete treatise, but simply to point out, by some very easy processes, at source of amusement and instruction, available to almost every intelligent reader. It is hoped that, in this subject, he has not entirely failed, and that all will find some entertainment from,

## "Art in Sport."

# SECRET WRITING.

The art of communicating secret information by means of writing, which is intended to be illegible except by the person for whom it is destined, is very ancient. The ancients sometimes shaved the head of a slave, and wrote upon the skin with some indelible coloring matter, and then sent him, after his hair had been grown again, to the place of his destination. This is not, however, properly secret writing, but only a concealment of writing. Another kind, which corresponds better with the name, is the following, used by the ancients. They took a small stick, and wound around it bark or papyrus, upon which they wrote. The bark was then unrolled and sent to the correspondent, who was furnished with a stick of the same size. He wound the bark again round this, and thus was enabled to read what had been written.

This mode of concealment is evidently very imperfect. Cryptography properly consists in writing with signs, which are legible only to him for whom the writing is intended, or who has a key or explanation of the signs. The most simple method is to choose for every letter of the alphabet some sign, or only another letter. But this sort of cryptography (chiffre) is also easy to be deciphered without a key. Hence many illusions are used. No separation is made between the words, or signs of no meaning are inserted between those of real meaning. Various keys are also used according to rules before agreed upon. By this means the deciphering of the writing becomes difficult for a third person not initiated, but it is also extremely troublesome to the correspondents themselves, and a slight mistake often makes it illegible even to them.

Another mode of communicating intelligence secretly, viz. to agree upon some printed book, and mark the words out, is also troublesome, and not at all safe. The method of concealing the words which are to convey the information intended in matter of a very different character, in a long letter which the correspondent is enabled to read by applying a paper to it, with holes corresponding to the places of the significant words, is attended with many disadvantages: the paper may be lost, the repetition of certain words may lead to a discovery, and the difficulty of connecting the important with the unimportant matter, so as to give to the whole the appearance of an ordinary letter, is considerable.

There are many kinds of sympathetic inks. They are so called because the writings or drawings made by them are illegible, till by the action of some chemical agents, such as light, heat, acids, or other substances are brought in contact with them, when they appear. A weak sulphate of iron will be invisible in writing till washed over with a weak solution of prussiate of potass, which turns it of a beautiful blue. If we write with the nitro-muriate of gold, and afterwards brush the letters over with dilute muriate of tin, the writing will appear of a beautiful purple. If we write with a diluted solution of muriate of copper, and when dry present it to the fire, it will be of a yellow color.

Chemistry was also in great request for secret writing, and various substances were found to afford a fluid which would leave no mark behind the pen, until some chemical agent were applied. For example, if a letter be written with a pen dipped in the juice of lemon, the words will be invisible until the paper is held before the fire. This is caused by the action of the heat. Again, if a solution of nitrate of iron be the fluid used, the writing cannot be seen until it is dipped into a solution of galls, or even into tea, which will act upon the iron, and become ink. It was found that if a plain sheet of paper were sent, and intercepted the very fact of its being plain rendered it suspicious, and every means were used to render visible any writing that might be on it. A letter was therefore written with ordinary ink, on indifferent subjects, and between the lines the required information was added in some sympathetic ink. But writing with these or other sympathetic inks is unsafe, because the agents employed to render them visible are too generally known. Hence, the chiffre indéchiffrable, as it is called, has come very much into use, because it is easily applied, difficult to be deciphered, and the key may be preserved in the memory and easily changed. It consists of a table in which the letters of the alphabet, or any other signs agreed upon, are arranged as follow:

```
z a b c d e f g h i k l m n o p q r s t u v w x y z
a b c d e f g h i k l m n o p q r s t u v w x y z a
b c d e f g h i k l m n o p q r s t u v w x y z a b
c d e f g h i k l m n o p q r s t u v w x y z a b c
d e f g h i k l m n o p q r s t u v w x y z a b c d
e f g h i k l m n o p q r s t u v w x y z a b c d e
f g h i k l m n o p q r s t u v w x y z a b c d e f
g h i k l m n o p q r s t u v w x y z a b c d e f g
h i k l m n o p q r s t u v w x y z a b c d e f g h
i k l m n o p q r s t u v w x y z a b c d e f g h i
k l m n o p q r s t u v w x y z a b c d e f g h i k
l m n o p q r s t u v w x y z a b c d e f g h i k l
m n o p q r s t u v w x y z a b c d e f g h i k l m
n o p q r s t u v w x y z a b c d e f g h i k l m n
o p q r s t u v w x y z a b c d e f g h i k l m n o
p q r s t u v w x y z a b c d e f g h i k l m n o p
q r s t u v w x y z a b c d e f g h i k l m n o p q
r s t u v w x y z a b c d e f g h i k l m n o p q r
s t u v w x y z a b c d e f g h i k l m n o p q r s
t u v w x y z a b c d e f g h i k l m n o p q r s t
u v w x y z a b c d e f g h i k l m n o p q r s t u
v w x y z a b c d e f g h i k l m n o p q r s t u v
w x y z a b c d e f g h i k l m n o p q r s t u v w
x y z a b c d e f g h i k l m n o p q r s t u v w x
y z a b c d e f g h i k l m n o p q r s t u v w x y
z a b c d e f g h i k l m n o p q r s t u v w x y z
```

Any word is now taken for a key. The word *Paris*, for example. This is a short word, and for the sake of secresy it would be well to choose for the key some one or more words less striking. Suppose we wish to write in this cypher with this key the phrase, "We lost a battle," we must write *Paris* over the phrase, repeating it as often as is necessary, thus:

Pa risP a risPar
We lost a battle.

We now take cypher for *w*, the letter which we find in the square opposite *w* in the left margin column, and under *p* on the top, which is *m*. Instead of *e* we take the letter opposite *e*, and under *a*, which is *f*; for *l*, the letter opposite *c*, and under *z*, and so on.

Proceeding thus, we should obtain the following series of letters:

mf cxli b tkmimw

The person who receives the epistle writes the key over the letters

P a r i s P a r i s P a r
m f c x l i b t k m i m w

He now goes down in the perpendicular line, at the top of which is *p*, until he meets *m*, opposite to which, in the left marginal column, he finds *w*. Next, going in the line of *a* down to *f*, he finds, on the left, *e*. In the same way *r* gives *l*, *i* gives *o*, and so on. Or you may reverse the process; begin with *p*, in the left marginal column, and look along horizontally till you find *m*, over which, in the top line, you will find *w*. It is easily seen that the same letter is not always designated by the same cypher; thus *e* and *a* occur twice in the phrase selected, and they are designated respectively by the cyphers *f* and *w*, *b* and *k*. Thus the possibility of finding out the secret writing is almost impossible.

The key may be changed from time to time, and a different key may be used with each correspondent. The utmost accuracy is necessary, because one character accidentally omitted changes the whole cypher. The best way of determining the key word is to arrange that any word which occurs at a certain distance from the beginning or end shall be the key word—the tenth from the beginning, for example. The key word will thus change every time, and any combination of letters will make it. This will make it impossible to be guessed.

230                THE MAGICIAN'S OWN BOOK.

The easiest method of working this square is to cut a piece of thin wood like a carpenter's square, and by applying it to the alphabet the letter is at once seen in the angle. For example, supposing such a square to be applied so that one side is on the letter *p* at the top, and the other on the letter *w* at the left hand, the letter *m* will be in the angle, so that the trouble of following the lines with the eye will be avoided.

Here is another specimen of secret writing.

A LOCK FOR MR. HOBBS TO PICK.

T:2 21rt:(,)t:2 s21(,)t:2 st1rr6 s,6(,)
1r2 86p : 2rs wr3t 76 : 1-9 93v3-2(,)
T : 1t : 1-9 w:38: t5-29 t:23r : 1r ? 4-6(,)
1-9 7192 t:23r v1r329 .!4r325 s:3-2(:)
3- t:2? 22- :21t:2-s 262 ?16 s22
S6?74!s 3- 5-2 .rl-9 tr3t: 84?75-2(;)
76t 3- t:2 744, 40 744,s t:2r2 !32s
1 ,26 34 r219 t:23r ?6st2r32s (.)

T:2- !2t -4t 013t:!2ss t4-.52 19v1-82
3ts s:l!!4w v15-ts(,)-4r s84002r 91r2
5p4- t:2 71s2 40 3.-4rl-82
T4 r13s2 1 str58t5r2 40 92sp13r(!)
T:45.: 044!s ?16 .3v2 t:2 w4r!9s t4 8:1-82(,)
92s3.- 1-9 pr4v392-82 1r2 t:2r2(.)
:4w 7!3-929(,)w:4 1t 921t: 1!4-2
T:23r 922p s3.-30381-86 4w-(!)

HERE IS THE ANSWER.

The letters are represented by the figures and symbols below them. With this key the lock may be opened.

a b c d e f g h i j k l m n o u y
1 7 8 9 2 0 . : 3 ; , ! ? - 4 5 6

The stops enclosed in brackets, are used in their capacity of stops: thus, (,) (;) &c.

The earth, the sea, the starry sky,
 Are cyphers writ by hand divine,
That hand which tuned their harmony,
 And bade their varied glories shine;

## SECRET WRITING.

In them e'en heathen's eye may see
    Symbols in one grand Truth combine;
But in the book of books there lies
    A key to read their mysteries.

Then let not faithless tongue advance
    Its shallow vaunts, nor scoffer dare
Upon the base of ignorance
    To raise a structure of despair!
Though fools may give the world to chance
    Design and Providence are there:
How blinded, who at death alone
    Their deep significancy own!

### THE CIRCULAR CYPHER.

To carry on a correspondence without the possibility of the meaning of the letter being detected, in case it should be opened by any other person, has employed the ingenuity of many. No method will be found more effectual for this purpose, or more easy, than the following.

Provide a piece of square card or pasteboard, and draw a circle on it, which circle is to be divided into 27 equal parts, in each of which parts must be written *one* of the capital let-

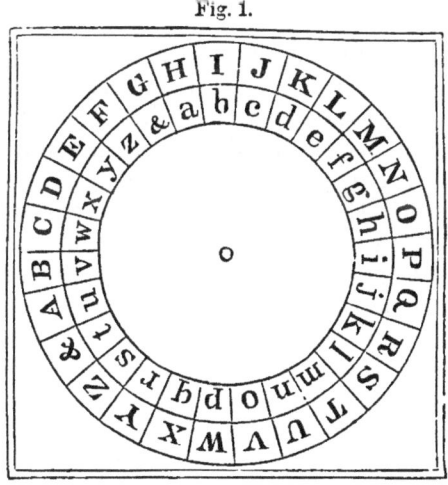
Fig. 1.

ters of the alphabet, and the &, as in the figure. Let the center of this circle be blank. Then draw another circle, also divided into 27 equal parts, in each of which write one of the small letters of the alphabet, and the &. This circle must be cut round, and made exactly to fit the blank space in the center of the large circle, and must run round a pivot or pin. The person with whom you correspond must have a similar dial, and at the beginning of your letter you must put the capital letter, and at the end the small letter, which answer to each other when you have fixed your dial.

Suppose what you wish to communicate is as follows :

*I am so watched I cannot see you as I promised; but I will meet you to-morrow in the park, with the letters, &c.*

You begin with the letter *T*, and end with the letter *m*, which shows how you have fixed the dial, and how your correspondent must fix his, that he may decipher your letter. Then, for *I am*, you write *b uf*, and so of the rest, as follows·

---

*T b uf lh pumwayx b wugghm lyy rhn ul b ikhfblyx vnm b pbee fyym rhn mh fhkkhp bg may iukd pbma may eymmykl, tw.    m.*

---

### Another Way.

Take two pieces of card, pasteboard, or stiff paper, through which you cut long squares at different distances. One of these you keep yourself, and the other you give to your correspondent. You lay the pasteboard on a paper, and, in the spaces cut out write what you would have understood by him only ; then fill the intermediate spaces with any words that will connect the whole together, and make a different sense. When he receives it, he lays his pasteboard over the whole, and those words which are between crotchets [ ] form the intelligence you wish to communicate. For example : suppose you want to express these words,

"*Don't trust Robert : I have found him a villain.*"

"[Don't] fail to send my books. I [trust] they will be ready when [Robert] calls on you. [I have] heard that you have [found] your dog. I call [him a villain] who stole him." You may place a pasteboard of this kind three other ways—the bottom at top—the top at bottom, or by turning it over; but in this case you must previously apprize your correspondent, or he may not be able to decipher your meaning.

## SECRET CORRESPONDENCE BY MUSIC.

Form a circle like Fig. 2, divided into twenty-six parts, with a letter of the alphabet written in each. The interior

Fig. 2.

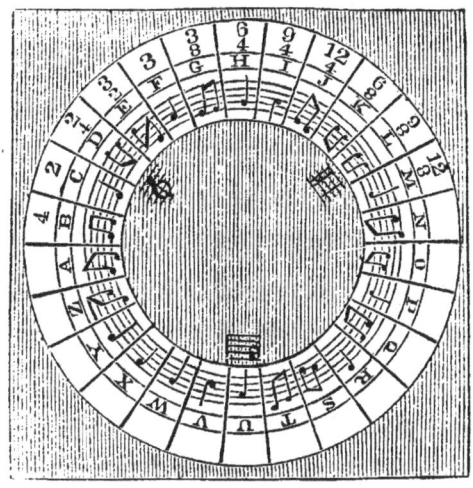

of the circle is movable, like that in Fig. 1, and the circumference is to be ruled like music paper. Place in each division a note different in figure or position.

Within the musical lines place the three keys, and on the outer circle the figures to denote time. Then get a ruled paper, and place one of the keys (suppose *ge-re-sol*) against the time 2-4ths, at the beginning of the paper, which will inform your correspondent how to place his circle. You

then copy the notes that answer to the letters of the words you intend to write, in the manner expressed above.

# THE MAGIC OF STRENGTH.

"Not two strong men the enormous weight could raise,
Such men as live in these degenerate days."—POPE'S HOMER.

The mechanical knowledge of the ancients was principally theoretical; and though they seem to have executed some minor pieces of mechanism which were sufficient to delude the ignorant, yet there is no reason for believing that they have executed any machinery that was capable of exciting much surprise, either by its ingenuity or its magnitude. The properties of the mechanical powers, however, seem to have been successfully employed in performing feats of strength which were beyond the reach even of strong men, and which could not fail to excite the greatest wonder when exhibited by persons of ordinary size.

Firmus, a native of Seleucia, who was executed by the Emperor Aurelian for espousing the cause of Zenobia, was celebrated for his feats of strength. In his account of the life of Firmus, who lived in the third century, Vopiscus informs us that he could suffer iron to be forged upon an anvil placed upon his breast. In doing this, he lay upon his back, and, resting his feet and shoulders against some support, his whole body formed an arch, as we shall afterward more particularly explain. Until the end of the sixteenth century, the exhibition of such feats does not seem to have been common. About the year 1703, a native of Kent, of the name of Joyce, exhibited such feats of strength in London and other parts of England, that he received the name of the second Samson. His own personal strength was very great; but he had also discovered, without the aid of theory, various positions of his body in which men even of common strength could perform very surprising feats. He drew against horses, and raised enormous weights; but as he actually exhibited his powers in ways which evinced the enormous strength of his own muscles, all his feats were ascribed to the same cause. In the course of eight or ten years, however, his methods were discovered, and many individuals of ordinary strength exhibited a number of his principal performances, though in a manner greatly inferior to Joyce.

Some time afterward, John Charles Van Eckeberg, a native of Harzgerode, in Anhault, traveled through Europe under the appellation of Samson, exhibiting very remarkable examples of his strength. This, we believe, is the same person whose feats are particularly described by Dr. Desaguliers. He was a man of the middle size, and of ordinary strength; and as Dr. Desaguliers was convinced that his feats were exhibitions of skill, and not of strength he was desirous of discovering his methods, and, with this view, he went to see him, accompanied with the Marquis of Tullibardine, Dr. Alexander Stuart, Dr. Pringle, and his own mechanical operator. They placed themselves round the German, so as to be able to observe accurately all that he did, and their success was so great, that they were able to perform most of the feats the same evening by themselves, and almost all the rest when they had provided the proper apparatus. Dr. Desaguliers exhibited some of the experiments before the Royal Society, and has given such a distinct explanation of the principles on which they depend, that we shall endeavor to give a popular account of them.

1. The performer sat upon an inclined board A B, placed upon a frame C D E, with his feet abutting against the up-

FIG. 1.

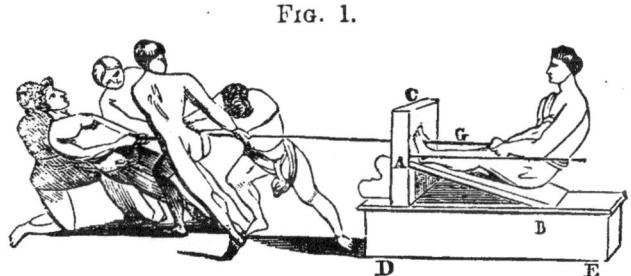

right board c. Round his loins was placed a strong girdle FG, to the iron ring of which at G was fastened a rope by means of a hook. The rope passed between his legs through a hole in board c, and several men, or two horses, pulling at the other end of the rope, were unable to draw the performer out of his place. His hands at G seemed to pull against the men, but they were of no advantage to him whatever.

2. Another of the German's feats is shown in Fig. 2.

Having fixed the rope above mentioned to a strong post at A, and made it pass through a fixed iron eye at B, to the

FIG. 2.

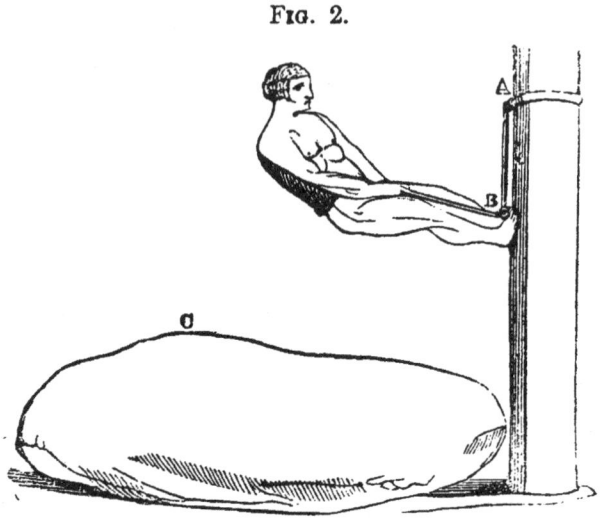

ring in his girdle, he planted his feet against the post at B, and raised himself from the ground by the rope, as shown in the figure. He then suddenly stretched out his legs and broke the rope, falling back on a feather bed at C, spread out to receive him.

FIG. 3.

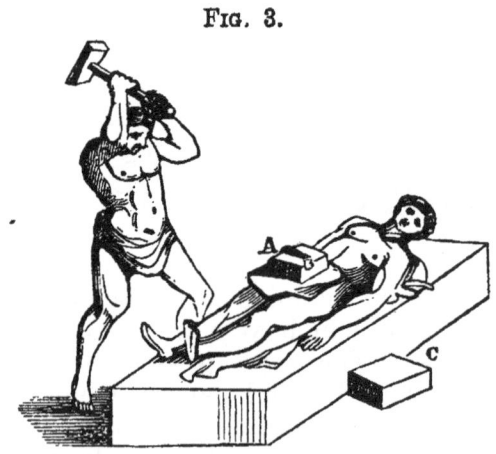

3. In imitation of Firmus, he laid himself down on the ground, as shown in Fig. 3, and when an anvil A was placed upon his breast, a man hammered with all his force

the piece of iron B, with a sledge hammer, and sometimes two smiths cut in two with chisels a great cold bar of iron laid upon the anvil. At other times a stone of huge dimensions, half of which is shown at C, was laid upon his belly, and broken with a blow of the great hammer.

Fig. 4.

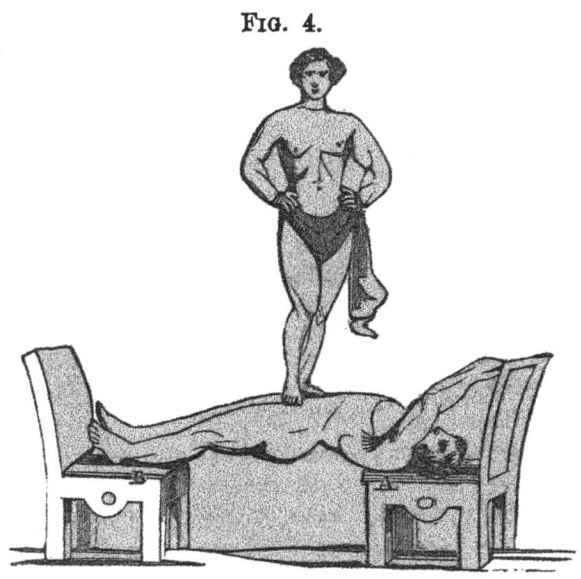

4. The performer then placed his shoulders upon one chair, and his heels upon another, as in Fig. 4, forming, with his back-bone, thighs, and legs, an arch springing from its abutments at A and B. One or two men then stood upon his belly, rising up and down while the performer breathed. A stone, one and a half feet long, one foot broad, and half a foot thick, was then laid upon his belly and broken by a sledge hammer, an operation which may be performed with much less danger than when his back touched the ground, as in Fig. 3.

5. His next feat was to lie down on the ground, as in Fig. 5. A man being then placed on his knees, he draws his heels towards his body, and, raising his knees, he lifts up the man gradually, till, having brought his knees perpendicularly under him, as in Fig. 6, he raises his own body up, and, placing his arms around the man's legs, he rises with him, and sets him down on some low table or eminence of the same height as his knees. This feat he sometimes performed with two men in place of one.

338    THE MAGICIAN'S OWN BOOK.

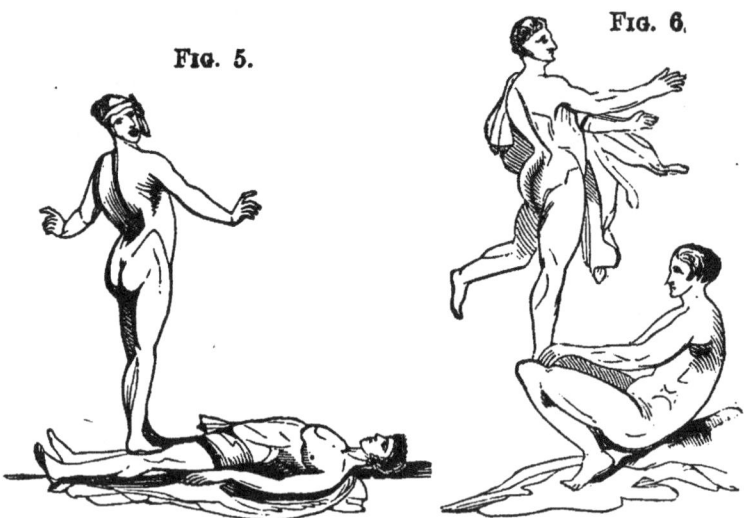

FIG. 5.   FIG. 6.

6. The last, and apparently the most wonderful, performance of the German, is shown in Fig. 7, where he appears to raise a cannon A, placed upon a scale, the four ropes of the scale being fixed to a rope or chain attached to his girdle, in the manner already described. Previous to the fixing of the ropes, the cannon and scale rest upon two rollers B C, but when all is ready, the two rollers are knocked from beneath the scale, and the cannon is sustained by the strength of his loins.

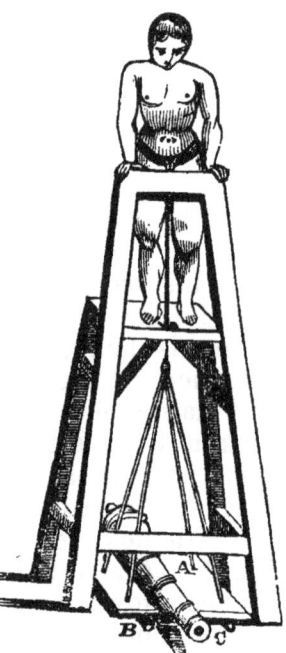

FIG. 7.

The German also exhibited his strength in twisting into a screw a flat piece of iron like A, Fig. 8. He first bent the iron into a right angle, as at B, and then wrapping his handkerchief about its broad upper end, he held that end in his left hand, and with his right applied to the other end, twisted about the angular point, as shown at C. Lord Tullibardine succeeded in doing the same thing, and even untwisted one of the irons which the German had twisted.

It would lead into details by no means popular, were I to

give a minute explanation of the mechanical principles upon which these feats depend. A few general observations will perhaps be sufficient for ordinary readers. The feats No. 1, 2, and 7, depend entirely on the natural strength of the bones of the pelvis, which form a double arch, which it would require an immense force to break, by any external pressure directed to the center of the arch; and, as the legs and thighs are capable of sustaining four or five thousand pounds when they stand quite upright, the performer has no difficulty in resisting the force of two horses, or of

FIG. 8.

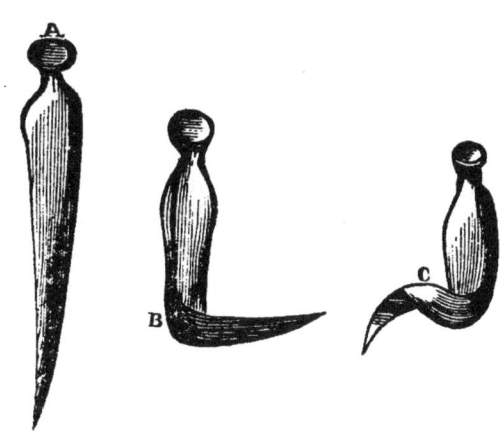

sustaining the weight of a cannon weighing two or three thousand pounds.

The feat of the anvil is certainly a very surprising one. The difficulty, however, really consists in sustaining the anvil; for when this is done, the effect of the hammering is nothing. If the anvil were a thin piece of iron, or even two or three times heavier than the hammer, the performer would be killed by a few blows; but the blows are scarcely felt when the anvil is very heavy, for the more matter the anvil has, the greater is its inertia, and it is the less liable to be struck out of its place; for when it has received by the blow the whole momentum of the hammer, its velocity will be so much less than that of the hammer, as its quantity of matter is greater. When the blow, indeed, is struck, the man feels less of the weight of the anvil than he did before, because, in the reaction of the stone, all the parts of it round about the hammer rise towards the blow. This property is illustrated by the well known experiment of laying a stick with its ends upon two drinking glasses full of water, and striking the stick downwards in the middle with an iron bar. The stick will in this case be broken without breaking the glasses, or spilling the water. But if the stick is struck upwards, as if to throw it up in the air, the glasses will break if the blow be strong, and if the blow is not very quick, the water will be spilled without breaking the glasses.

When the performer supports a man upon his belly, as in Fig. 4, he does it by means of the strong arch formed by his backbone, and the bones of his legs and thighs. If there were room for them, he could bear three or four, or, in their stead, a great stone to be broken with one blow.

A number of feats of real and extraordinary strength were exhibited about a century ago, in London, by Thomas Topham, who was five feet ten inches high, and about thirty-one years of age. He was entirely ignorant of any of the methods for making his strength appear more surprising; and he often performed, by his own natural powers, what he learned had been done by others by artificial means. A distressing example of this occurred in his attempt to imitate the feat of the German Samson by pulling against horses. Ignorant of the method which we have already described, he seated himself on the ground with his feet against two stirrups, and by the weight of his body he succeeded in pulling against a single horse; but in attempting to pull against two horses, he was lifted out of his place, and one of his knees was shattered against the stirrups, so as to deprive him of most of the strength of one of his legs. The following are the feats of real strength which Dr. Desaguliers saw him perform.

1. Having rubbed his fingers with coal-ashes to keep them from slipping, he rolled up a very strong and large pewter plate.

2. Having laid seven or eight short and strong pieces of tobacco-pipe on the first and third fingers, he broke them by the force of his middle finger.

3. He broke the bowl of a strong tobacco-pipe placed between his first and third fingers, by pressing his fingers together sideways.

4. Having thrust such another bowl under his garter, his

legs being bent, he broke it to pieces by the tendons of his hams, without altering the bending of his leg.

5. He lifted with his teeth, and held in a horizontal position for a considerable time, a table six feet long, with half a hundred weight hanging at the end of it. The feet of the table rested against his knees.

6. Holding in his right hand an iron kitchen poker three feet long and three inches round, he struck upon his bare left arm, between the elbow and the wrist, till he bent the poker nearly to a right angle.

7. Taking a similar poker, and holding the ends of it in his hands, and the middle against the back of his neck, he brought both ends of it together before him, and he then pulled it almost straight again. This last feat was the most difficult, because the muscles which separate the arms horizontally from each other are not so strong as those which bring them together.

8. He broke a rope about two inches in circumference, which was partly wound about a cylinder four inches in diameter, having fastened the other end of it to straps that went over his shoulder.

9. Dr. Desaguliers saw him lift a rolling stone of about 800 pounds' weight with his hands only, standing in a frame above it, and taking hold of a frame fastened to it. Hence Dr. Desaguliers gives the following relative view of the strengths of individuals :

  Strength of the weakest men, . . 125 pounds.
  Strength of very strong men, . . 400
  Strength of Topham, . . . . . 800

The weight of Topham was about 200.

One of the most remarkable and inexplicable experiments relative to the strength of the human frame, which we have ourselves seen and admired, is that in which a heavy man is raised with the greatest facility, when he is lifted up the instant that his own lungs, and those of the persons who raise him, are inflated with air. This experiment was, I believe, first shown in England a few years ago by Major H., who saw it performed in a large party at Venice under the direction of an officer of the American navy. As Major H. performed it more than once in my presence, I shall describe, as nearly as possible, the method which he prescribed. The heaviest person in the party lies down upon two chairs, his legs being supported by the one and his back by the other. Four persons, one at each leg and one at each shoulder, then try to raise him, and they find his dead weight to be very great, from the difficulty they experience in supporting him. When he is replaced in the chairs, each of the four persons takes hold of the body as before, and the person to be lifted gives two signals by clapping his hands. At the first signal he himself and the four lifters begin to draw a long and full breath, and when the inhalation is completed, or the lungs filled, the second signal is given, for raising the person from the chairs. To his own surprise and that of his bearers, he rises with the greatest facility, as if he were no heavier than a feather. On several occasions I have observed that when one of the bearers performs his part ill, by making the inhalation out of time, the part of the body which he tries to raise is left, as it were, behind. As we have repeatedly seen this experiment, and have performed the part both of the load and of the bearer, we can testify how remarkable the effects appear to all parties, and how complete is the conviction, either that the load has been lightened, or the bearer strengthened by the prescribed process.

At Venice, the experiment was performed in a much more imposing manner. The heaviest man in the party was raised and sustained upon the points of the fore fingers of six persons. Major H. declared that the experiment would not succeed if the person lifted were placed upon a board, and the strength of the individuals applied to the board. He conceived it necessary that the bearers should communicate directly with the body to be raised. I have not had an opportunity of making any experiments relative to these curious facts; but whether the general effect is an illusion, or the result of known or of new principles, the subject merits a careful investigation.

Among the remarkable exhibitions of mechanical strength and dexterity, we may enumerate that of supporting pyramids of men. This exhibition is a very ancient one. The simplest form of this feat consists in placing a number of men upon each other's shoulders, so that each row consists of a man fewer till they form a pyramid terminating in a single person, upon whose head a boy is sometimes placed with his feet upwards.

# MISCELLANEOUS

# CURIOUS TRICKS AND FANCIES.

"Youth loves and lives on change,
Till the soul sighs for sameness, which at last
Becomes variety, and takes its place."

### AN ARTIFICIAL MEMORY.

The reader must have observed, that to perform several of the recreations in this book, it is necessary to have a good memory; but as that is a gift every one has not from nature, many methods have been contrived to supply that defect by art—the most material of which we shall here describe.

An artificial memory respects either figures or words; for the former, let the five vowels, a, e, i, o, u, represent the first five digits; the diphthongs that begin with the first four vowels, as au, ea, ie, ou, representing the remaining four digits, let y stand for an 0, or cypher. Let the ten first consonants also stand for the nine digits and the cypher, as in the following table:

| a | e | i | o | u | au | ea | ie | ou | y |
|---|---|---|---|---|----|----|----|----|---|
| 1 | 2 | 3 | 4 | 5 | 6  | 7  | 8  | 9  | 0 |
| b | c | d | f | g | h  | k  | l  | m  | n |

Then to represent any number, let the first letter be a vowel or diphthong, the second a consonant, the third a vowel, the fourth a consonant, &c. Thus for the number 1763, you write or remember the word *akaud*; if there are several sums to be retained, you place the words in form of verses, which will make them more pleasing to repeat and more easy to remember; for example, if you would remember the dates of the discovery of America by Columbus, the settlement of Virginia by Captain Smith, the landing of the Pilgrims at Plymouth, the Battle of Bunker Hill, the Declaration of Independence, and the Battle of New Orleans, which were in 1492, 1605, 1620, 1775, 1776, and 1815, you write as follows—for you are to observe that in this, as well as similar cases, when the first figure is always the same, it is unnecessary to write it after the first time:

Afouc hyh hen keag keah lag.

When several cyphers come together, instead of repeating y or *n*, you may write y or *n* 2, 3, &c.; thus, for 3400, write *ify*2, and for 256,000, write *ehun*3.

To remember any number of words, select the initial letters of those words, and to the first add a, if it begins with a consonant, or b, if it begins with a vowel. In like manner e or c to the second initial letter; to the third add i or d; to the fourth o or f; to the fifth u or g, so that of the five initials you make five syllables, which are joined together in one word—then of the next five initials you make, in the same manner, another word, and of every two words you make a verse; for example, suppose you would remember the names of all the kings of England since the Norman conquest in the order in which they reigned, you then write as follows:

W*a* we h*i* so h*u*   R*a* je h*i* ef *eg*
E*b* r*e* h*i* ho h*u*   E*b* ec r*i* ho h*u*
E*b* me e*d* jo c*u*   C*a* je w*i* a*f* g*u* G*a* ge g*i* go w*u* V*a*.

Or, if you would remember the letters that begin any number of verses, suppose the twenty first lines of Pope's Essay on Man, you write as follows:

A*btelitoeg*   A*bacodtotu*
T*aocedaflu*   B*asewioffu*.

### THE MAGICIAN'S MIRROR.

Construct a box of wood, of a cubical shape, A B C D, of about fifteen inches every way. Let it be fixed to the pedestal P, at the usual height of a man's head. In each side of

## MISCELLANEOUS TRICKS AND FANCIES.

this box let there be an opening, of an oval form, ten inches high, and seven wide. In this box place two mirrors, A D, with their backs against each other. Let them cross the box in a diagonal line, and in a vertical position. Decorate the openings in the side of this box with four oval frames and transparent glasses, and cover each with a curtain so contrived as all to draw up together.

Place four persons in front of the four sides, and at equal distances from the box, and then draw them up that they may see themselves in the mirrors, when each of them, instead of his own figure, will see that of the person next to him, but who will appear to him to be placed on the opposite side. Their confusion will be the greater, as it will be very difficult, if not impossible, for them to discover the mirrors concealed in the box. The reason of this phenomenon is evident; for though the rays of light may be turned aside by a mirror, yet they always *appear* to proceed in right lines.

### THE PERSPECTIVE MIRROR.

Provide a box, A B C D, of about two feet long, fifteen inches wide, and 12 inches high. At the end A C, place the concave mirror, the focus of whose parallel rays is eighteen inches from the reflecting surface. At I L place a pasteboard, blacked, in which a hole is cut, sufficiently large to see on

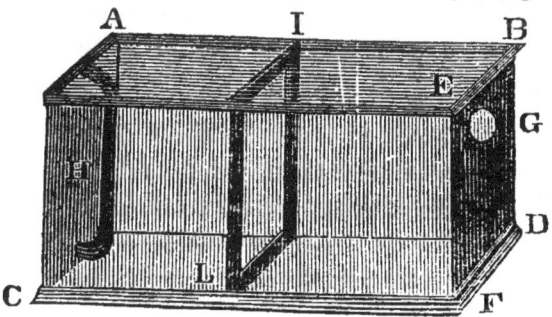

the mirror H the object placed at B E F D. Cover the top of the box, from A to I, close, that the mirror H may be entirely darkened. The other part, I B, must be covered with glass, under which is placed a gauze or oiled paper, to prevent the inside from being seen. Make an aperture at G, near the top of the side E B, beneath which, on the inside, place in succession, paintings of vistas, landscapes, figures, &c. so that they may be in front of the mirror H. Let the box be placed that the object may be strongly illuminated by the sun, or by wax-lights placed under the inclosed part of the box A I. By this simple construction, the objects placed at G D will be thrown into their natural perspective, and if the subjects be properly chosen and well executed, the appearance will be both wonderful and pleasing.

### THE MAGICAL GYROSCOPE.

A little instrument has been constructed lately, exhibiting such remarkable results in connection with rotary motion, that it has greatly puzzled most of those who have witnessed its strange performances. Although many of our readers may have seen the instrument, yet from the numberless inquiries that have been made for the rationale of its peculiar feats, and also from the fact that we have not yet heard a solution that appears to be the true one, we are induced to furnish a brief description and explanation of the whole.

It consists of a brass wheel, B, four or five inches in diameter, with a thick lead rim, or circumference, so as to impart to

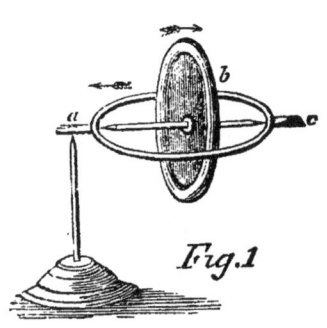
Fig. 1

the wheel when revolving rapidly sufficient momentum to cause it to spin for some minutes. The axis of this wheel terminates in pivots, set in a circular ring at right angles to the wheel, as the figure represents. Two small flat pieces of brass (A and c) are soldered outside to opposite sides of this ring, and a small cavity is made on the under side of each piece, so that the whole may rest on a pointed upright wire, placed in one of these cavities, this wire being inserted in a heavy metallic base to give it solidity. A small hole is made in the axis of the wheel, so that the end of a cord may be thrust through, the cord wound around it, and rapid motion imparted to the wheel like the spinning of a top. This constitutes the whole of the apparatus, which is shown in Fig. 1.

Now, by placing the wheel and its ring, on the upper end

of the pointed wire, as shown in the figure, *only one side being supported*, the wheel and ring would of course, immediately fall by the force of gravity, there being no support at the other side, c. But if a rapid spinning motion is given to the wheel by means of the cord already described, and it be placed on the point at A, *it will not fall*, but will move slowly around on the upright point, performing a steady, revolving horizontal motion, as long as the rapid rotary motion of the wheel continues. So steady and uniform is this horizontal movement, that it generally suggests the motion of the planets round the sun.

This *self-upholding* property constitutes the wonder and puzzle of the instrument, and many explanations have been attempted. Some ascribe it to atmospheric influence ; others to electricity ; while others confidently remark, " Ah, yes, I understand it—it is the *motion* which keeps it from falling —it is the momentum—the centrifugal force ; " but *why* this result is produced by centrifugal force, we are not told.

The true explanation is this :

1. The wheel when at rest, may of course be easily moved about so as to alter the position of its axis, in any direction. But this is not so when it is made to spin rapidly ; if the ring is held in the hands, the wheel will be found strongly to resist any side or twisting movement—so much so, that a novice will start, and almost let it drop, supposing there is something *alive* in it or, as they sometimes remark ; " Why ! it feels as if there was a *snake* in the wheel ! " This is owing to nothing but the strong momentum of the *lead rim* (already described) tending to keep the wheel in its position ; for an attempt to alter its position, throws all this swiftly flying matter into a different course, which, it is evident, cannot easily be done.

2. The *slowly revolving*, horizontal motion on the pivot at A is in a contrary direction to the *spinning* motion of the *top* of the wheel, as the arrows show in Fig. 1. In other words, the forward portion of the wheel flies upwards, and the back portion downwards. This will be found to be always the case.

3. Now, when the wheel is moving on horizontally around the pivot at *a*, the forward portion of the rim is continually moving to the *left*, and the hinder portion to the right, as represented in Fig. 2. The combined motion of the forward part of the wheel both upward and to the left, is therefore

not perpendicularly upward, but inclined to the left, and the tendency of its momentum is to throw the top of the wheel also to the left. In the same way, the downward momentum behind throws the bottom to the right. Throwing the top to the left and the bottom to the right, of course raises the wheel as it rests on the pivot A. In other words, the combined motion of the wheel on its axis, and on the pivot A, constantly tends to raise it, thus overcoming gravity, and maintaining the wheel in its position, supported only at one end.

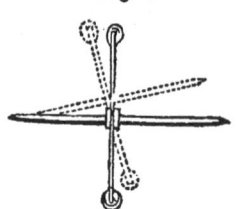

Fig. 2

4. The momentum of the lead rim, as described in (1.) tending to keep the wheel in its position, keeps it also in a uniformly horizontal attitude; if placed by the hand, inclining upwards, it will move around on the pivot at *a*, without altering this inclination; or the same result takes place, if inclined below the horizontal.

5. The reason of the forward horizontal movement, is this: the spinning force of the wheel tends to throw it to the left, and consequently to lift it upwards, as shown in (3.)—gravity, on the opposite hand, tends to draw it downward; the *resultant* (or mid-way) motion is therefore between them, or horzontally. As a proof that gravity thus produces the onward movement — when the wheel spins with the greatest rapidity, and consequently has the greatest relative force to gravity, the horizontal movement is slowest; but it continues constantly to increase as the motion of the wheel is retarded, and as gravity assumes a greater proportionate force.

### THE ARTIFICIAL LANDSCAPE.

Procure a box, as in cut, of about a foot long, eight inches wide, and six inches high, or any other dimensions you please, so they do not greatly vary from these proportions. At each of its opposite ends, on the inside of this box, place a piece of looking-glass, that shall exactly fit; but at that end where the sight hole A is, scrape the quicksilver off the glass, through which the eye can view the objects.

Cover the box with gauze, over which place a piece of transparent glass, which is to be well fastened in. Let there be two grooves at each of the places C D E F, to receive two printed scenes, as follow : On two pieces of pasteboard, let there be skillfully painted, on both sides, any subject you think proper, as woods, bowers, gardens, houses,

&c. ; and on two other boards, the same subject on one side only, and cut out all the white parts : observe also, that there ought to be in one of them some object relative to the subject, placed at A, that the mirror placed at B may not reflect the hole on the opposite side.

The boards painted on both sides are to slide in the grooves C D E F, and those painted on one side are to be placed against the opposite mirrors A and B ; then cover the box with its transparent top. This box should be placed in a strong light, to have a good effect.

When it is viewed through the sight hole, it will present and unlimited prospect of rural scenery, gradually losing itself in obscurity ; and be found well worth the pains bestowed on its construction.

### EASY AND CURIOUS METHODS OF FORETELLING RAINY OR FINE WEATHER.

If a line be made of good whipcord, that is well dried, and a plummet affixed to the end of it, and then hung against a wainscot, and a line drawn under it, exactly where the plummet reaches, in very moderate weather it will be found to rise above it before rain, and to sink below when the weather is likely to become fair. But the best instrument of all, is a good pair of scales, in one of which let there be a brass weight of a pound, and in the other a pound of salt, or of saltpeter, well dried ; a stand being placed under the scale so as to hinder it falling to low

When it is inclined to rain, the salt will swell, and sink the scale: when the weather is growing fair, the brass weight will regain its ascendancy.

Another very simple method is, to take a strip of pine wood, about twenty inches long, one wide, and a quarter thick, and cut across the grain. Then take a strip of cedar, of the same dimensions, but cut along the grain. Glue them firmly face to face, and set them upright in a stand. Some time before rain falls, the pores of the pine will absorb moisture from the atmosphere, and swell until the whole forms a bow, which will straighten itself as fine weather approaches. It is needless to say that the rods should not be painted or varnished.

### THE MAGICAL MEASURE.

The line to be measured must not be extravagantly long, otherwise it will be difficult to measure it accurately; for the least failure of a just aim, or departure from an upright position, would make very sensible errors in the measure of a very long line, especially if the ground was very uneven. To measure then the line A B, accessible at the extremity A, suppose the breadth of a small river, he who

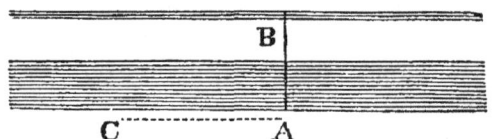

pretends to measure must stand very straight at the extremity A, and support his chin with a little stick resting upon one of the buttons of his coat, so as to keep his head steady in one position. He must pull his hat down upon his forehead till the brim of his hat covers from his view the inaccessible extremity B of the line to be measured A B, then he must turn himself to a level, uniform piece of ground, and with the same position of his hat, observe the point of the ground where his view terminates, as C, then measuring with a line or chain the distance A C, he has the length of the line proposed A B.

### THE BOUNDLESS PROSPECT.

Take a square box, about six inches long and twelve high, or of any other proportionate dimensions. Cover the inside with four flat pieces of looking glass placed perpendicular to the flottom of the box. Place at the bottom any objects you please, as a piece of fortification, a castle, tents, soldiers, &c. On the top, place a frame of glass shaped like the bottom of a pyramid, as in the figure, and so formed as

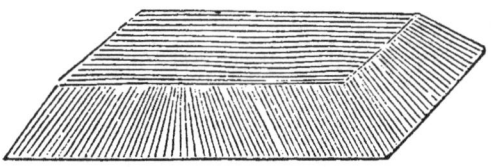

to fit on the box like a cover. The four sides of this cover are to be composed of ground glass, or covered inside with gauze, so that the light may enter, and yet the inside be invisible, except at the top, which must be covered with transparent glass : when you look through this glass, the inside will present a pleasing prospect of a boundless extent ; and, if managed with care, will afford a deal of amusement.

THE HOUR OF THE DAY OR NIGHT TOLD BY A SUSPENDED SHILLING.

However improbable the following experiment may appear, it has been proved by repeated trials :

Sling a shilling or sixpence at the end of a piece of thread by means of a loop. Then resting your elbow on a table, hold the other end of the thread betwixt your fore finger and thumb, observing to let it pass across the ball of the thumb, and thus suspend the shilling into an empty goblet. Observe, your hand must be perfectly steady ; and if you find it difficult to keep it in an immovable posture, it is useless to attempt the experiment. Premising, however, that the shilling is properly suspended, you will observe, that when it has recovered its equilibrium, it will for a moment be stationary : it will then of its own accord, and without the least agency from the person holding it, assume the action of a pendulum, vibrating from side to side of the glass, and, after a few seconds, will strike the hour nearest to the time of day; for instance, if the time be twenty-five minutes past six, it will strike six ; if thirty-five minutes past six, it will strike seven ; and so on of any other hour.

It is necessary to observe, that the thread should lie over the pulse of the thumb, and this may in some measure account for the *vibration* of the shilling ; but to what cause its striking the precise hour is to be traced, remains unexplained; for it is no less astonishing than true, that when it has struck the proper number, its vibration ceases, it acquires a kind of rotary motion, and at last becomes stationary, as before.

CONTRIVANCE FOR A WATCH LAMP, PERFECTLY SAFE, WHICH WILL SHOW THE HOUR OF THE NIGHT, WITHOUT ANY TROUBLE, TO A PERSON LYING IN BED.

It consists of a stand, with three claws, the pillar of which is made hollow, for the purpose of receiving a water candlestick of an inch diameter. On the top of the pillar, by means of two hinges and a bolt, is fixed on a small proportionate table, a box of six sides, lined with brass, tin, or any shining metal, nine inches deep, and six inches in diameter. In the center of one of these sides is fixed a lens, double convex, of at least three inches and a half diameter. The center of the side directly opposite to the lens is perforated so as to receive the dial-plate of the watch, the body of which is confined on the outside, by means of a hollow slide. When the box is lighted by a common watch-light, the figures are magnified nearly to the size of those of an ordinary clock.

### THE ENCHANTED PALACE.

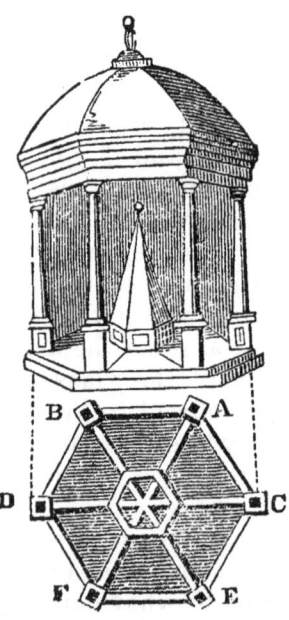

On the six-sided plane A B C D E F of the figure, draw six semi-diameters; and on each of these place perpendicularly two plane mirrors, which must join exactly at the center, and which, placed back to back, must be thin as possible. Decorate the exterior boundary of this piece, (which is at the extremity of the angles of the hexagon,) with six columns, that at the same time serve to support the mirrors by grooves formed on their inner sides. Add to these columns their entablatures, and cover the edifice in whatever manner you please. In each one of these six triangular spaces, contained between two mirrors, place little figures of pasteboard, in relief, rep resenting such subjects, as when seen in an hexagonal form, will produce an agreeable effect. To these add small figures of enamel, and take particular care to conceal by some object that has no relation to the subject, the place where the mirrors join, which, as before observed, all meet in the common center.

When you look into any one of the six openings of this palace, the objects there contained, beng reflected six times, will seem entirely to fill up the whole of the building. This illusion will appear very remarkable, especially if the objects chosen are properly adapted to the effect which the mirrors are intended to produce.

If you place between two of these mirrors part of a fortification, as a curtain, and two demi-bastions, you will see an entire citadel with six bastions ; or if you place part of a ball-room, ornamented with chandeliers and figures, all these objects being here mithltiplied, will afford a very pleasing prospect.

### TO KNOW WHICH OF TWO DIFFERENT WATERS IS THE LIGHTEST WITHOUT ANY SCALES.

Take a solid body, the specific gravity of which is less than that of water, pine, or fir wood, for instance, and put it into each of the two waters, and rest assured that it will sink deeper in the lighter than in the heavier water ; and so by observing the difference of the sinking, you will know which is the lightest water, and consequently the most wholesome for drinking.

### TO KNOW IF A SUSPICIOUS PIECE OF MONEY IS GOOD OR BAD.

If it be a piece of silver that is not very thick, as a dollar or a half dollar, the goodness of which you want to try, take another piece of good silver of equal balance with it, and tie both pieces with thread or horse-hair to the scales of an exact balance (to avoid the wetting of the scales themselves) and dip the two pieces thus tied in water ; for then, if they are of equal goodness, that is, of equal purity, they will hang in equilibrio in the water as well as in the air ; but if the piece in question is lighter in the water than the other, it is certainly false, that is, there is some other metal mixed with it that has less specific gravity than silver, such as copper. If it is heavier than the other, it is likewise bad, as being mixed with a metal of greater specific gravity than silver, such as lead.

If the piece proposed is very thick, such as that crown of gold that Hiero, king of Syracuse, sent to Archimedes to know if the goldsmith had put into it all the eighteen pounds of gold that he had given him for that end, take a piece of pure gold of equal weight with the crown proposed, viz., eighteen pounds, and without taking the trouble of weighing them in water, put them into a vessel full of water, one after another, and that which drives out most water must necessarily be mixed with another metal of less specific gravity than gold, as taking up more space, though of equal weight.

### PYRAMID OF ALUM.

Put a lump of alum into a tumbler of water, and as the alum dissolves it will assume the shape of a pyramid. The cause of the alum decreasing in this peculiar form is briefly as follows : at first, the water dissolves the alum very fast, but as the alum becomes united with the water, the solvent power of the latter diminishes. The water, which combines first with the alum, becomes heavier by the union, and falls to the bottom of the glass, where it ceases to dissolve any more, although the water which it has displaced from the bottom has risen to the top of the glass, and is there acting upon the alum. When the solution has nearly terminated, if you closely examine the lump, you will find it covered with geometrical figures, cut out, as it were, in relief upon the mass ; showing, not only that the cohesion of the atoms of the alum resists the power of solution in the water, but that, in the present instance, it resists it more in some directions than in others. Indeed, this experiment beautifully illustrates the opposite action of cohesion and solution.

### THE DANCING AUTOMATON.

Procure a piece of silk thread about six feet long, and fasten a small wire hook at one end, and a fine needle at the other, then make a knot in the thread about ten inches from the end upon which the hook is fastened. You also procure a small pasteboard figure about four inches long, and pierce a hole through the center of the same just large enough to easily admit the needle. Having done this, take a convenient opportunity and fasten the hook in the carpet about five and a half feet from the chair upon which you intend to sit while performing the trick. You then can inform your audience that you intend to make the figure dance and keep time to any tune they may name You then slip the needle through the hole in the figure and throw it down on the floor, with sufficient force to make it slip on the thread until it reaches the knot, being careful to retain the needle still in your hand, then whistle any air the company may suggest, and appear to beat time with your hands upon your knees. This will make the figure dance, to the great astonishment of the spectators After you have continued this for a few minutes, you must drop the needle and pick up the figure, when the needle will again slide through the hole in the figure, and the automaton being free from the thread, you can hand it to the audience for examination. This is an excellent trick for the parlor, and, if well performed, will defy detection.

### TO MELT A PIECE OF MONEY IN A WALNUT SHELL. WITHOUT INJURING THE SHELL.

Bend any thin coin, and put it into half a walnut shell; place the shell on a little sand, to keep it steady. Then fill the shell with a mixture made of three parts of very dry pounded niter, one part of flowers of sulphur, and a little sawdust well sifted. If you then set light to the mixture, you will find, when it is melted, that the metal will also be melted at the bottom of the shell, in form of a button, which will become hard when the burning matter round it is consumed : the shell will have sustained very little injury.

### THE INVISIBLE SPRINGS.

Take two pieces of white cotton *cord*, precisely alike in length; double each of them separately, so that their ends meet; then tie them together very neatly, with a bit of fine cotton *thread*, at the part where they double (*i. e.* the middle). This must all be done beforehand. When you are going to exhibit the trick, hand round two other pieces of cord, exactly similar in length and appearance to those which you have prepared, but not tied, and desire your company to examine them. You then return to your table, placing these cords at the edge, so that they fall (apparently accidentally) to the ground, behind the table; stoop to pick them up, but take up the prepared ones instead, which you had previously placed there, and lay *them* on the table. You then take round for examination three ivory rings; those given to children when teething, and which may be had at any of the toyshops, are the best for your purpose. When the rings have undergone a sufficient scrutiny, pass the prepared double cords through them, and give the two ends of one cord to one person to hold, and the two ends of the other to another. Do not let them pull hard, or the thread will break, and your trick be discovered. Request the two persons to approach each other, and desire each to give you one end of the cord which he holds, leaving to him the choice.

You then say that, to make all fast, you will tie these two ends together, which you do, bringing the knot down so as to touch the rings; and returning to each person the end of the cord next to him, you state that this trick is performed by the rule of contrary, and that when you desire them to pull hard, they are to slacken, and *vice versa*, which is likely to create much laughter, as they are certain to make many mistakes at first. During this time you are holding the rings on the fore fingers of each hand, and with the other fingers preventing your assistants from separating the cords prematurely, during their mistakes; you at length desire them, in a loud voice, to slack, when they will pull hard, which will break the thread, the rings remaining in your hands, whilst the strings will remain unbroken: let them be again examined, and desire them to look for the springs in the rings.

### THE FLIGHT OF THE RING.

You may cause a ring to shift from one hand to another and make it go on any finger required on the other hand, while somebody holds both your arms, in order to prevent communication between them, by attending to these instructions: Desire some lady in company to lend you a gold ring, recommending her at the same time to make a mark on it, that she may know it again. Have a gold ring of your own, which fasten by a small piece of catgut string to a watch barrel, and sew it to the left sleeve of your coat. Take the ring that is given you in your right hand; then putting, with dexterity, the other ring fastened to the watch-barrel near the entrance of your sleeve, draw it privately to the fingers' ends of your left hand. During this operation, hide the ring that has been lent you between the fingers of your right hand, and fasten it dexterously on a little hook sewed for the purpose, on your waistcoat, and hidden by your coat. After that, show your ring, which hold in your left hand; then ask the company on which finger of the other hand they wish it to pass. During this interval, and as soon as the answer has been given, put the before mentioned finger on the little hook, in order to slip the ring on it: at that moment let go the other ring, by opening your fingers. The spring which is in the watch-barrel, being confined no longer, will contract, and make the ring slip under the sleeve, without any body perceiving it, not even those who hold your arms, as their attention will be occupied to prevent your hands from communicating. After this operation, show the assembly that the ring is come on the other hand, and make them remark that it is the same that had been lent to you, or that the mark is right. Much dexterity is required in this trick, so that the deception may not be suspected.

### MUSICAL FIGURES RESULTING FROM SOUND.

Cover the mouth of a wine glass, having a foot-stalk, with a thin sheet of membrane, over which scatter a layer of fine sand. The vibrations excited in the air by the sound of a musical instrument, held within a few inches of the membrane, will cause the sand on its surface to form regular lines and figures with astonishing celerity, which vary with the sound produced.

### TO MAKE A CARD JUMP OUT OF THE PACK.

Let any person draw a card, and afterwards put it into the pack, but take care that you know where to find it at pleasure. This you may do by having *forced* it. Then put a piece of wax under the thumb-nail of your right hand, and fasten a hair by it to your thumb, and the other end of the hair, by the same means, to the card chosen: spread the pack upon the table, and, making use of any words you think fit, make it jump from the pack about the table.

### THE TELL-TALE CARDS.

Tell any one to shuffle the pack, to take off the upper card, and to notice it, then to lay it on the table, with its face downward, and put so many cards upon it as will make up thirteen with the number of spots on the noted card.

For instance : if the card which the person first looked at was a king, queen, knave, or ten, bid him lay that card with its face downward, calling it ten ; upon that let him lay another, calling it eleven ; upon that, another, calling it twelve ; and upon that, another, calling it thirteen ; then bid him take off the next uppermost card : suppose it to be an eight, let him lay it down on another part of the table, calling it eight ; upon the latter another, calling it nine, and so on in the same way, until he makes that heap up to thirteen ; then let him go to the next uppermost card, and so proceed to lay out the third parcel in the same way as the two preceding, and should the uppermost card be an ace, he must lay it down, calling it one, the next two, &c.

All this should be done either while you are out of the room, or your back is turned ; upon your turning round, you take the cards which have been left ; your object being to count, without its being perceived, how many there are remaining, you throw aside the three top cards, and lay the next three on the table, with their faces upward ; then throw away one, then turn up one, and so on in the same way, until you ascertain how many cards they are ; we will suppose that you find twenty-five cards left ; deduct ten, when the remaining fifteen will be the number of all the spots contained in all the bottom cards of the three heaps, counting the court cards as ten ; you must recollect that ten is, in all cases, the number to be deducted from the cards remaining. Having found that fifteen is the number of spots on the cards, do not declare it at once; but select from those cards which lie on the table, face uppermost, three or four which added together will make fifteen.

For instance : should there be a deuce, a five, and an eight, lay them aside for a moment, and taking the other cards from which you selected the three, put them along with those which you previously rejected ; you now hand the three telltale cards to any person, assuring him that the number of pips on those cards will be the same as those on the bottom cards of the three heaps, which will be found to be the case.

### THE DOUBLE DOZEN.

Present a pack of cards to one of the company, desiring him to shuffle them well, and to get them shuffled by whomsoever he pleases ; then make several persons cut them ; after which you will propose to one of the company to take the pack and think of a card, and remember it, and likewise its order in the pack, by counting one, two, three, four, &c., till he comes, exclusively, to the one thought of; offer to go into another room, or to be blindfolded, while he is doing this. Now declare in what order the card shall be in the pack; say, for instance the twenty-fourth; and, by attending to the following instructions, it will prove to be so :—Suppose the person who thinks of the card stops at thirteen, and that the thirteenth card was the queen of hearts, the number you have stated it shall be in the pack being twenty-four; you return to the room, in case you had left it, or desire the handkerchief to be removed, if you have been blindfolded; and, without asking any question of the person who has thought of the card, ask only for the pack, and apply it to your nose, as if to smell it; then passing it behind your back, or under the table, take, from the bottom of the pack, twenty-three cards; that is to say, one less than the number you have stated the card thought of shall be; place these twenty-three cards on the top. This being done, return the pack to the person who had thought of the card, requesting him to reckon the cards from the top of the pack, beginning by the number of the card he thought of. His card being the thirteenth, he will be compelled to count fourteen, and you are to stop him when he comes to twenty-three, reminding him that the number you have mentioned is twenty-four, and that, consequently, the twenty-fourth card, which he is going to take up, will be the card thought of; and so it will most certainly be.*

### THE HOUSEBREAKERS.

Take a pack of cards, and place all the aces together, the twos, the threes, and so on up to the kings. There will then be thirteen different heaps. You say, " Here are four houses (laying down the four aces separately), which four knaves enter for the purpose of robbing (laying a knave upon each ace), and take with them their implements for housebreaking (and upon each of the knaves you lay a two, three, four, five, six, seven, and eight). The mistresses of the houses come home (laying a queen upon each of the heaps), bringing their money with them (laying a nine upon each queen). Shortly after, their husbands also return (laying a king up-

---

* Be sure and have the number you name greater than that of the first position of the card in the pack; for instance, twenty-four is greater than thirteen.

on each queen), also bringing money with them" (laying a ten upon each heap). You have now disposed of all the cards, which form four distinct heaps. Then lay one heap over the other, and let as many persons cut them as please. When this is done, if you commence at the top of the pack, and lay the cards face downwards, one by one, so as to make thirteen separate heaps, you will find all the aces together, the twos, and so on, as you originally placed them.

### THE MAGIC BOOK.

Provide an octavo book of plain paper, of whatever thickness you please. Turn over seven leaves from the beginning, and paint a group of flowers; then turn over seven more leaves, and paint the same again, and so on, until you have turned the book through to the end. Then paste a slip of paper or parchment to each of the painted leaves. Turn the book over again, and paint upon every sixth leaf a parrot, and then paste strips upon them as you did upon the first, only a little lower down. Proceed in this manner until you have painted the book full of pictures of various sorts, taking care one side of the leaves is left white paper. When you use the book, hold it in your left hand, and set the thumb of your right hand upon the first of the parchment stays; run the book through, and it will appear full of flowers; then stop and, blowing upon the book, run it through again, with the thumb upon the second slips of parchment, and it will appear full of parrots. Afterwards, reverse the book, and run it through as before, and it will appear composed of blank paper.

### THE TAPE TRICK.

This trick consists in suffering a person to tie your thumbs together tightly, and yet that you shall be able to release them in a moment, and tie them together again. The mode of performing this trick is as follows:—Lay a piece of tape across the palms of your hands, placed side by side, letting the ends hang down; then bring your palms quickly together, at the same time privately catching hold of the middle of the tape with your fourth and fifth fingers. Then direct any person to tie your thumbs together as tight as he pleases, but he will not, of course, in reality be tying them, because you have hold of the tape, yet it will nevertheless appear to him that he is doing so. Request him to place a hat over your hands; then blow upon the hat, and say, "Be loose," slipping your thumbs from under the tape; direct him to remove the hat, and show your thumbs free. You then request the hat may again be placed over your hands, and blowing upon it, you say "Be tied," slipping your thumbs under the tape again; and when the hat is removed, your thumbs will appear tied as at first. After performing the trick, convey the tape away, lest it be detected.

### MORE THAN FULL.

Fill a glass to the brim with water, and you may add to it spirit of wine without causing the water to overflow.

### FLOATING NEEDLES.

Fill a cup with water, gently lay on its surface small fine needles, and they will float.

### THE KNOTTED THREAD.

Considerable amusement, not unmixed with wonder, may be occasioned among a party of ladies, by a clever performance of this trick. It is most frequently performed by a female, but the effect of it is considerably increased when it is displayed by a youth. A piece of calico, muslin, or linen, is taken in the left hand, a needle is threaded in the presence of the spectators, and the usual, or even a double or treble knot, made at the extremity of one of the ends of it. The operator commences his work by drawing the needle and the thread in it quite through the linen, notwithstanding the knot, and continues to make several stitches in like manner successively.

The mode of performing this seeming wonder is as follows: A bit of thread, about a quarter of a yard long, is turned once round the top of the middle finger of the right hand, upon which a thimble is then placed, to keep it secure. This must be done privately, and the thread kept concealed, while a needle is threaded with a bit of thread of a similar length. The thread in the needle must have one of its ends drawn up nearly close, and be concealed between the forefinger and thumb; the other should hang down nearly as long as, and by the side of the thread, which is fastened under the thimble, so that these two may appear to be the two ends of the thread. The end of the piece that is fastened under the thimble is then knotted, and the performer begins to sew, by moving his hand quickly after he has taken up the stitch.

It will appear as though he actually passed the knotted thread through the cloth.

### THE BACCHUS EXPERIMENT.

This experiment, showing the elasticity of air, is performed with a pleasing toy. It represents a figure of Bacchus sitting across a cask, in which are two separate compartments. Put into one of them a portion of wine or colored liquid, and place the apparatus under the exhausted receiver of an air-pump, when the elastic force of the confined air will cause the liquid to ascend a transparent glass tube (fitted on purpose), into the mouth of the Bacchanalian figure. To render the experiment more striking, a bladder, with a small quantity of air therein, is fastened around the figure, and covered with a loose silken robe, when the air in the bladder will expand, and produce an apparent increase in the bulk of the figure, as if occasioned by the excess of liquor drunk.

### CURIOUS METHOD OF MEASURING THE HEIGHT OF A TREE.

To ascertain the height of an object a peculiar method of measurement is in use among the Isthmus Indians. In measuring the height of a tree, for instance, a man proceeds from its base to a point where, on turning the back towards it, and putting the head between the legs, he can just see the top ; at the spot where he is able to do this he makes a mark on the ground to the base of the tree ; this distance will be equal to the height.

### THE TRANSPOSABLE PIECES.

Take two quarter eagles and two dimes, and grind part of them away, on one side only, so that they may be but half the common thickness ; and observe, that they must be quite thin at the edge ; then rivet a quarter eagle and a dime together. Lay one of these double pieces, with the dime upwards, on the palm of your hand, at the bottom of your three first fingers, and lay the other piece with the quarter eagle upwards in like manner, in the other hand Let the company take notice in which hand is the quarter eagle, and in which is the dime. Then, as you shut your hands, you naturally turn the pieces over, and when you open them again, the dime and the quarter eagle will appear to have changed their places.

# INQUIRE WITHIN
## For Anything You Wish to Know:
—OR,—
## OVER 3,700 FACTS FOR THE PEOPLE.
A large Vol. of 436 pp., cloth, gilt, Price $1. Sent free of postage.

This Book, as its title imports, will give you correct information on every possible subject that you ever heard or thought of! It tells you how to *cook a dinner*—to *cure a sick friend*, or *cut an acquaintance*—to *get up a dinner party*, or *dine abroad*—to *play at cards, chess,* or *any other populur game*,—whether you wish to establish yourself in life according to the *rules of etiquette*—to get up a *sumptuous entree for the dinner table*, or *arrange a plain dinner*—to *fold fancy napkins*—to *start business*—to *make money*—to *dress with taste*—to *conduct a courtship*—to *tie any kind of a knot*—to *get married*—to *give an evening party to your friends*—to *behave well in company*—to *keep house properly*—to *dance*—to *make ornamental vases*, by the new art of Potichomanie, or Wax work, and other *fancy employments for the ladies*—to *establish acquaintances according to the rules of etiquette*—to *enjoy an hour at curious puzzles* and *arithmetical questions*—to *do up a neat parcel*—to *relieve the invalid*—to acquaint yourself with the *technical terms in literature, law, and medicine*—in short, to *do every useful thing that can be thought of or imagined*, whether at *home* or *abroad*, or among your friends, or in *your business*, or *on your farm*, or *in your garden*, or at *a public meeting*, or at a *private assembly*. It contains tables of all weights and measures; *Interest Tables* from $1 to $10,000 at six and seven per cent, besides innumerable tables on interesting and curious subjects. It gives complete directions how to *wash, starch, and iron*—how to *keep the eyes, hair, teeth, and complexion in perfect order*—how to *punctuate, spell, and write corrrctly*—how to *compose all kinds of letters,* from the billet-doux to the business letter—how to *clean furniture*, take care of *pet animals*—how to *measure all kinds of mechanics' work*—how to *detect fradulent scales*—and all about the properties and uses of different medicines. Indeed this is really and truly one of the most wonderful and valuable books ever printed. Besides all this information—and we have not room to give an idea of a hundredth part of it—*it contains so many valuable and useful receipts* that an enumeration of them requires

### SEVENTY-TWO COLUMNS OF FINE TYPE FOR THE INDEX.

It is *no collection of ancient sayings and receipts*, but the whole are *fresh and new*, and *suited to the present times*. As a book to keep in the family for reference, it is unequaled, *comprising as it does all kinds of Books of Information in a single volume.*

Send cash orders to **DICK & FITZGERALD,**
No. 18 Ann Street, N. Y.

# THE REASON WHY SERIES

These useful works will, when completed, supply all the "Reasons" which the human mind has discovered for the varied and interesting phenomena of Nature; and for events, and their consequences, in religious and civil history. Such a series, entirely original in their plan, and executed with the most conscientious care---embracing the very essence of demonstrative truth and inductive reasoning---must become as widely diffused as the language in which they are written. Each work is complete in itself.

**The Reason Why : General Science.** A careful collection of some thousands of reasons for things, which, though generally known, are imperfectly understood. A book of condensed scientific knowledge for the million. By the author of "Inquire Within." It is a handsome 12mo volume, of 356 pages, printed on fine paper, bound in cloth, gilt, and embellished with a large number of wood cuts, illustrating the various subjects treated of. Price ONE DOLLAR. This work assigns reasons for the thousands of things that daily fall under the eye of the intelligent observer, and of which he seeks a simple and clear explanation.

EXAMPLE.

*Why does silver tarnish when exposed to the light? Why is the sky blue?*

This volume answers 1,325 similar questions.

**The Biblical Reason Why:** A HAND-BOOK FOR BIBLICAL STUDENTS, and a Guide to Family Scripture Readings. By the author of "Inquire Within," &c. Beautifully illustrated, large 12mo, cloth, gilt side and back. Price ONE DOLLAR. This work gives Reasons, founded upon the Bible, and assigned by the most eminent Divines and Christian Philosophers, for the great and all-absorbing events recorded in the History of the Bible, the Life of our Saviour, and the Acts of his Apostles.

EXAMPLE.

*Why did the first patriarchs attain such extreme longevity?*
*Why is the Book of the Prophecies of Isaiah a strong proof of the authenticity of the whole Bible?*

This volume answers upwards of 1,400 similar questions.

**The Reason Why : Natural History.** By the author of "Inquire Within," "The Biblical Reason Why," &c. 12mo, cloth, gilt side and back. Price ONE DOLLAR. Giving Reasons for hundreds of interesting facts in connection with Zoology, and throwing a light upon the peculiar habits and instincts of the various Orders of the Animal Kingdom.

EXAMPLE.

*Why do dogs turn around two or three times before they lie down?*
*Why do birds often roost upon one leg?*

This volume answers about 1,500 similar questions.

THE FOLLOWING BOOKS OF THIS SERIES ARE IN PRESS, AND WILL BE ISSUED IN RAPID SUCCESSION:

| | |
|---|---|
| The Denominational Reason Why. | The Geological Reason Why. |
| The Gardener's and Farmer's Reason Why. | The Astronomical Reason Why. |
| The Housekeeper's Reason Why. | The Chemical Reason Why. |
| The Botanical Reason Why. | The Grammatical Reason Why. |

# The Reason Why: Natural History.

BY THE AUTHOR OF "INQUIRE WITHIN," "THE BIBLICAL REASON WHY," "REASON WHY OF GENERAL SCIENCE," "THAT'S IT, OR, PLAIN TEACHINGS," &c., &c.

**Profusely Illustrated. 12mo, Cloth, Gilt Side and Back. Price $1.**

Giving reasons for hundreds of interesting facts in connection with Zoology, and throwing a light upon the peculiar habits and instincts of the various Orders of the Animal Kingdom.

## EXAMPLE.

*Why has the lion such a large mane?*
*Why does the otter, when hunting for fish, swim against the stream?*
*Why do dogs turn around two or three times before they lie down?*
*Why have flat fishes their upper sides dark, and their under sides white?*
*Why do sporting dogs make what is termed " a point?"*

*Why do birds often roost upon one leg?*
*Why do frogs keep their mouths closed while breathing?*
*Why do cats, when being played with, lie on their backs, seize the hand of the person playing with them with their fore paws, and strike with their hind feet?*
*Why does the wren build several nests, but occupies only one?*

This volume answers about 1500 similar questions.

---

# The Corner Cupboard; or, Facts for Everybody.

*By the Author of "Inquire Within," "The Reason Why," &c.*

**Large 12mo, 400 pages, Cloth, Gilt Side and Back. Illustrated with over One Thousand Engravings.**

PRICE ONE DOLLAR.

Embracing Facts about I. Things not generally known, II. Things that ought to be known. III. Things worth knowing. The "Corner Cupboard" is

*A Complete Confectioner.*
*A Complete Cook.*
*A Complete Family Doctor.*
*A Complete Gardener.*
*A Complete Father's Book.*
*A Complete Mother's Book.*
*A Complete Family Book.*

*A Complete Lady's Book.*
*A Complete Gentleman's Book.*
*A Complete Boy's Book.*
*A Complete Girl's Book.*
*A Complete Master's Book.*
*A Complete Servant's Book.*
*A Complete Amusement Book.*

*A Friend at Everybody's Elbow in Time of Need.*

It tells about the food we consume, the clothes we wear, the house we live in, and facts from the Arts and Sciences, as well as from Literature, Manufacture, Commerce, Anatomy, Physiology, the Garden and Field, the whole forming a complete Encyclopedia of Useful Knowledge. Whether in the parlor or the kitchen, the chamber or the boudoir, at home or abroad, it may be very appropriately called the Family's Ready Adviser.

---

# 10,000 WONDERFUL THINGS.

Comprising the Marvellous and Rare, Odd, Curious, Quaint, Eccentric and Extraordinary, in all Ages and Nations, in Art, Nature and Science, including many Wonders of the World, enriched with Hundreds of Authentic Illustrations.

EDITED BY EDMUND FILLINGHAM KING, M.A., AUTHOR OF "LIFE OF NEWTON," &C.

**12mo, Cloth, Gilt Side and Back. Price One Dollar.**

In the present work, interesting scenes from Nature, curiosities of art, costume, and customs of a bygone period, rather predominate; but we have devoted many of its pages to descriptions of remarkable occurrences, beautiful landscapes, stupendous waterfalls, and sublime sea pieces. It contains not a line that the nicest judgment could pronounce obnoxious; and yet, in every page is a mass of material to create both surprise and laughter. It is impossible to read the volume through, without feeling, not only that you have been well entertained, but well instructed.

☞ Copies of either of the above books sent to any address in the United States or Canada, free of postage. Send cash orders to

**DICK & FITZGERALD, 18 Ann Street, New York.**

# The Reason Why:
## GENERAL SCIENCE.
### A CAREFUL COLLECTION OF
## Some Thousands of Reasons
**FOR THINGS WHICH, THOUGH GENERALLY KNOWN, ARE IMPERFECTLY UNDERSTOOD.**

A Book of Condensed Scientific Knowledge for the Million.

### BY THE AUTHOR OF "INQUIRE WITHIN."

"What 'Haydn's Dictionary of Dates' is in regard to Historical events, this wonderful book is in respect to scientific facts. The plan of the book and its execution leave nothing to be desired."
[Church of England Monthly Review.

This Work assigns REASONS, for the thousands of things that daily fall under the eye of the intelligent observer, and of which he seeks a simple and clear explanation.

#### EXAMPLE.

Why does silver tarnish when exposed to the light?
Why do some colors fade and others darken when exposed to the sun?
What develops electricity in the clouds?

Why does lightning sometimes appear red, at others yellow, at others white?
Why does dew form round drops on the leaves of plants?
Why is the sky blue?

This volume answers 1,325 similar questions.

"THE REASON WHY" is a handsome 12mo volume, of 356 pages, printed on fine paper, bound in cloth, gilt, and embellished with a large number of Wood Cuts, illustrating the various subjects treated of.

### PRICE ONE DOLLAR.

☞ Copies Mailed to any address in the United States or Canada, free of postage.

---

# Live and Learn;
### A GUIDE TO ALL WHO WISH TO
## SPEAK AND WRITE CORRECTLY.

Particularly intended as a book of reference for the solution of difficulties connected with Grammar, Composition, Punctuation, &c., with explanations of Latin and French words and phrases of frequent occurrence in newspapers, reviews, periodicals, and books in general; containing examples of

### ONE THOUSAND MISTAKES

Of daily occurrence in Speaking, Writing, and Pronunciation, together with detailed Instructions for Writing for the Press, and forms of articles in the various departments of Newspaper Literature.

"Such a book as this has long been wanted by those who entertain the wish alluded to in the title. It is suitable for all classes. We have attentively conned its pages, and can recommended it as one of the best works of reference for the young student, or even the ripe scholar, and as deserving to be generally consulted. The work is altogether useful and indispensable." [Tribune.

216 Pages, Bound in Cloth, 12mo.

### PRICE FIFTY CENTS,

And sent to any address Free of Postage. Send Cash Orders to

**DICK & FITZGERALD, 18 Ann Street, N. Y.**

# The Secret Out;

OR,

## 1,000 TRICKS WITH CARDS AND OTHER RECREATIONS.

### ILLUSTRATED WITH OVER 300 ENGRAVINGS.

And containing clear and comprehensive explanations how to perform with ease all the Curious Card Deceptions and Sleight-of-Hand Tricks extant. With an endless variety of Entertaining Experiments in Drawing-Room, or White Magic, including the celebrated Science of Second Sight. Together with a choice collection of Intricate and Puzzling Questions. Amusements in Chance, Natural Magic, etc., etc., etc.

By the Author of "The Sociable," "The Magician's Own Book," "Parlor Theatricals," etc.

*Large 12mo, Cloth, Gilt Side and Back. Price One Dollar.*

A Book which explains all the Tricks and Deceptions with Playing Cards, ever known or invented, and gives, besides, a great many new and interesting ones—the whole being described so accurately and carefully, with engravings to illustrate them, that anybody can easily learn how to practise these Tricks.

This book contains, in addition to its numerous Card Tricks above described, full and easily understood explanations of some **Two Hundred and Forty** of the most

### Curious, Amusing & Interesting Sleight-of-Hand & Legerdemain Tricks

Ever invented, and which are illustrated with Engravings to make each trick understood with ease.

---

# The Magician's Own Book

OR,

## THE WHOLE ART OF CONJURING.

Being a Complete Hand-Book of Parlor Magic, containing over One Thousand Optical, Chemical, Mechanical, Magnetical, and Magical Experiments, Amusing Transmutations, Astonishing Sleights and Subtleties, Celebrated Card Deceptions, Ingenious Tricks with Numbers, Curious and Entertaining Puzzles—together with all the most Noted Tricks of Modern Performers.

### The whole Illustrated with over 500 Wood Cuts,

And intended as a source of Amusement for

### ONE THOUSAND AND ONE EVENINGS.

12mo, cloth, 400 pages, gilt side and back stamp. Price ONE DOLLAR, sent free of postage.

Here is a book for the long winter evenings, and one that will make all merry and happy. It contains over a THOUSAND TRICKS, of every description; and they are all explained so clear and explicitly, that any person can comprehend and perform them with ease. It also contains numerous CURIOUS PUZZLES, with patterns showing how they are done, any one of which will afford amusement enough for a whole evening.

Copies sent to any address free of postage. Send Cash Orders to

### DICK & FITZGERALD,

18 ANN STREET, NEW YORK.

A Book of Never-Ending Entertainment.

# THE SOCIABLE;

OR,

## One Thousand and One Home Amusements.

CONTAINING

ACTING PROVERBS, DRAMATIC CHARADES, ACTING CHARADES, OR DRAWING-ROOM PANTOMIMES, MUSICAL BURLESQUES, TABLEAUX VIVANTS. PARLOR GAMES, GAMES OF ACTION, FORFEITS, SCIENCE IN SPORT AND PARLOR MAGIC, AND A CHOICE COLLECTION OF CURIOUS MENTAL AND MECHANICAL PUZZLES, &c.

By the author of "The Magician's Own Book."

Illustrated with nearly 300 Engravings and Diagrams,

THE WHOLE BEING A FUND OF NEVER-ENDING ENTERTAINMENT.

Nearly 400 pages, 12mo., Cloth, gilt side stamp, $1.00.

---

"The Sociable" will be found one of the most extensively popular family books ever issued from the press. As its title implies, it is a collection—a complete *repertoire*—of the

### AMUSEMENTS OF HOME,

Embracing a large and comprehensive list of recreative pastime, arranged as follows:

Parlor Theatricals, including Acting Proverbs, Acting Charades, Dramatic Charades and Tableaux Vivants; Games of Action; Games requiring Memory and Attention; Games requiring Wit and Intelligence; Ruses, or Catch Games; Forfeits; Puzzles; Fireside Games for Winter Evenings, and Science in Sport, and Parlor Magic. Many of these Games—the majority of them—are ENTIRELY NEW, as are, also, the

### PARLOR THEATRICALS
AND
### TABLEAUX VIVANTS,

Which were PREPARED EXPRESSLY FOR THIS WORK. Everything in the book is superior of its kind—the greatest care having been taken to exclude everthing that was not above the standard of mediocrity in interest and ingenuity. It is

### THE ONLY BOOK
OF THIS KIND
### Ever Published in America,

And as it will be invaluable to Families, Schools, Social Clubs, etc., as a book of reference on all matters of Amusement and Recreation, there must be a steady and permanent demand for it at all seasons and in all years, although few of the so-called "Holiday Books" are as appropriate for Gifts as THE SOCIABLE.

Each department is AMPLY ILLUSTRATED with

### BEAUTIFUL WOOD ENGRAVINGS

Which render the Text clear, and fully explain all the Puzzles, the Mechanical Contrivances mentioned, and other things difficult to describe in writing. It is elegantly bound, so as to be an ornament to any center-table, and its typographical execution is a specimen of the highest excellence.

The need of such a collection of HOME GAMES has long been felt, and the publishers believe that this endeavor on their part, to supply that want, must meet with the fullest success. They have spared neither trouble nor expense to render it a complete and invaluable *vade mecum* of Domestic Amusements, so that its name may be familiar as a "Household Word" in all families, north, south, east and west, where the value of wholesome and innocent recreation is recognized.

Price only One Dollar, bound in cloth, with gilt side and back stamp, sent to any address in the United States, free of postage. Send cash orders to

**DICK & FITZGERALD, Publishers,**

18 Ann Street, New York.

# The Perfect Gentleman;
### Or, ETIQUETTE AND ELOQUENCE.

A Book of Information and Instruction for those who desire to become Brilliant or Conspicuous in General Society, or at Parties, Dinners or Popular Gatherings, &c.

A handsome volume of 335 pages, beautifully bound and gilt. Price $1 00.

This is not only a valuable book of reference, but it contains minute Instructions for Gentlemen in all those modern accomplishments which have become almost a necessity in this age of refinement. It gives directions how to use Wine at Table, with rules for judging the quality thereof—Rules for Carving, and a complete Etiquette of the Dinner Table, including Dinner Speeches, Toasts and Sentiments, Wit and Conversation at Table, &c. It has also an American Code of Etiquette and Politeness for all occasions—Model Speeches, with directions how to deliver them—Duties of the Chairman at Public Meetings, Forms of Preambles and Resolutions, &c. In short, this book will give a man every possible information he may desire to enable him to appear to good advantage in either public or private life. It is a choice book that any gentleman will find a valuable addition to his library. We expect to sell at least one hundred thousand copies of this work, and the price is correspondingly low.

---

## Art of Dancing without a Master;
### Or, Ball Room Guide and Instructor.
#### TO WHICH IS ADDED
**Hints on Etiquette; also, The Figures, Music and Necessary Instruction for the Performance of the most Modern and Improved Dances.**

By EDWARD FERRERO, Professor of Dancing at West Point.

By the aid of which any one can attain a knowledge of the Art of Dancing without a Master. This work also contains

### ONE HUNDRED AND FIVE PAGES OF THE CHOICEST MUSIC,

Arranged for the Piano Forte by the most celebrated Professors. The whole forming the most valuable and useful *melange* for the centre-table of the drawing-room ever published. The MUSIC alone, if purchased in separate sheets at any of the music stores, would cost ten times the price of the book. Thus you can obtain **a History of Dancing, Hints on Etiquette, the Figures and Steps of all Dances, and Ten Dollars' worth of the Choicest Music FOR ONE DOLLAR.**

---

## SONGS OF IRELAND.

Embracing Songs of the Affections, Convivial and Comic Songs, Patriotic and Military Songs, Historical and Political Songs, Moral, Sentimental, Satirical, and Miscellaneous Songs. Edited and Annotated by SAMUEL LOVER, Esq., Author of "Handy Andy," "Rory O'More," "Legends and Stories of Ireland," &c. Embellished with numerous fine Illustrations, engraved by the celebrated Dalziel. 12mo, Cloth, Gilt Side and Back. Price $1.25.

☞ *Copies of the above Books sent to any address in the United States free of postage. Send cash orders to*

**DICK & FITZGERALD, 18 Ann Street, N. Y.**

DICK & FITZGERALD'S LIST OF PUBLICATIONS.

## Judge Haliburton's Works.

**Sam Slick in Search of a Wife.**
12mo., Paper - - - - $0 50
Cloth, - - - - - price 1 00
Everybody has heard of "Sam Slick, the Clockmaker," and he has given his opinion on almost everything. This book contains his opinion about "*Courtin the Gals!*" and his laughable adventures after the petticoats. Buy this book if you want many good hearty laughs. There is a book called "The Horse," and another "The Cow," and "The Dog," and so on ; why shouldn't there be one on "The Gals?" They are about the most difficult to choose and to manage of any created critter, and there aint any dependable directions about pickin' and choosin' of them. Is it any wonder then so many fellows get taken in when they go for to swap hearts with them ?

**Sam Slick's Nature and Human**
*Nature.* Large 12mo., Paper - 50
Cloth - - - - price 1 00

**The Attache ; or, *Sam Slick in England.* Large 12mo., Paper - - 50
Cloth - - - - - price 1 00

**Sam Slick's Sayings and Doings.**
Paper - - - - - - 50
Cloth - - - - - price 1 00
This is the most amusing collection of the Opinions, Sayings and Doings of the famous Sam Slick, that has ever been published. It gives the experiences of the Yankee Clockmaker, and the incidents that occurred in his journeyings over the world, together with his observations on men and things in general; also containing his opinions on Matrimony.

## Miscellaneous Books.

**Courtship Made Easy; or, the**
*Mysteries of Making Love Fully Explained.* With specimen Love Letters. Containing also a Treatise on the general qualifications necessary for Marriage, and the proper age and condition for Wedlock, &c. By HARRY HAZEN, Jr., a widower who has been thrice married, but is still young enough to be an especial favorite of the ladies. - - price 13

**The Ladies' Love Oracle; or, Coun-**
*sellor to the Fair Sex.* Being a complete Fortune Teller and Interpreter to all questions upon the different events and situations of life, but more especially relating to all circumstances connected with Love, Courtship and Marriage. By MADAM LE MARCHAND. Illustrated cover, printed in colors. - price $0 25

**Chesterfield's Art of Letter-writing**
*Simplified.* A Guide to Friendly, Affectionate, Polite and Busines Correspondence. - - - price 13
Containing a large collection of the most valuable information relative to the Art of Letter-Writing, with clear and complete instructions how to begin and end Correspondence, Rules for Punctuation and Spelling, &c.,together with numerous examples of Letters and Notes on every subject of Epistolary intercourse, with several Important Hints on Love Letters.

**The Laws of Love. A Complete**
Code of Gallantry. 12mo. Paper, price 25
Containing concise rules for the conduct of Courtship through its entire progress, aphorisms of love, rules for telling the characters and dispositions of women, remedies for love, and an Epistolary Code.

**Gamblers' Tricks with Cards Ex-**
*posed and Explained.* By J. H. GREEN, Reformed Gambler. 12mo. Paper. - - - - price 25
This work contains one hundred tricks with cards, explained, and shows the numerous cheats which Gamblers practice upon their unwary dupes. The uninitiated will stare when they here see how easily they can be swindled by dealing, cutting, and shuffling cards.

**How to Win and How to Woo;**
Containing Rules for the Etiquette of Courtship, with directions showing how to win the favor of Ladies, how to begin and end a Courtship, and how Love Letters should be written. - - - - price 13

**Bridal Etiquette; A Sensible Guide**
to the Etiquette and Observances of the Marriage Ceremonies ; containing complete directions for Bridal Receptions, and the necessary rules for bridesmaids, groomsmen, sending cards, &c., &c. - - price 13

**How to Behave; or, The Spirit of**
*Etiquette:* A complete guide to Polite Society, for Ladies and Gentlemen ; containing rules for good behavior at the dinner table, in the parlor, and in the street; with important hints on introduction, and the art of conversation. - price 13

☞ Any Book on this List will be sent to any address in the United States or Canada, *Free of Postage.* Send Cash Orders to DICK & FITZGERALD, 18 Ann St., N. Y.

## DICK & FITZGERALD'S LIST OF PUBLICATIONS.

**Dashes of American Humor.** With numerous laughable illustrations, on tinted paper, from designs from John Leach, 320 pages, paper cover, $0 50
Cloth, gilt, - - - price 1 00
This work contains in its 320 pages, some thirty of the most amusing articles we have ever perused, redolent with not only humor, but with wisdom and pathos; the happiest days and most innocent recreations of our youth are here recalled.

**Dr. Valentine's Comic Lectures.** A Budget of Wit and Humor; or, Morsels of Mirth for the Melancholy. A certain cure for the Blues, and all other serious complaints. Comprising Comic Lectures on Heads, Faces, Noses, Mouths, Animal Magnetism, etc., with Specimens of Eloquence, Transactions of Learned Societies, Delineations of Eccentric Characters. Comic Songs, etc., etc. By Dr. W. VALENTINE, the favorite delineator of Eccentric Characters. Illustrated with twelve portraits of Dr. Valentine in his most celebrated characters. 12mo., Cloth, gilt -1 00
Ornamented paper cover - price 50

**Dr. Valentine's Comic Metamorphoses.** Being the second series of Dr. Valentine's Lectures, with characters as given by the late Yankee Hill. Embellished with numerous portraits. Ornamental Paper Cover 50
Cloth, gilt - - - - price 1 00

**Laughable Adventures of Messrs.** Brown, Jones and Robinson, showing where they went, and how they went; what they did, and how they did it. With nearly 200 most thrillingly comic engravings. - price 25

**Laughing Gas.** An Encyclopedia of Wit, Wisdom and Wind. By SAM SLICK, Jr. Comically illustrated with 100 original and laughable engravings, and near 500 side-extending jokes, and other things to get fat on ; and the best of it is, that everything about the book is new and fresh—all new; new designs, new stories, new type—no comic almanac stuff. It will be found a complete antidote to "hard times." price - - - - - - 25

**The Courtship of Chevalier Sly-Fox-Wikoff,** showing his heart-rending, astounding, and most wonderful love adventures with Fanny Elssler and Miss Gambol. Illustrated with 200 comic engravings - price $0 25

**The Extraordinary and Mirth-Provoking** Adventures by Sea and Land, of Oscar Shanghai. Illustrated by nearly 200 comic engravings - - - - - price 25
All told in a series of nearly two hundred of the most risible, quizzible, provoking, peculiar, saucy and spicy cuts ever gathered within the leaves of any one book. All fond of a hearty laugh, here is amusement for many a merry hour.

**Charley White's Ethiopian Joke Book.** Being a perfect Casket of Fun, the first and only work of the kind ever published. Containing a full expose of all the most laughable Jokes, Stories, Witticisms, &c., as told by the celebrated Ethiopian Comedian, Charles White. 18mo., 94 pages - - - - price 12½

**Black Wit and Darkey Conversations.** By Charles White. Containing a large collection of Laughable Anecdotes, Jokes, Stories, Witticisms, and Darkey Conversations. 18mo., - - - - price 12½

**Chips from Uncle Sam's Jack Knife.** Illustrated with over one hundred Comical Engravings, and comprising a collection of over 500 Laughable Stories, Funny Adventures, Comic Poetry, Queer Conundrums, Terrific Puns, Witty Sayings, Sublime Jokes and Sentimental Sentences. The whole being a most perfect portfolio for those who love to laugh. Large Octavo - price 25

**The Comical Adventures of David Dufficks.** Illustrated with over 100 Funny engravings. Large Octavo, price - - - - - - 25

**Yale College Scrapes ; or How the** Boys Go It at New Haven. - price 25
This is a book of 114 pages, containing accounts of all the noted and famous " Scrapes " and " Sprees," of which students at Old Yale have been guilty for the last quarter of a century.

**The Comic Wandering Jew.** Full of Fun and containing 100 Humorous engravings - - - price 25

☞ Any Book on this List will be sent to any address in the United States or Canada, *Free of Postage.* Send Cash Orders to **DICK & FITZGERALD, 18 Ann St., N. Y.**

# The Harp of a Thousand Strings

## OR, LAUGHTER FOR A LIFETIME.

And peculiarly prepared to produce prolific PEALS OF LAUGHTER. The very quintessence of HUMAN WIT, WAGGERY and WISDOM.

400 Pages of the most Mirth-Provoking Literature ever printed.

**It contains more than a Million Laughs, and is Illustrated with 200 Comic Cuts.**

The pictures are all original, designed by some of our best artists (including Darley), and the collection of droll conceits and queer stories is unsurpassed, having been several years in preparation.

*Large 12mo, nearly 400 pages, Illustrated with 200 Comic Engravings, and bound in fine Cloth, with gilt side and back stamp.*

**PRICE ONE DOLLAR AND TWENTY-FIVE CENTS.**

---

THE BOOK OF

# One Thousand Comical Stories

### Or, ENDLESS REPAST OF FUN.

*A rich Banquet for Every Day in the Year, with several courses and a dessert.*

BILL OF FARE: Comprising Tales of Humor, Laughable Anecdotes, Irresistible Drolleries, Jovial Jokes, Comical Conceits, Puns and Pickings, Quibbles and Queries, Bon Mots and Broadgrins, Oddities, Epigrams, &c., &c. Merry Songs for Merry Moments; Conundrums for the Million; an inexhaustible store of Nuts to Crack, and Sports and Pastimes for all Seasons—forming a Welcome Guest for Spring, a Cheerful Friend for Summer, a Jovial Host for Autumn, a Pleasant Companion for Winter, and a varied Feast of Mirth for Everybody's Enjoyment.

*Appropriately Illustrated with 300 Comic Engravings. By the author of "Mrs. Partington's Carpet Bag of Fun."*

**Large 12mo. Cloth. Price One Dollar.**

---

# Mrs. Partington's Carpet Bag of Fun.

Illustrated with over 150 of the most laughable engravings ever designed, from drawings by Darley, McLennan, Leach, Phiz, Henning, Hine, Tenniel, Crowquill, Cruikshank, Meadows, Doyle, Goder and others; and a collection of over 1,000 of the most Comical Stories, Amusing Adventures, Side-splitting Jokes, Cheek-extending Poetry, Funny Conundrums, QUEER SAYINGS OF MRS. PARTINGTON, Heart-rending Puns, Witty Repartees, etc., etc.

**Bound in Paper, Price 50 Cents; Cloth, $1 00.**

In offering this book to the public, we must caution all weakly and nervous people against buying it. It is only intended for those hearty and robust persons who can laugh long and loud, and grow fat, being a perfect Encyclopedia of Wit and Witty Sayings. To those fond of Fun it will be a treasure.

☞ *Copies of either of the above Books sent to any address in the United States, free of postage.*

**DICK & FITZGERALD, 18 Ann Street, N. Y.**

## POPULAR BOOKS SENT FREE OF POSTA

**The Game of Draughts, or Checkers,** Simplified and Explained. With Practical Diagrams and Illustrations, together with a Checker board, numbered and printed in red. Containing the Eighteen Standard Games, with over 200 of the best variations, selected from the various authors, together with many original ones never before published. By D. SCATTERGOOD. Bound in cloth, with flexible cover............................................0 38

**Romantic Incidents in the Lives of** *the Queens of England.* By J. F. SMITH, Author of "Stanfield Hall," "Amy Lawrence," "Minnie Gray," "Gus Howard," etc. 12mo, Extra Cloth, Gilt............1 00

This is a beautiful volume of 350 pages. It contains truthful and admirably drawn literary portraits of Elizabeth Woodville, Queen Consort of Edward IV, Eleanora of Aquaitaine, Queen Consort of Henry II, Matilda of Flanders, Queen Consort of William the Conqueror, and Matilda Atheling, Queen Consort of Henry I. The writer, in giving us the history of these eminent women, has remarkably exemplified the old adage that "truth is stranger than fiction;" for no pure romance could excel it in stirring incident, and the various vicissitudes of love, pleasure, sorrow, and suffering, which form the staple of all works of fiction. Each sketch is a complete narrative in itself, possessing all the charms of a novel, with the additional value and merit of historical truth. The book may be read with equal entertainment and profit.

**The Family Aquarium.** A new Pleasure for the Domestic Circle. Being a familiar and Complete Instructor upon the subject of the construction, fitting up, stocking, and maintenance of the Marine and Fresh Water Aquaria, or River and Ocean Gardens. By H. D. BUTLER, Esq. 12mo, cloth, gilt side stamp. This work is a complete adaptation to American peculiarities of every species of useful information upon Marine and Fresh Water Aquariums, to be met with in the elaborate volumes of European authority, together with a careful concentration of all the practical results of the author's great experience in the structure and management of Aquaria. Price.........0 50

**The Ladies' Guide to Beauty:** A Companion for the Toilet. Containg practical advice on improving the complexion, the hair, the hands, the form, the teeth, the eyes, the feet, the features, so as to insure the highest degree of perfection of which they are susceptible. And also upwards of one hundred recipes for various cosmetics, oils, pomades, etc., etc., being a result of a combination of practical and scientific skill. By Sir JAMES CLARK, Private Physician to Queen Victoria. Revised and edited by an American Physician and Chemist. Price......0 25

**Parlor Theatricals;** *or, Winter Evenings' Entertainment.* Containing Acti Proverbs, Dramatic Charades, Acti Charades, or Drawing-Room Pantomimes, Musical Burlesques, Tableau Vivants, &c. By the author of "T Sociable," "The Magician's Own Book" "The Secret Out," &c. 12mo. cloth, g side and back, illustrated with descripti engravings and diagrams. Price........

**The Book of 500 Curious Puzzles.** Co taining a large collection of Entertaini Paradoxes, Perplexing Deceptions Numbers and Amusing Tricks in Geo etry. By the author of "The Sociable "The Secret Out," "The Magician's O Book," "Parlor Games," and "Parl Theatricals." Illustrated with a gre variety of engravings. 12mo. fancy p per cover. Price.............................

**The Book of Fireside Games:** A Rep tory of Social Amusements. Containi an Explanation of the most Entertaini Games, suited to the Family Circle a Recreation, such as: Games of Action Games which merely require attention Games which require Memory—Cat Games, which have for their obje Tricks or Mystification—Games in whi an opportunity is afforded to display G lantry, Wit, or some slight knowledge certain Sciences—Amusing Forfeits Fireside Games for Winter Eveni Amusement, &c. By the Author of "T Sociable," "The Secret Out," &c. Bea tifully illustrated, 12mo. fancy paper cc er. Price.............................

**The Game of Whist:** Rules, Directio and Maxims to be observed in playing Containing also Primary Rules for E ginners, Explanations and Directions Old Players, and the Laws of the Ga Compiled from Hoyle and Matthe Also, Loo, Euchre, and Poker, as n generally played—with an explanati of Marked Cards, &c. This is the late work on Whist Playing, and it gives m ute directions for every phase of t Game. Besides Hoyle's Laws and Rul revised, it gives complete, the Directio and Maxims of Mathews, the celebrat Whist Player. and it is probably the b work on the subject that has ever be printed. The Directions for the Gam of Euchre, Loo, and Poker, are written plain langurge, so as to be easily und stood. The book contains, also, an E planation of Marked Cards, showing h the cards are marked by gamblers cheat with, and pointing out the mar by which they distinguish the high car by a glance at the backs of them. A ne ly printed book of 64 pages. Price...

**The Chairman and Speaker's Guid** *or, Rules for the Orderly Conduct of P lic Meetings.* Price.............................

☞ Any Book on this List will be sent to any address in the United States or Canada *Postage.* Send Cash Orders to **DICK & FITZGERALD, 18 Ann St.**

## POPULAR BOOKS SENT FREE OF POSTA

**The Game of Draughts, or Checkers,** Simplified and Explained. With Practical Diagrams and Illustrations, together with a Checker board, numbered and printed in red. Containing the Eighteen Standard Games, with over 200 of the best variations, selected from the various authors, together with many original ones never before published. By D. SCATTERGOOD. Bound in cloth, with flexible cover........................................0 38

**Romantic Incidents in the Lives of** *the Queens of England.* By J. F. SMITH, Author of "Stanfield Hall," "Amy Lawrence," "Minnie Gray," "Gus Howard," etc. 12mo, Extra Cloth, Gilt............1 00
This is a beautiful volume of 350 pages. It contains truthful and admirably drawn literary portraits of Elizabeth Woodville, Queen Consort of Edward IV, Eleanora of Aquaitaine, Queen Consort of Henry II, Matilda of Flanders, Queen Consort of William the Conqueror, and Matilda Atheling, Queen Consort of Henry I. The writer, in giving us the history of these eminent women, has remarkably exemplified the old adage that "truth is stranger than fiction;" for no pure romance could excel it in stirring incident, and the various vicissitudes of love, pleasure, sorrow, and suffering, which form the staple of all works of fiction. Each sketch is a complete narrative In itself, possessing all the charms of a novel, with the additional value and merit of historical truth. The book may be read with equal entertainment and profit.

**The Family Aquarium.** A new Pleasure for the Domestic Circle. Being a familiar and Complete Instructor upon the subject of the construction, fitting up, stocking, and maintenance of the Marine and Fresh Water Aquaria, or River and Ocean Gardens. By H. D. BUTLER, Esq. 12mo, cloth, gilt side stamp. This work is a complete adaptation to American peculiarities of every species of useful information upon Marine and Fresh Water Aquariums, to be met with in the elaborate volumes of European authority, together with a careful concentration of all the practical results of the author's great experience in the structure and management of Aquaria. Price........0 50

**The Ladies' Guide to Beauty:** A Companion for the Toilet. Containing practical advice on improving the complexion, the hair, the hands, the form, the teeth, the eyes, the feet, the features, so as to insure the highest degree of perfection of which they are susceptible. And also upwards of one hundred recipes for various cosmetics, oils, pomades, etc., etc., being a result of a combination of practical and scientific skill. By Sir JAMES CLARK, Private Physician to Queen Victoria. Revised and edited by an American Physician and Chemist. Price.....0 25

**Parlor Theatricals:** *or, Winter Eve ings' Entertainment.* Containing Acti Proverbs, Dramatic Charades, Acti Charades, or Drawing-Room Pant mimes, Musical Burlesques, Tableau Vivants, &c. By the author of "T Sociable," "The Magician's Own Book "The Secret Out," &c. 12mo. cloth, g side and back, illustrated with descripti engravings and diagrams. Price......

**The Book of 500 Curious Puzzles.** Co taining a large collection of Entertaini Paradoxes, Perplexing Deceptions Numbers and Amusing Tricks in Geor etry. By the author of " The Sociable "The Secret Out," "The Magician's Ov Book," "Parlor Games," and "Parl Theatricals." Illustrated with a gre variety of engravings. 12mo. fancy p per cover. Price.......................

**The Book of Fireside Games:** A Rep tory of Social Amusements. Containi an Explanation of the most Entertaini Games, suited to the Family Circle a Recreation, such as: Games of Action Games which merely require attention Games which require Memory—Cat Games, which have for their obje Tricks or Mystification—Games in whi an opportunity is afforded to display G lantry, Wit, or some slight knowledge certain Sciences—Amusing Forfeits Fireside Games for Winter Eveni Amusement, &c. By the Author of "T Sociable," "The Secret Out," &c. Bea tifully illustrated, 12mo. fancy paper cc er. Price.........

**The Game of Whist:** Rules, Directio and Maxims to be observed in playing Containing also Primary Rules for E ginners, Explanations and Directions Old Players, and the Laws of the Ga Compiled from Hoyle and Matthe Also, Loo, Euchre, and Poker, as no generally played—with an explanati of Marked Cards, &c. This is the late work on Whist Playing, and it gives mi ute directions for every phase of t Game. Besides Hoyle's Laws and Rul revised, it gives complete, the Directio and Maxims of Mathews, the celebrat Whist Player. and it is probably the b work on the subject that has ever be printed. The Directions for the Gam of Euchre, Loo, and Poker, are written plain langurge, so as to be easily und stood. The book contains, also, an E p!anation of Marked Cards, showing h the cards are marked by gamblers cheat with, and pointing out the mar by which they distinguish the high car by a glance at the backs of them. A ne ly printed book of 64 pages. Price...

**The Chairman and Speaker's Guid** *or, Rules for the Orderly Conduct of P lic Meetings.* Price...............

☞ Any Book on this List will be sent to any address in the United States or Canada Postage. Send Cash Orders to **DICK & FITZGERALD, 18 Ann St**

## POPUL

**The Dictionary of Love.** Containing a definition of all the terms used in the HISTORY OF THE TENDER PASSION, with rare quotations from the Ancient and Modern Poets of all nations; together with specimens of curious Model Love Letters, and many other interesting matters appertaining to Love, never before published; the whole forming a remarkable Text-Book for all Loves, as well as a Complete Guide to Matrimony, and a Companion of Married Life. Translated, in part, from the French, Spanish, German and Italian, with several Original Translations from the Greek and Latin. By THEOCRATUS, JUNIOR. 12mo, gilt side and back, price........................................$1 00

**Every Woman her own Lawyer.** A private Guide in all Matters of Law, of essential interest to women, and by the aid of which every female may, in whatever situation, understand her legal course and redress, and be her own Legal Adviser; containing the Laws of the differerent States relative to Marriage and Divorce, Property in Marriage, Guardians and Wards, Rights in Property of a Wife, Rights of Widows, False Pretenses in Courtship, &c By GEORGE BISHOP. price..............................$1 00

This book should be in the hands of every woman, young or old, married or single, in the United States. Now-a-days, especially, when women are beginning to be so universally recognized as competent to attend to all sorts of business matters which relate to themselves, such a work is invaluable. It is compiled from the very best and most reliable authorities, and the legal advice, forms and information it contains, are for all the States of the Union.

**Anecdotes of Love.** Being a true account of the most remarkable events connected with the History of Love in all Ages and among all Nations. By LOLA MONTEZ, Countess of Landsfelt, Large 12mo, cloth, price............................$1 00

These romantic and surprising anecdotes really contain all of the most tragic and comic events connected with the history of the tender passion among all nations and in all ages of the world. It is precisely the kind of book which a man will find it impossible to relinquish until he has read it through from the first to the last chapter. And besides the exciting love histories embraced in this volume, it really contains a great deal of valuable historic lore, which is not to be found except by reading through interminable volumes.

**Blunders in Behavior Corrected.** Price 0 12
A concise code of Deportment for both sexes.—"It will polish and refine either sex, and is Chesterfield superseded.— *Home Companion.*

**Art of Beauty; or, Secrets of a Lady** *Toilet.* With Hints to Gentlemen on t Art of Fascinating. By Madame LO MONTEZ, Countess of Landsfeldt. Clot gilt side, price.........................

This book contains and account, in deta of all the arts employed by the fashionat ladies of all the chief cities of Europe, f the purpose of developing and preservi their charms. Independent of its rare a really useful matter, the book is a curiosi as a piece of art, itself, for the most delica subjects are handled with a skill, and unexceptionable propriety of languag which is really surprising.

This work is also full of the curious a useful recipes used by the beauties of E rope, and will enable our ladies to supp their toilets, at a trifling cost, with wh cannot be purchased at the perfumers any cost.

**The Bordeaux Wine and Liquor De** *ers' Guide.* A Treatise on the Manufa ture and Adulteration of Liquors. By practical Liquor Manufacturer. 12m cloth, price.............................

In this work *not one* article in the sma est degree approximating to a poison recommended, and yet the book teach how Cognac Brandy, Scotch and Irish Wh ky, Foreign and Domestic Rum, all kin of Wines, Cordials, &c., from the choic to the commonest, can be imitated to th perfection that the best judges cannot tect the method of manufacture.

**The Great Wizard of the North's Han** *Book of Natural Magic.* Being a ser of the newest Tricks of Deception. ranged for Amateurs and Lovers of t Art. To which is added an exposure the practice made use of by Professio Card-players, Blacklegs, and Gamble Eighty-fifth Edition. By Professor J. ANDERSON, the Great Wizard of t North. Price .........................

**Laccur on the Manufacture of Liquo** *Wines, and Cordials, without the aid Distillation.* Also the Manufacture Effervescing Beverages and Syrups, Vi gar and Bitters. Prepared and arrang expressly for the Trade by PIERRE I COUR. 12mo, cloth, price..............

Procure a copy of "Lacour on the Ma facture of Liquors," or, if you do not w to purchase, look through the book fo few moments as a matter of curiosity. Physicians' and Druggists' pharmaceu cal knowledge cannot be complete witho a copy of this work.

**How to Cut and Contrive Childre** *Clothes at a Small Cost.* With numero explanatory engravings. Price.....

---

☞ Any Book on this List will be sent to any address in the United States or Canada Postage. Send Cash Orders to **DICK & FITZGERALD, 18 Ann S**